Paradox®3.5 Made Easy

Paradox® 3.5 Made Easy

Edward Jones

BORLAND·OSBORNE/McGRAW·HILL

B U S I N E S S   S E R I E S

Osborne **McGraw-Hill**
2600 Tenth Street
Berkeley, California 94710
U.S.A.

Osborne/McGraw-Hill offers software for sale. For information on software, translations or book distributors outside of the U.S.A., please write to Osborne **McGraw-Hill** at the above address.

This book is printed on recycled paper.
This book was produced using Ventura 2.0.

Paradox® 3.5 Made Easy

1234567890 DOC 99876543210

ISBN 0-07-881710-2

Acquisitions Editor: Elizabeth Fisher
Technical Reviewers: John Machado and Lisa Biow
Copy Editor: Kay Luthin
Proofreaders: Julie Anjos, Jeff Green
Composition: Bonnie Bozorg
Production Supervisor: Kevin Shafer

DEDICATION

To Nancy Carlston for all those long hours that helped make "best seller" a part of my vocabulary.

CONTENTS AT A GLANCE

CONTENTS

FOREWORD

Paradox, the relational database management system from Borland International, has rapidly become the favorite of database users at all levels of experience. *Paradox 3.5 Made Easy* is a clear and practical guide providing hands-on applications that quickly show the beginning user how to access the power of Paradox. By the end of Chapter 3, you will be creating queries, producing reports, and managing your information with ease.

This new edition of *Paradox Made Easy* is updated to include the new capabilities of Paradox version 3.5, as well as the capabilities of the earlier version 3.0. Users will find expanded information on presentation graphics, multiform capability, custom configuration, validity checks, calculated fields, and modifying field displays.

For database users, the important work begins when it is time to ask questions that will produce the answers needed to generate complex reports. Query by example, a unique technology included in Paradox, makes extracting the needed data simple, painlessly providing you with all the detailed information you need from your database in the format you specify. Author Edward Jones's careful explanation of this technology allows even novice users to take advantage of the power of query-by-example functionality.

By using this well-organized and clearly written book, you can confidently make Paradox one of your most valued software tools.

Philippe Kahn
President
Borland International, Inc.

ACKNOWLEDGMENTS

Any technical book represents the combined efforts of a number of people, and this one is no different. Thanks to Liz Fisher, at Osborne/McGraw-Hill, who conceived the project and artfully guided it around a maze of other projects, schedule conflicts, and the assorted roadblocks that have a way of appearing during book production. Thanks for the arduous task of manuscript preparation and layout go to Kevin Shafer, who knows that this isn't the first time he has done wondrous things to help make this author look good. Regarding the task of copy edit, thanks to Kay Luthin are well deserved for the (challenging!) task of juggling comments from more than one technical reviewer. Thanks also to Gwen Goss, associate editor at Osborne/McGraw-Hill, for her coordination efforts. And, no small amount of thanks to the people of Borland, for proving that it is still possible to produce software that one can get excited about.

INTRODUCTION

In a short period of time, Paradox has established itself as the number two player among database managers for IBM-compatible PCs. Considering the intense competition in the software industry, that says a lot about the nature of Paradox. It is that nature—that ability to provide true database power along with ease of use—that this book is designed to imitate from the ground up.

Since the beginning of the PC software industry, database managers have earned a reputation for being difficult to use. Paradox, with its highly visual interface and its query-by-example technology, is very different. It has gained a strong following among corporate users because you need not be a "programming guru" to decipher its use. And even though it is easy to use, Paradox offers a great deal of relational database management power. This book is designed to help you utilize that power.

What is in this book? Chapter 1 offers an introduction to Paradox by showing ways in which the product can be used and by describing the features and capabilities of the product. In Chapter 2, important tips are offered on the subject of database design, and you are introduced to some basic database concepts.

You will begin putting Paradox to use quickly in Chapter 3, which details how to get started with the program, how to create a database, and how to add records, perform simple queries, and print simple reports. Chapter 4 further explores the concepts of managing your data by showing you how you can edit records, find and delete records, change the layout of a table, sort tables, and view multiple tables simultaneously.

Chapter 5 covers the use of custom forms, a flexible tool offered by Paradox for the display of your data in any conceivable format. In Chapter 6, you are introduced to the significant power offered by Ask, the Paradox option that uses query-by-example technology to find the data you are looking for. Chapter 7 covers the basics of creating reports, and Chapter 8 covers the use of graphics. Chapter 9 shows how you can work with relational information while using Paradox.

In Chapter 10, you will learn how to use the built-in macro capabilities of Paradox, called *scripts*, to automate often-used procedures. Chapter 11 covers the area of file management by showing how tables can be modified and how you can perform helpful DOS functions without exiting from Paradox. Chapter 12 takes a further look at the complex subject of reporting, continuing where Chapter 7 left off by showing you techniques for free-form reports, mailing labels, invoices, and other specific report formats.

Chapter 13 introduces the Personal Programmer, a feature of Paradox that writes complete applications for you. Chapter 14 provides an introduction to PAL, the

Paradox Application Language, used for writing complex applications within Paradox. Chapter 15 provides users with important tips and techniques that will help them make optimal use of Paradox on a local area network. Finally, Chapter 16 provides instructions for building two sample applications within Paradox. Appendix A contains a command listing. Appendix B details the use of the Custom Configuration Program (CCP), which is used to change various default settings within Paradox.

The style of this book encourages learning by doing. You will get the best results if you have your PC and your copy of Paradox at hand and if you follow along with the hands-on practice sessions outlined in most chapters. However, ample illustrations have been provided, so even if you do not have a PC and Paradox, you can still become familiar with the program by reading this book.

WHAT IS PARADOX?

Welcome to Paradox, a true high-performance database manager for the IBM PC and compatible machines. If you have never used a relational database manager for a microcomputer before, you can feel confident that your choice of Paradox as a database management tool is an excellent one. If you have used other relational database managers prior to Paradox, you are in for a major change in expectations.

For the first decade of personal computer use, relational database managers all shared a very common trait, often expressed as "no pain, no gain." These powerful programs were universally difficult to use. And while advances gradually made these programs easier to use, it was still the case that if you wanted real power in a database manager, you had to sacrifice ease of use.

```
Viewing Items table: Record 1 of 10                          Main ▲—

SALES┌──────Last Name──────┬Init┬──────Street──────┬──────City──────┐
     7 │ Hawes-Anderson    │ D  │ Waves Cottage    │ Palm Springs   │ **
     8 │ Matthews          │ J  │ 1050 12th Street │ San Francisco  │ **
     9 │ Matthews          │ R  │ P. O. Box 28336  │ Albuquerque    │ **
    10 │ Mayor             │ K  │ 40 Winding Way   │ Salt Lake City │ **
    11 │ McDougal          │ L  │ 4950 Pullman Ave NE │ Seattle     │ **
    12 │ Ranier            │ T  │ 8947 San Andreas │ Klamath Falls  │ **
    13 │ Ranier            │ T  │ 8947 San Andreas │ Klamath Falls  │ **
    14 │ Simms             │ R  │ Box 13, RFD 2    │ Topeka         │ **
    15 │ Simpson           │ H  │ 3 Pooks Hill     │ Dallas         │ **

ITEMS┌──Stock #──┬──────Description──────┬In Stock┬──────Price──────┐
     1 │  632     │ Portable suntan machine │ 350  │    12,000.95
     2 │  130     │ Stretch VW Beetle       │   3  │    38,495.95
     3 │  235     │ Diamond-filled bathtub  │   1  │ 1,500,000.95
     4 │  244     │ Mink handkerchiefs (13) │  13  │    12,995.95
     5 │  422     │ Platinum snuff box      │  88  │   124,995.95
     6 │  519     │ Robot-valet             │  50  │   149,995.95
     7 │  558     │ Digital grandfather clock │ 266 │    4,995.95
     8 │  890     │ Matching panthers/leashes │   3 │  385,000.95
     9 │  983     │ Gourmet Kenya film safari │     │   50,000.95
    10 │  289     │ Gucci exec workstation  │  19  │   449,999.95
```

FIGURE 1-1.   Paradox in use

Paradox has changed all that. The word "paradox" is defined as "something that cannot be, but is," and Paradox lives up to its name. High-powered database managers are not supposed to be easy to use, but Paradox is.

Paradox uses a series of well-designed menus and a query-by-example feature that makes asking for specific data a simple task. Paradox normally displays information in table format, as shown in the example in Figure 1-1. The data in each table is composed of *fields*, or categories. If these terms are unfamiliar to you, they will be covered in more detail later in this chapter. You can use Paradox to create databases of tables containing the necessary fields. And you can display information in a format that best meets your needs with the custom forms capabilities built into Paradox.

HOW YOU WILL USE PARADOX

From the very start, Paradox will prove easy to use. Thanks to an automatic installation procedure, the program installs itself on your hard disk, creating the needed subdirectory for you. When you load the program, Paradox displays a two-line *main menu* on the screen (Figure 1-2). This menu provides access to all of Paradox's powerful features.

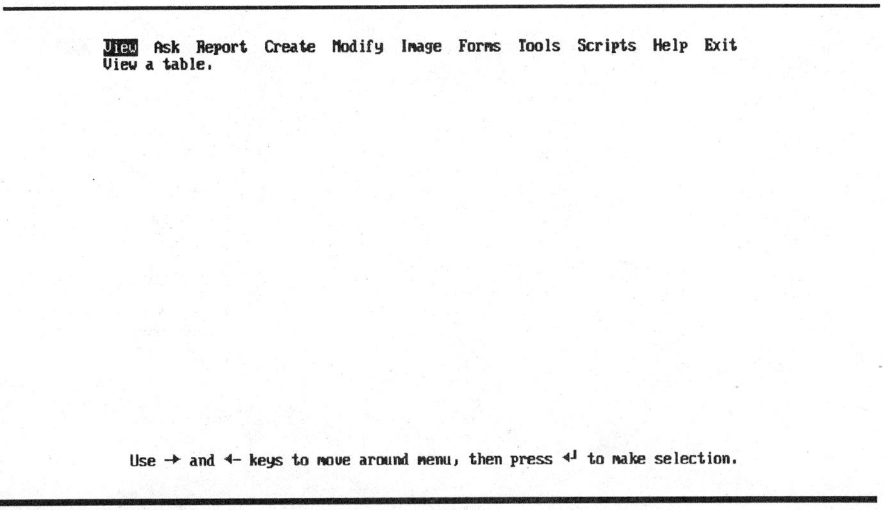

```
View  Ask  Report  Create  Modify  Image  Forms  Tools  Scripts  Help  Exit
View a table.
```

```
Use → and ← keys to move around menu, then press ↵ to make selection.
```

FIGURE 1-2.   Paradox main menu

If you have used Lotus 1-2-3 or similar programs, you will find Paradox's menu design to be familiar. As with 1-2-3, you can select menu choices by typing the first letter of the command or by highlighting the choice with the cursor keys and pressing RETURN. Most menu options, when selected, will display an explanation of the choice on the line immediately below the choice itself.

Creating a table in which to store your data is a simple task. After choosing the Create option from the main menu, you enter a name for the table. You then define the names and types of fields (categories) you will use. Unlike the limits imposed on you by competing programs, Paradox field names can be up to 25 characters in length and can include spaces. Five different data types can be used in Paradox: alphanumeric (combinations of alphabetic and numeric characters), number, currency, date, and short number (a special type of number field that stores values between -32,767 and 32,767). Figure 1-3 shows the process of creating a table in Paradox.

Once your table exists, you can select the Modify option from the main menu and choose Data Entry from the next menu that appears. You are then ready to begin entering data into the table. Paradox lets you enter data into a tablelike view or into a form. You can quickly create a standard form for any table by pressing a single function key. You can also design custom forms, which contain fields at the locations you desire along with borders or descriptive text.

To perform queries within Paradox that will extract data from your table, you can use the Ask command on the main menu. After using the Ask command to display a Query Form, you check off the fields you want to see in the query answer, and you enter matching data in any fields of the Query Form to isolate the subset of records. Figure 1-4 shows a Query Form and the resulting answer to the query.

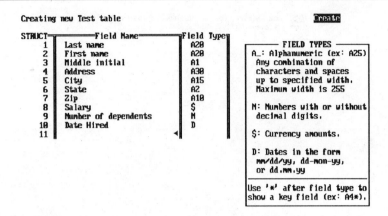

FIGURE 1-3.   Creating a Paradox table

To get more detailed information from your Paradox tables, you will want to build detailed reports. Paradox provides a report *hot key* that lets you create a quick tabular-style report simply by pressing ALT-F7. If you need additional flexibility, you

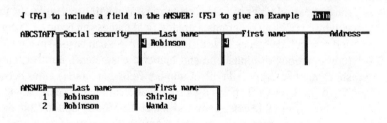

FIGURE 1-4.   Example of a query

can use the powerful Report Generator built into Paradox to design custom reports in either a tabular or a free-form format.

Paradox also offers powerful presentation graphics. Numeric data contained in a Paradox table can be visually represented in the form of a graph. Paradox offers a wide variety of graphs, including bar, pie, line, and marker graphs. The graphs that you create can be displayed or printed, and you can customize many parts of a graph, such as the colors of various objects, shading, and the fonts used as labels within the graph. Figure 1-5 shows an example of a graph created with Paradox.

Finally, advanced users will find no shortage of available power in Paradox. You can make use of *scripts,* which are automated actions stored in a file that Paradox carries out as if individual commands had been entered at the keyboard. Paradox scripts are stored as *PAL,* the Paradox Application Language. You can use PAL to build complete, menu-driven custom applications that novices can use without special training. On the other hand, if you have no desire to learn to write applications in this or any other language, you can use the Personal Programmer, an automated system that writes a Paradox application for you after you use a series of menus to answer questions about the application.

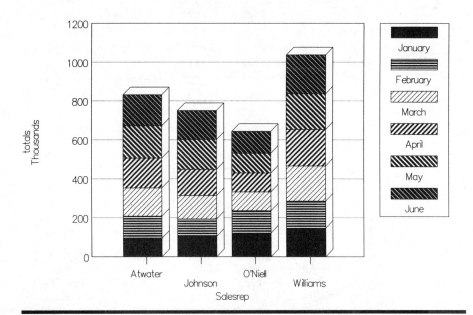

FIGURE 1-5. A Paradox graph

EASE OF NETWORK USE

You can use Paradox on a local area network, and the program can be used by multiple users as easily as it can by single users. Unlike some database managers, Paradox automatically handles most network tasks in the background, leaving users free to manage data. Paradox automatically places and removes the types of network locks that will prove most beneficial. You always have the option of manually placing more restrictive types of network locks on a table, but it is not necessary to think about this as you would have to with competitive packages. Paradox also updates data viewed by one network user as another user makes changes to that data.

WHAT IS A DATABASE?

Although "database management" is a computer term, it can also apply to the ways in which information is cataloged, stored, and used. At the center of any information management system is a *database*. Any collection of related information grouped together as a single item, as in Figure 1-6, is a database. A metal filing cabinet containing customer records, a card file of names and phone numbers, and a notebook with a penciled listing of a store inventory are all databases. However, a file cabinet or a notebook does not itself constitute a database—the way information is organized makes it a database. Objects like cabinets and notebooks only aid in organizing information, and Paradox is one such aid.

Information in a database is usually organized and stored in the form of tables, with rows and columns in each table. As an example, in the mailing list shown in Figure 1-6, each row contains a name, an address, a phone number, and a customer number. Each row is related to the others because they all contain the same types of information.

Name	Address	City	State	ZIP	Phone No.	Cust. No.
J. Billings	2323 State St.	Bertram	CA	91113	234-8980	0005
R. Foster	Rt. 1 Box 52	Frink	CA	93336	245-4312	0001
L. Miller	P.O. Box 345	Dagget	CA	94567	484-9966	0002
B. O'Neill	21 Way St. #C	Hotlum	CA	92346	555-1032	0004
C. Roberts	1914 19th St.	Bodie	CA	97665	525-4494	0006
A. Wilson	27 Haven Way	Weed	CA	90004	566-7823	0003

FIGURE 1-6.   A simple database

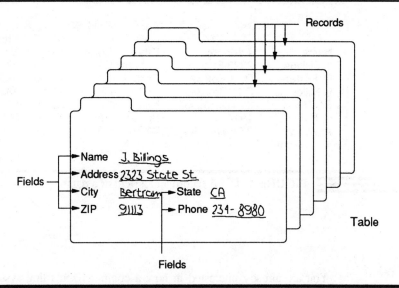

FIGURE 1-7.   Each card represents a record; information is separated into fields

And because the mailing list is a collection of information arranged in a specific order—a column of names, a column of addresses, a column of customer numbers—it is a table. One or more tables containing information arranged in an organized manner is a database.

Rows in a table are called *records,* and columns are called fields. Figure 1-7 illustrates this idea by showing a comparison of a one-table database to an address filing system kept on 3 X 5 file cards. Each card in the box is a single record, and each category of information on a card is a field.

Fields can contain any type of information that can be categorized. In the card box, each record contains six fields: name, address, city, state, ZIP code, and phone number. Since every card in the box has the same type of information, the card box is a database. Figure 1-8 identifies a record and a field in the mailing-list database.

USING A DATABASE

In theory, any database is arranged in such a way that information is easy to find. In Figure 1-8, for example, names are arranged alphabetically. If you want to find the phone number of a customer, simply locate the name and read across to the corresponding phone number.

		Field			Phone	Cust.
Name	**Address**	**City**	**State**	**ZIP**	**No.**	**No.**
J. Billings	2323 State St.	Bertram	CA	91113	234-8980	0005
R. Foster	Rt. 1 Box 52	Frink	CA	93336	245-4312	0001
L. Miller	P.O. Box 345	Dagget	CA	94567	484-9966	0002
B. O'Neill	21 Way St. #C	Hotlum	CA	92346	555-1032	0004
C. Roberts	1914 19th St.	Bodie	CA	97665	525-4494	0006
A. Wilson	27 Haven Way	Weed	CA	90004	566-7823	0003

Record

FIGURE 1-8.   A record and a field of a database

You are already interested in how a computerized filing system or a database system can make information storage and retrieval more efficient than a traditional filing system. You will find that Paradox offers many advantages. A telephone book, for example, is fine for finding telephone numbers; but if all you have is the address of the person who lives there and not the name, the telephone directory becomes useless for finding that person's number. A similar problem plagues conventional office filing systems. If the information is organized by name and you want to find all of the clients located in a particular area, for example, you are in for a tedious search. In addition, organizing massive amounts of information into written directories and filing cabinets can consume a great deal of space.

A manual database can also be difficult to modify. For example, adding a new phone number to the listing may mean rearranging the list. If the phone company were to assign a new area code, someone would have to search for all of the phone numbers having the old area code and replace each with a new one.

When a database is teamed with a computer, many of these problems are eliminated. A computerized database provides speed: finding a phone number from among a thousand entries or putting a file in alphabetical order takes just seconds with Paradox. Also, a computerized database is compact: a database with thousands of records can be stored on a single floppy disk. Finally, a computerized database is flexible: it enables users to examine information from a number of angles, so you can, for example, search for a phone number by name or by address.

Tasks that are time-consuming when done manually are more practical with the aid of a computer. In principle, a database in a computer is no different from a database recorded on paper and filed in a cabinet. But the computer does the tedious work of maintaining and accessing a database, and it does it quickly. A program that enables you to do all of this is known as a *database management system*, or *DBMS* for short.

RELATIONAL DATABASES

There are a number of systems that store information in a computer, but not all of these are *relational* database management systems. A word-processing program can be used to organize data in the form of a list; however, it will offer only limited flexibility. You must still sort, rearrange, and access the information. Moving a level above word processors, you get to the simple file managers and the spreadsheets with simple database management capabilities. Most file managers (and spreadsheets with data management capabilities) can also perform sorting and other data management tasks.

Relational database managers can also store information in database files. However, in addition to being more sophisticated than file managers, they can access two or more tables simultaneously by linking records on a common field such as customer number or an account code. By comparison, file managers can access only one table at a time. This type of constraint can be severely limiting. If a file manager is accessing information from one table but needs three pieces of information from a second table, it cannot continue unless the second table is available. Only when the file manager has finished with the first table can it proceed to the second table. But what good is this when the file manager needs information from both tables simultaneously? The only solution is to duplicate the three fields from the second table in the first table. Fortunately, this is not a problem with a relational database manager like Paradox.

Let's look at an example. Suppose a mailing list stores customer information for a warehouse that distributes kitchen appliances. The warehouse database would also have a separate table within it for customer orders, which would include fields for customer number, merchandise number, price per unit, quantity ordered, and total cost. The mailing list and customer order tables comprise a relational database because they have the customer number field in common, as shown in Figure 1-9. By searching for the customer number in the mailing list and matching it to the customer number in the order form, the database manager can determine who the purchaser is and where the purchaser is located from one table, and what the purchaser ordered and the total cost of the purchase from the other table. A database manager that can draw information like this, from different tables linked by a common field, is known as a *relational database manager*.

To handle the same task with a file manager would be very difficult—a file manager could not access the mailing list when it was time to find out where the merchandise should be shipped. The only alternative would be to combine the two tables, but this would result in a clumsy and inefficient database. For example, to represent both of R. Foster's purchases, you would have to duplicate his name, address, and phone number, as shown in Figure 1-10. If R. Foster had purchased 100 items instead, the extra typing could take much longer and use up valuable memory space.

Mailing List

Name	Address	City	State	ZIP	Phone No.	Cust. No.
J. Billings	2323 State St.	Bertram	CA	91113	234-8980	0005
R. Foster	Rt. 1 Box 52	Frink	CA	93336	245-4312	0001
L. Miller	P.O. Box 345	Dagget	CA	94567	484-9966	0002
B. O'Neill	21 Way St. #C	Hotlum	CA	92346	555-1032	0004
C. Roberts	1914 19th St.	Bodie	CA	97665	525-4494	0006
A. Wilson	27 Haven Way	Weed	CA	90004	566-7823	0003

Customer Order

Cust. No.	Merchandise No.	Price per Unit	Quantity	Total Price
0001	15A	1500.00	5	7500.00
0001	15B	1750.00	10	17500.00
0002	311	500.00	3	1500.00
0003	555	1000.00	4	4000.00
0004	69	650.00	7	4550.00
0005	1111	300.00	2	600.00
0006	15A	1500.00	1	1500.00

FIGURE 1-9.   Relationship between tables

HOW PARADOX COMPARES TO THE COMPETITION

Paradox is one of a number of competing products in a market built on the popularity of the IBM PC and its descendants, and on the usefulness of relational database managers for microcomputers. There are many excellent products on the market that are comparable in power to Paradox, including dBASE III/IV, R:base, Revelation, FoxPro, and others. All of these products offer relational database management, integral programming languages for applications development, and similar top-of-the-line features. However, Paradox excels at providing the features and the power while maintaining a simple, friendly user interface.

A major difference between Paradox and its competitors is the highly visual nature of the program. Some database managers force you to build strings of commands to carry out operations; these commands must follow a precise syntax. (Some products offer menu systems that help you build parts of the commands, but you must nevertheless supply the commands correctly to carry out your tasks.) In comparison,

Name	Address	Phone No.	Merch-andise No.	Price per Unit	Quan-tity	Total Price
J. Billings	2323 State St. Bertram CA 91113	234-8980	1111	300.00	2	600.00
R. Foster	Rt. 1 Box 52 Frink CA 93336	245-4312	15A	1500.00	5	7500.00
R. Foster	Rt. 1 Box 52 Frink CA 93336	245-4312	15B	1750.00	10	17500.00
L. Miller	P.O. Box 345 Dagget CA 94567	484-9966	311	500.00	3	500.00
B. O'Neill	21 Way St. #C Hotlum CA 92346	555-1032	69	650.00	7	4550.00
C. Roberts	1914 19th St. Bodie CA 97665	525-4494	15A	1500.00	1	1500.00
A. Wilson	27 Haven Way Weed CA 90004	566-7823	555	1000.00	4	4000.00

FIGURE 1-10. Combined customer order invoice and mailing list database (unnecessary customer number field was eliminated)

Paradox lets you perform much of your work by manipulating objects on the screen. And for those interested in custom applications, the Paradox Personal Programmer (described in Chapter 13) makes it easy for nonprogrammers to create complex custom applications that are free of "bugs."

SYSTEM REQUIREMENTS

To use Paradox, you will need an IBM PC, XT, AT, or PS/2; or a PC compatible like the Compaq Portable or Portable Plus, a Deskpro, a Compaq Portable II, Portable III, or Compaq 386; a Tandy 1000, 3000, or 4000; or an Epson I, II, or III. Any personal computer that is software-compatible with the IBM PC should be able to use Paradox. Your computer must have a minimum of 512K (kilobytes) of memory, and it must be equipped with one floppy disk drive and one hard disk drive. Users of Paradox version 2.0 or earlier can use dual-floppy systems, but if you are using version 3.0 or above, you must have a hard disk. You must be using DOS 2.0 or a newer version. Paradox can be used with either a monochrome or a color monitor, and with any compatible printer. Paradox is designed to take advantage of extra memory. It uses the AST RAMPage, Intel Above Board, or any other memory board that meets the EMS (LIM) or EEMS specifications. Of the two specifications, EEMS is recommended for better performance. Extended memory of up to 16MB is supported by Paradox 3.5.

To use Paradox or the Paradox Multi Pack on a local area network, you will need work stations with a minimum of 640K of memory; any combination of disk drives (or no drives); and DOS 3.1 or above. The operating system can be any of the following:

- Novell Advanced Netware, version 2.0A or above

- IBM PC Network or Token Ring Network with IBM PC Local Area Network Program, version 1.12 or above

- 3Com 3Plus Network or 3Com 3+ Open Network with 3Com 3Plus operating system, version 1.1 or above

- AT&T Starlan Network with AT&T P6300 Network Program, version 1.1 or above

- Other networks that are NETBIOS compatible with the above may work with Paradox, but they have not been tested and support is limited.

SPECIFICATIONS

Specifications for Paradox include the following:

Maximum number of records:	2 billion
Maximum number of fields:	255
Maximum number of characters per field:	255
Maximum number of characters per unindexed record:	4000
Maximum number of forms per table:	15
Maximum number of reports per table:	15

DATABASE DESIGN

Data and Fields
Three Phases of Database Design

At this point, you may be anxious to load Paradox into your computer and begin using the program. However, you should resist the temptation to use Paradox for a task you have never done by computer before. There is an excellent reason for approaching the job of designing a database with patience: planning is vital to effective database management. Many a buyer of database management software has gotten started with the software, created a database, and stored data within that database only to discover that the database did not provide all of the needed information. While powerful databases like Paradox let you make up for mistakes committed during the design process, correcting such errors can nevertheless be a tedious job. To help you avoid such time-consuming mistakes, this chapter focuses on the design of a database.

 Creating a database without proper planning often results in a database with too many or too few fields.

Database design requires that you think about how the data should be stored and how you and others will ask for data from the database file. During this process, your problem (which Paradox was purchased to help solve) will be outlined on paper. Just as one would not haphazardly toss a bunch of files into a filing cabinet without designing some type of filing system, one cannot place information into a database file without first designing the database. As you design it, you must define the kinds of information that should be stored in the database. Output requirements can be a significant help in designing your database. Think about what you want to get from a database, in the form of printed reports, screen forms, or graphs. Your output needs will help you better plan what goes into your database.

DATA AND FIELDS

Data and fields are two important terms in database design. Fields are the types of data that make up the database. A field is another name for a category, so an entire category of data, such as a group of names, is considered to be a field. Names, phone numbers, customer numbers, descriptions, locations, and stock numbers are common fields that your database might contain. *Data* is the information that is stored in the fields you have defined. An individual's last name (Smith, for example) is data.

In addition to thinking about what kinds of information will go into the database, you must give careful consideration to the ways in which information will come out of the database, or *output*. Output most often comes from a database in the form of *reports*. A report is a summary of information. When you ask the computer for a list of all homes in the area priced between $100,000 and $150,000 or for a list of employees earning less than $15.00 per hour, you are asking for a report. When you ask for John Smith's address, you are also asking for a report. Whether the computer displays a few lines on the screen, a graph, or hundreds of lines on a stack of paper, it is providing a report based on the data contained within the database file.

The practice sessions in this book demonstrate how you can design and use a database. The problems and needs of a hypothetical company called ABC Temporaries will be used throughout the book to illustrate the effectiveness of Paradox for database management. ABC Temporaries is a temporary services firm that must not only keep track of the number of employees working for a firm, but must also track which client companies temporary employees are assigned to.

For some time, ABC Temporaries has handled this task by using ordinary 3 X 5 file cards, but the paperwork load has finally grown too large to be efficiently handled in this manner. A major task at ABC Temporaries is to track just how much time each temporary employee spends at a particular client company so that accurate bills can be generated. The relational capabilities of Paradox will make such tracking a simple matter.

Successive chapters of this text will show how the staff at ABC Temporaries uses Paradox to manage information. By following along with these examples, you will learn how to put Paradox to work within your particular application.

THREE PHASES OF DATABASE DESIGN

Designing a database file, whether for ABC Temporaries or for yourself, involves three major steps:

1. Data definition (an analysis of existing or required data)

2. Data refinement (refining necessary data)

3. Establishing relationships between fields

Data Definition

During the first phase of database design, you must make a list, on a piece of paper, of all the important fields involved in your application. To do this you must examine your application in detail and determine exactly what kinds of information must be stored in the database.

In discussing the design for the database, the staff at ABC Temporaries determined that certain items must be known about each temporary worker: the name of the employee, the employee's address, date of birth, date hired, and salary, and the name of the client firm the employee is assigned to. The resulting list of fields is shown in Figure 2-1.

During this phase of database design, you should list all the possible fields your database might contain. Listing more fields than your particular application actually

```
Fields

1.  Employee name
2.  Employee address
3.  Employee salary
4.  Assigned to firm
5.  Date of birth
6.  Date hired
```

FIGURE 2-1.   Initial list of fields

needs is not a problem—unnecessary fields will be eliminated during the data refinement phase.

Data Refinement

In this phase you refine your initial list of fields so that the fields form an accurate description of the types of data needed in the database. It is vital to include at this stage suggestions from as many other users of the database as possible. The people who use the database are likely to know what kinds of information they need to get from the database. When the staff of ABC Temporaries took a close look at their initial list of fields, for example, they realized that most of the refinements were obvious. The Address field, for example, needed to be divided into street address, city, state, and ZIP code. Such division of an initial field into more than one field is particularly important when record sorting or selection based on those fields will occur. Any item used to sort or select records should be in a field by itself.

Note ≡   Get suggestions from those who will use a database before starting its design.

In your own case, some refinements may quickly become evident and others may not. Going over your written list of fields will help make any necessary refinements more obvious. For example, when the staff of ABC Temporaries further examined the initial field list, they realized that the index-card system of employees contained multiple occurrences of employees with the same last name. To avoid confusion, the Name field was further divided into last name and first name. Suggestions were also made to add the phone number, salary, number of dependents, and hourly billing rate charged to the client. Figure 2-2 shows the refined list of fields.

Establishing the Relationships

During the third phase of database design, drawing relationships between the fields can help determine which fields are important and which are not as important. One way to determine such relationships is to ask yourself the same questions that you will ask your database. If a manager wishes to know how many different employees worked on temporary assignments for Mammoth Telephone & Telegraph, the database must draw a relationship between an employee identifier (such as the social security number) and the names of the clients for whom that employee worked.

Relationships can be more complex. The company president might want to know how many employees worked as data entry operators for Mammoth Telephone

```
Fields

 1. Employee last name
 2. Employee first name
 3. Street address
 4. City
 5. State
 6. ZIP code
 7. Phone
 8. Salary
 9. No. of dependents
10. Assigned to firm
11. Rate charged to firm
12. Date of birth
13. Date hired
```

FIGURE 2-2.   Refined list of fields

between July and October. The database management system must compare the "client worked for" fields with fields for the type of job and the time the job was performed. These types of questions can help reveal which fields are unimportant, so that they can be eliminated from the database.

During this phase you must determine which relationships between data (if any) will call for the use of multiple tables, keeping in mind that Paradox is a relational database, which means that the data within one table can be related to the data in another. When designing a database, you should not lose sight of the opportunity that relational capabilities offer you. Too many users take relational database management software and proceed to create bulky, nonrelational databases—an approach that drastically increases the amount of work involved.

The proposed staff table to be used by ABC Temporaries has fields that will be used to describe each employee. A major goal of computerizing the personnel records at the firm is to provide automated billing. By creating another table that shows which employees worked at a given assignment during a certain week, the company can easily generate bills for the services that ABC Temporaries provides to its clients. If the ABC staff took the nonrelational approach of adding a "week ending" date field and a "number of hours worked" field, they could store all of the information needed in each record. However, they would also have to fill in the name and address, as well as other information, for each employee, week after week. The better solution is to create two tables, one containing the fields described, detailing each employee, and the other containing the number of hours worked, a "week ending" date, the client the work was done for, and a way of identifying the employee. You should consider

```
Fields

 1. Employee social security number
 2. Employee last name
 3. Employee first name
 4. Street address
 5. City
 6. State
 7. ZIP code
 8. Phone
 9. Salary
10. No. of dependents
11. Assigned to firm
12. Rate charged to firm
13. Date of birth
14. Date hired
```

FIGURE 2-3.   Final list of fields

breaking a database into separate tables whenever one or more tables contain redundant data—data that is the same for a large number of records.

When establishing the relationships, you may determine that an additional field is necessary. In the case of ABC Temporaries, employees are identified by social security number, so an appropriate field was added to the proposed list of fields, resulting in the finalized list of fields (Figure 2-3). It is from this list that the table created in the next chapter is based.

During the design phases, potential users should be consulted to determine what kinds of information they will expect the database to supply. Just what kinds of reports are wanted from the database? What kinds of queries will employees make of the database? By continually asking these types of questions, you will think in terms of your database, and this should help you determine what is important and what is unimportant.

You may have noticed that throughout the entire process, the specific data, such as employees' names, addresses, and so forth, has not been discussed. It is not necessary to identify any specific data at this point; only the fields need to be defined. Once you have finalized a given design, you should test that design using samples of existing data. Testing with real data can reveal problems with the database design, such as foreign postal codes (when a field was designed for U.S. ZIP codes) or name titles such as M.D. that were not originally planned for.

Note ≡ Look at examples of your data before finalizing your list of fields.

Keep in mind that even after the database design phases, the design of the database file is not set in stone. Changes to the design of a database file can be made later if necessary. However, if you follow the systematic approach of database design for your application, you will not create a database that fails to provide much of the information you need and must therefore be extensively redesigned. Although Paradox lets you change the design of a table at any time, such changes are often inconvenient to make once the database is designed.

Here is an example. If you used Paradox to create a database file that handled a customer mailing list, you might include fields for names, addresses, cities, states, and ZIP codes. At first glance, this might seem sufficient. You could then begin entering customer information into the database and gradually build a sizeable mailing list. However, suppose your company later decided to begin telemarketing based on the same mailing list. You might suddenly realize that you had not included a field for telephone numbers. Using Paradox, you could easily change the design to include a field for them, but you would still face the mammoth task of going back and adding a telephone number for every name in the mailing list. If this information had been added as you developed the mailing list, you would not face the inconvenience of having to enter the phone numbers as a separate operation. Thus, careful planning and the time spent during your database design process can help avoid later pitfalls.

GETTING STARTED

Paradox comes in the form of assorted manuals, quick reference guides, nine 5.25-inch floppy disks, and eight 3.5-inch microfloppy disks. The disks can be divided into two groups: those that contain the Personal Programmer, and those that do not. (The Personal Programmer is an automated system for building applications; it is covered in more detail in a later chapter.) If you have not yet installed Paradox on your system, you can place all the disks labeled "Personal Programmer" aside until later.

If you are using 5.25-inch disks, the remaining disks should include the Installation and Sample Tables Disk, System Disks 1, 2, and 3, the Custom Configuration Disk, and the Data Entry Toolkit Disk. If you are using 3.5-inch disks, the remaining disks should include the Installation and Sample Tables Disk, System Disk 1/2 and System Disk, Custom Configuration Disk 1/2, and the Data Entry Toolkit Disk. Note that if you are installing a version of Paradox older than version 3.5, your disk count may differ. In that case, you should refer to your Paradox documentation to make sure that you have the correct number of disks. If you are installing Paradox on a network, your disk count will differ. Refer to your Network Administrator's Guide for details.

HARD-DISK INSTALLATION

Installing Paradox on a hard disk is a simple matter, thanks to the installation program contained on the Installation Disk and the detailed instructions contained in the "Introduction" booklet packaged with your software. (If you do not have the booklet, you should locate it now.) Because versions of Paradox change and the instructions may change along with software updates, this text will provide only some general tips regarding installation. Refer to your latest Paradox documentation for detailed specifics on installing the program.

The installation program supplied as a part of Paradox creates the necessary subdirectory on your hard disk and copies the necessary files into that subdirectory. Before installing Paradox version 3.5, you should make sure that you have at least three megabytes of free disk space remaining on your hard disk. Optional software, such as sample tables, requires an additional 3MB. Earlier versions of Paradox will require less disk space; refer to your Paradox documentation for details. (You can tell the amount of free space by using the DIR command; the description "XXXXX bytes free," which appears at the bottom of the directory listing, indicates the amount of free space remaining.) (The installation requires nearly two megabytes of disk space; however, you will certainly need adequate space for storage of your databases and for sorting tables.)

If you are using Paradox for the first time, you should also be aware of the memory requirements of the program. Paradox requires 512K of installed memory. While your machine may be equipped with 640K, some memory is consumed by DOS, and memory resident programs like Sidekick, Sidekick Plus, or Superkey will also consume available memory. In addition, although Paradox will operate in as little as 512K of RAM, when working with files of any size it will need to access the disk much more often than it does when it has more memory to work with. For best performance, you should have 640K of memory in your machine, and you should not have memory resident programs loaded while using Paradox (unless those programs are designed to use extended or expanded memory, which you may also have installed above 640K).

To install the Paradox program, turn on your computer and get to the DOS prompt in the usual manner. Your hard-disk drive should be the default drive; if it is not, log on to the hard disk before attempting to install Paradox. As an example, if your hard disk is in drive C, type C: and press RETURN to log on to drive C. Then perform the following steps:

1. Insert the Installation Disk (or the Installation and Sample Tables Disk if your system uses 3.5-inch disks) into drive A.

2. Enter the command

   A:INSTALL

   to start the installation process. Refer to the "Read Me First" booklet supplied with your Paradox documentation, and follow the instructions starting on page 8 of that document to complete the installation process.

USING PARADOX FROM A FLOPPY DISK (VERSION 2.0 ONLY)

Earlier versions of Paradox can be installed on a floppy disk system, although on a system that lacks a hard disk you must be prepared to deal with a healthy amount of disk swapping at times. In order to install Paradox version 2.0 or earlier for floppy disk use, you must run a special program, called FINSTALL, from the Installation and Sample Tables Disk, as detailed in the "Introduction" booklet supplied with Paradox version 2.0. Follow the directions on page 9 of the booklet, if you wish to install Paradox for floppy disk use.

Note that your machine must have at least two disk drives. Unless you have a RAM disk available, you will not be able to use Paradox successfully on single-drive laptops or on other one-drive machines, because the needed program files will consume so much space on the disk that there will not be sufficient room for your own databases.

STARTING PARADOX ON A HARD-DISK SYSTEM

To start Paradox, you must first switch to the subdirectory containing the program (usually C:\PDOX35) and then enter **PARADOX** (if you are using version 3.5), or **PARADOX3** (if you are using version 3.0) or **PARADOX2** (if you are using version 2.0) from the DOS prompt. As an example, if your hard disk is in drive C and the program is stored in a subdirectory named PDOX35, you would start the program by entering the following commands from the DOS prompt:

```
CD\PDOX35
PARADOX
```

Once the program starts, you will briefly see an introductory screen and a copyright message. In a moment, the Paradox main menu will appear, as shown in Figure 3-1.

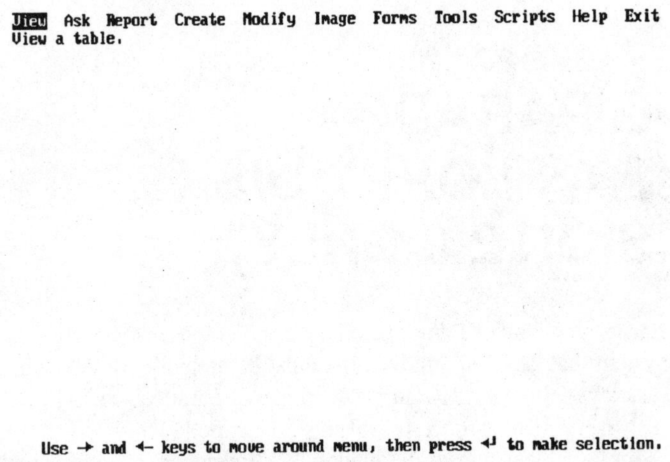

```
View  Ask  Report  Create  Modify  Image  Forms  Tools  Scripts  Help  Exit
View a table.
```

```
Use → and ← keys to move around menu, then press ↵ to make selection.
```

FIGURE 3-1.   Paradox main menu

STARTING PARADOX ON A FLOPPY DISK SYSTEM (VERSION 2.0 ONLY)

Start your computer with your normal DOS disk. When the A prompt appears, remove the DOS disk and insert the Paradox System Disk 1 into drive A. Start Paradox by entering the command

PARADOX2

Once you have started the program, you will see an introductory screen and a copyright message. In a moment, you will be asked to remove System Disk 1 and to replace it with System Disk 2. Insert the proper disk and press RETURN. In a moment, the Paradox main menu will appear, as shown in Figure 3-1.

CREATING A BATCH FILE TO START THE PROGRAM

You can create a batch file to make starting Paradox and changing to the desired subdirectory an easier task. If you have installed Paradox in a subdirectory named PDOX35 on drive C of your hard disk, the commands that follow can be used to accomplish this task. If your hard disk is not C: substitute your hard disk letter for the letter C: in the following commands. If you installed Paradox in a subdirectory named something other than PDOX35, refer to your DOS manual for specifics on creating batch files.

≡ Note ≡ Batch files make starting Paradox an easier process.

To create the batch file, first enter the following commands from the DOS prompt, pressing RETURN at the end of each line.

```
C:
CD\
MD\PDOX35\DATA
COPY CON PARADOX.BAT
```

When you complete the fourth command, the cursor will move down a line, and will wait for additional entries. Type the following lines, pressing RETURN after each line

```
C:
PATH=C:\PDOX35;C:\DOS
CD\PDOX35\DATA
```

then press the F6 key, or CTRL-Z followed by the RETURN key. You should see the message, "1 file(s) copied." From this point on, you will always be able to start Paradox and switch to the PDOX35\DATA subdirectory by simply entering **PARADOX** at the DOS prompt. Creating a subdirectory to contain your data files (in this case, C:\PDOX35\DATA) is a wise idea, because it will help you keep your data files separate from the other program files used by Paradox.

ABOUT THE SCREEN

The top line of your screen shows a series of menu choices. Paradox uses a detailed system of these choices to let you easily select options for creating databases, adding and changing information, printing reports, and performing most of the functions that can be performed within Paradox.

The screen can be divided into four general areas: the *menu highlight,* which appears at the top of the screen and contains the menu choices; the *menu* explanation, which appears directly below the menu highlight and displays additional information regarding a menu choice; the *workspace,* which is the large area in the center of the screen; and the *message window,* which is an area occupying the bottom two lines of the screen. Paradox will display various messages within the message window to help you as you use the program. You will also often see *status messages,* which appear from time to time in the menu area.

When you first load the program, the cursor highlights the View option. The cursor will always point to the next available option or to the field or characters you are selecting or editing. The left and right arrow keys can be used to move the cursor around the screen.

Try pressing the right arrow key once, and you will see the highlighted menu option change from View to Ask. At the same time, a brief description of the option will appear in the menu area immediately below the top line of the screen. If you continue pressing the right or left arrow key, you will notice descriptions of the various menu options. Pressing RETURN with a menu option highlighted will select that option. As an example, if you use the left or right arrow key to highlight the menu option entitled Report and then press RETURN, the available choices dealing with reports will appear as a menu. (You can press the ESCAPE key to exit the Report menu.)

Note that you can also choose a menu option by entering the first character of its name. For example, if you type **T**, the menu options for the Tools choice will be displayed in the menu area. As you become more experienced, you will probably want to choose menu options by pressing the letter keys. Remember that you can press ESCAPE at any menu to redisplay Paradox's main menu options. You may need to press it more than once, however, depending on what menu you are in because the ESC key "backs up" one menu level each time you press it.

Note that Paradox 3.5 has "incremental menus." This means that you can type further letters to distinguish between choices with the same first letter. For example, if Directory and Delete appear on the same menu, typing DI chooses Directory while DE chooses Delete.

ABOUT THE KEYBOARD

If you are already familiar with the PC keyboard, you should skip this section and move on to the next. Paradox uses a number of special-purpose keys for various functions. In addition to the ordinary letter and number keys, you will use the *function keys* often. On most older IBM PC and PC-compatible computers, the function keys are the double row of gray keys at the left side of the PC keyboard, as shown in Figure 3-2. On newer IBM PCs and most newer compatibles, the function keys are placed in a horizontal row at the top of the keyboard, as shown in Figure 3-3. The function keys on older PCs are labeled F1 through F10, for Function 1 through Function 10. The newer machines have 12 function keys. Four often-used keys—the ESCAPE key (abbreviated as ESC), the TAB key (which may have the double arrows on it), the SHIFT key (which may have a hollow upward-pointing arrow), and the ALTERNATE key (abbreviated as ALT)—are usually grouped on the left side of the keyboard. Some keyboards have the ESCAPE key in a different location. Find these keys before going further, as they will prove helpful for various operations.

You should locate the function key template supplied with your package of Paradox and place it where you can refer to it for the uses of the function keys. These uses will be detailed in later chapters as each operation is discussed.

Toward the right side of the keyboard is another SHIFT key. Below it is a key labeled CAPS LOCK, which is used to change all typed letters to uppercase. Newer IBM PCs and many compatible keyboards will have the CAPS LOCK key located above the left SHIFT key. (The CAPS LOCK key does not change the format of the numbers in the top row of the keyboard.) Just above the right SHIFT key is the RETURN or ENTER key; it

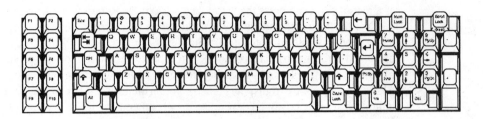

FIGURE 3-2.   The IBM PC keyboard

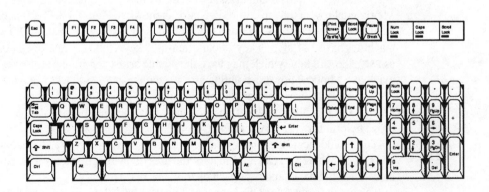

FIGURE 3-3.   The enhanced IBM PC keyboard

performs a function that is similar to the Return key on a typewriter. Above the RETURN key is the BACKSPACE key.

On the right side of the keyboard, in the numeric keys area, is a key labeled DEL. This key can be used to delete characters or other objects when in Paradox (such as deleting records when you are in Edit mode). Finally, on the far-right side of the keyboard are two gray keys with plus (+) and minus (-) labels. These keys usually produce the plus and minus symbols when pressed.

The far-right side of the keyboard contains a *numeric keypad*. On some computers, this area can serve a dual purpose. The keys in this area—the up, down, left, and right arrows—can be used to move around in a workspace. By pressing the NUM LOCK key, you can use the same keys to enter numbers. Some keyboards have a separate area with arrow keys and a separate area with a numeric keypad.

 When NUM LOCK is pressed, the arrow keys on many keyboards create numbers instead of moving the cursor. If you press on an arrow key and get an unwanted number, check the status of the NUM LOCK key.

 The ESC key is your most useful key whenever you are somewhere you don't want to be. In many cases, repeatedly pressing ESC will get you out of an operation. Remember that ESC won't UNDO or CANCEL an edit session.

USING THE FUNCTION KEYS

Function keys are used for a variety of tasks within Paradox. Table 3-1 shows the purpose of each function key and function key combination. Many of the terms in the table may not make sense at this point, but they will be explained in further detail throughout this text. For your reference, the function key assignments can also be found on the Command Card at the back of this book.

GETTING HELP

Should you need help, Paradox provides detailed information on subjects ranging from basic Paradox concepts to programming in PAL, the Paradox Application Language, all of which is stored in a Help file that is accessed through Paradox. A series of menus

Key	Name	Assignments
F1	Help	
F2	Do-It!	Performs current operation
F3	Up Image	Moves up by one image
F4	Down Image	Moves down by one image
F5	Example	Enters a query example
F6	Check	Includes current column in query result
F7	Form	Toggles switch between Form and Table view
F8	Clear	Clears current image
F9	Edit	Starts Edit mode
F10	Menu	
ALT-F3	Instant Script Record	Begins/ends recording
ALT-F4	Instant Script Play	Begins playback
ALT-F5	Field View	Permits cursor movement within field
ALT-F6	Check Plus	Includes all records, including duplicates
ALT-F7	Instant Report	Prints report based on current table
ALT-F8	Clear All	Clears all images
ALT-F9	Coedit	Starts CoEdit mode
CTRL-F6	Check Descending	Same as Check, but also sorts in descending order
CTRL-F7	Graph	Draws graph based on current column
SHIFT-F6	Group By	Groups field, but does not display values in the query answer

TABLE 3-1.   Function Key Assignments

will assist you in finding the information you are searching for. For example, if you are working with Paradox and need information on a certain key combination you cannot recall, you can press the Help (F1) key and choose the Keys choice from the main menu within the Help System for a more detailed explanation. If you press F1 now, you will see the help screen shown in Figure 3-4.

Note   At any point in Paradox, pressing F1 reveals a help screen.

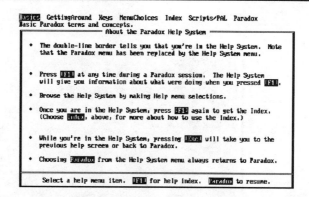

FIGURE 3-4. Help screen

The Help System uses the same type of menu bar as the rest of Paradox, and you can select from among these options in the same manner. The Help System is divided into six basic areas, shown in Table 3-2. You can choose from any of the six areas by selecting the choice from the menu (again, either by typing the first letter in the name of the choice or by highlighting the choice with the cursor keys and pressing RETURN).

Once you select any one of the six areas, another help screen will appear. It will usually display additional choices of help topics, which can be selected in the same manner. From any of the help screens, you can select the Paradox option from the

Area	Description
Basics	Help with basic terms and concepts
Getting Around	Movement between menus, tables, and within Help System
Keys	Explanation of the Paradox keyboard
Menu Choices	Explanation of all menu choices
Index	Detailed index to all Help topics
Scripts/PAL	Explanation of script editing and help when programming with PAL

TABLE 3-2. The Six Areas of the Help System

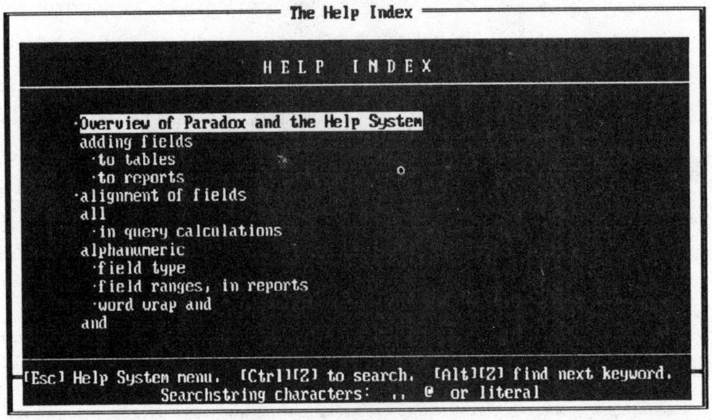

FIGURE 3-5.   Help Index

menu to exit the Help System and return to the program, or you can press the ESCAPE key to move to the previous menu.

One particular area of the Help System that you may find useful is the Help Index, which is arranged by topic in alphabetical order. To view this index, go to the main Help System menu and choose Index from the menu. Another screen that details how the index can be used will appear, and from this screen you can press F1 to display the Help Index, shown in Figure 3-5.

You can use the PGUP and PGDN keys to browse through the Help Index. Any specific topic preceded by a period has an accompanying help screen, which can be displayed by pressing RETURN. After reading the information, you can select Paradox from the menu to resume using the program, or you can press F1 to get back to the Help Index.

To gain a familiarity with the Help System, you may wish to take a few minutes to browse through the help screens. When you are done viewing the screens, choose Paradox from the menu to get back to the program.

CREATING A TABLE

As mentioned earlier, Paradox stores data in the form of tables. To create a table, you must choose Create from the main menu. Remember, you can display the menu with F10 and then use the cursor keys or press the first letter of the desired menu name (in this case, C for Create).

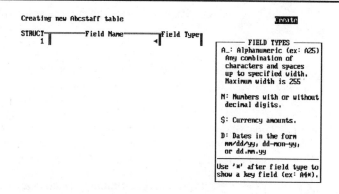

Creating new Abcstaff table   Create

STRUCT┬──────Field Name──────┬─Field Type┐
    1 ║   │◄   │
                                            ┌─── FIELD TYPES ───┐
                                            │A_: Alphanumeric (ex: A25)│
                                            │ Any combination of│
                                            │ characters and spaces│
                                            │ up to specified width.│
                                            │ Maximum width is 255│
                                            │   │
                                            │N: Numbers with or without│
                                            │ decimal digits.   │
                                            │   │
                                            │$: Currency amounts.│
                                            │   │
                                            │D: Dates in the form│
                                            │ mm/dd/yy, dd-mon-yy,│
                                            │ or dd.mm.yy   │
                                            ├───────────────────┤
                                            │Use 'x' after field type to│
                                            │show a key field (ex: A4x).│
                                            └───────────────────┘

FIGURE 3-6.   Table structure image

Once you choose Create from the menu, Paradox prompts you for the name of the table. Each table must have a name, and the name must conform to the rules for all DOS filenames. A *filename* consists of letters, numbers, or the underscore character. It cannot contain more than eight characters. Paradox automatically assigns table names the .DB extension because it only searches for files with the .DB (database) extension. Note that Paradox uses temporary tables named ANSWER, STRUCT, and KEYVIOL at various times. You should not try to assign these names to any tables that you create.

Enter **ABCSTAFF** for the name of the table. Within a moment, Paradox will display a screen known as the table structure image (which is shown in Figure 3-6). This screen contains areas in which you define both the names of the fields and the field types.

When naming a field, use a name that best describes the contents of that field. Like names for tables, field names can be composed of letters and numbers. However, you have considerably more flexibility in naming fields than tables. Field names can be up to 25 characters in length, and they can contain spaces (however, they cannot *start* with a space). You can include any printable character except for double quotation marks, square brackets, left and right parentheses, curly braces, or the -> character combination. Although Paradox lets you create long field names, it is a good idea to keep them relatively short. Doing so will keep the headings in your simpler reports from occupying too much space.

Now that you have learned some of the Paradox basics, let's return to the example created in Chapter 2 for ABC Temporaries and begin to create a table. The first attribute on the list is the employee's social security number, so enter **Social security** for the first field name. Once you press RETURN, the cursor automatically moves over to the Field Type column. Paradox allows the entry of four types of fields. They are as follows:

- *Alphanumeric fields* are used to store any characters, including letters, numbers, special symbols, and blank spaces. An alphanumeric field has a maximum size of 255 characters.

- *Number fields* use numbers, with or without decimal places. You can enter numbers of up to 15 significant digits, so unless you are performing scientific calculations, you should not have a problem with numerical accuracy.

- *Currency fields* are a special type of number field, designed to handle currency. Paradox automatically formats values stored in a currency field with two decimal places and commas as thousands separators. (You can change the type of separators by choosing International Sort Order.) The currency format also automatically puts any negative numbers stored in the field within parentheses.

- *Date fields* are used to store dates. Paradox lets you enter the dates in any of three formats: mm/dd/yy, dd-mon-yy, or dd.mm.yy. Paradox defaults to dates in the twentieth century; for other dates, you can enter all four numbers of the year as a part of the date. While Paradox accepts dates between 1/1/100 and 12/31/9999, amateur genealogists and others concerned with dates should note that date tracking in Paradox is based on the Gregorian calendar in present use, so dates earlier than the sixteenth century may vary when compared to the calendar you decide to use.

Paradox also offers another type of field, which does not appear in the Field Types description on the right side of the screen. These are *short number fields*, a special type of field used for storing short numbers, or numbers within the range from -32,767 to +32,767. You should not use a short number field unless you are an advanced Paradox user or developer; while this type of field takes less space in a database, there are serious limitations affecting the display of short number fields in Paradox forms.

Most fields in a table will be either of the alphanumeric or the number type, although there will undoubtedly be times when you will need most or all of the different field types that Paradox offers. Keep in mind that if a field that contains numbers will not be used in calculations, you should define that field as an alphanumeric field. Such fields commonly contain such items as social security numbers, part numbers, phone numbers, and so forth.

 Use numeric fields for numbers that must be calculated. Numbers that you never need to perform calculations on (like phone numbers) should be stored in alphanumeric fields.

Since the Social security field will contain alphanumeric characters, enter **A** (for alphanumeric) and press RETURN. Note that when you press RETURN, Paradox asks for the field width. Remember, alphanumeric fields can be up to 255 characters in length. Earlier, in Chapter 2, ABC Temporaries calculated that the Social security field would require 11 characters, so type 11 but do not press RETURN.) Add an asterisk (*) to designate the field as a key field, and *then* press RETURN.

The Key Field Concept

Paradox lets you define one or more initial fields as *key fields,* which Paradox will treat differently than non-key fields. Probably the most important thing to remember is that key fields will contain unique information; Paradox will not let you put the same entry into the key of two records. Also, when designing the structure of the table, note that you *must* place all key fields together, beginning at field number 1. (You cannot place key fields in a random order all over the structure of a table.) Note that when you save the file, records are arranged by key field. The requirement that key-field data be unique means you should be careful when deciding what should be a key field. If the first two fields of a table were Last name and First name, making both fields key fields would mean you could never enter two records with an identical last and first name. In such a case, you might want to use a combination of Last name, First name, and Middle name as key fields. Also, remember that you don't have to make any field a key field; doing so can boost performance but is not generally required.

In addition to preventing duplications, designating a field as a key field causes Paradox to keep an internal index that helps to speed sorts and queries that are based on the contents of that field. Since social security numbers are unique, the asterisk is placed after the field type to designate the field as a key field, as shown in Figure 3-7.

Enter **Last name** for the second field name. When the cursor moves to the Field Type area, enter **A15** to designate the field type and width at the same time. (This saves you the trouble of pressing RETURN and waiting for Paradox to ask for the field width.) For the third item in the attribute list, the employee's first name, enter **First name**. Again, when the cursor moves to the Field Type area, enter **A15**.

Moving down the list, enter **Address** for the fourth field definition and **A25** for the field type and width. For the fifth field enter **City** and enter **A15** for the field type and width. For the next field enter **State** and enter **A2** for the field type and field width.

The next field will be ZIP Code. ZIP codes consist of numbers, so at first you might think you should use the numeric field type. However, this is not really practical. If you make use of the nine-digit business ZIP codes, Paradox will not allow the entry of the hyphen. It will also delete beginning zeros in ZIP codes such as 00123.

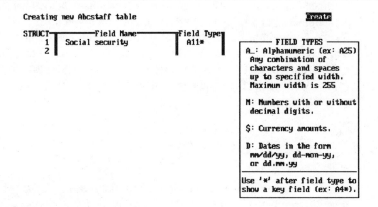

Creating new Abcstaff table   Create

STRUCT ┬──────Field Name──────┬─Field Type─┐
     1 │ Social security   │ A11*   │
     2 │   │   │

┌──────── FIELD TYPES ────────┐
│ A_: Alphanumeric (ex: A25) │
│   Any combination of   │
│   characters and spaces   │
│   up to specified width.   │
│   Maximum width is 255   │
│   │
│ N: Numbers with or without │
│   decimal digits.   │
│   │
│ $: Currency amounts.   │
│   │
│ D: Dates in the form   │
│   mm/dd/yy, dd-mon-yy,   │
│   or dd.mm.yy   │
├─────────────────────────────┤
│ Use '*' after field type to │
│ show a key field (ex: A4*). │
└─────────────────────────────┘

FIGURE 3-7.   Key field designation

You will never use a ZIP code in a numerical calculation, so it makes sense to store the ZIP code as an alphanumeric field rather than as a numeric field. A number stored in an alphanumeric field cannot be used directly in a numerical calculation, although you can convert the value to a number with a Paradox function. Now enter **ZIP Code** as the field name. Enter **A10** to designate an alphanumeric field that is ten characters wide.

You may recall from Chapter 2 that two fields in the personnel database take the form of a date. Paradox lets you use date fields to enter these dates. Enter **Date of birth** for the name of the field, and type **D** in the Field Type column to indicate a date field. Enter **Date hired** for the name of the field, and type **D** in the Field Type column to indicate a date field.

For the next field name, enter **Dependents**. For the field type, enter **N** for numeric. You may notice that unlike some database managers, Paradox does not require you to specify the width of a numeric field or the number of decimal places needed to store the number. Paradox will make allowances for storing the number automatically.

Enter **Salary** for the name of the next field, and enter a dollar sign ($) to designate this field as a currency field. This field will be used to track the salaries of the employees in dollar amounts. Finally, enter the remaining information, as shown here, for the next three fields:

Field Name	Type	Width	Key field?
Assignment	Alphanumeric	20	No
Hourly Rate	Currency		No
Phone	Alphanumeric	12	No

Correcting Mistakes

If you make any mistakes while defining the structure of the table, you can correct them before you complete the table definition process. Use the cursor keys to move to the field name or field type containing the offending characters, and use the BACKSPACE key along with the character keys to make any desired corrections. CTRL-BACKSPACE can be used to clear the entire field. You can also use DEL to delete an entry, INS to insert a line, and ALT-F5 to edit an entry. See Chapter 6 for how to make corrections after the table is complete.

Completing the Table Definition

To tell Paradox that you have finished defining the table structure, press F10 and then press the Do-It! (F2) key. You will briefly see the message "Creating ABCSTAFF," and then the main menu will reappear.

DISPLAYING A TABLE STRUCTURE

You could begin entering the records for the employees of ABC Temporaries at this time, but instead, display the table structure first. From the menu, you can use Tools/Info/Structure to examine the structure of a table. If you cannot recall the precise fields you used when creating a table, or if you cannot remember what a particular table is used for, you can get an idea by displaying the table's structure.

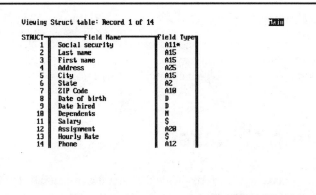

FIGURE 3-8.   Table structure for ABCSTAFF

From the main menu, type **T** to open the Tools menu, and then choose Info. From the next menu that appears, choose Structure. Paradox will ask for a table name. Pressing RETURN at this point will display a list of all tables contained in the Paradox subdirectory of your disk. Select ABCSTAFF from the list of available tables. Paradox will show the table's structure within a temporary table named STRUCT, as shown in Figure 3-8.

Since you will not need to retain this data in any permanent fashion, press Clear Image (F8) to clear the display. You now have the new table, but it remains empty. To add records to the table, you will use the Edit command, found within the Modify menu.

THE EDIT COMMAND

The Edit command is used both for editing existing records and for adding new records to a table in Paradox. To try this command, choose Modify from the main menu. The Modify menu will appear; from this menu, one of the available choices is Edit.

Select the Edit command. (Note that F9 can be used as a shortcut for the Edit command.) Paradox will ask you for the name of the table you wish to edit; you can enter the table name, or you can press RETURN to display all available tables. Choose

ABCSTAFF as the table from the list, or enter **ABCSTAFF** and press RETURN. In a moment, the ABCSTAFF table will appear. In the upper-right corner of the screen the word "Edit" will appear, informing you that Paradox is now in Edit mode. The cursor is flashing in the Social security field.

For each field in the record, enter the following information, pressing RETURN after each entry is completed:

Social security: **123-44-8976**
Last name: **Morse**
First name: **Marcia**
Address: **4260 Park Avenue**
City: **Chevy Chase**
State: **MD**
ZIP Code: **20815-0988**
Date of birth: **3/01/54**
Date hired: **7/25/85**
Dependents: **2**
Salary: **8.50**
Assignment: **National Oil Co.**
Hourly Rate: **15.00**
Phone: **301-555-9802**

As you finish filling in the record, you will notice that once the record has been completely filled in, the cursor automatically moves down to the row that will contain the next record. You don't need to type decimal places into currency fields if there are no cents in the amount.

If you make a mistake during the data entry process, you can reach the offending field with the cursor keys and use the BACKSPACE key to correct and retype the entry. Proceed now to fill in the additional records for the ABC Temporaries staff table, as shown in Figure 3-9.

SAVING
THE INFORMATION

As long as you are in Edit mode in Paradox, the information that you have entered has not been saved on your disk. To save the data, you can use the Do-It! (F2) key. Press F2 now, and the edits will be saved.

Social security: 121-33-9876
Last name: Westman
First name: Andrea
Address: 4807 East Avenue
City: Silver Spring
State: MD
ZIP Code: 20910-0124
Date of birth: 5/29/61
Date hired: 7/04/86
Dependents: 2
Salary: 15.00
Assignment: National Oil Co.
Hourly Rate: 24.00
Phone: 301-555-5682

Social security: 232-55-1234
Last name: Jackson
First name: David
Address: 4102 Valley Lane
City: Falls Church
State: VA
ZIP Code: 22044
Date of birth: 12/22/55
Date hired: 9/05/85
Dependents: 1
Salary: 7.50
Assignment: City Revenue Dept.
Hourly Rate: 12.00
Phone: 703-555-2345

Social security: 901-77-3456
Last name: Mitchell
First name: Mary Jo
Address: 617 North Oakland Street
City: Arlington
State: VA
ZIP Code: 22203
Date of birth: 8/17/58
Date hired: 12/01/87
Dependents: 1
Salary: 7.50
Assignment: Smith Builders
Hourly Rate: 12.00
Phone: 703-555-7654

FIGURE 3-9.   Additional records for ABCSTAFF

TABLE VIEW
VERSUS FORM VIEW

Viewing and entering records as you have been doing gets the job done, but as you can see, it is impossible to view all of the fields in the table at the same time—they will not all fit on the screen. Paradox normally displays information in table view, because most users find it easier to grasp the concept of a database when it is shown in this fashion. It is easy to see a number of records, and the records and fields are clearly distinguished. However, not being able to see all of the fields also presents a clear drawback. For example, when you are viewing the name of an employee, you will find that the City, State, and remaining fields are hidden. To view these fields, you could use the right arrow key, but then the Name fields disappear off to the left side. This makes it hard to recall which line containing date-hired, date-of-birth, and salary information matches a particular employee name.

To avoid this problem, some database managers display information in an on-screen form rather than in a table. Paradox provides the flexibility of using either method. You can quickly move between the two with the Form Toggle (F7) key. Press F7 now, and Paradox will display the record in the database in a form view, as shown in Figure 3-10.

Moving around in the table is different when in Form view than when in Table view. Try PGUP and PGDN, and then try using the up and down arrow keys. Whereas in Table view, PGUP and PGDN move you up and down by a screenful of records, they now move you up and down one record at a time. And the up and down arrow keys

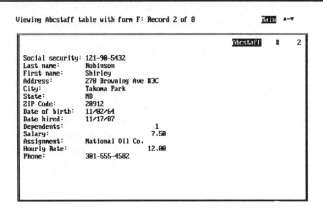

FIGURE 3-10.   Form view of record

now move the cursor between fields instead of between records. While viewing the records in either view, you can use the F7 key to switch back and forth between Table and Form view.

Use the view of your choice to proceed, and add the remaining records to the table now. (Press F9 to begin editing, then use the PGDN key to get to a new, blank record.) Figure 3-11 contains the remaining records. After the last record has been entered, press the F2 key to save the records, and press Menu (F10) to display the main menu.

AN INTRODUCTION
TO QUERIES

Your data is now stored in Paradox, ready for use. Successive chapters will detail how you can make use of data once it has been entered into a table, but a quick introduction to how you will ask Paradox for information and produce simple reports is appropriate.

Database users frequently need to obtain sets of facts. Suppose you need a list of all employees living in Maryland. Paradox makes such a query simple with its Ask command. To quickly try an example, choose Ask from the main menu. Paradox will ask for the name of the table you are asking about; enter **ABCSTAFF** and a Query Form will appear, as shown in Figure 3-12.

The use of the Query Form is covered in more detail in Chapter 6. By moving the cursor to each desired field and pressing F6, you place check marks in the fields that you want to see included in the answer Paradox will provide. You also type a matching criteria to select the desired records in the field of your choice.

To see how this works, use the left or right cursor key to place the cursor in the Last name field, and then press F6. When you do this, a check mark will appear in the field. Move to the First name field and press F6 again; then do the same for the City and State fields. This action tells Paradox that you will want to see the Last name, First name, City, and State fields included in the list Paradox provides in response to your query.

With the cursor still in the State field, enter **MD** to tell Paradox that you want the query to select only those records that contain the letters "MD" in the State field. What you have just done is basically all that you need do to provide Paradox with a query. There are no arcane commands or strange syntax to try to decipher; just check the fields you need to see, fill in an example of what data you want in any desired field, and press Do-It! (F2) to perform the query.

Social security: 121-90-5432
Last name: Robinson
First name: Shirley
Address: 270 Browning Ave #3C
City: Takoma Park
State: MD
ZIP Code: 20912
Date of birth: 11/02/64
Date hired: 11/17/87
Dependents: 1
Salary: 7.50
Assignment: National Oil Co.
Hourly Rate: 12.00
Phone: 301-555-4582

Social security: 343-55-9821
Last name: Robinson
First name: Wanda
Address: 1607 21st Street, NW
City: Washington
State: DC
ZIP Code: 20009
Date of birth: 6/22/66
Date hired: 9/17/87
Dependents: 0
Salary: 7.50
Assignment: City Revenue Dept.
Hourly Rate: 12.00
Phone: 202-555-9876

Social security: 876-54-3210
Last name: Hart
First name: Edward
Address: 6200 Germantown Road
City: Fairfax
State: VA
ZIP Code: 22025
Date of birth: 12/20/55

FIGURE 3-11.   Remaining records for ABCSTAFF

Date hired: 10/19/86
Dependents: 3
Salary: 8.50
Assignment: Smith Builders
Hourly Rate: 14.00
Phone: 703-555-7834

Social security: 909-88-7654
Last name: Jones
First name: Judi
Address: 5203 North Shore Drive
City: Reston
State: VA
ZIP Code: 22090
Date of birth: 9/18/61
Date hired: 8/12/86
Dependents: 1
Salary: 12.00
Assignment: National Oil Co.
Hourly Rate: 17.50
Phone: 703-555-2638

FIGURE 3-11.   Remaining records for ABCSTAFF (*continued*)

If you have not yet done so, press F2. Paradox will perform the query, and it will display the results in a temporary table named ANSWER, which appears below the Query Form, as shown in Figure 3-13. (If your results do not match the ones shown, check the entry in the State field of the query to be sure that the entry matches the way you originally entered "MD" in the table. Use Up Image, F3, to move back to the Query Form, correct any typos, and press F2 to retry the query.)

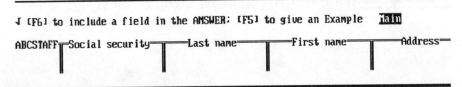

Figure 3-12.   Query form

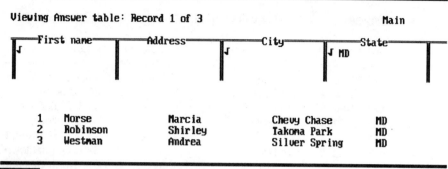

Viewing Answer table: Record 1 of 3   Main

	First name	Address	City	State
√			√ MD	

1	Morse	Marcia	Chevy Chase	MD
2	Robinson	Shirley	Takoma Park	MD
3	Westman	Andrea	Silver Spring	MD

Figure 3-13.   Results of query

Note Chapter 6 provides more details on how you can design queries to retrieve specific information.

GETTING AN INSTANT REPORT

If you need a quick printed report of the results of a query, or of any table, you can easily get one with a single key combination. Paradox uses the ALT-F7 key combination as the instant report key. If you have a printer, make sure it is turned on and that paper is loaded. Then press ALT-F7. You should get a printed report based on the temporary table created by the query. The report will resemble the example shown here:

2/02/88	Standard Report		Page 1

Last name	First name	City	State
Morse	Marcia	Chevy Chase	MD
Robinson	Shirley	Takoma Park	MD
Westman	Andrea	Silver Spring	MD

Press Clear All (ALT-F8) to clear the results of the query and to clear the Query Form and return to the main menu. Then choose View, and enter **ABCSTAFF** for the name of the table. The screen will again display the table you created during this chapter.

2/02/88	Standard Report		Page 1

Social security	Last name	First name	Address
121-33-9876	Westman	Andrea	4807 East Avenue
121-90-5432	Robinson	Shirley	267 Browning Ave #2A
123-44-8976	Morse	Marcia	4260 Park Avenue
232-55-1234	Jackson	David	4102 Valley Lane
343-55-9821	Robinson	Wanda	1607 21st Street, NW
876-54-3210	Hart	Edward	6200 Germantown Rd.
901-77-3456	Mitchell	Mary Jo	617 North Oakland Street
909-88-7654	Jones	Judi	5203 North Shore Drive

City	State	ZIP Code	Date of birth	Date hired	Depen-dents
Silver Spring	MD	20910-0124	5/29/61	7/04/86	2
Takoma Park	MD	20912	11/02/64	11/17/87	1
Chevy Chase	MD	20815-0988	3/01/54	7/25/85	2
Falls Church	VA	22044	12/22/55	9/05/85	2
Washingtong	DC	20009	6/22/89	9/17/87	0
Fairfax	VA	22025	12/20/55	10/19/86	3
Arlington	VA	22203	8/17/58	12/01/87	1
Reston	VA	22090	9/18/61	8/12/86	1

Salary	Assignment	Hourly Rate	Phone
15.00	National Oil Co.	24.00	301-555-5682
7.50	National Oil Co.	12.00	301-555-4582
8.50	National Oil Co.	15.00	301-555-9876
7.50	City Revenue Dept.	12.00	703-555-2345
7.50	City Revenue Dept.	12.00	202-555-9876
8.50	Smith Builders	14.00	703-555-7834
7.50	Smith Builders	12.00	703-555-7654
12.00	National Oil Co.	17.50	703-555-2638

Figure 3-14.   Results of instant report using ABCSTAFF table

You can use the same ALT-F7 key combination to produce a report of your entire database. Turn on your printer, load paper if necessary, and press ALT-F7. This time, you should get a printed report based on the ABCSTAFF table created by the query. The report will resemble the example that is shown in Figure 3-14.

You can produce very detailed reports in Paradox. Such reports can include customized headers and footers, customized placement of fields, word wrapping of large amounts of text, and numeric results based on calculations of fields. Such reports are covered in detail in Chapter 7.

GETTING AN INSTANT GRAPH

Paradox can also be used to produce presentation graphs. You will learn more about this subject in Chapter 8, but for now, keep in mind that an instant graph can provide a quick look at the presentation capabilities of Paradox. To display an instant graph, simply place the cursor in the numeric field to be graphed and press CTRL-F7. As an example, perhaps you would like to see a bar graph showing the staff salaries. First use the right arrow key to move the cursor to the Salary field, and then press CTRL-F7. Figure 3-15 shows the resulting graph. (Note that the social security numbers run

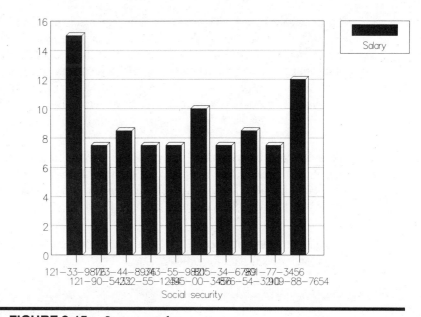

FIGURE 3-15.   Instant graph

together; Chapter 8 will detail ways in which you can correct this.) For now, press any key to exit the graph.

If this is a good time for a break, press F10 to display the main menu, choose Exit, and choose Yes when asked if you wish to exit Paradox. Note that whenever you exit Paradox, any temporary tables (such as ANSWER) are normally lost.

Now that you have a table containing data, you will want to know how you can manipulate that data to better obtain the results you want. The next chapter covers this area in more detail.

Remember   Always exit from Paradox by choosing Exit from the menu. Never exit by turning off your computer while still in Paradox!

QUICK SUMMARY

To start Paradox   Switch to the directory containing your data files, and set a path to the directory containing Paradox. Then enter **PARADOX** at the DOS prompt. (Remember, you can create a batch file to do all of this automatically.)

To get help   From anywhere in Paradox, press F1.

To create a table   Press F10 to display the menu, and choose Create. Enter the name for the table. When the table structure image appears, enter the desired field names and field types. (Remember, with alphanumeric fields, you must include a number that indicates the width of the field; for example, A12 indicates an alphanumeric field that is 12 characters wide.) Add an asterisk after the field type if you wish to indicate that a field is a key field. When you are finished defining the table, press Do-It! (F2) to save the table definition.

To add data to a table   Press F10 for the menu, choose Modify, then choose DataEntry. Enter the name of the table (or press ENTER, and choose from the list of tables which appears). You can proceed to enter the data directly while in Table View. To change to a form for the data entry, press Form Toggle (F7).

To get an instant report   While viewing the table, make sure your printer is ready, and press Instant Report (ALT-F7).

MANAGING YOUR DATABASE

As you work with your data within Paradox, you will find that much of your time is spent adding new records, finding specific information, making changes, rearranging records, producing simple lists, and performing similar tasks that keep your database current. This chapter will show you how you can perform those tasks effectively.

LISTING EXISTING TABLES

To keep track of your tables and other assorted files, you can use the Tools/Info/Inventory choice. On a broader scale, the Info choice of the Tools menu provides you with information about Paradox tables, any forms and reports you build that are associated with a table, and other information of interest to network users. Choose Tools/Info/Inventory/Tables from the main menu, and Paradox will ask you for the name of the desired directory. If you press RETURN to accept the default directory (the one currently in use), Paradox will display a LIST table, which shows the names of all tables and their creation dates. Figure 4-1 gives an example of a LIST table. Here, Paradox displays information in the form of a temporary table. As with all tables, you can clear the information from the screen by pressing Clear Image (F8).

Other menu choices from Tools/Info/Inventory may prove helpful for locating other files that may be contained on your disk. You can use the Paradox Info choice to view files without leaving the program and returning to DOS. Choose Tools/Info/Inventory/Files from the main menu, and Paradox will respond with the following prompt:

Pattern:
Enter DOS directory pattern (e.g. *.TXT), or press RETURN for working directory).

At this point, you can press RETURN to see a table containing all files in the current (PDOX35) subdirectory, or you can enter any accepted DOS wild cards and extensions

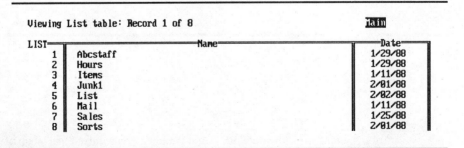

Figure 4-1.   LIST table

```
Viewing List table: Record 1 of 70                              Main

        1     Abcstaff.db                                   3/01/89
        2     Abcstaff.f                                    2/28/89
        3     Abcstaff.f1                                   3/07/89
        4     Abcstaff.f2                                   3/07/89
        5     Abcstaff.f3                                   3/08/89
        6     Abcstaff.px                                   3/01/89
        7     Abcstaff.r                                    2/28/89
        8     Abcstaff.val                                  3/01/89
        9     Advertis.db                                   3/13/89
       10     Advertis.r                                    3/13/89
       11     Advertis.r1                                   3/13/89
       12     Answer.db                                     3/20/89
       13     Att.bgi                                      12/21/88
       14     Bold.chr                                     12/21/88
       15     Carmodel.db                                   3/15/89
       16     Carmodel.r                                    3/15/89
       17     Carsales.db                                   3/11/89
       18     Carsales.f                                    3/11/89
       19     Cga.bgi                                      12/21/88
       20     Colors.lib                                   12/21/88
       21     Config.bgi                                   12/21/88
       22     Custom.lib                                   12/21/88
```

FIGURE 4-2.   LIST table containing all files

to limit the types of files viewed. For example, entering *.f would display all files with the extension of .F, which are standard screen form files used by Paradox. If there are too many filenames to be viewed on a single screen, you can use the PGUP and PGDN keys to view additional ones.

You can also enter other directory names at this prompt to see the contents of other subdirectories on your hard disk. This can be particularly useful if you keep different Paradox databases in multiple subdirectories on your hard disk. Figure 4-2 shows a sample of the list of files obtained by pressing RETURN to view all files. Pressing Clear Image (F8) clears this list from view.

MORE ABOUT EDITING

Chapter 3 provided an introduction to editing records within Paradox. Because updating information is a major task with any database, it is worth the time you spend to learn the ways you can edit with Paradox.

Paradox lets you edit records in two ways: by pressing the Edit (F9) key after you use the View choice from the main menu, or by using the Modify choice from the main menu and selecting Edit. If you choose View from the main menu, Paradox prompts you for a table name. You can enter the table name directly, or press RETURN

```
Editing Abcstaff table: Record 1 of 8                              Edit

ABCSTAFF Social security   Last name        First name            Address
    1    121-33-9876       Westman          Andrea          4807 East Avenu
    2    121-90-5432       Robinson         Shirley         270 Browning Av
    3    123-44-8976       Morse            Marcia          4260 Park Avenu
    4    232-55-1234       Jackson          David           4102 Valley Lan
    5    343-55-9821       Robinson         Wanda           1607 21st Stree
    6    876-54-3210       Hart             Edward          6200 Germantown
    7    901-77-3456       Mitchell         Mary Jo         617 North Oakla
    8    909-88-7654       Jones            Judi            5203 North Shor
```

Figure 4-3.   ABCSTAFF table in Edit mode

to view a list of tables. Once the table appears, press Edit (F9) and you are in Paradox's Edit mode. As an alternative method, choose Modify from the main menu, and then choose Edit from the next menu that appears. (Another menu choice available at this point, called CoEdit, is used for editing on a network; this is described in greater detail in Chapter 14.)

Paradox will prompt you for a table name. Once the table has been selected, Paradox automatically places you in Edit mode, as Figure 4-3 demonstrates.

Whenever you are in Edit mode, Paradox informs you of this fact by displaying "Edit" in the upper-right corner of the screen. As you learned earlier, you can press Form Toggle (F7) to move back and forth between a table view (which shows you the records in a tabular fashion) and a form view (which shows the records one at a time in an on-screen form).

While you are in Edit mode, the cursor is always at the *end* of the current entry. You cannot move the cursor to individual characters while you are in this mode, but you can use the BACKSPACE key as necessary to delete characters, and retype them in order to correct mistakes. (A way to do a full cursor edit is described shortly.) As a helpful shortcut, you can also use the CTRL-BACKSPACE key combination to delete an entire value in any field.

Remember   When editing, use F7 to move between form and table views.

The DEL and INS keys perform a more powerful function than you might suspect if you have used other PC programs, so you should be careful with these keys. When you are in Edit mode, the DEL key will delete an entire record or row from the Paradox database. If you do this by accident and you want to cancel the effects of such an edit, you can press F10 to display the current menu and choose Undo from that menu. Doing

Name of Key	Results While in Field View
Left, right arrow	Moves from character to character
HOME	Moves to start of field
END	Moves to end of field
DEL	Deletes character at cursor location
INS	Switches between insert and overwrite
RETURN	Leaves Field View mode

TABLE 4-1. Editing Keys Available in Field View Mode

so will undo the effects of your last action. (You can also use CTRL-U as an "Undo" key; the CTRL-U key combination has the same effect as the menu's Undo option.) If you accidentally delete a record and then perform some other editing actions before you notice your error, you can still regain the deleted record by pressing F10 to display the menu and choosing Cancel to cancel the effects of the edits. Note, however, that this action will cancel any other edits you have made, restoring the table to the condition it was in before you entered Edit mode.

While editing, you may come across an error at or near the beginning of a field, and you may prefer to correct that character without backspacing over the entire field. Paradox has a special key, known as Field View (ALT-F5, or CTRL-F), for this purpose. Just place the cursor at the desired field and press Field View (ALT-F5 or CTRL-F). The cursor will assume the shape of a small rectangle, and the keys listed in Table 4-1 can be used for editing. When you are done editing in Field View mode, just press RETURN and you will be back in normal Edit mode.

The INS key adds a new record just above the current record in the table. While this provides a quick way of keeping your records in order, you should not be concerned with inserting records at any specific spot to maintain a particular order. It is much easier to add records at the end of a table or with the DataEntry menu option (described later) and let the powerful sorting features of Paradox keep your records in order for you. However, INS can be useful if you want to duplicate information from the previous record into a new record. Another quick way to add a record while in Edit mode is to move to the last field in the table and press RETURN or the down arrow key. The cursor will move into the next blank record, and you can proceed to add the information.

Once you have completed your edits, you can exit Edit mode and save the changes simultaneously by pressing the Do-It! (F2) key. As an alternative you can press the Menu (F10) key and choose Do-It! from the menu that appears. To cancel your edits without saving the changes, press Menu (F10) and choose Cancel from the main menu.

HANDS-ON PRACTICE: ADDING AND EDITING RECORDS

To add a new record to the ABC Temporaries table, choose Modify and then Edit. Enter **ABCSTAFF** in response to the name for the table, and Paradox will place you in Edit mode. Move the cursor past the last entry with the down arrow key, and a new record number will appear on the blank line. Enter the following information to fill in the new record:

Social security: 495-00-3456
Last name: Abernathy
First name: Sandra
Address: 1512 Redskins Park Drive
City: Herndon
State: VA
ZIP Code: 22071
Date of birth: 10/02/59
Date hired: 02/17/88
Dependents: 1
Salary: 10.00
Assignment: City Revenue Dept.
Hourly Rate: 18.00
Phone: 703-555-7337

Suppose that while you are in Edit mode, you learn that Ms. Shirley Robinson has moved to a different apartment on the same street, and you wish to correct the address without retyping the entire line. Move the cursor to the address for Shirley Robinson and press Field View (ALT-F5). Change the address to **267 Browning Ave, #2A**, and then press RETURN to leave Field View. You have made the needed additions and changes, but they have not been saved to disk; if you were to shut off the PC (never recommended while inside a program), the changes would be lost. To save the changes, press Do-It! (F2), and the edits will be written to disk.

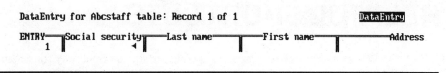

Figure 4-4.   Table used for data entry

USING DATAENTRY
TO ADD RECORDS

Although you can add records to a table when you are in Edit mode, that is not the best way to do it. As you have seen, Edit mode lets you change or delete records, something you normally do not do while adding new records. In Edit mode, there is always the possibility that you could hit the wrong key and make a change to an existing table. For adding a large number of records, Paradox provides the DataEntry choice, available from the Modify menu. The difference between using DataEntry and Edit is that existing records are not displayed when you use DataEntry, so you cannot delete or alter those records.

To add records with DataEntry, simply choose Modify from the main menu and then choose DataEntry from the next menu. Paradox will prompt you for the name of the table into which you wish to enter data; enter the desired name, or press RETURN for a list of tables to select from. Once you have chosen the desired table, a new table will appear, which you will use for adding new records, as shown in Figure 4-4.

When you use DataEntry mode, Paradox creates a temporary table named ENTRY with a structure that matches the table you just selected. All of the new records that you enter will be stored in this temporary table. After adding the last record, you may want to use ALT- F7 to get an instant report of the temporary table; you can then check your work for any errors. Once you complete the record entry, you can press Do-It! (F2), and the records will be inserted automatically into the permanent table.

HELPFUL SHORTCUTS

While adding new records, you may find certain "shortcut" key combinations offered by Paradox to be quite useful. One such combination is the Ditto key combination (CTRL-D), used to repeat a prior entry without retyping. Pressing CTRL-D when in a blank field of a new record will tell Paradox to repeat the entry stored in the field immediately above. Another useful shortcut key, which only applies to date fields, is the spacebar. If you press the spacebar while in a date field, Paradox will automatically enter the month, then the day, and then the year (as measured by the PC's clock) into the date field.

HANDS-ON PRACTICE: USING THE SHORTCUT KEYS

An example of the usefulness of the shortcut keys is illustrated by ABC Temporaries' hiring of the spouse of an existing employee, Marcia Morse. Instead of manually typing all of the characters for William Morse, you can insert a new record under the one for Marcia Morse and then use the shortcut keys to duplicate much of the information and to enter today's date as the date of hire. If you are not in Edit mode now, go to it by pressing F9, and move the cursor to the record immediately following the one for Marcia Morse. Press the INS key once, and a new record will appear, as shown in Figure 4-5.

```
Editing Abcstaff table: Record 4 of 10                          Edit

┌─Last name───┬─First name──┬─────────Address─────────┬─City─────
 Westman        Andrea        4807 East Avenue           Silver Spr
 Robinson       Shirley       267 Browning Ave #2A       Takoma Par
 Morse          Marcia        4260 Park Avenue           Chevy Chas

 Jackson     ◄  David         4102 Valley Lane           Falls Chur
 Robinson       Wanda         1607 21st Street, NW       Washington
 Abernathy      Sandra        1512 Redskins Park Drive   Herndon
 Hart           Edward        6200 Germantown Road       Fairfax
 Mitchell       Mary Jo       617 North Oakland Street   Arlington
 Jones          Judi          5203 North Shore Drive     Reston
```

Figure 4-5.   New record inserted into existing table

Place the cursor in the Social security field and enter **805-34-6789**. Move the cursor to the First name field and enter **William**. For most of the remaining fields, you can duplicate the fields in the previous record. In succession, move the cursor to the Last name, Address, City, State, and ZIP Code fields, and press CTRL-D each time to duplicate the entry from the prior record. For the Date of birth field, enter **8/17/52**.

For the Date hired field, press the spacebar three times. Each time you press the spacebar, Paradox will insert part of the current date; the month, followed by the day, and finally, the year. To complete the entry of the new record, enter **1** for Dependents, **7.50** for Salary, **Smith Builders** for Assignment, and **12.00** for Hourly Rate; then move to the Phone field and again use CTRL-D to duplicate the prior entry.

FINDING A RECORD QUICKLY

With a table as small as the one we have created in our example so far, you can easily find a record by looking for a specific name within the table. However, when there are hundreds or thousands of names and items in your tables, finding a record will not be that simple. Paradox offers sophisticated query features for selecting one or more records; these are detailed in Chapter 6. However, you can also use a quick method to search for the first record that contains desired information: the Zoom key (CTRL-Z).

To use the Zoom key, simply place the cursor in the field you wish to search, press CTRL-Z, and enter the value that you wish to search for. Capitalization must be exactly the same here as it is in the record. For example, if you place the cursor in the Social security field and press CTRL-Z, Paradox will display the following prompt:

Value:
Enter value or pattern to search for.

If you enter **876-54-3210**, the cursor will move to the matching social security number, which is for Mr. Hart. In a similar fashion, you can place the cursor in the Last name field, press CTRL-Z, and enter **Westman** in response to the prompt, and the cursor will move to the record for Ms. Westman. This works well for simple searches or for searches in which you are searching a unique key field (such as Social security).

Remember   Place the cursor in the field you want to search before using the Zoom (CTRL-Z) key.

The Zoom key finds the first occurrence of the item, so if you search for Robinson in the Last name column, you will find the first "Robinson" in the table, which may or may not be the one you are looking for. You could use the ALT-Z key combination (Zoom Next) to find the next occurrence of the same search value. When you want to search for items that are dependent on more than one field (as in a combination of last and first name), you must resort to the more powerful query features offered by Paradox.

DELETING A RECORD

If you want to delete an existing record, get into Edit mode with F9, place the cursor in any field of the record, and press the DEL key. The record will be removed from the table, and the next record below it (if there is one) will assume the deleted record's place in the table. You can use Undo (CTRL-U) to undo a deletion if desired. When you have saved the edits by pressing the Do-It! key, the deletion will become permanent.

CHANGING THE TABLE'S LAYOUT

While working with your data, you may find that you frequently need to see particular kinds of information at a glance. For example, the ABC Temporaries table contains a number of fields, not all of which can be viewed in tabular form at the same time. However, for most day-to-day needs, the staff can get the needed data from four fields: Last name, Social security, Phone, and Assignment. If these fields could be viewed at once, most requests for information could be satisfied with one quick glance at the screen.

To meet such needs, Paradox lets you change the appearance of the table on the screen. You can move columns around, or shrink or expand the width of columns, to present an optimal viewing area. The underlying data in your table does not change when you do this; only the appearance of the table on the screen is affected.

To move a column you use the Move command, available from the Image menu. From the main menu you can select Image and then Move, and Paradox will display a list of the fields in the table. You can select the field you wish to move, and then place the cursor in any field. (The field to be moved will appear where the cursor is, and all other fields will shift to the right.) Press RETURN, and the field will be moved. Note that CTRL-R can also be used to move one column at a time.

You can also change the width of a column to provide additional room for the display of other columns. To change column widths, you use the ColumnSize command, also available from the Image menu. (By now it is probably clear that most

```
TableSize ColumnSize Format Zoom Move PickForm KeepSet Graph
Change the number of records to show in the current image.
```

Use → and ← keys to move around menu, then press ↵ to make selection.

FIGURE 4-6.   Image menu

of the commands available from the Image menu are used to affect the image on your screen.) From the main menu you can select Image and then ColumnSize; then you can move the cursor to the column you wish to resize. With the cursor positioned in the desired column, press RETURN. Paradox will tell you to use the left and right arrow keys to resize the column. As you press the left or right arrow key, the column will expand or contract in width on the screen. (Unaltered alphanumeric fields can only be contracted, while numeric fields can be expanded.) When the field is the size you want, press RETURN, and the change will be complete.

There are other useful commands available from the Image menu, all worth considering. When you choose Image from the main menu, the Image menu appears, containing the choices shown in Figure 4-6. As you know, ColumnSize and Move are used to resize or move a column. TableSize is used to change the number of records that Paradox will display in the current table; this can be useful when you are working with more than one table on the screen. (Successive chapters will show you how this can be done.)

The Format command lets you change the display format for numeric, currency, and date fields. For numbers and currency fields, Paradox lets you format a column in standard format (all numbers justified), fixed number of decimal places, numbers with commas inserted, or scientific (exponential) format. Dates can be formatted as mm/dd/yy, dd-mon-yy (with the month spelled as a three-character abbreviation), or dd.mm.yy.

To try reformatting a column, press F10 for the menu, and choose Image and then Format. Paradox will ask you to move the cursor to the field to be reformatted. Place the cursor in the Date of birth field, and press RETURN.

Paradox will next display the three available date formats on the screen. Select dd-mon-yy from the list, and you will see the dates change to the European date format. If you prefer, you can change them back by again pressing F10 for the menu and choosing Image/Format, reselecting the Date of birth field, and choosing the mm/dd/yy format from the list of available formats.

The Zoom command (called GoTo in earlier versions of Paradox) is available from the main menu, or from the Image menu while in Edit or DataEntry mode. The Zoom command provides another way to move the cursor to an item. Using Zoom, you can quickly move the cursor to a named field, a specific record, or a field containing a certain value. Zoom can be useful when you are viewing a table with a large number of fields and want to move to a certain field quickly. To use this option, begin your data entry or editing; then press F10, choose Image, and choose Zoom. The next menu to appear provides three options: Field, Record Number, and Value. Choose Value and enter the desired data to find that value. (Field takes you to a field you give by name, while Record Number takes you to the record number you specify.)

The PickForm command lets you use a specific form to view the table. (Forms will be discussed in greater detail in the next chapter.) The KeepSet command will make permanent any changes that you make in the way the table appears. Keep in mind that your changes do not affect the actual data contained in the table; only the appearance of that data is altered by the commands that you use from the Image menu.

The Graph command lets you change, load, or save graph settings. Topics regarding graphs will be covered in Chapter 8.

Changes you make in the way Paradox displays a table with the Image command are not permanent unless you save those changes. Normally, Paradox disposes of any image settings in effect when you choose Exit from the main menu to leave the program. When you next load Paradox and view the same table, Paradox will use the default table to display the data. With the KeepSet command, accessible from the Image menu, you can save your changes to the image.

To save the image, choose Image from the main menu, and then choose KeepSet. Paradox will briefly display the message "settings recorded." The current image settings will be saved in a file named after your database, but with an extension of .SET. Whenever you load that table, Paradox will use the image settings recorded in the .SET file.

HANDS-ON PRACTICE: CHANGING THE TABLE'S LAYOUT

Since the ABC Temporaries staff wants to see the Social security, Last name, Phone, and Assignment fields most frequently, you can move the columns containing these fields to the left side of the table. If the main menu is not currently displayed, press F10 to see it. Choose Image and then Move, and Paradox will ask for the name of the field to be moved.

Choose Phone from the list. When you select the field, Paradox will ask you to use the left and right arrow keys to show the new position for the field. Place the cursor in the First name field, and then press RETURN to move the field. Paradox will place the Phone field to the left of the cursor, between the Last name and First name fields.

Press F10 to display the main menu, and again choose Image and then Move. For the desired field, choose Assignment. Place the cursor in the First name field, and press RETURN. The column containing the employee assignments will be moved to its new location, as shown in Figure 4-7.

```
Viewing Abcstaff table: Record 1 of 10                              Main

   ┌─Last name─────────Phone─────────Assignment────────First name─┐
   │ Westman        301-555-5682   National Oil Co.   Andrea      │
   │ Robinson       301-555-4582   National Oil Co.   Shirley     │
   │ Morse          301-555-9876   National Oil Co.   Marcia      │
   │ Jackson        703-555-2345   City Revenue Dept. David       │
   │ Robinson       202-555-9876   City Revenue Dept. Wanda       │
   │ Abernathy      703-555-7337   City Revenue Dept. Sandra      │
   │ Morse          301-555-9876   Smith Builders     William     │
   │ Hart           703-555-7834   Smith Builders     Edward      │
   │ Mitchell       703-555-7654   Smith Builders     Mary Jo     │
   │ Jones          703-555-2638   National Oil Co.   Judi        │
```

Figure 4-7. New location of columns

One last point noted by the staff of ABC Temporaries is that if the Last name column were shortened a bit, enough of the first name column would appear to be useful. Press F10 to display the main menu, and choose Image and then ColumnSize. Paradox will ask you to place the cursor in the column to be resized.

Move the cursor to the Last name column, and press RETURN. Paradox next asks that you use the left and right arrow keys to change the column's size. Press the left arrow key five times to shorten the column's width by five characters. Then press RETURN to complete the change. To make this change in appearance permanent, press F10 for the menu, choose Image, and then choose KeepSet.

VIEWING MORE THAN ONE TABLE

Because Paradox is a relational database, you can use it to work extensively with multiple tables at the same time. Later chapters will explain how relationships can be drawn between multiple tables. For now, however, the ability to simply view more than one table on the screen will come in handy.

ABC Temporaries needs an additional table that will show how many hours were worked by a given employee for a given firm while on assignment. This table, called HOURS, will be used along with the ABCSTAFF table throughout the remainder of this text, so we will create it in this section.

After some analysis, the management staff at ABC Temporaries decides that the fields shown in Table 4-2 need to be tracked. Note that in this table, a key field designation will *not* be assigned to any field. There will be intentional duplicates in every field in this table; any record may have the same social security number as other records, and the same fact goes for the Assignment, Weekend date, and Hours worked fields.

Field Name	Field Type	Length
Assignment	Alphanumeric	20
Social security	Alphanumeric	11
Weekend date	Date	
Hours worked	Numeric	

TABLE 4-2.   Fields for HOURS Table

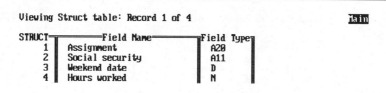

STRUCT	Field Name	Field Type
1	Assignment	A20
2	Social security	A11
3	Weekend date	D
4	Hours worked	N

Hours table has 15 records

FIGURE 4-8. Structure for HOURS table

Press F10 to display the main menu, choose Create to create a new table, and enter **HOURS** for the name of the table. Using Table 4-2 as a guide, create the four fields of the table. When you have finished defining the fields, the structure should look like the example in Figure 4-8. Press Do-It! (F2), and the new table will be created. Paradox will return to the display of the existing table you were working with earlier.

Now that you have two tables, you can view both simultaneously. Press F10 to display the main menu, and choose View. For the name of the table, enter **HOURS**. The empty table will appear ready for use below the ABCSTAFF table, as shown in Figure 4-9.

You can tell which table is current (in use) by the location of the cursor. Unless you have moved it, the cursor is currently in the new HOURS table. Press Edit (F9), and the cursor will appear in the first record of the new table. Since you will not be disturbing any existing records, it is safe to add new records directly from Edit mode. If you prefer to use a form for entry, press F7 to switch to a form. Add the records shown in Table 4-3 to the new table; remember the helpful shortcut CTRL-D key combination for duplicating data. When you have finished adding the records, press Do-It! (F2) to save the new records to disk.

With two tables on the screen, as you now have, things get a little more complex. You cannot possibly see all of the records from both tables at the same time, so you must make some decisions about what you want to work with. Of major importance when dealing with more than one table are the Up Image (F3) and Down Image (F4)

```
Viewing Hours table: Table is empty                              Main

ABCSTAFF┬Social security┬─────Last name─────┬─────First name─────┬────────Address
      1 ║ 121-33-9876    │ Westman           │ Andrea             │ 4807 East Avenu
      2 ║ 121-90-5432    │ Robinson          │ Shirley            │ 267 Browning Av
      3 ║ 123-44-8976    │ Morse             │ Marcia             │ 4260 Park Avenu
      4 ║ 232-55-1234    │ Jackson           │ David              │ 4182 Valley Lan
      5 ║ 343-55-9821    │ Robinson          │ Wanda              │ 1607 21st Stree
      6 ║ 495-00-3456    │ Abernathy         │ Sandra             │ 1512 Redskins P
      7 ║ 805-34-6789    │ Morse             │ William            │ 4260 Park Avenu
      8 ║ 876-54-3210    │ Hart              │ Edward             │ 6200 Germantown
      9 ║ 901-77-3456    │ Mitchell          │ Mary Jo            │ 617 North Oakla
     10 ║ 909-88-7654    │ Jones             │ Judi               │ 5203 North Shor


HOURS─┬──────Assignment──────┬Social security┬Weekend date┬Hours worked─┐
```

Figure 4-9.   Appearance of two tables

keys, which are used to move between images on the screen. Since you are currently viewing tables, these tables are your screen "images." (If you are viewing the records through a form, press F7 to get back to a table view.)

Assignment	Social security	Weekend date	Hours worked
National Oil Co.	909-88-7654	1/16/88	35
National Oil Co.	121-33-9876	1/16/88	30
National Oil Co.	121-90-5432	1/16/88	27
National Oil Co.	123-44-8976	1/16/88	32
City Revenue Dept.	343-55-9821	1/16/88	35
City Revenue Dept.	495-00-3456	1/16/88	28
City Revenue Dept.	232-55-1234	1/16/88	30
Smith Builders	876-54-3210	1/23/88	30
Smith Builders	901-77-3456	1/23/88	28
Smith Builders	805-34-6789	1/23/88	35
City Revenue Dept.	232-55-1234	1/23/88	30
City Revenue Dept.	495-00-3456	1/23/88	32
City Revenue Dept.	343-55-9821	1/23/88	32
National Oil Co.	121-33-9876	1/23/88	35
National Oil Co.	909-88-7654	1/23/88	33

TABLE 4-3.   New Records for HOURS Table

Try pressing F3 and F4 repeatedly, and note that the keys move the cursor back and forth between the two tables. All of your Paradox menu commands will apply to the active table, or the table that the cursor is currently located within.

HANDS-ON PRACTICE: RESIZING A TABLE

You can resize the tables in order to give more of the screen to one table than to another. For example, you may decide that you only need to see a few employee names at a time, while you would like to view simultaneously as many records of the hours worked as will comfortably fit on the screen.

To reduce the size of the ABCSTAFF table, first press Up Image (F3) so that the cursor is in the ABCSTAFF table. Press F10 to display the main menu. Choose Image and then TableSize. Paradox will ask you to use the up or down arrow key to increase or decrease the size of the table in rows. Press the up arrow key five times, and then press RETURN. The ABCSTAFF table will assume the new size, providing additional space to the HOURS table, as shown in Figure 4-10.

CHECKING A FIELD'S VALIDITY

A powerful feature of Paradox, called ValCheck, lets you define conditions that entries into fields must meet before they will be accepted. Using this feature, you could, for example, specify a minimum and a maximum salary for a salary field, or you could specify that a date field not allow any entries earlier than a certain date. You can even define *lookup tables*, which are other Paradox tables that can be used as a cross-reference for data entry or editing. (These tables must be created before you use the ValCheck option.) With a lookup table of valid state abbreviations, for example, you could specify that all entries into a state field be accepted only if a match for the entry were found in another database containing the valid state names. Validity checks apply to records that are changed as well as those that are added. To set validity checks, you use Modify/DataEntry to begin the data entry. You then press F10 for the menu, and choose ValCheck. For editing, you choose Modify/Edit to begin the editing process, press F10 for the menu, and choose ValCheck.

≡Note≡ Validity checks can reduce data-entry errors.

```
Viewing Abcstaff table: Record 5 of 10                          Main  —▼

ABCSTAFF┬Social security┬────Last name────┬────First name───┬──────────Address─────
     1  │ 121-33-9876   │ Westman         │ Andrea          │ 4807 East Avenu
     2  │ 121-90-5432   │ Robinson        │ Shirley         │ 267 Browning Av
     3  │ 123-44-8976   │ Morse           │ Marcia          │ 4260 Park Avenu
     4  │ 232-55-1234   │ Jackson         │ David           │ 4102 Valley Lan
     5  │ 343-55-9821   │ Robinson        │ Wanda           │ 1607 21st Stree


HOURS─┬──────Assignment──────┬─Social security─┬─Weekend date─┬─Hours worked─
     1│ National Oil Co.      │ 909-88-7654     │ 1/16/88      │    35
     2│ National Oil Co.      │ 121-33-9876     │ 1/16/88      │    30
     3│ National Oil Co.      │ 121-90-5432     │ 1/16/88      │    27
     4│ National Oil Co.      │ 123-44-8976     │ 1/16/88      │    32
     5│ City Revenue Dept.    │ 343-55-9821     │ 1/16/88      │    35
     6│ City Revenue Dept.    │ 495-00-3456     │ 1/16/88      │    28
     7│ City Revenue Dept.    │ 232-55-1234     │ 1/16/88      │    30
     8│ Smith Builders        │ 876-54-3210     │ 1/23/88      │    30
     9│ Smith Builders        │ 901-77-3456     │ 1/23/88      │    28
    10│ Smith Builders        │ 805-34-6789     │ 1/23/88      │    35
    11│ City Revenue Dept.    │ 232-55-1234     │ 1/23/88      │    30
    12│ City Revenue Dept.    │ 495-00-3456     │ 1/23/88      │    32
    13│ City Revenue Dept.    │ 343-55-9821     │ 1/23/88      │    32
    14│ National Oil Co.      │ 121-33-9876     │ 1/23/88      │    35
```

FIGURE 4-10. Tables after resizing

As an example, consider setting a minimum and maximum salary for employees of ABC Temporaries. Press F10 for the main menu, and choose Modify/DataEntry. For the name of the table, enter **ABCSTAFF**. (While you may or may not want to add data at this time, you must be in DataEntry or Edit mode to set validity checks, because the ValCheck option is reached from the DataEntry or Edit menu.)

Now that you are in DataEntry mode, press F10 for the menu. You will see that ValCheck is one of the available options. Choose ValCheck now. Paradox presents the following options:

Define   Clear
Define a range, lookup table, or picture check for a field in current image.

The Clear option clears an existing validity check; the Define option sets new validity checks. Choose Define now. Paradox asks you to move the cursor to the field to which the validity check is to apply. Since you want to limit the possible salaries, use the cursor keys to place the cursor in the Salary field, then press RETURN. You will see the following options:

LowValue HighValue Default TableLookup Picture Required
Specify the lowest acceptable value for the field.

Before proceeding, a word of explanation about the options is in order. The LowValue and HighValue options are used to specify a minimum and maximum value, as you will do for the Salary field. Such values can be numbers, dates, or even letters (for example, A for a low value and M for a high value could limit names to those starting with the letter A through M). The Default option lets you set a default value that Paradox will place automatically in a particular field. For example, you might want to place the minimum wage as a default value in a salary field if most employees were paid that amount.

The TableLookup option lets you specify the name of another Paradox table, which will provide acceptable values for the validity check. For example, you might want to limit entries in a ZIP code field to a certain group of ZIP codes. You could create another Paradox table containing only one field with the same field structure, store the acceptable ZIP codes in the records of that table, and use that table's name with the TableLookup option. (You must first create the table that will serve as a lookup table before you can use the TableLookup option.)

The Picture option lets you specify a valid format that entries must match before they will be accepted. For example, you could limit telephone numbers to a ten-number format, with the area code surrounded by parentheses and the prefix and suffix separated by hyphens, by using a picture format like the following:

(###)###-####

Paradox would supply the literal characters (the hyphen and parentheses) automatically; the user would not need to type these in each record. You can use any of the symbols shown in Table 4-4 within a picture format.

Symbol	Function
#	Represents any numeric digit
?	Represents any letter
&	Converts letters to uppercase
!	Accepts any characters; converts letters to uppercase
;	Takes the next character literally
*	Repetition counts (use to repeat a character)
[ ]	Specifies items that are optional
{ }	Grouping operator
,	Separates alternate values

TABLE 4-4.   Picture Formats

The repetition count character (*) is the equivalent of repeating another picture symbol a specified number of times. For example, the following pictures perform the same task, that of allowing up to ten numeric digits in a field:

```
##########
*10#
```

The [ ] brackets for optional elements tell Paradox that the entry in this area is optional. For example, you could specify a picture for a telephone number, with the area code as optional, with a format like this one:

```
[###] ###-####
```

The comma can be used to separate alternate values, which is useful for multiple-choice types of applications. For example, if four different prices of 1.99, 2.99, 5.99, and 7.99 are the only acceptable entries in a dollar field, you could use a picture like the following:

```
{1.99,2.99,5.99,7.99}
```

The curly braces are grouping operators. The braces surround any group of acceptable items in a picture.

Finally, the Required option is used to specify whether a field may be left blank. Keep in mind that you must move the cursor into the field for the validity check to be tested. If the user never moves the cursor into a required field, the record could be saved without filling in the required field.

Keep in mind that you can use the various validity check options in combination with others. For example, a field could have a low value, a high value, and be a required field.

Getting back to the example, the Salary field needs a minimum (low) and a maximum (high) value. Choose LowValue from the menu. Paradox asks for a value. Enter **4.50** for the minimum value. You will see the message "Low value recorded" appear at the lower-right corner of the screen.

Press F10 for the menu and choose ValCheck again; then choose Define. Since the cursor is still in the Salary field, you can press RETURN to select this field again. Choose HighValue and enter **18.00** as the maximum acceptable salary. This time, the message "High value recorded" will appear in the lower-right corner of the screen.

You can now press Do-It! (F2) to leave DataEntry mode and return to viewing the ABCSTAFF table. The values recorded by the ValCheck options will take effect for any additions or edits you make to the ABCSTAFF table.

SORTING A TABLE

After a database is built, you may need to arrange it in different ways. As an example, consider the needs of the staff at ABC Temporaries. Judi, who does the accounting, often wants to refer to a list of employees arranged by the amount of salary. Marge, the personnel administrator, prefers to keep a list organized in alphabetical order by name, while Bill, who mails assignments and paychecks to the staff, wants to keep a list arranged by ZIP codes. You can arrange a table by *sorting,* which means changing the order of the table.

When Paradox sorts a table, it rearranges all records in the table according to the specified new order. If the table you sort contains a key field, Paradox writes the sorted records to a new table. If the table is not keyed, you are given the option of placing the sorted records in a new table or in the existing table. If you were to sort a table of names arranged in random order, the sorted table would contain all the records that were in the old table, but they would be arranged in alphabetical order, as shown in Figure 4-11.

You must choose one or more fields on which to sort. In some cases, you will need to sort a database on more than one field. As an example, if you sort a database with last names as the sort field, you may get groups of records with the same last names but with the first names in random order. In such a case, you can sort the database with one field (such as last names) as the primary sort field and another field (such as first names) as the secondary sort field.

To sort a table, you will use the Sort option of the Modify menu. Display the main menu with F10 if necessary, and choose Modify/Sort. Paradox will ask you for the name of the table that is to be sorted; you can enter the name or press RETURN to display a list of tables to choose from. If the table you choose to sort has a key field, Paradox will next ask you to give a name to the new table that will result from the sort. If the table is not keyed, you next must choose Same, which places the results of the sort in the same table, or New, which places the results of the sort in a new table. Supply the name for the new table if you are making one, and the Sort Form will appear (as shown in Figure 4-12).

The Sort Form allows you to sort a table by any field, or combination of fields, in ascending or descending order. The arrow keys are used to move the cursor throughout the fields. Numbers indicating the sorting priority (1, 2, 3, and so on) are placed next to each desired field. As an example, if you wished to sort a table by ZIP codes, you would place a 1 next to the ZIP Code field. If you wished to sort by ZIP codes and, where the ZIP codes were the same, by last names, you would place a 1 next to the ZIP Code field and a 2 next to the Last name field.

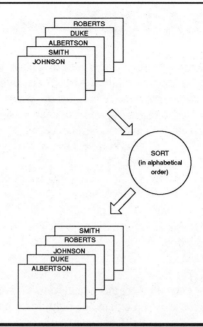

FIGURE 4-11.   Sorting records in a database

Sorting Abcstaff table into new SORTS table   Sort

Number fields to set up sort order (1, 2, etc.). If you want a field sorted
  in descending sequence, follow the number with a 'D' (e.g., '2D').
        Ascending is the normal sequence and need not be indicated.

    ◄ Social security
      Last name
      First name
      Address
      City
      State
      ZIP Code
      Date of birth
      Date hired
      Dependents
      Salary
      Assignment
      Hourly Rate
      Phone

FIGURE 4-12.   Sort Form

Indicating the Sort Order

Paradox assumes you wish to sort fields in ascending order. Ascending order means from A through Z if the sorted field is an alphanumeric field, from lowest to highest number for numeric or currency fields, and from earliest to latest date for date fields. In most cases, this is how you will want the table to be sorted. When you prefer descending order, however, you can indicate your preference by adding the letter "D" beside the number that indicates the sort priority. For example, entering the designation 1D beside the Last name field of a table would tell Paradox that you wished to sort on the last names in descending order (the letters Z through A). The designation 1A would indicate ascending order. If you omit the letter entirely, Paradox assumes ascending order. (When sorting, also note that uppercase letters are placed before lowercase ones.) Paradox sorts using the ASCII Sort Order, which is punctuation marks, then uppercase letters, then lowercase letters, then extended characters, in order of the character's ASCII value.

Performing the Sort

Once you have entered the desired designations in the Sort Form, press Do-It! (F2). Paradox will perform the sort, and the results will appear in the new table on your screen.

 If you want records in a report to print in a particular order, sort the table first, then produce the report using the sorted table.

HANDS-ON PRACTICE: SORTING A TABLE

Things are always clearer with an example, so try one now. Press ALT-F8 to clear any remaining tables from the screen. Then choose the Modify option from the main menu, choose Sort from the Modify menu, and enter **ABCSTAFF** for the name of the table to sort. When Paradox asks for a name for the new (sorted) table, enter **SORTS** as the name. Paradox will then display the Sort Form.

To satisfy Judi's request for a list of employees arranged by amount of salary, move the cursor down until it is beside the Salary field and enter **1**. The number 1 indicates the priority of fields, in order of importance, that will determine how the database will

```
Viewing Sorts table: Record 1 of 10                          Main

┌─Date hired─┬─Dependents─┬──Salary─┬─────Assignment─────┬─Ho─
│  11/17/87  │     1      │   7.50  │ National Oil Co.    │ ***
│   9/05/85  │     1      │   7.50  │ City Revenue Dept.  │ ***
│   9/17/87  │     0      │   7.50  │ City Revenue Dept.  │ ***
│   2/02/88  │     1      │   7.50  │ Smith Builders      │ ***
│  12/01/87  │     1      │   7.50  │ Smith Builders      │ ***
│   7/25/85  │     2      │   8.50  │ National Oil Co.    │ ***
│  10/19/86  │     3      │   8.50  │ Smith Builders      │ ***
│   2/17/88  │     1      │  10.00  │ City Revenue Dept.  │ ***
│   8/12/86  │     1      │  12.00  │ National Oil Co.    │ ***
│   7/04/86  │     2      │  15.00  │ National Oil Co.    │ ***
```

FIGURE 4-13.   Sorted database

be sorted. When a database is sorted on a single field, this order has no real meaning, but when you sort a table on more than one field (as you will in later examples), you can use this column to choose which fields will take priority over other fields.

Once the criteria for the sort have been entered in the Sort Form, the sort can be performed by pressing Do-It! (F2). Press F2 now, and the table will be sorted. The new table will appear, arranged by the amount of salary in ascending order (as shown in Figure 4-13).

Note If records are added to a table following a sort, the new records are not automatically placed in any sorted order. If you want those records to fall into a proper order, you must again sort the table after the addition of the records.

Sorting on Multiple Fields

Let's say you have printed the table and passed it along to Judi, who immediately decided that wherever the salaries were the same, the names should appear in alphabetical order. This requires a sort on more than one field.

Press F8 to clear the table from the screen. Then again choose Modify/Sort from the main menu and enter **ABCSTAFF** for the name of the table to sort. When Paradox asks for a name for the new (sorted) table, enter **SORTS**. Paradox will respond to your attempt to make use of the same name with this prompt:

Cancel   Replace
A table with this name already exists, do not reuse name.

```
Viewing Sorts table: Record 1 of 10                        Main

SORTS─Social security─  ─Last name─        ─Salary─   ─First name─
   1    232-55-1234    Jackson              7.50      David
   2    901-77-3456    Mitchell             7.50      Mary Jo
   3    805-34-6789    Morse                7.50      William
   4    121-90-5432    Robinson             7.50      Shirley
   5    343-55-9821    Robinson             7.50      Wanda
   6    876-54-3210    Hart                 8.50      Edward
   7    123-44-8976    Morse                8.50      Marcia
   8    495-00-3456    Abernathy           10.00      Sandra
   9    909-88-7654    Jones               12.00      Judi
  10    121-33-9876    Westman             15.00      Andrea
```

FIGURE 4-14. Table sorted by amount, last name

As a precaution, Paradox is asking for confirmation before it will replace the prior table named SORTS with another one. Choose Replace from the menu to tell Paradox to proceed, and the Sort Form will appear.

Place the cursor beside the Salary field and enter **1**. Then place the cursor beside the Last name field and enter **2**. Again, since the letter "D" was not entered in either case, Paradox will assume that ascending order is desired.

The order that you have entered indicates that the table should be sorted in two ways. First, it will be arranged by the salary amount, in ascending numeric order. Second, where salaries are equal, the records will be sorted by last name in ascending alphabetical order. To see the results, press F2, and the new sorted table will appear, as shown in Figure 4-14. In the figure, the columns have been rearranged to show the Last name and Salary fields simultaneously.

Changing the Sort Direction

Now assume that Judi is happy with the printed table you have supplied, but Marge, who would like to see a list arranged by date hired with the earliest dates at the bottom of the list, doesn't care for the current order. To sort in descending order, you will need to change the direction of the sort.

Press F8 to clear the table from the screen, and then choose Modify/Sort from the main menu and enter **ABCSTAFF** for the name of the table to sort. When Paradox asks for a name for the new (sorted) table, enter **SORTS** as the name. Choose Replace from the next menu that appears. This tells Paradox to proceed, and the Sort Form will appear.

```
Viewing Sorts table: Record 1 of 10                                    Main
```

State	ZIP Code	Date of birth	Date hired	Dependents	Salary
VA	22071	10/02/59	2/17/88	1	10.00
MD	20815-0988	8/17/52	2/02/88	1	7.50
VA	22203	8/17/58	12/01/87	1	7.50
MD	20912	11/02/64	11/17/87	1	7.50
DC	20009	6/22/66	9/17/87	0	7.50
VA	22025	12/20/55	10/19/86	3	8.50
VA	22090	9/18/61	8/12/86	1	12.00
MD	20910-0124	5/29/61	7/04/86	2	15.00
VA	22044	12/22/55	9/05/85	1	7.50
MD	20815-0988	3/01/54	7/25/85	2	8.50

FIGURE 4-15.   Table sorted in descending order by date hired

Since you need to sort on the Date hired field this time, move the cursor to the Date hired field and enter **1D**. Then press F2 to implement the sort. The new table will display the records in order of the date of hire, with the earliest dates at the bottom of the table, as illustrated in Figure 4-15.

Future chapters will demonstrate how you can use Paradox to draw relationships between the two tables you have created, so you can produce reports showing the fees that should be billed to each of ABC Temporaries' clients. If this is a good time for a break, be sure to save your work first with Do-It! (F2). Then use Exit from the main menu to leave Paradox.

 Remember   When you sort a table with a key field, you must sort to a new table. When you sort a table with no key fields, Paradox gives you the option of sorting to the same table, or to a new table.

QUICK SUMMARY

To edit records in a table   Press F10 for the menu, and choose Modify/Edit. When prompted, enter the name of the table to edit. Paradox places you in the Edit mode. You can also press F9 while viewing a table.

To add a group of records to a table   Press F10 for the menu, and choose Modify/DataEntry. When prompted, enter the name of the table. A new (temporary) table appears, and you can proceed to add records to that table. When done, press the Do-It! (F2) key.

To quickly find a record   Place the cursor in the field to search, and press Zoom (CTRL-Z). Paradox will ask for a search value. Enter the desired value to search for. The cursor will move to the first occurrence of the value. Use Zoom Next (ALT-Z) to search for repeated occurrences of the same value.

To delete a record   Press Edit (F9). Place the cursor in any field of the record to be deleted, and press the DEL key.

To sort a table   Press F10 for the menu, and choose Modify/Sort. Enter the name of the table to be sorted. If asked, choose Same (to sort to the same table) or new (to sort to a new table). If asked, enter a name for the new table. When the Sort Form appears, enter the numbers indicating the sort order next to the desired fields. Press Do-It! (F2) to perform the sort.

USING
CUSTOM FORMS

So far, when you have been adding new records with DataEntry or making changes to a table with Edit, you have been using the Form Toggle key (F7) to switch from a table view to a simple on-screen entry form. This form listed the various fields and displayed highlighted areas that contained the actual data. For demonstrating how to add or change data within a database, this approach has been sufficient. However, there can be problems with such a straightforward approach to adding data to a table.

One drawback is the "unfriendly" screen that this approach presents to the computer user. If an ABC Temporaries employee does not know whether the hourly salary or the weekly salary belongs in the Salary field, the help screens or the Paradox manual will not offer any assistance. Another drawback is the lack of editing control you have

```
Editing Abcstaff table with form F2: Record 2 of 10          Edit  ▲—▼

    ┌─────────────────────────────────────────────────────┐
    │                             Social Security No.      │
    │  Last name: Robinson      ◄  121-90-5432             │
    │                                                      │
    │  First name: Shirley                                 │
    │                                                      │
    │  Address:267 Browning Ave #2A                        │
    │                                                      │
    │  City:Takoma Park      State:MD  ZIP Code:20912      │
    └─────────────────────────────────────────────────────┘
```

FIGURE 5-1.   Example of a custom form

within Paradox's default entry form. If for any reason you wish to prevent the editing of a particular field, you cannot do so with Edit.

To overcome such limitations, Paradox provides a flexible way to build *custom forms*. A custom form is simply a form of your own design that appears on the screen for data display and entry. Using Paradox, you can build custom forms that resemble the printed forms commonly used in an office. Figure 5-1 shows an example of such a form. You can also restrict entry by omitting or including certain fields in the form, or by making fields visible but unchangeable. And you can use Image/Pickform to use a specific custom form by default so that the form appears automatically when you use DataEntry and Edit commands.

If you are not already in Paradox, load the program now, and go to the main menu.

Note ≡ If you desire, you can design forms that resemble paper-based forms used in your office.

CREATING A CUSTOM FORM

Custom forms can be created with the Design command from the Form menu. There are four basic steps in this process:

1. Choose the table with which the form will be used.

2. Assign a number and a description to the form.

3. Using the screen as a drawing area, place the desired fields and enter any accompanying text and borders.

4. Store the form.

The first step is straightforward. From the main menu, choose Forms and then Design. Paradox will prompt you for a table name; enter **ABCSTAFF**, or press RETURN and choose ABCSTAFF from the list of available tables.

Paradox will next display a menu containing 14 numbers, along with the letter "F," a designation for "standard form." (The standard form is the one that Paradox normally displays when you use the Form Toggle key, F7, to switch from a table view to a form view. It is generally not a good idea to modify this form. If the standard form does not yet exist, Paradox automatically creates it for any table in use when you press F7.) You can assign any of the 14 number choices as names for your custom forms. This provides you with a total of 15 possible forms for each table. If you select a number that has previously been used for a custom form, Paradox will verify that you want to replace the previous form with the new one you are designing.

When you choose a number for the form, Paradox next asks for a description of the form. You can enter up to 40 characters (including spaces) as the description, which will appear as a part of the menu whenever you select a form. Once you enter the description, the screen clears, revealing only the current cursor position and a prompt that indicates that you are designing a form, as shown in Figure 5-2.

The Drawing Area

At the top right side of the screen appears the word "Form" in reverse highlighting. If you repeatedly press the INS key, you will see the "Ins" designation appear and disappear. This is the Insert Toggle indicator, which indicates whether you are in Insert mode (where typed characters push existing ones to the right) or in Overwrite mode

```
Designing new F1 form for Abcstaff                    Form ◄      1/1
    < 1, 1>
```

FIGURE 5-2. Drawing area

(where typed characters overwrite existing characters). To the right of the Insert Toggle indicator is the Page indicator, which shows which page of a multiple-page form currently appears on the screen. Paradox lets you design forms that appear on more than one screen (or "page"); the Page indicator is useful for determining where you are when working with such forms. The first number indicates the current page number, and the second number indicates the total number of pages in the form.

At the far left appears the Cursor Position indicator, which indicates the current row and column position of the cursor. As many as 23 lines can appear on each screen (or page) of the form.

Entering Labels

You can use the cursor keys to place descriptive text (such as the names for fields) anywhere you wish. To add labels and other descriptive text, simply enter the text at the desired location. The DEL and BACKSPACE keys can be used to remove unwanted characters, and you can move text strings to the right by inserting spaces ahead of the text while in Insert mode.

Placing Fields

To place fields in the form, use the Field command from the Form menu. To display the Form menu, press Menu (F10) while you are in the drawing area. The Form menu contains nine choices, as shown in Figure 5-3. The Field command is used to place or erase fields from the form, reformat a field's width, edit an expression used in a calculated field, or wrap text within a long field. The Area command lets you move

```
Field  Area  Border  Page  Style  Multi  Help  DO-IT!  Cancel  Form      1/1
Place, erase, reformat, recalculate, or wrap a field.
```

FIGURE 5-3.   Form menu

or erase an area on the form. The Border command lets you draw borders, and the Page command lets you add or delete pages.

The Style command lets you set the colors and the style of displayed characters by means of such options as screen intensity and reverse highlighting. The Multi command is used to define multitable or multirecord forms. Multitable forms are covered in Chapter 9, while multirecord forms are covered later in this chapter. The Help command provides the help screens associated with form design, while the Do-It! command saves the form. Finally, you can use the Cancel command to cancel the form design operation. You can also press ESCAPE to leave the menu and return to the drawing of the form.

For each field desired, press F10 to display the menu (if it does not already appear on the screen), choose Field, and then choose Place to place the field. From the next menu that appears, you can choose Regular if you desire a normal field, which can be edited; DisplayOnly for a field in which the contents appear but cannot be edited; Calculated for a field that will contain a value based on a calculation that uses the contents of other fields; or #Record to display the record number.

Field Choices

Regular fields are fields used for normal data entry and editing. They are actual fields from the table, as opposed to temporary values based on a calculation, and each field can be used in a form no more than once. You would not want to edit the same field twice anyway, so there should be no need to place the same regular field on a form more than one time.

Display-only fields contain the same information as regular fields, but they are used only to display the data and cannot be edited. Display-only fields are most common on multiple-page forms, where you want to show pertinent information. An example is showing a customer's name on every page of a four-page form, although the customer's name only needs to be entered or edited on the first page of the form.

Calculated fields are used to display the results of calculations that usually are based on the contents of other fields in the table. When you make a calculated field, Paradox will ask for an expression that provides the basis of the calculation. For example, if your table contained both an hourly salary field named Salary and an hours-worked field named Hours, using the expression [Salary] * [Hours] would display a calculated field containing the result of the Salary field multiplied by the Hours field. The asterisk indicates multiplication and brackets are always used to enclose field names in expressions. Calculated fields will be explained in more detail later in this chapter.

#Record, the final field choice, is used to insert the record number field at the desired location. The record number field will always display the record number of the current record.

Once you choose the type of field, you must in most cases tell Paradox which field will be placed on the screen. If you choose Regular or DisplayOnly, Paradox will show a list of all available fields in the table, and you can select from among the list. If you choose Calculated, Paradox will ask for the expression that provides the basis of the calculation. If you choose #Record, it assumes that you want to show the record number.

Once you choose the field type, Paradox asks you to place the cursor at the starting location for the field. You can use the cursor keys as well as HOME and END to move the cursor. HOME will move the cursor to the top of the screen, and END will move it to the bottom. Moving the cursor past the right edge is a shortcut for moving to the left edge of the screen, and moving the cursor past the left edge gets you to the right edge of the screen. With the cursor at the desired screen location, press RETURN. A solid underline representing the field will appear. You can use the left and right arrow keys to adjust the width of the field. The width defaults to the width needed to display the entire field, but you can shorten it and use Field/WordWrap to wrap long text fields. If you shorten a field but do not use WordWrap, you can scroll through data using the right arrow key. If you want to shorten a number field, it must be two digits longer than the maximum number currently stored in any record in the database.

Drawing Borders

In addition to placing fields and descriptive text on the form, you may wish to add borders. These can be easily added with the Border command from the Form menu. Press F10 to display the menu, if necessary, and choose Border and then Place to place the border on the screen. Paradox then provides the choices of Single-Line, Double-Line, or using a border character of your choice. When you select Other to use border characters of your choosing, ASCII graphics can be used by pressing ALT and typing the decimal number from the keypad. (For a listing of ASCII characters, see Appendix D of the PAL manual.) Make the desired selection, and then use the cursor keys to place the cursor at one corner of the border and press RETURN. Then move the cursor to the other corner, and press RETURN again. If the two cursor positions have the same horizontal or vertical coordinate, a line will be drawn using the specified character or single or double line. If the coordinates are at different horizontal and vertical locations, a box will be drawn.

Dealing with Wordwrap

Depending on your application, you may encounter amounts of text that are too large to fit comfortably on a single line of a screen. As an example, consider the following database for tracking billings at a law firm:

Date	Rate	Hours	Description
10/02/87	150	2	Filing, preparation for appeal in case of United States government vs. John Doe
10/16/87	65	6.5	Westlaw, library research on Internal Revenue Service statutes and precedents in prior rulings

When entering such data into a form, it would be helpful if the entire Description field could be viewed without your having to scroll with the cursor keys. However, the text is clearly going to extend past a single line in most cases. The solution is to use the WordWrap option, which is available once you select the Field option from the Form menu.

To wrap a field within a custom form, first reformat the field to the desired width on the form. Then press F10 if necessary to display the Form menu. Choose Field and then WordWrap. Paradox will ask you to move to the desired field. Place the cursor in the field you want to wrap, and press RETURN to select that field. Paradox will now display the following prompt:

Number of lines: 0
Enter the number of lines to wrap onto, or press ↵ to leave unchanged.

Paradox is asking for the maximum number of lines that the wrapped text will be allowed to occupy on the form. Enter the desired number of lines to complete the placement of the wrapped field.

Note that you cannot add fields, text, or borders in the area needed for the maximum amount of wrapped text. For example, if you place a field on line 15 and allow it to wrap a maximum of 3 lines, down to line 18, you cannot place other fields on line 18 in the area that the wrapped field occupies. If you attempt to do so, Paradox will display a warning message when you attempt to save the form, and you must correct the error before the form can be saved.

Also keep in mind that the maximum field width (the width specified in your table structure) must exceed the displayed width for wordwrap to take effect. To calculate the number of lines needed to wrap text, use the formula, MAX WIDTH/DISPLAY WIDTH = NO. OF LINES.

Wrapped fields can be used for data entry or for editing records. If a value is still too long to fit in the field, you can use Field View (ALT-F5) to view and edit the entire value. If this happens often, you always have the option of changing the form's design so that still more lines are allowed in the wrapped field.

Saving the Form

When all the desired fields, borders, text, and other elements have been placed, you can choose Do-It! from the menu, and the form will be stored. To use the form, view a table in the normal manner. From the main menu choose Image and then PickForm, and select the desired form from the list of choices. Use Image KeepSet to invoke the form automatically.

HANDS-ON PRACTICE: DESIGNING A TWO-PAGE PERSONNEL FORM

A detailed multipage form can be demonstrated by building such a form for use with the ABC Temporaries staff table. Since most updates to the staff table are performed when an employee moves to a new address, the personnel department wishes to use a two-page form for updating records in the table. The first page of the form will display the name and address information for each employee, while the second page will display the remaining information. Since employees do not normally change social security numbers, the personnel manager wants the Social security field to be display-only. And the manager also wants a "profitability" field, which will contain the result of the salary subtracted from the hourly rate for each employee. When completed, the form will resemble the example shown in Figure 5-4.

To begin designing the form, get to the main menu and choose Forms and Design. Enter **ABCSTAFF** for the name of the table, or press RETURN and select ABCSTAFF

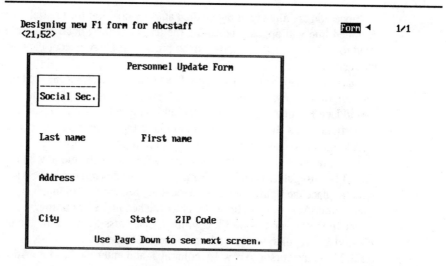

FIGURE 5-4.   Example of personnel form

from the list provided. From the next menu, which shows the 14 available numbers, select 1 to identify the form. Paradox will prompt you for a description of the form. Enter **Personnel Update Form** as the description, and the drawing area will appear.

Note that although you can choose a field to place and then move the cursor after you have selected the field, it may be better to first locate the cursor at the desired starting location. Once you start using the menus, you will not be able to see the Cursor Position indicator. If the Form menu is currently on the screen, press ESCAPE to hide the menu. Then place the cursor at row 5, column 5. This will serve as the starting position for the first field, Social security.

Note ≡ The row and column indicators are helpful for determining cursor location when designing forms.

Press F10 to display the Form menu. Choose Field and then Place to insert the first field. This will be the Social Sec. field, which should not be edited, so choose DisplayOnly from the next menu. Paradox will show a list of available fields from the ABCSTAFF table. Choose Social security from the list, and Paradox will display the following prompt:

Use ← → ↑ ↓ to move where you want the field to begin...then press ↵ to place it...

Since you are already at the desired starting position for the field, press RETURN. A dotted line will appear, indicating the length of the Social Sec. field. It does not need to be lengthened or shortened, so press RETURN to accept the current width of the field.

Place the cursor at row 6, column 5, and enter **Social Sec.** as the text. Then move the cursor to row 9, column 5, and press F10 to display the menu. Choose Field/Place/Regular to place a regular field at the cursor location, and choose the Last name field. Press RETURN to start the field at the current cursor location, and press RETURN again to end the field at row 9, column 20.

Now place the cursor at row 9, column 25. Display the menu with F10, and choose Field/Place/Regular. Then select First name as the desired field. Press the RETURN key twice to place the field at the desired location. At row 10, column 5, enter the heading **Last name**. At row 10, column 25, enter the heading **First name**.

Move the cursor to row 13, column 5, and press F10 to show the menu. Choose Field/Place/Regular, select Address as the field, and press RETURN twice to place the field. Move the cursor to row 14, column 5, and enter the heading **Address**. Use the locations and commands described in Table 5-1 to complete the fields and headings on the first page of the form.

Two borders are desired. One will be used to visually highlight the employee's social security number, and the other will enclose all of the fields in the first page of the form. Place the cursor at row 4, column 4, and press F10 to display the menu. Choose Border/Place/Single-Line, and press RETURN to start the border at row 4, column 4. Move the cursor approximately to row 7, column 17, so that the Social Sec. field and the entire label are enclosed within the highlighted box, and press RETURN.

At Location:	Select These Commands:	Then Choose This:
17,5	Field/Place/Regular	City
17,23	Field/Place/Regular	State
17,32	Field/Place/Regular	ZIP Code

At Location:	Enter This Heading:
18,5	City
18,23	State
18,32	ZIP Code
3,22	Personnel Update Form
20,16	Use PAGE DOWN to see next screen.

TABLE 5-1.   Remaining Field Locations for First Page

Move the cursor to row 2, column 2, and press F10 for the menu. Choose Border/Place/Double-Line and press RETURN to begin the border. Move the cursor to approximately row 23, column 58, so that the box encloses all of the fields and the headings, and then press RETURN to complete the border. This will complete the first page of the custom form, which should resemble the page shown in Figure 5-4.

Adding a New Page

Paradox usually adds another page for every 22 lines used in a form to place fields. However, you can add new pages at any time by using the Page command from the Form menu.

If the Form menu is not currently displayed, press F10 to display it; then choose Page and Insert. Paradox will display the following menu options and prompt:

After Before
Insert a new page after the current page.

You can insert new pages either before or after the current page in the form. In this case, choose After. The screen will clear, and the Page indicator at the upper-right side of the screen will indicate that you are now on Page 2 of a two-page form.

To help the employee using the form keep track of which employee's record is being edited, we will need to again display the Last name and First name fields. However, there is no need to allow editing, since these fields were editable on the first page of the form. Place the cursor at row 3, column 5, press F10 for the menu, and choose Field/Place/Display Only. For the field name, choose Last name, and then press RETURN twice to locate the field. Place the cursor at row 3, column 22, press F10 for the menu, and choose Field/Place/Display Only. For the field name, choose First name, and then press RETURN twice to locate the field.

For the name headings, at row 4, column 5, enter **Last name** and at row 4, column 23, enter **First name**. At row 6, column 5, press F10 for the menu, and choose Field/Place/Regular; then select Date of birth and press RETURN twice to place the field. Move to row 6, column 20, press F10, and choose Field/Place/Regular. Select Date hired, and press RETURN twice to place the field. Finally, move to row 6, column 36, press F10, and then choose Field/Place/Regular. Select Dependents as the field, and press RETURN once.

You will note that the Dependents field displays a full 22 characters. Because this is a numeric field, Paradox allows a maximum of digits for the field, which in this case is overkill. Use the left arrow key to narrow the field until a maximum of 8 digits can be displayed, and then press RETURN to set the width at 8 digits.

At Location:	Select These Commands:	Then Choose This:
10,5	Field/Place/Regular	Assignment
13,5	Field/Place/Regular	Salary (adjust width to 8)
13,25	Field/Place/Regular	Hourly Rate (adjust width to 8)

At Location:	Enter This Heading:
11,5	Assignment
14,5	Salary
14,25	Hourly rate

TABLE 5-2.   Additional Field Locations for Second Page

For the headings, at row 7, column 5, enter **Date of birth**. At row 7, column 20, enter **Date hired**. At row 7, column 36, enter **Dependents**. Use the locations and commands described in Table 5-2 to add the remaining fields and headings to the second page of the form.

Adding a Calculated Field

As mentioned earlier in the chapter, Paradox lets you add *calculated fields* to a form. These fields are used to display the results of calculations that are usually based on the contents of other fields in the database. Calculated fields are not actual fields in a database; they do not consume space because they are not stored in any permanent location. Adding a calculated field simply tells Paradox to perform a calculation and to display the results in the calculated field of the form.

When you create a calculated field, Paradox will ask for the expression that provides the basis of the calculation. Such expressions can be up to 175 characters in length. As a part of an expression, you are allowed to use field names that are enclosed in [ ] brackets and that are typed exactly as they appear in the table structure; math operators, which include + (addition), - (subtraction), * (multiplication), and / (division); and constants, such as "James", 4.75, or 3/12/89. Here are some examples of valid expressions:

"Mr./Ms. " + [First name] + " " + [Last name]
[Date] + 365
[Hourly salary] * [Hours worked]

As these examples indicate, you can use the + operator to combine text strings (including text stored in alphanumeric fields), and you can add a number of days to a valid date value. You cannot perform calculations between incompatible data types; for example, you could not add a value in a numeric field to a text string in a character (alphanumeric) field. If you try to base a calculated field on an incompatible operation, or if you misspell a field name used as the basis for the calculation, Paradox will warn you about it by displaying an error message.

Note that in Paradox 3.5, you can include most PAL functions in calculated fields, as well as in forms and reports. PAL is introduced in Chapter 14.

In our example, the managers at ABC Temporaries desire a "profitability" field, which will display the difference between the hourly rate charged to the customer and the employee's salary. To add a new field to the table for this information would be a waste of time, since the information can be readily obtained by subtracting the salary amount from the hourly rate amount. The result can be displayed as a calculated field.

The calculated field for the hourly profit is still needed. Place the cursor at row 13, column 44, and press F10. Choose Field/Place/Calculated from the menu. In response to the prompt for an expression, enter the following:

[Hourly rate] - [Salary]

Be sure to include the left and right bracket symbols around the field names. Press RETURN once to begin the field, use the left arrow key to shorten the field width to eight characters, and press RETURN again to set the field's width. Finally, place the cursor at row 14, column 44, and enter the heading **Hourly profit**. If you were observant enough to notice that we have forgotten the Phone field, do not add it yet; it will be added to the form later.

To draw a border, first place the cursor at row 16, column 58, press F10, and choose Border/Place/Double-Line. Press RETURN to start the border. Place the cursor at approximately row 2, column 2, so that the entire form, including the headings, is enclosed by the border, and then press RETURN to complete the border.

The completed form only needs to be saved to be ready for use. Press F10 to display the menu, and choose Do-It! (F2) to save the form.

Remember   Because calculated fields do not exist in the table, you cannot edit them while viewing the form. Calculated fields are "display-only" fields.

Using the Example Form

To use the form you have just created, press F10 if necessary to display the main menu. Choose View, and enter **ABCSTAFF** as the table to view. Press F10 for the menu, choose Image and then PickForm, and select 1 from the available forms. A record in the table will appear. If you try moving through the form with the left or right arrow key, you will notice that you cannot move the cursor to the Social Sec. field on the first page of the form or to the Last name and First name fields on the second page—you set them to display-only.

EDITING AN EXISTING FORM

The Change command, available from the Form menu, allows you to modify existing forms. Any changes that you wish to make to the form can be made in a manner similar to that used to create the form. Use the same options from the Form menu to place or remove fields, add borders, insert or delete pages, or to change styles.

To change a form, choose Forms/Change from the main menu, enter the name of the table associated with the form, and pick the number assigned to the form from the menu of up to 14 numbers that appears. Once you have chosen the form, the form description you originally entered will appear. You can change the description, or you can press RETURN to accept it without changes. The Form menu will then appear. You are provided with the same options for placing fields and borders, changing styles, and inserting or deleting pages as you were provided when you originally designed the form. Some specific menu commands that may prove useful when you want to make changes to an existing form are discussed in additional detail here.

Reformatting Fields

If you want to change the width of existing fields, use the Reformat command, available from the Field menu. While editing the form, press F10 if needed to display the Form menu, and choose Field/Reformat. Paradox will ask you to select the desired field; move the cursor to the field whose width you wish to change, and press RETURN to select the field. You can then use the left and right arrow keys to adjust the field's width. When you are satisfied with the width, press RETURN to set the new field width. When a field will not expand further by pressing the right arrow key it has reached its maximum width.

Moving an Area

If you do not like the location of a portion of your form, you can move it to a new location by using the Move command, available from the Area command of the Form menu. To do this, begin editing the form as described earlier, press F10 to display the menu, and choose Area/Move. Paradox will ask you to place the cursor on any corner of the desired area; do so, and press RETURN. Next, move the cursor to the opposite corner. As you move the cursor, the area on the screen will be highlighted.

Once the highlight encloses the desired area, press RETURN again. Then use the cursor keys to drag the area to the new location, and press RETURN once more to reposition the area. Note that you can use the PGUP and PGDN keys to move entire areas between pages of a multipage form.

Erasing an Area

The Erase command, available from the Area command of the Form menu, offers a convenient way to erase a portion of a form. Begin editing the form as described earlier. Press F10 to display the menu, and choose Area/Erase. Paradox will ask you to place the cursor on any corner of the desired area; do so, and press RETURN. Next, move the cursor to the opposite corner. As you move the cursor, the area on the screen will be highlighted.

Once the highlight encloses the desired area, press RETURN once more to erase the area.

While you could undo the effects of this operation by choosing Cancel from the menu, such a choice would also cancel any constructive changes you had made while you were editing the form. You should be sure that an area of the form is no longer needed before you erase it.

Deleting Pages

In just as final a manner, you can delete pages from a multiple-page form. To do so, edit the form, and use the PGUP or PGDN key to reach the page that you want to delete. Then press F10 to display the Form menu, and choose Page/Delete. When you select the Delete command, the page will be removed. Although deleting a page is final, you can cancel the effects of the deletions—and any other edits you have performed—if you cancel the form design process without saving your changes.

Adding Some Style

You can assign style attributes to selected areas of a form after entering text and placing your desired fields. While designing the form, press F10 for the menu. The menu choices available from the menu that appears when you select Style are Color, Monochrome, FieldNames, and ShowHighlight. If you are using an older version of Paradox, the choices are Intensity, Blink, Reversal, FieldNames, and Default.

The Color option lets you select foreground and background colors for a selected area of the form or a border. The Monochrome option lets you set the intensity, reverse, normal, and blink attributes for a selected area of the form or for a border. If you select the FieldNames option, Paradox will superimpose field names on the fields you place on the form. This can be helpful for designing complex screens, because it is easier to keep up with which fields are which when they are labeled. Once the form has been saved and you begin using the form to add or edit records, the field names are no longer visible. The ShowHighlight option tells Paradox to display the areas of multirecord forms while you are designing or changing a form. You will learn more about multirecord forms later in this chapter.

The Intensity option tells Paradox to show selected text and borders in boldface on monochrome monitors or in color on color monitors. The Blink option causes text and borders to blink, and the Reversal option causes text and borders to be shown in reverse video. The Default option lets you quickly turn off a previously chosen display attribute. This option, when chosen, will turn off blinking and reverse video, disable any display of field names during form design, and restore text and borders to normal intensity. If you want to assign a style attribute to existing text, use the Area option and then select the desired style.

Note ≡ Use colors or highlighting to highlight important fields in your forms.

Working with Colors And Intensity

Assuming you are using Paradox version 3.0 or above, you can change the colors used in a form (unless you have a monochrome system, in which case the color options are ignored by Paradox). With prior versions of Paradox, you do not have the color options, but you can change the intensity and blinking attributes as described earlier by using the Intensity and Blink options of Form/Style. The rest of this section assumes you are using Paradox version 3.0 or above.

When you select Style from the Forms menu, you can then select the style and the colors for selected areas of the form or for borders. You might want to use this option to visually highlight a portion of a form; for example, you might want an employee's name to appear in a different color than the rest of the form, or you might want the salary to appear blinking. Selecting the Style option of the Forms menu reveals the following choices:

Color Monochrome Fieldnames ShowHighlight
Select foreground and background colors for an area or border.

The FieldNames and ShowHighlight options were described earlier. For changing the visual attributes of part of a form, you are interested in the Color and Monochrome options.If you are using a color system and you want to change the colors for a field, fields, or a border, choose Color. You will then see the following options:

Area Border
Color an area of the form.

If you want the color changes to affect a portion of a form (such as one or more fields), choose Area. Then place the cursor at the start of the area to change the color, and press RETURN to begin selecting the area. Move the cursor to the diagonal corner of the area (it will be highlighted as you do so), and press RETURN again to mark the end of the area. Once you have marked the area, a color palette showing the available foreground and background colors will appear in the upper-right corner of the screen. Use the up and down arrow keys to change the background color, and use the left and right arrow keys to change the foreground color. (As you press the arrow keys, the new colors will appear in the selected area on the form; this makes it easier to decide on the most desirable color choice.) When you have selected the desired colors, press RETURN, and the new colors will take effect. Note that you can color the entire form by selecting Area and blocking out the entire screen. You would then enter your text, place fields, and designate other colors, if desired, for specific portions of the form.

≡Tip≡   Use ALT-C to toggle the color palette on and off.

In a similar manner, you can change the colors for the border of a form by choosing Style/Color/Border. Move the cursor to one corner of the border and press RETURN to begin selecting it; then move the cursor to the diagonal corner of the border and press RETURN to finish defining the border. The color palette will appear in the upper-right corner of the screen. Use the arrow keys to select the desired foreground and background colors, and press RETURN when you've found the desired colors.

If you are not using a color monitor, you can still take advantage of the Style/Mono-chrome option. As with the Color option, selecting the Monochrome option provides you with two choices: Area and Border. Choose Area if you want to change the display attributes for a portion of the screen (such as one or more fields), or choose Border to change the display attributes for a border. Move the cursor to one corner of the area or the border, and press RETURN; then move the cursor to the diagonal corner of the area or the border, and press RETURN to complete the selection. Once you've made the selection, Paradox will tell you to use the left or right arrow key to switch between the available monochome attributes, or styles. You can switch between intense display, reverse video, intense and reverse, blinking, nonblinking, and normal (which cancels the effects of intense or reverse if it was chosen earlier). Continue pressing either the left arrow or the right arrow key until the desired display style appears on the screen. Then press RETURN to accept that style of display.

Whatever color and style choices you make are stored when you save the form with the Do-It! option. You can move forms between systems of the same types and they will be displayed in the same fashion. You can also move forms designed on a monochrome system to a color system and the form will appear in black-and-white, with the same intensity, reverse, or blinking attributes that you designed on the monochrome system.

Taking forms designed on a color system to a monochrome system may present some problems. Paradox saves your color information, and monochrome equivalents for that information, along with the form. However, since you did not design the form on a monochrome system, you have no way of knowing exactly what it will look like on a monochrome system before trying it. Also, some color combinations make data difficult to read on a monochrome system. If you are designing a form on a color system that will be used on monochrome systems, you may want to first use the Video/Colors option of the Custom Configuration Program to see the equivalent monochrome attributes for various colors. For more details on the use of the Custom Configuration Program, see Appendix B.

The same sort of problem can apply to most laptop computers. If you design a form with different colors on a color system and then move that form to a laptop, you may have trouble seeing some of the data clearly on the laptop's screen. If you know laptop users will be using the form, it may be best to stick with white on black or black on white color combinations.

HANDS-ON PRACTICE: EDITING THE PERSONNEL FORM

The Change command in the Form menu lets you make changes to the design of an existing form. Get to the main menu, choose Forms/Change, and enter **ABCSTAFF** for the name of the table. Paradox will display the list of available forms; choose 1 as the form to edit, and when prompted for a description, press RETURN to keep the same description for the form.

For the example form, the phone number needs to be added to the first page of the form. Place the cursor at the start of the descriptive text "Use Page Down to see next screen," and press F10 to display the Form menu.

With the Area command, you can move portions of the form from one area to another. (Note that the area to which you move an object must be a blank area.) Choose Area/Move, and press RETURN to mark the beginning of the area. Move the cursor to the end of the descriptive text, and press RETURN again to define the area. Press the down arrow key twice to move the descriptive text to row 22, and press RETURN to relocate the area.

Place the cursor at row 20, column 5, and press F10 for the menu. Choose Field/Place/Regular, and select Phone from the list of fields. Press RETURN twice to place the field. Finally, place the cursor at row 21, column 5, and enter **Phone** as the heading. You can also try changing the display characteristics of the Social Sec. field to set off this field visually from the remainder of the form. Place the cursor at the upper-left corner of the border around the Social Sec. field (row 4, column 4). Press F10 for the menu, and choose Style. If you are using a color system, choose Color; otherwise choose Monochrome.

From the next menu to appear, choose Area. Since the cursor is already at the start of the area you want to change, press RETURN. Then move the cursor to the lower-right corner of the border surrounding the Social Sec. field and press RETURN again.

If you are using a color system, the color palette will appear (unless it has been turned off using the Custom Configuration Program). If the color palette does not

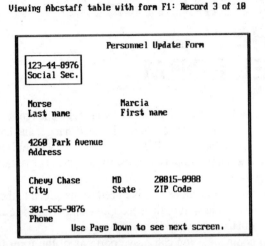

Personnel Update Form

123-44-8976
Social Sec.

Morse   Marcia
Last name   First name

4260 Park Avenue
Address

Chevy Chase   MD   20815-0988
City   State   ZIP Code

301-555-9876
Phone
         Use Page Down to see next screen.

FIGURE 5-5.   Personnel form with Phone field added

appear, press ALT-C to show it. Use the up or down arrow key to pick a background color. Press RETURN when done, and the new colors will take effect. Then press F10 for the menu, and choose Do-It! from the menu to save the modified form.

If you are using a monochrome system, use the left or right arrow key to display the Intensity-Reverse option, and then press RETURN for the option to take effect. Then, press F10 for the menu, and choose Do-It! from the menu to save the modified form.

If you were viewing the table when you chose the Change command to modify the form, you will again see the records in the table through the form when you complete the change process. Note that the Phone field now appears at the bottom of the first page of the form, as shown in Figure 5-5.

Deleting Fields

If you need to remove an existing field from a form, you can do so with the Change command, available from the Form menu. While in the drawing area, display the menu with F10. Choose Field/Erase, and Paradox will ask you to place the cursor at the field that is to be removed. Place the cursor anywhere in the desired field, and press RETURN. The field will be removed from the form.

DESIGNING A MULTIRECORD FORM

Paradox version 3.5 and 3.0 offer the capability of *multirecord forms*. Such forms show more than one record at a time, much like the tabular display that appears by default when you first begin viewing a table. One important difference between an ordinary table view and a multirecord form is that you can design the form to show the data in the format you prefer. Another important difference is that, as with any form, you can add calculated fields. Note, however, that you cannot have multirecord forms that span more than one page (unlike other types of forms).

Multirecord forms can be very useful when you want to be able to scroll up and down and see many records on the screen at once. They are also useful when a number of records, such as those containing "week ending" dates and hours worked, are related to a single record in another table, such as the name of an employee. Designing this type of multirecord form (a form that is linked to another table) will be covered in Chapter 9.

Any multirecord form has two areas: an *original record*, where fields from the first record to appear are placed on the form, and *copies* of the original record. The copies of the original record appear directly below the original record.

To create a multirecord form, you start designing the form in the usual manner by choosing Forms/Design from the menu, entering a table name, and selecting a number for the new form. After entering the form description, you are placed in the Form Design screen. You next press F10 for the Form menu and choose Multi/Records and then Define.

Paradox next asks you to place the cursor at the corner of the region to be used for the original record of the multirecord form. You move the cursor to the start of the area and press RETURN; then you move the cursor to the diagonal corner of the area, and press RETURN again. Paradox then asks you to use the up or down arrow key to add or delete repeating rows; these are used to display the copies, or additional records, that will appear in the multirecord form. Press the up or down arrow key as many times as necessary, and press RETURN when you are done.

At this point, the original area and the copies area will appear in different colors or styles of highlighting. You can then proceed to use Field/Place as described previously to place the desired fields in the original area. As you place each field, copies of that field will automatically appear in the copies area. Once you have finished placing the fields and adding any desired headings, save the form with the Do-It! option of the Form menu. When you select the form with Image/PickForm, you will see multiple records displayed in the form, and you will be able to use the up and down arrow keys to move among the records.

HANDS-ON PRACTICE: DESIGNING A MULTIRECORD FORM

The managers at ABC Temporaries would like to be able to use a tabular form for editing employee records. The fields most often edited are the Salary, Assignment, and Hourly Rate fields, so these fields are to be included in the form. Also, the name fields are needed so the managers will be able to see which employee record is being edited.

Press F10 for the menu, and choose Forms/Design. Enter **ABCSTAFF** as the name of the table. Choose 2 as the form name, and for a description, enter **Tabular form for employees**.

Move the cursor to row 5, column 10. Press F10 for the Form menu, and choose Multi/Records/Define. Since the cursor is already at the desired starting location, press RETURN. Move the cursor down 2 lines and to the right 64 spaces. Press RETURN again to mark this as the area for the original record.

Paradox now asks you to use the up or down arrow key to add or delete repeating rows in the region. Press the down arrow key five times to add room for five additional records. Then press RETURN. The screen will now contain two highlighted areas: a two-line area for the original record and a ten-line area for the copies. (Depending on your monitor type and your graphics hardware, you may or may not be able to see the distinction clearly. With monochrome monitors, adjusting your contrast may improve the distinction.)

Move the cursor to row 5, column 10, and type the heading

Last:

Press F10 for the menu, and choose Field/Place/DisplayOnly. From the list of fields to appear, choose Last name. Then press RETURN twice to place the field at the desired location.

Move the cursor to row 5, column 32, and type the heading

First:

Press F10 for the menu, and choose Field/Place/DisplayOnly. From the list of fields to appear, choose First name. Then press RETURN twice to place the field at the desired location.

Move the cursor to row 6, column 10. Type the heading

Assignment:

Press F10 for the menu, and choose Field/Place/Regular. From the list of fields to appear, choose Assignment. Then press RETURN twice to place the field at the desired location.

Move the cursor to row 6, column 43. Type the heading

Salary:

Press F10 for the menu, and choose Field/Place/Regular. From the list of fields to appear, choose Salary. Then press RETURN once. Use the left arrow key to shorten the field width to eight characters, and then press RETURN again.

Move the cursor to row 6, column 60. Type the heading

Rate:

Press F10 for the menu, and choose Field/Place/Regular. From the list of fields to appear, choose Hourly Rate and press RETURN once. Use the left arrow key to shorten the field width to eight characters, and then press RETURN again. The final line of the original area will remain blank, providing a visual divider between successive records when they appear in the completed form.

Move the cursor to row 4, column 8. Press F10 for the menu, and choose Border/Place/Double-Line. Press RETURN to start the border. Move the cursor just to the right and below the other diagonal corner of the highlighted area for the copied records (approximately row 23, column 77) and press RETURN again to complete the border.

Save the form with Do-It! (F2). When you are back viewing the table, press F10 for the main menu and choose Image/PickForm. From the next menu that appears, select 2. You should see the new multirecord form on your screen, and you can try using the up and down arrow keys to move among the various records.

Note that you can make changes to a multirecord form at any time in a manner similar to that for other forms. From the Form menu, you can choose Multi/Records/Adjust to change the size of the original and copies areas. Use Multi/Records/Remove to remove all copies of an original record from the form. Changing attributes (such as intensity or colors) is done in the same manner as with other forms, as described earlier in this chapter.

BOXES, LINES, AND YOUR PRINTER

If you use the SHIFT-PRTSCR key combination to print screen images to your printer, any form containing lines or boxes created by Paradox may not print out as you might expect. In most cases, the lines on the form will print as alphabetic characters on your printer. Only printers that can print the IBM extended graphic character set will print these lines as they actually appear on a form.

A NOTE ABOUT FILES

Paradox stores your screen forms as Paradox objects in disk files. In order to better keep track of the files, it provides the same name as you assigned to the associated table, but Paradox uses an extension of .F for the standard form, .F1 for the first custom form, .F2 for the second custom form, and so on. You should keep these files in the same directory with other Paradox objects so that the program can find them when you want to use them.

QUICK SUMMARY

To design a form   Press F10 for the menu, and choose Forms/Design. Enter the table name on which the form will be based. Choose a number for the form, then enter a description. When the Drawing Area appears, place the desired fields and enter any accompanying text or borders. Save the form by pressing Do-It! (F2).

To modify an existing form   Press F10 for the menu, and then choose Forms/Change. Enter the table name on which the form will be based. Choose the number of the existing form, then enter a new description, or press RETURN to accept the previous description. When the Drawing Area appears, make any desired changes to the form. Save the form by pressing Do-It! (F2).

To place fields in a form   When at the Drawing Area, press F10 for the Form Menu, and choose Field/Place. From the next menu, choose Regular to place fields; Display-Only to place fields which cannot be edited; or Calculated to place fields that are calculations based on other fields or PAL functions.

To add labels or text in a form   Place the cursor at the desired location, and type the labels or the descriptive text.

To draw borders or lines in a form   When at the Drawing Area, press F10 for the Form Menu, and choose Border/Place. From the next menu, choose the desired type of border (Single Line, Double Line, or a character of your choosing). Place the cursor at one corner of the border (or one end of a line) and press RETURN, then move the cursor to the other corner or end and press RETURN again.

THE POWER
OF ASK

Now that you have significant sets of data stored within a Paradox database, it is time to examine more complex and better methods to get at the precise data you will need. You have already used the helpful Zoom key to quickly locate a record, but this is only a simple form of query. You will often need to isolate one or more records that meet a condition. For example, you may need to generate a list of all employees working at a particular assignment, or all employees earning over $8.00 an hour.

In this chapter you will learn to use the main menu's Ask command to compose queries. This powerful Paradox feature uses a query-by-example design and artificial intelligence technology to make complex requests easy for the user. You will not have to think of the arcane logic behind a detailed set of commands, as you must with other database products. With Paradox, you simply check off the fields you want included in the results and provide examples or ranges of the data that you wish to extract. Paradox does the rest for you.

You can also use queries to add or delete records, with the additions or deletions based on the results of the query. In addition, you can update values in one table, based on a query directed to another table.

DISPLAYING A QUERY FORM

Queries are built in a Query Form, which resembles the table you are using to supply the data. To display a Query Form, choose Ask from the main menu, and Paradox will prompt you for the name of the table. Enter the name, or choose a table from the list by pressing RETURN. The Query Form that appears will be similar to the one that is shown in Figure 6-1.

The Query Form will duplicate the table you choose in its structure. In the example in Figure 6-1, the Query Form was produced from the ABCSTAFF table. Queries of a relational nature will be covered in Chapter 9, but for now, note that you can repeat the Ask process for additional tables and make use of examples to link common fields in order to build a query that is dependent on multiple tables.

To fill out a Query Form, you usually need to perform just two basic steps. You select the fields you want displayed in the answer by moving the cursor to those fields and adding a checkmark with F6. If you wish to see all of the fields in the answer, you can move to the leftmost field of the Query Form and press F6 to place a checkmark in all fields. If you place a checkmark in a field and then decide you do not need to

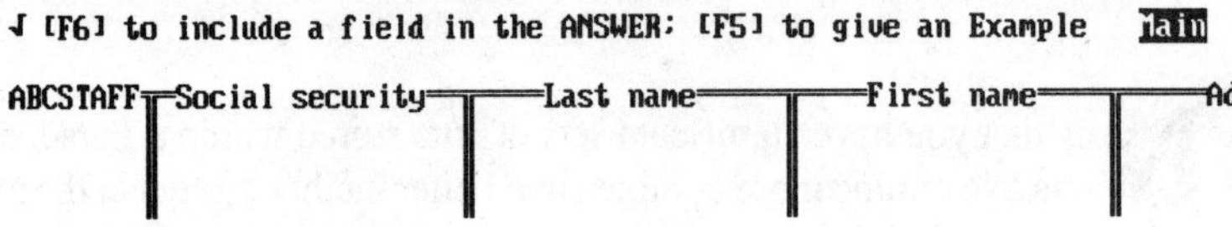

√ [F6] to include a field in the ANSWER; [F5] to give an Example   Main

ABCSTAFF┬Social security┬─Last name┬─First name┬─Address─

FIGURE 6-1.   Query Form

see that field in the answer, place the cursor in the field again and press F6 to remove the checkmark. Note that all existing checkmarks can be removed from a table by moving to the leftmost field and pressing F6. The F6 key acts as a *toggle*; if checkmarks exist, they are removed, and if no checkmarks exist, F6 adds them.

For the second step, simply enter a matching expression in any desired field, in the same row as the checkmark. (This is only necessary if you want to limit your query to include a specific subset of records; if you want to see all records, you can omit this step.)

As an example, if you wanted to see all employees with a last name of Robinson, you would move the cursor to the Last name field and type **Robinson** (no quotes are necessary). To select records for employees hired before January 1, 1987, you would enter **<1/1/87** in the Date hired field. And if you wanted all employees who earned between $7.50 and $9.00 an hour, you could enter **>=7.50, <=9.00** in the Salary field, as shown in Figure 6-2. There are many other variations that can be used, but these are the basic steps for constructing a query.

PERFORMING THE QUERY

Once the Query Form has been filled in, the touch of one key, Do- It! (F2), will perform the query. The results will appear in a new table, which is automatically named ANSWER. Figure 6-3 shows the results of the query described in Figure 6-2.

The new ANSWER table is a temporary table. If you perform another query, the resulting answer will overwrite the existing ANSWER table. If, however, you want to store the results permanently, you can use Tools/Rename to rename the temporary table so that it is not overwritten by the next query. Also, if you want to use a form or

```
√ [F6] to include a field in the ANSWER; [F5] to give an Example    Main

┌─Date of birth──────┬──Date hired──────┬──Dependents──────┬────Salary────────┬─
│                    │                  │                  │  >=7.50, <=9.00   │
│                    │                  │                  │                   │
│                    │                  │                  │                   │
```

FIGURE 6-2.   Example of filled-in Query Form

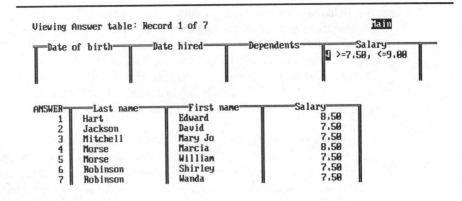

Viewing Answer table: Record 1 of 7   Main

┌─Date of birth──┬──Date hired──┬──Dependents──┬──Salary──────┐
│   │   │   │▓ >=7.50, <=9.00│

ANSWER──┬───Last name──┬──First name──┬──Salary──┐
    1   │ Hart   │ Edward   │   8.50
    2   │ Jackson   │ David   │   7.50
    3   │ Mitchell   │ Mary Jo   │   7.50
    4   │ Morse   │ Marcia   │   8.50
    5   │ Morse   │ William   │   7.50
    6   │ Robinson   │ Shirley   │   7.50
    7   │ Robinson   │ Wanda   │   7.50

FIGURE 6-3.   Results of example query

report designed for the original table with the query results, you can use
Tools/Copy/Form or Tools/Copy/Report to copy an existing form or report for use
with the ANSWER table.

=Remember   An existing table named ANSWER will be overwritten by a new ANSWER
table whenever you perform a query.

These steps are all that is necessary, in many cases, to get the kind of information
that you need from your database. You can quickly produce reports of critical data by
designing a query with the desired fields and filling in any desired conditions to isolate
the needed set of matching records. (You may want to limit the fields so they will fit
on a single page.) Execute the query with Do-It! (F2), and the results you need will be
displayed in the ANSWER table; then press ALT-F7 for an instant report based on your
query. You can move fields in the ANSWER table, if you desire, with Image/Move
or by using CTRL-R.

Unlike a table, a Query Form always contains four columns, regardless of the actual
widths of the fields. While the fields in the Query Form may appear narrow, they are
no more limited in size than a normal field within a Paradox table. You can enter any
valid expression, up to 255 characters in length, into any field of a Query Form. If you
wish to see all of the expression as you are entering it, you can use the Field View key
(ALT- F5) to edit the field of the Query Form. When using the Field View key, you
must press RETURN twice when done: once to exit the field view, and once to store the
expression within the field of the Query Form.

Note Use the Instant Report (ALT-F7) key if you need a report based on the results of a query.

VALID QUERY SYMBOLS

The symbols, operators, and reserved words listed in Table 6-1 assist you in building your queries. They let you select records based on a wide variety of numeric conditions, pattern matches, and ranges. Of special interest are the pattern-matching

Symbol	Meaning
+	Addition
-	Subtraction
*	Multiplication
/	Division
( )	Operators
=	Equal to
>	Greater than
<	Less than
=>	Greater than or equal to
<=	Less than or equal to
..	Pattern matching for any characters
@	Pattern matching for any single character
like	Similar to (spelling need not be exact)
not	Not a match
blank	Contains no value
today	Date in field matches today's date
average	Average of values
max	Maximum of values
min	Minimum of values
sum	Sum of values
count	Number of values
OR	Specifies OR conditions in a field
AS	Specifies name of field in answer

TABLE 6-1.   Valid Query Symbols and Operators

wild-card operators and the blank operator, discussed next. Other symbols and operators, including those used for calculations, are discussed later in this chapter.

Pattern Matching

On occasion, you may need to find a group of records in which the characters match a specific pattern. Paradox lets you use certain *wild cards* as a part of a query expression. Valid wild-card operators are a double period (..), which represents any number of characters, and the "at" sign (@), which indicates any single characters. The wild cards can be used in alphanumeric, number, or date fields.

As an example, you could use the expression

J..n

to query a name field for names, which might include Jackson, Jonson, and James-Albertson. Whenever you base queries on alphanumeric fields, remember that uppercase letters are considered to be different from lowercase ones. However, when you use a pattern such as the one just shown, case does not matter.

To use the double-period wild card along with a query of a numeric field, while not confusing Paradox about where the decimal point is, you can enclose the decimal point in quotes. As an example, the expression

..".""50

could be used to query a currency field for all amounts ending in fifty cents (.50). In this example, the first two periods act as wild cards, telling Paradox to accept any characters to the left of the decimal point, as long as the characters "50" appear to the right of the decimal place in the field.

For dates, you could enter an expression that is similar to

10/../88

to qualify records with any day in October of 1988 in the date field.

To see some examples of pattern matching, press Clear All (ALT-F8) to clear the screen. Choose Ask from the menu, and enter **ABCSTAFF** for the table. Use the F6 key to place checkmarks in the Social security, Last name, First name, Date hired, and Salary fields. In the Social security field, enter this expression:

@@@-55-@@@@

Press F2 to implement the query. The resulting records are those that have social security numbers with 55 as the center digits.

Get back to the Query Form with F3, and press CTRL-BACKSPACE to delete the entry. (If you accidentally press DEL instead of CTRL-BACKSPACE, the entire line will be erased.) Then try this expression in the Last name field:

..n

Press F2 to process the query, and this time you will see every last name ending in the letter "n."

Press F3 and then CTRL-BACKSPACE to delete the last entry, and place the following expression in the Salary field:

..".".50

Pressing F2 now displays an answer that shows every employee earning any dollar amount that ends in .50.

Finally, to try some date logic, press F3. Delete the prior entry with CTRL-BACK-SPACE, and enter this expression in the Date hired field:

9/../87

Press F2 to see all employees hired during the month of September 1987.

If you need to include any punctuation marks in the pattern, enclose them in double quotation marks as described earlier.

The Blank Operator

If you need to find records in which there may not be an entry in a particular field, you can use the reserved word "blank" as a part of the expression. This tells Paradox to find records where the field is blank.

Note that this is *not* the same as leaving a field in a Query Form empty. An empty field indicates that it does not matter what is in that field of a particular record. The word "blank" in the query field indicates that the field *must be blank* (contain no entry) before the record will be selected and placed in the ANSWER table.

A WARNING ABOUT RESERVED WORDS AND WILD-CARD SYMBOLS

Because Paradox uses certain reserved words and wild-card symbols (such as blank, like, not, today, *, and @ as shown in Table 6-1), you may someday run into a special problem. You might try to perform a query in which you want a record with a literal word or symbol, but Paradox will think that you are trying to use one that is reserved. For example, you might be searching for a text string that specifically contains the @ sign, but Paradox might take the symbol to mean any single character, possibly providing incorrect results. For such occurrences, you can surround the desired character or word in double quotation marks. As an example, entering **"today"** in a query expression would ensure that Paradox searches for the literal word "today" and not for the date stored in the PC's clock.

HANDS-ON PRACTICE: PERFORMING QUERIES

Your first task as the personnel manager for ABC Temporaries is to find a person living in Maryland whose last name is Robinson. Get into Paradox and go to the main menu if you are not already there. If a table is currently displayed on the screen, you may want to clear the working area with Clear Image (F8) so that there is sufficient room on the screen to view both the Query Forms and the temporary ANSWER tables that result.

To begin the query, choose Ask from the main menu and enter **ABCSTAFF** for the table. Once you choose the desired table, the Query Form will appear at the top of the screen. In the query answer you are seeking, you will want to see the Last name and State fields, so place the cursor in the Last name field, press F6 to place the checkmark, and enter **Robinson**. Then move the cursor to State, press F6, and enter **MD**. Press Do-It! (F2), and the answer to the query will appear, as in Figure 6-4.

If your results do not match those of the figure, make sure that your matching criteria in the Query Form matches the actual data in the table. For example, if you are trying to locate a record in which the last name has been entered as Robinson, you cannot find the record if you enter robinson or ROBINSON in the Query Form.

Note that the message area contains the prompt "Viewing Answer table: Record 1 of 1." Since ANSWER is an actual Paradox table, you can treat it like any other

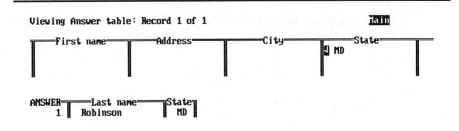

```
Viewing Answer table: Record 1 of 1                              Main

   ┌─First name──────┬──Address─────┬──City──┬─────State────┬─
   │                 │              │        ││ MD           │
   │                 │              │        ││              │
   │                 │              │        ││              │
   │                 │              │        ││              │


ANSWER──┬──Last name──┬─State┐
   1  ││  Robinson   │  MD  │
```

 FIGURE 6-4. Results of first practice query

Paradox table; you can add to, edit, or delete its records, and you can generate reports based on it. The most important difference to remember is that this table will be erased if you change directories or leave Paradox, and it will be replaced by the results of successive queries unless you change its name. Remember, ANSWER is a temporary table. Rename the ANSWER table if you wish to save its results.

Note When modifying existing Queries, you can use CTRL- BACKSPACE to delete an entry in a query field.

Matching on Two Or More Fields

To search for records that meet criteria in two or more fields, simply enter the criteria in the proper format within each field of the Query Form. If, for example, you need to see the records of all employees who live in Virginia and earn more than $10.00 an hour, you will need to place **VA** in the State field and **>10.00** in the Salary field of the Query Form.

To try this, first press Clear All (ALT-F8) to clear both the ANSWER table and the existing Query Form. You could have edited the existing form, but ALT-F8 is the fastest way to clear the entire workspace. Choose Ask from the main menu, and choose ABCSTAFF for the table. Use F6 to place checkmarks in the Last name, First name, and State fields. While within the State field, enter **VA**. Move to the Salary field and press F6 to add the checkmark, and then enter **>10.00**. Finally, press Do-It! (F2) to process the query. The results will appear in the answer, as shown in Figure 6-5.

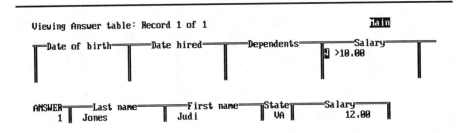

Viewing Answer table: Record 1 of 1   Main

┌─Date of birth─────┬────Date hired────┬────Dependents────┬────Salary────┬──
│   │   │   │ >10.00   │
│   │   │   │   │
│   │   │   │   │
│   │   │   │   │

ANSWER─┬────Last name────┬────First name────┬─State─┬────Salary────┐
   1   │   Jones   │   Judi   │ VA   │   12.00   │

FIGURE 6-5.   Results of second practice query

Including Duplicates

Paradox automatically filters out any records that it considers to be duplicate records. Depending on how you structure your query, this tendency may or may not give you precisely what you want. Try this example to see how Paradox treats duplicates. First press ALT-F8 to clear the table and the Query Form. Perhaps you want a quick count of the number of employees living in Maryland. (There are other ways to get a count in Paradox, but for the sake of this example, use this method.) Choose Ask from the main menu, and enter **ABCSTAFF** as the table name. You are only interested in the number of records, so you really do not need to see any fields other than the State field. Move the cursor to the State field, press F6 to supply the checkmark, and enter **MD**. Press F2 to process the query, and the results will look like those in Figure 6-6.

If you do not understand how Paradox operates, the answer may seem deceiving. There is obviously more than one employee living in Maryland, yet the answer indicates just one. Because you asked for only the State field in the answer, Paradox considers all other records with MD in the state after the first one found to be duplicates of the first one. Had you asked for more fields than just the State field, Paradox would have displayed additional records, because the other records would not be considered duplicates. Paradox considers records duplicates when they contain the same values in all the fields included in the ANSWER table.

There will be times like this when you have intentional duplicates, as in item numbers from an inventory. You can tell Paradox to display all duplicates by using ALT-F6, instead of F6, to place a checkmark followed by a plus symbol (+) in the field of the Query Form. In Paradox, this is called the *check-plus*.

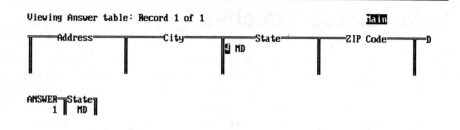

FIGURE 6-6. Results of third practice query

To try this, press F3 to move back to the State field of the Query Form. Press F6 once to remove the existing checkmark. Then press ALT-F6, and a checkmark followed by the plus symbol will appear. The check-plus tells Paradox to include all records that match the example conditions in the ANSWER table, regardless of what it considers to be duplicates. Press F2 to process the query. The resulting answer, shown in Figure 6-7, shows how many times an entry of "MD" occurs in the STATE field.

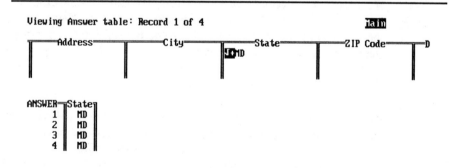

FIGURE 6-7. Results of practice query with check-plus

Using Inexact Matches

One very useful feature of the query-by-example nature of Paradox is its ability to use the like operator as a condition for finding inexact matches. For example, the term "like Morrs," when used in the Last name field of a query of the ABCSTAFF table, should find a record that actually sounds like "Morrs"—in short, Marsha Morse.

Try this now. Press ALT-F8 to clear any existing tables, choose Ask from the main menu, and enter **ABCSTAFF** for the table. Use the F6 key to place checkmarks in the Last name and First name fields. Enter the following in the Last name field of the Query Form:

like Morrs

Press F2 to process the query. The answer should show the records for Ms. Marcia Morse and Mr. William Morse, because the last name "Morse" sounds like "Morrs." This Paradox capability can be quite useful for finding names when you are not quite sure of the spelling. The like operator is also helpful for maintaining mailing lists, where you are trying to weed out accidental duplicates of the same record.

Using Ranges

The range operators, shown with the operators in Table 6-1, are very useful for ensuring that records fall within a selective range. You can use the range operators with all types of Paradox fields; they are by no means limited to numeric values.

Consider a list of employees whose last names fall between the letters "M" and "Z." Press F3 to move up to the Query Form (you can leave the existing checkmarks intact, or if you have already cleared them, open a new Query Form and place checkmarks in the Last name and First name fields). In the Last name field of the Query Form, enter the following expression:

>M,<=Zz

This stands for "Greater than M and less than or equal to Zz." Note the inclusion of the second letter "z." If it were omitted, Paradox would find names up to "Z," but none after the letter "Z" alone (in effect, omitting all last names of more than one character starting with "Z"). Press F2 to process the query, and the results shown in Figure 6-8 will appear.

In this example, note that a comma is used to separate the two possibilities. Remember that whenever you want to enter more than one selection criterion in a field, you must separate each with a comma.

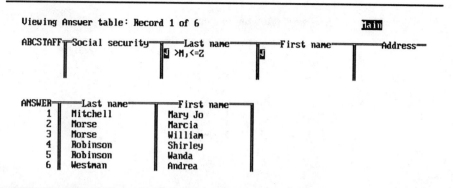

Viewing Answer table: Record 1 of 6   Main

```
ABCSTAFF┬─Social security─┬──────Last name─────┬─────First name─────┬────Address──
        │                 │  >M,<=Z            │                    │
        │                 │                    │                    │
        │                 │                    │                    │


ANSWER┬────Last name────┬────First name────┐
    1 │ Mitchell        │ Mary Jo          │
    2 │ Morse           │ Marcia           │
    3 │ Morse           │ William          │
    4 │ Robinson        │ Shirley          │
    5 │ Robinson        │ Wanda            │
    6 │ Westman         │ Andrea           │
```

FIGURE 6-8.   Results of practice query with operators limiting names

Another example, this time performed with dates, illustrates this point. Suppose you need a report of all employees who were hired during 1986. Press F3 to move up to the Last name field of the Query Form, and press CTRL-BACKSPACE to delete the prior entry. Move the cursor to the Date hired field, and enter the following expression:

>=1/1/86, <=12/31/86

Press F2 to process the completed query. The results, shown in Figure 6-9, display the employees hired by ABC Temporaries in 1986. Yet another way to enter this expression would be **..86**, which would also indicate any date value falling in 1986.

You may have noticed another point while you were making this query. The limiting criterion for records was the date hired, yet the Date hired field was not checked for inclusion in the resulting table. Paradox does not necessarily need to have the fields that are used to select the records included in the results, but it's usually a good idea to include fields containing the criteria at first so you can check the results.

You can also use the operators listed in Table 6-1 to build queries based on other types of ranges. Consider the common personnel problem of deciding who qualifies for vacation and who does not. At ABC Temporaries, every employee with one year or more of service qualifies for vacation. If you suddenly need a list of employees eligible for vacation, a simple query will do the task. Press F3 to move back up to the Query Form and into the Date hired field. Use CTRL-BACKSPACE to delete the previous query, and enter the following expression:

<= TODAY-365

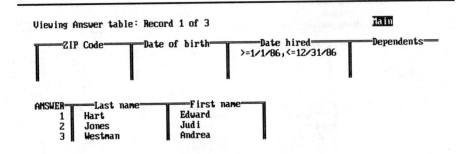

FIGURE 6-9.   Results of query of 1986 employees

This translates as "Less than or equal to today's date, minus 365 days." If you refer back to Table 6-1, you will note that Paradox uses the word "today" as a reserved word that indicates today's date (as measured by the computer's clock). Press F2 to process the query, and you will see a list of employees who have been with the firm for a year or more. Depending on the date maintained by your PC's clock and the dates you entered for the employees, this list may or may not include every employee of the company.

The Not Operator

If you want to select a group of records that do not meet a specific condition, you can place the reserved word "not" ahead of your desired criteria. For example, if you wanted to see a list of all employees not earning $7.50 per hour, you could place the expression

not 7.50

in the Salary field of the query. Like other operators, the not operator can be combined with other selection criteria.

Matching Records Based On OR Criteria

The types of queries you have done so far will work fine for conditions in which a record must meet all of the specified criteria. Such cases of criteria are also referred to as *AND logic*, because you are qualifying a record where one condition is met, AND another condition is met.

Sometimes, however, you need a different sort of qualification. Suppose you want to find records that meet any one of multiple criteria, such as all employees who live in either Maryland or Virginia. This calls for a different type of logic, known as *OR logic*. You want to find records for employees in Maryland OR in Virginia. Fashioning such queries in Paradox is simple. You just add as many lines to the Query Form as necessary; each line contains a separate condition, which the records must meet in order to qualify.

For an example, press ALT-F8 to clear both tables, choose Ask from the main menu, and choose ABCSTAFF for the table. With the cursor in the first field of the Query Form, press F6. Because the cursor is in the first field, this action will tell Paradox to place a checkmark in every field of the Query Form, so that every field will be included in the answer.

Move the cursor down one line by pressing the down arrow key once, and press F6 again. You should now have two rows in the Query Form, each with checkmarks contained in every field. Next, place the cursor in the State field and in the first row, and enter **MD**. Move the cursor down one line by pressing the down arrow key once, and enter **VA**. Finally, press Do-It! (F2) to process the query. The results should show all of the employees who live in either Maryland or Virginia.

You can have up to 22 lines in a single Query Form. This gives you sufficient room to execute the most complex of queries by using OR logic.

Note that Paradox version 3.0 or greater also lets you use the OR operator as an alternate way of composing queries based on OR criteria. If you use the OR operator, you place the query condition on a single line, with the reserved word OR between the desired conditions. For example, you could enter the expressions

Jones or Morse

in the last name field of a query, and the answer would provide records containing the last name of Jones or of Morse.

Complex Matching

You can use Paradox's powerful query-by-example facility to define criteria for several fields, thereby setting up very complex searches. You can also combine AND and OR logic to isolate the results in precisely those records you will need. As an example, suppose that you wish to see all of the employees who live in Virginia or in Maryland, were hired in 1986, and are earning at least $9.00 an hour. If this sounds like overkill, rest assured that it is not; often, real-world management reports require more complex conditions than these before upper management is satisfied with the results.

In this example, what Paradox needs as selection criteria are a State equal to MD or VA; a Date hired that is >=1/1/86 AND <=12/31/86; and a Salary value that is >=$9.00. To begin, press ALT-F8 to get a fresh screen. Then choose Ask from the main menu, and enter **ABCSTAFF** as the desired table. Using the arrow keys to position the cursor, enter the following matching criteria:

1. In the Last name and First name fields of *both* rows 1 and 2, enter a checkmark with F6.

2. In the State, Date hired, and Salary fields of *both* rows 1 and 2, enter a checkmark with F6.

3. In the State field, on the first row, enter **VA**. On the second row of the same field, enter **MD**.

4. In the Date hired field, on both the first and second rows, enter this expression:

   >=1/1/86, <=12/31/86

5. In the Salary field, on both the first and second rows, enter this expression:

   >= 9

6. Finally, implement the query by pressing Do-It! (F2). The results should be similar to the example shown in Figure 6-10.

Using Calculations in Queries

You may find the reserved words that apply to numeric calculations to be of use in your own applications. These words can be used as a part of a query to find totals, minimum and maximum values, averages, or counts of occurrences. To see how these

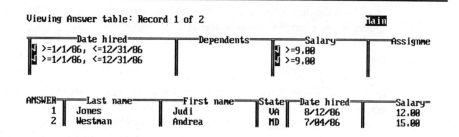

Viewing Answer table: Record 1 of 2   Main

```
       ┌─────Date hired─────┐  ┌────Dependents────┐  ┌────Salary────┐  ┌──Assignme
       │ >=1/1/86, <=12/31/86            │  │          │ >=9.00       │  │
       │ >=1/1/86, <=12/31/86            │  │          │ >=9.00       │  │


ANSWER─┬────Last name────┬────First name───┬State┬─Date hired─┬───Salary─
     1 │   Jones         │   Judi          │ VA  │  8/12/86   │  12.00
     2 │   Westman       │   Andrea        │ MD  │  7/04/86   │  15.00
```

FIGURE 6-10.   Results of complex query

reserved words can be used, press ALT-F8 to clear the screen, choose Ask from the main menu, and enter **ABCSTAFF** as the desired table.

For insurance purposes, perhaps you need to know the average number of dependents carried by the staff. Move the cursor to the Dependents field of the Query Form, and enter

CALC AVERAGE

in the field. Then press F2 to process the query. The resulting answer shows the average number of dependents per employee of ABC Temporaries.

Press F3 once to move back to the Query Form, and then change the expression to

CALC SUM

Press F2. This time, Paradox displays the total number of dependents for the entire staff. Press F3 to move back to the Dependents field of the Query Form, and press CTRL-BACKSPACE to delete the entry. Then move to the Salary field, enter the expression,

CALC MAX

and press F2. The resulting answer shows the salary of the highest-paid employee of ABC Temporaries. If you had entered **CALC MIN** as the expression, the result would have been the minimum salary. If you press F3 to move back to the Salary field of the Query Form, change the expression to

CALC SUM

and press F2, Paradox will sum the salaries of all employees and display the total hourly payroll cost of the firm. Note that you can combine these statistical operators with your selection criteria. For example, you could average the salary for all employees on a particular assignment by placing the assignment name in the Assignment field and placing CALC AVERAGE in the Salary field.

A REMINDER

The following information has been mentioned before, but it is of such importance that one more reminder may save you problems later. All of your queries are stored in a temporary table named ANSWER, which is erased or overwritten whenever you leave Paradox, change directories, or perform yet another query. If you want to save the results of any query, be sure to rename the ANSWER table by selecting Tools/Rename/Table from the main menu.

PERFORMING OPERATIONS

Besides using queries to extract data directly, you can use certain reserved words to cause a query to perform an *operation* on a table. Operations allow you to selectively add, delete, update, and find certain records. To perform such operations, you use special reserved words within certain columns of the Query Form. The reserved words and their purposes are shown here.

Word	Purpose
INSERT	Inserts new records with certain values into a table
DELETE	Deletes all records meeting certain criteria from a table
FIND	Finds records that meet certain criteria in a table
CHANGETO	Updates (changes) values in specified fields within all records that meet certain criteria in a table

Using INSERT

With INSERT, you can copy records from one table to another. Which records are added is determined by the structure of the query. Using INSERT within queries is a good way to move data selectively from one table to another when the structures do not precisely match.

The use of INSERT usually involves one or more *source tables* (from which data is copied), a *target table* (where the copied data is to be inserted), and *example elements* in Query Forms. In addition, you can also include specific criteria in the Query Forms, which will allow you to select records to be inserted into the target table.

Whenever a query involves more than one table, example elements are used. You'll learn more about example elements in Chapter 9, but for now it helps to know that example elements are common expressions you enter into the columns of the Query Form by pressing F5 and entering the element. The element does not have to be any special word; it can consist of any characters, such as "ABC" or "test" or "Johnny5." All that matters is that the same example element be used in the fields being linked in the two tables.

First, fill out a Query Form for the source table or tables; place example elements in the fields you will want, and place any selection criteria you desire within the query. Next, fill out the Query Form for the target table. Place the reserved word **INSERT** in the far left column of this form. Then place any expressions containing the example elements in the fields where you want the data inserted. Finally, use Do-It! (F2) to process the query, and records will be inserted into the target table based on the query.

As an example, perhaps the national headquarters for ABC Temporaries wants a copy of the table from the local office, but they need just two fields: Social security and Name (a combination of the Last name and First name fields). To supply the headquarters office with a table that contains the data in this format, you first create a new table, called HQDATA, with just two fields: Social security and Name.

Creating the table is the easy part; how do you get the data into the table when it exists? The job can be done with INSERT, which will insert records from ABCSTAFF into the new HQDATA table. You would first build a query for the source table (ABCSTAFF), placing example elements in all of the fields that need to be inserted into the target table. In this case, example elements in the Social security, Last name, and First name fields would be sufficient, as shown in Figure 6-11. Next, you would build a query for the target table (HQDATA) by first placing the reserved word **INSERT** in the far left column of the Query Form and then placing the example elements in the fields that are to receive the inserted records. Since in this example the Last name and First name fields must be combined into a single Name field, you can use an expression (in this case, Last + ", " + First) made up of the example elements to combine the names into one field. An example of the filled-in Query Form appears in Figure 6-12.

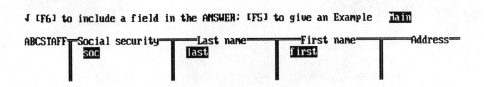

FIGURE 6-11.   Query of source table

When the query is executed, the results will look like Figure 6-13. The records are inserted into the target table. Note that you will not see the target table on the screen unless you were viewing it when you performed the query that made the insertions. Also note that copies of the inserted records are stored in a temporary table named (appropriately enough) INSERTED. This temporary table is overwritten at the next insert, or it is discarded when you change directories or exit Paradox. It is also possible to make inserts to a table that already contains some records; simply specify the existing table containing the records as the target table.

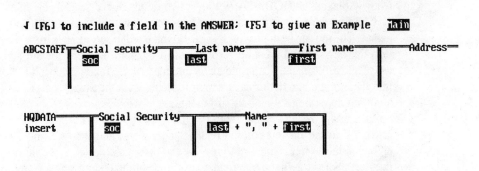

FIGURE 6-12.   Query of target table

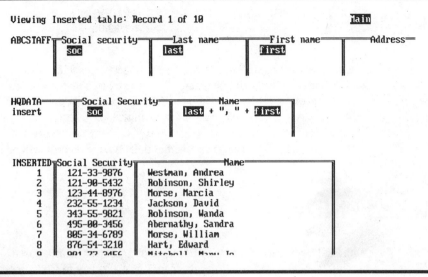

Viewing Inserted table: Record 1 of 10   Main

ABCSTAFF Social security   Last name   First name   Address
          soc   last   first

HQDATA   Social Security   Name
insert   soc   last + ", " + first

INSERTED Social Security   Name
   1   121-33-9876   Westman, Andrea
   2   121-90-5432   Robinson, Shirley
   3   123-44-8976   Morse, Marcia
   4   232-55-1234   Jackson, David
   5   343-55-9821   Robinson, Wanda
   6   495-00-3456   Abernathy, Sandra
   7   805-34-6789   Morse, William
   8   876-54-3218   Hart, Edward
   9   901-77-3456   Mitchell, Mary Jo

FIGURE 6-13.   Inserted records

Using DELETE

With DELETE, you can delete records from a table, based on a particular query. This is particularly useful when you are performing the type of update that requires the removal of a large number of records, as in all students who graduated in a particular year.

To use DELETE with a query, simply place the reserved word **DELETE** in the leftmost column of the Query Form. This tells Paradox that any records meeting the other conditions specified in the query are to be deleted from the table. After entering **DELETE** in the leftmost column, proceed to construct the remainder of the query as desired. (Note that if you do not enter any conditions in the Query Form, all records will be deleted.)

As an example, if (in a moment of temporary insanity) the manager of ABC Temporaries decides to give all clients a free week's worth of work with no billings, one way to do so after the hourly records had been entered into the existing HOURS table would be to delete all of the records in which the "week ending" date contained a value for the desired week. If that week were 1/23/88, the resulting query would resemble the following:

```
HOURS-----ASSIGNMENT----SOCIAL SEC----WEEKEND
DELETE                                1/23/88
```

Once the Query Form is filled in and the query is executed, the records meeting the specified condition will be deleted from the table. The deleted records are stored in a temporary table named DELETED, so you can recover them with Tools/More/Add if you make an accidental, unwanted deletion. Keep in mind that the DELETED table is a temporary table, so if you change directories, exit Paradox, or overwrite the table by performing another deletion, the records will be gone forever.

Using FIND

With FIND, you can locate a specific record or a group of records based on the contents of a query. While you could use the Zoom (CTRL-Z) key to find a record, the Zoom key limits you to finding the record based on the value in a single field. With FIND as a part of a query, you can find records based on conditions specified for any number of fields.

To use FIND, enter the reserved word **FIND** in the leftmost column of the Query Form. After entering **FIND** in the leftmost column, proceed to construct the remainder of the query as desired. When you perform the query by pressing Do-It! (F2), Paradox will display the table that you queried—not the ANSWER table—with the cursor at the first record in the table that meets the conditions specified by the query. At the same time, Paradox will place all records meeting the specified criteria in an ANSWER table. In this case, the ANSWER table is not displayed automatically, but you can view it whenever you wish with the View option.

As an example, you might want to edit a record in the ABCSTAFF table for Marcia Morse. There is more than one person named Morse in the table, so using the Zoom key to find a last name of "Morse" might or might not result in the selection of the correct record. Instead, you can fill in a query in a manner similar to this example:

```
ABCSTAFF--SOCIAL SEC---LAST NAME----------FIRST NAME----

FIND                    Morse              Marcia
```

When this is executed, the cursor will move to the record for Marcia Morse in the ABCSTAFF table. Keep in mind that FIND is unique in that the cursor appears in the table you are querying, and not in a temporary ANSWER table as with most queries. At this point, you can press Edit (F9) or CoEdit (ALT-F9) to make any desired changes in the data. Also note that FIND finds only the first match. To check for additional matches, view the ANSWER table.

Using CHANGETO

With CHANGETO, you can update (change) a number of records, based on a query. This is very handy for global updates—for example, when you want to change the salary of every employee in a certain department by a given bonus amount, or when you want to change all telephone area codes for records of a certain city.

The operator CHANGETO is different from the other operators in that you can put CHANGETO in any column *except* the leftmost column of the Query Form; the other operators, when used in a query, *always* appear in the leftmost column of the query. The column that you place CHANGETO in will determine the field whose contents are changed by the query. You follow the operator with an expression, which tells Paradox how the data should be changed. As an example, the following combination of operator and expression changes the value shown, 212, to the new value 718:

212, CHANGETO 718

In most cases, you will want some sort of selection criteria in one or more fields of the Query Form to determine when the change takes effect. Consider an example of a table containing names, cities, area codes, and telephone numbers, as illustrated here:

Name	City	Area Code	Phone
E. Smith	Brooklyn	212	555-4931
R. Jackson	New York	212	555-2387
L. Rodgers	Queens	212	555-4945
L. Fairfax	Brooklyn	212	555-9354

If the telephone company makes a change that results in all residents of Brooklyn and Queens being assigned a new area code of 718, you certainly do not want to manually update a few dozen (or hundred) records in a table like this one. Instead, the change can be performed with a single query and CHANGETO, as in the following example:

Name	City	Area Code	Phone
	Brooklyn	212, CHANGETO 718	
	Queens	212, CHANGETO 718	

In this example, the query translates to "For all records in which the city equals Brooklyn, change area code 212 to 718; and for all records in which the city equals Queens, change area code 212 to 718." When the query is executed, the records meeting the criteria (in this case, all those with either Brooklyn or Queens in the City field) will have the 212 area code replaced with 718.

Copies of the original records (before the changes) will be stored in a temporary table named CHANGED. You can examine this temporary table after executing the query to make sure that the correct records have been changed.

A NOTE ABOUT REPETITIVE QUERIES

As you use the power of Paradox Queries to retrieve selected data, you may find yourself repeating the same queries over and over. To save time, you can save a query for later use, with the Scripts/QuerySave command from the main menu. With the query visible on the screen, press F10 for the menu, and choose Scripts/QuerySave. Enter a name for the query to be saved. When you want to reuse the query, choose Scripts/Play from the menu, and enter the name that you saved the query under. Then, press Do-It! (F2) to process the query. More information about scripts can be found in Chapter 10.

QUICK SUMMARY

To build a query   Press F10 for the menu, and choose Ask. Enter the name of the table to query, and the Query Form will appear. To include fields in the answer table, move the cursor into the desired fields, and press Check (F6). To limit the records included in the answer table, enter a matching expression in any desired field (omit this step if you want to see all records). Press Do-It! (F2) to process the query and display the answer table.

To include duplicates in a query   Use the Check-Plus key (ALT-F6) instead of the Check key (F6) when indicating the desired fields.

To perform calculations in queries   Use the reserved word CALC, followed by the reserved word for the type of calculation (AVERAGE, SUM, MIN, or MAX) in the desired numeric fields of the query form.

To save a query for later use   Press F10 for the menu, and choose Scripts/QuerySave. Enter a name for the query. To reuse the saved query, from the menu choose Scripts/Play and enter the name of the query.

INTRODUCING
REPORTS

Creating reports is, for many users, what database management is all about. Although a Query Form is a powerful tool for gaining immediate answers to specific questions, much of your work with Paradox will probably involve generating reports. Detailed reports are easy to produce with Paradox, due in no small part to the program's philosophy of relying on visual examples to get the job done.

To select records for inclusion in a report, you design a query using the tools you have already learned about in the previous chapter. Once those records are contained in a table, you can print a report by using the standard report form provided with any table you create. For greater flexibility, you can use the report creation features of Paradox to design custom reports that meet your specific needs.

Paradox offers two types of reports: *standard* and *custom*. Standard reports are reports created automatically by Paradox when you need them. They contain all of the fields in a table, and the field names that you supplied during the table design are used as headings for the fields.

Custom reports, by comparison, are reports that you modify in some way to better fit your specific needs. A major advantage of Paradox over many competing database managers is that it does not force you to design a custom report from scratch, starting with a blank screen. Paradox uses the standard report as the basis for all custom reports you design. You can add or remove fields from the standard report, change headings, lengthen or shorten columns, change formatting attributes, and save the modified design as a custom report. This approach saves much of the time it would usually take to design a custom report from a blank screen.

To design a custom report, you simply choose the Design option from the Report menu and choose a number to identify the custom report. Paradox then creates a report based on the standard report format, and you can choose to modify that report in any way you desire.

On the other hand, if a standard report will do fine, Paradox automatically creates a standard report for any table when you press the Instant Report (ALT-F7) key. The same report can also be chosen by selecting menu options from the Report choice on the main menu.

Both types of reports, standard and custom, are also available in two general formats: *tabular* and *free-form*. Tabular reports are columnar reports that contain any data you desire from the fields of the table. They can also include numeric information, such as totals or other calculations based on numeric fields. Tabular reports normally include headings that contain the specified title of the report, the date (determined by the PC's clock), and the page number for each page.

Free-form reports do not need to follow a columnar format. In a free-form report, fields can be placed in different locations on the screen. Figure 7-1 shows an example of a tabular report, and Figure 7-2 shows an example of a free-form report. Tabular reports will be discussed throughout this chapter, and free-form reports will be discussed in Chapter 12.

Assignment	Social security	Weekend date	Hours worked
National Oil Co.	909-88-7654	1/16/88	35
National Oil Co.	121-33-9876	1/16/88	30
National Oil Co.	121-90-5432	1/16/88	27
National Oil Co.	123-44-8976	1/16/88	32
City Revenue Dept.	343-55-9821	1/16/88	35
City Revenue Dept.	495-00-3456	1/16/88	28
City Revenue Dept.	232-55-1234	1/16/88	30
Smith Builders	876-54-3210	1/23/88	30
Smith Builders	901-77-3456	1/23/88	28
Smith Builders	805-34-6789	1/23/88	35
City Revenue Dept.	232-55-1234	1/23/88	30
City Revenue Dept.	495-00-3456	1/23/88	32
City Revenue Dept.	343-55-9821	1/23/88	32
National Oil Co.	121-33-9876	1/23/88	35
National Oil Co.	909-88-7654	1/23/88	33

2/08/88   Standard report   Page   1

FIGURE 7-1.   Tabular report produced by Paradox

GENERATING A STANDARD REPORT

By far the fastest way to produce printed reports in Paradox is to use the standard report, because this report needs no designing in advance. To produce a standard report, simply view the desired table, turn on your printer, and press Instant Report (ALT-F7). You can also generate a standard report by choosing Report from the main menu and then choosing Output, followed by the name of the table, then R, and then Printer.

ABC Temporaries

2/08/88   Free-form Example Report   Page 1

Assignment: National Oil Co.
Social security: 909-88-7654
Weekend date: 1/16/88
Hours worked: 35

Assignment: National Oil Co.
Social security: 121-33-9876
Weekend date: 1/16/88
Hours worked: 30

Assignment: National Oil Co.
Social security: 121-90-5432
Weekend date: 1/16/88
Hours worked: 27

Assignment: National Oil Co.
Social security: 123-44-8976
Weekend date: 1/16/88
Hours worked: 32

Assignment: City Revenue Dept.
Social security: 343-55-9821
Weekend date: 1/16/88
Hours worked: 35

Assignment: City Revenue Dept.
Social security: 495-00-3456
Weekend date: 1/16/88
Hours worked: 28

Assignment: City Revenue Dept.
Social security: 232-55-1234
Weekend date: 1/16/88
Hours worked: 30

FIGURE 7-2.   Free-form report produced by Paradox

Assignment: Smith Builders
Social security: 876-54-3210
Weekend date: 1/23/88
Hours worked: 30

Assignment: Smith Builders
Social security: 901-77-3456
Weekend date: 1/23/88
Hours worked: 28

FIGURE 7-2.   Free-form report produced by Paradox (*continued*)

The report shown in Figure 7-1 was produced from the HOURS table by means of
the Instant Report key. Note that the report illustrates the design of a standard report.
The date appears at the top left of each page; a report heading, "Standard Report,"
appears at the top center; and a page number appears at the top right. The names of
the fields appear as column headings, and the data appears in single-spaced rows
beneath the headings. For alphanumeric fields, Paradox uses the field width as defined
in the table structure to determine the width of the column within the report. Numeric
and short-number (integer) fields are assigned a default width of 6, currency fields a
width of 14, and date fields a width of 9 (to allow for the possible dd-mon-yy format).
If the name of the field is wider than the default width, Paradox will make the column
as wide as the field name so that the entire heading will fit.

If you study the example in Figure 7-1 (or generate your own report by viewing
the ABCSTAFF table and pressing ALT-F7), you will notice one trait of a standard
report which may not be very appealing to you. Depending on the design of the
structure, one or more columns may be divided by the right margin of the report, with
part of the column appearing on one page and the remainder on the following page.
You can quickly solve this problem by changing the width or moving the location of
the columns in a custom report. If you are printing from a query, you can solve the
problem by eliminating some fields from the ANSWER table.

≡Note≡   If a report needs to be in a specific order, sort the table before producing the
report.

SENDING REPORTS TO THE SCREEN OR TO A FILE

While reports created by pressing ALT-F7 will go by default to the printer, you can choose to direct the output of any report to the screen or to a disk file as ASCII (American Standard Code for Information Interchange) text. To send a report to the screen or to a file, you cannot use the ALT-F7 key combination; you must instead use the report choices from the Paradox menus.

≡Note≡   Reports sent to a file can be used by most word processors.

To send a report to the screen, press F10 to display the main menu; then choose Report/Output and enter the name of the table that will be used to produce the report. From the next menu that appears, choose R for Standard Report; this may be the only menu choice shown unless you have created additional reports.

Next, the following menu choices appear:

Printer Screen File
Send the report to the printer.

This menu provides the options used for redirecting the output of the report. By choosing Screen from this menu, you can display the report on the screen. By selecting File, you can store the contents of the report in a disk file.

If you select Screen, the first page of the report appears momentarily on the screen. If there is more than one page of the report, you will see a "Press any key to continue" message, and you can repeatedly press a key to display successive pages of the report.

If you select File, Paradox will ask for a valid DOS filename. Enter any valid name, and the text of the report will be stored to the file. If a file by the supplied name already exists, Paradox will warn you of this fact and will ask for confirmation before overwriting the existing file. Note that the ASCII text is stored in the file in the same format as it appears printed or on screen: with the headings, title, and page numbers, and large amounts of white space (or blank lines) between successive pages. This option of sending data to a disk file can be very useful for merging the contents of a report with a document; nearly all word processors for the IBM PC and compatibles can read in an ASCII file produced in this manner by Paradox. Consult your word processor's manual for details on how to do this.

HANDS-ON PRACTICE: PRODUCING SELECTIVE REPORTS WITH EASE

If you want maximum results in a minimum amount of time, keep in mind the flexibility that Paradox provides by storing the results of queries in the form of temporary tables. You can use these tables to generate your reports. And, in many cases, you can solve your formatting problems by including selected fields in the ANSWER table, while omitting unwanted fields.

Remember   For a fast, selective report, perform a query and then press ALT-F7.

Take the instant report produced if you view the ABCSTAFF table, and press ALT-F7 to print a report. In the resulting report the City field has been cut off unattractively. Perhaps all you are really interested in are the Last name, Salary, Hourly Rate, and Assignment fields, and you know that these will comfortably fit on a single sheet of standard paper.

Press F10 to get to the main menu, and choose Ask. Then enter **ABCSTAFF** for the table name. Use the F6 key to place checkmarks in the Last name, Salary, Hourly Rate, and Assignment fields, and then press Do-It! (F2) to produce the result. The ANSWER table contains all of the records from the staff table, but with only the desired fields. Press ALT-F7, and the instant report that is printed will resemble the one shown in Figure 7-3, with all of the desired data on a single page's width.

If you wanted specific records in the report, you could use the query-by-example methods detailed in the previous chapter to produce a subset of records in the ANSWER table. Also, if you wanted to see the instant report in some specific order, you could sort the ANSWER table and then produce the report. The built-in flexibility of Paradox lets you generate complex reports with little or no customizing.

One important point to remember about generating reports from an ANSWER table: reports are stored as a part of the table. If you dispose of an ANSWER table without storing it under another name, the report will be disposed of as well. Since Paradox creates the standard report when you press ALT-F7, this is not a problem. However, if you design a custom report for use along with an ANSWER table, be aware that you must rename the table by using the Tools/Rename/Table option if you want to keep and reuse the custom report (see "A Note About Reports" in Chapter 9).

Before proceeding, press ALT-F8 to clear the tables and the Query Form from your screen.

2/08/88		Standard Report		Page 1
Last name	Salary	Assignment	Hourly Rate	
Abernathy	10.00	City Revenue Dept.	18.00	
Hart	8.50	Smith Builders	14.00	
Jackson	7.50	City Revenue Dept.	12.00	
Jones	12.00	National Oil Co.	17.50	
Mitchell	7.50	Smith Builders	12.00	
Morse	7.50	Smith Builders	12.00	
Morse	8.50	National Oil Co.	15.00	
Robinson	7.50	City Revenue Dept.	12.00	
Robinson	7.50	National Oil Co.	12.00	
Westman	15.00	National Oil Co.	24.00	

FIGURE 7-3. Instant report based on query with selected fields

DESIGNING A CUSTOM TABULAR REPORT

There will be times when you prefer the flexibility of customizing a report by placing fields, changing formatting attributes, adding custom headers and footers, and so on. Designing a custom report is the desired route when you need this kind of flexibility. A simplified list of the steps you must take to design such a report is shown here:

1. Choose the table for the report.

2. Choose a name (numeric designator) and description for the report.

3. Select a tabular or a free-form report.

4. Modify the Report Specification that appears on the screen, as desired.

5. Save the Report Specification.

Depending on how complex your needs are, the precise steps may vary in complexity. The basic process in designing a custom report, following the tabular format used by the standard report, will be presented here.

You first choose Report/Design from the main menu to begin the report's design process. After entering the name of the table to be used, select one of the available Report Specification numbers that appear in the form of a menu, resembling the following:

R 1 2 3 4 5 6 7 8 9 10 11 12 13 14
Standard Report

Paradox provides up to 14 possible designators for your custom reports. Once you have selected a number to assign to the report you are creating, Paradox will ask for a description. You can enter up to 40 characters, including spaces, to describe the report.

After you enter a description, Paradox displays the following menu:

Tabular Free-form
Print the information in rows or columns

You can choose Tabular to design a report in the tabular, or columnar, style. (The other option, Free-form, is covered in Chapter 12.) Once you make the selection, Paradox displays the Report Specification, as shown in Figure 7-4. This Report Specification is derived from the standard report produced with the Instant Report

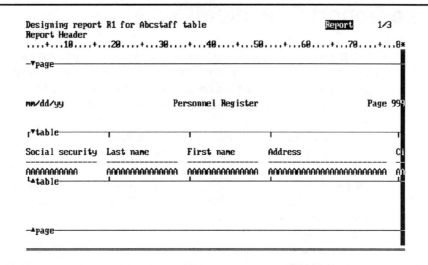

FIGURE 7-4.   Report Specification

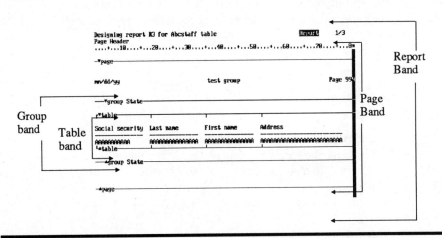

FIGURE 7-5.   Parts of a Report Specification

key; in the process of designing a custom report, you can move fields, delete entire columns, and make other changes to the report.

The Report Specification

The Report Specification is made up of several important parts, as illustrated in Figure 7-5. Paradox views each portion of the report as a horizontal area known as a *band*. There is a report band, a page band, a group band, and a table band, as shown in the illustration. These bands control what the report contains and how it will appear when printed.

The overall screen contains the report band, which is printed once and contains everything that appears between the start and the end of the report. Inside of the report band is the page band, which appears once for each page of the report. At the start of the page band (or, the top of the page) will appear any page headers that you specify; the date, title, and page number in a standard report are default page headers. At the end of the page band (the bottom of the page) will appear any page footers that you include in the report's design.

Contained within the page bands are the group bands. Group bands, which are optional, are printed once for every group of records in a report. You may or may not want to group records in a report; as an example of grouping, you might decide to print a list of employees for ABC Temporaries by assignment. If you decide to include groups, Paradox lets you have up to 16 group bands in a single report.

Finally, there are table bands. (In free-form reports, these are known as form bands.) Table bands indicate the actual information (usually fields) that will appear in the body of the report. The values in the table bands are represented by symbols called *field masks,* such as AAAAAAA for alphanumeric fields, 999999 for number fields, and mm/dd/yy for date fields. Table bands also contain the headings or field labels that appear at the top of the columns of printed data.

MAKING CHANGES TO A REPORT SPECIFICATION   Once the Report Specification appears on the screen, you can use various options of the Design menu to rearrange or remove fields and columns, set display formats, add bands for grouping, or make other desired changes. If you press F10 while the Report Specification is visible, you will see the Design menu, as shown at the top of Figure 7-6.

The Design Menu Options

The Field option controls general field placement and appearance; you can use this choice to place new fields in a report, remove existing fields from the report, change

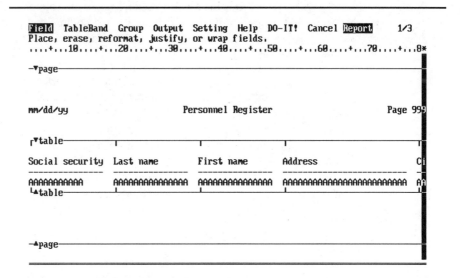

FIGURE 7-6.   Design menu

a field's format, set justification (left, center, and right), edit an expression used in a calculated field, or wordwrap a text field. The Field option also provides a Lookup choice that lets you include related tables in a report. This option is covered in detail in Chapter 9.

The TableBand option lets you insert or remove entire columns from the table band, resize columns, and move or copy columns to other locations. (The actual fields are placed inside the columns.) The Group option, designed for use with the optional groupings, lets you insert or delete groups, specify your group headings, change the sort order for a group, and change the types of groupings used. The Output option permits you to specify the printer, the screen, or a disk file as the default output device for the report.

The Setting option will be discussed in additional detail later. In a nutshell, this option lets you control a number of settings for the report, including page length and width, the left margin, setup strings for specialized font control of printers, and more. Finally, the DO-IT! option saves the modifications to the Report Specification, and the Help and Cancel options perform the same functions as they do elsewhere in Paradox.

From here on, the steps you perform will depend on what you want the report to look like. You use the various options shown on the Design menu to modify the report. A hands-on practice session that further illustrates many of these options is provided later in the chapter. The features you will use are described here:

- *To Move Columns:* From the Design menu, choose the option called Table-Band/Move and then place the cursor in the desired column and press RETURN. Move the cursor to the new location for the column and press RETURN again, and the column will be moved.

- *To Copy Columns:* From the Design menu, choose TableBand/Copy and then place the cursor in the desired column and press RETURN. Move the cursor to the desired location for the copied column, and press RETURN again. The copy of the column will appear in the designated location. Note that there is no limit to the number of times you can copy a column containing the same field to different locations in a report. This can be very helpful with tabular reports that must display many fields; you can place common information, such as the name of an employee, in the first column of each page, while other fields appear in the remaining columns.

- *To Remove Columns:* From the Design menu, choose the option called Table-Band/Erase. Then place the cursor in the desired column and press RETURN to erase the column.

- *To Resize Columns:* From the Design menu, choose the option called Table-Band/Resize. Then place the cursor at either edge of the desired column and press RETURN. Use the cursor keys to contract or expand the size of the column to the desired width, and then press RETURN again to complete the resizing.

- *To Edit Headings or Footers in the Page Band:* Place the cursor in the desired portion of the page band, and enter the desired heading or edit existing headings. "Page Number" and "System Date" are fields, not literal text; these can be removed or added by choosing Fields from the Design menu and using Place to place the fields or Erase to erase them.

- *To Reformat Fields:* From the Design menu, choose Field/Reformat, and then place the cursor in the field you want to reformat. Press RETURN to select the field. Use arrow keys to change the width, or select from the menu the desired format for the field.

- *To Place New Fields:* From the Design menu, choose Field/Place and then choose the type of field desired (regular, summary, calculated, current date, current time, page number, or record number). If you chose a regular field, you will be prompted for the name of the field; if you choose a summary or calculated field, you can enter an expression that will calculate the field. The date and time fields will display a menu of varying formats, and you can select the format desired. Finally, place the field in the desired location and press RETURN. You may need to add a column with TableBand/Insert to make room for the field.

- *To Remove Fields:* From the Design menu, choose Field/Erase. Then place the cursor on the desired field and press RETURN.

Saving the Report

Once you have made the desired changes to the Report Specification, press Do-It! (F2) or choose DO-IT! from the Design menu to save it.

 To design a report that prints using compressed print, choose Setting/Setup/Pre-defined from the menu while designing the report. Then, select the compressed option that matches your type of printer.

HANDS-ON PRACTICE: DESIGNING A CUSTOM PERSONNEL REPORT

ABC Temporaries needs a personnel report with more to offer than the standard report. The report must include the Last name, First name, Phone, and Date hired fields as the first set of columns per page, and the Last name, Social security, Salary, and Hourly Rate fields as the second set of columns per page. The date and time of the report should appear in the upper-right corner of the first page, and a report title should be centered at the top of the first page. Page numbers should be centered at the bottom of each page. Also, the Salary and Hourly Rate fields are to be totaled, producing figures that reflect the total hourly rate of income generated (assuming all employees are working) and the total cost of salary for the entire staff.

To begin designing the report, press F10 to display the main menu, and choose Report/Design. Enter **ABCSTAFF** as the table name, and choose 1 for the Report Specification. (If you have already used 1 for a different report, you can select a different number or replace the prior report.)

Paradox will prompt you for a description of the report; enter **Personnel Register** as the description. From the next menu that appears, choose Tabular to indicate that this will be a tabular report. In a moment, the Report Specification, based on the standard report for the ABCSTAFF table, will appear (Figure 7-7).

Note that you can quickly move between the pages of a report that contains multiple fields (like this one) with the CTRL-left arrow and CTRL-right arrow key combinations. Try using the CTRL-right arrow key repeatedly, and note the effect as the additional pages of the report come into view on the right. Use the CTRL-left arrow key combination to get back to the far left edge of the report.

The headings need to be customized for this report; the page number, which currently appears at the top of the report, needs to be relocated to the bottom. The

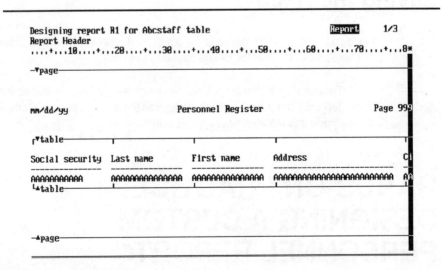

FIGURE 7-7. Report Specification

current date needs to be positioned at the right side of the top, rather than the left; and the custom heading needs to be amended to include the name of the company.

To display the Design menu, press F10. Choose Field/Erase, and then place the cursor anywhere in the "999" designation that indicates the page-number field. Press RETURN to erase the field, and then use the BACKSPACE key to erase the "Page" designation.

Move the cursor to the left slightly, roughly to position 70. The top of the screen provides a guide that indicates the relative column position of the cursor. To place the date and time fields in this area, press F10 for the menu and choose Field/Place. Then select Date from the list of field types. Paradox will display a list of possible date formats; press RETURN to select the first format shown. Then, with the cursor at position 70, press RETURN to place the field.

Move the cursor down one line and back to position 70. Press F10 for the menu, and choose Field/Place. Then select Time from the list of field types. Paradox will display a list of possible time formats; select the second format shown in the menu. Then, with the cursor at position 70, press RETURN to place the field.

Use CTRL-left arrow to quickly get back to the left side of the report. Directly above the "Personnel Register" title, add **ABC Temporaries**.

The date field at the left side of the report is no longer needed, so go to the menu with F10, choose Field/Erase, and place the cursor in the date field at the left side of the header. Then press RETURN to remove the field.

Deleting Unwanted Columns

To quickly rid the report of undesired fields and columns at the same time, you can use the Erase option from the TableBand choice on the Design menu. Press F10 for the menu, choose TableBand/Erase, and place the cursor in the Address field. Press RETURN to remove the column.

In a similar fashion, choose TableBand/Erase from the menu, and with the cursor positioned in the City field, press RETURN to delete the column. Perform the same step for the State, Zip Code, Date of birth, Dependents, and Assignment fields.

Moving a Column

The column containing the Phone field needs to be relocated to the right of the First name field. Press F10 for the menu, and choose TableBand/Move. Place the cursor in the column containing the Phone field, and press RETURN to select the column; Paradox will prompt you to show the new location for the field.

Use CTRL-left arrow to get back to the left side of the report. Place the cursor anywhere in the Date hired field, and press RETURN to insert the column containing the Phone field into this location.

In a similar fashion, press F10 for the menu, and choose TableBand/Move. Place the cursor in the Social security field, and press RETURN to select the field. Then move the cursor to the Date hired field and press RETURN to move the field to its new location (now between the Date hired and the Salary fields).

Resizing a Column

As the report design now stands, the column containing the Salary field is split by the vertical bar that indicates the division between pages of a report. By widening the column containing the Social security field, this can be corrected. From the menu, choose TableBand/Resize, place the cursor at the left edge of the Social security field, and press RETURN to select the field. Press the right arrow key three times to widen the column by three spaces, and press RETURN to set the new column width.

 Note When resizing columns, the cursor cannot be inside the field within the column, as Paradox will not let you split a field in two.

Duplicating a Column

The report now contains most of the desired fields on the first page, with the Salary and Hourly Rate fields occupying the second page. In this format, it would be difficult to tell which name belongs to which salary and hourly rate. Duplicating the last name in the second page of the report will make it easier to keep track of the fields.

From the menu, choose TableBand/Copy. Place the cursor anywhere in the column containing the Last name field, and press RETURN to select the field. Place the cursor anywhere in the Salary field, and press RETURN to insert the Last name field at this location.

Adding Report Totals

All that is needed at this point are the totals of the Salary and Hourly Rate fields. From the menu, choose Field/Place to place a new field. Paradox next prompts you for the type of field desired; choose Summary/Regular, and then select Salary from the list of fields. Choose Sum and then Overall.

Paradox will then ask you to indicate the position for the summary total of the salary values. Place the cursor in the footer section of the report band, just above the double line at the bottom of the screen and directly underneath the location of the Salary field within the table band. Press RETURN to place the field, press the left arrow key three times to shorten the width of the field, and press RETURN twice—once to set the number of decimal places, and once to complete the placement of the new field.

Again, choose Field/Place from the main menu to place a new field. From the next menu that appears, choose Summary/Regular, and then select Hourly Rate from the list of fields. From the next menu to appear, choose Sum. (The remaining choices on this menu are Count, Average, High, and Low. Average would provide an average value, Count would give the number of occurrences in the group, High would provide a maximum value, and Low would provide a minimum value.) After choosing Sum, select Overall from the next menu.

Paradox will then ask you to indicate the position for the summary total of the hourly rate values. Place the cursor in the footer section of the report band, just above the bottom of the screen and directly underneath the location of the Hourly Rate field within the table band. Press RETURN to place the field, press the left-arrow key three times to shorten the width of the field, and press RETURN twice—once to set the number of decimal places, and once to complete the placement of the new field. Move the cursor eight characters to the left of the start of the summary field you just placed, and enter **TOTALS:** as a label for this field.

To test the report before you save it, press F10 for the menu and choose Output/Screen. The report will appear on the screen, and if any errors exist, you can go back and correct them before saving the report.

When you are done previewing the report, choose DO-IT! from the menu or press F2. To see the results, choose Report/Output from the menu and enter **ABCSTAFF** as the desired table for the report. Select 1 from the menu for the desired Report Specification, and choose Printer (or Screen, if you prefer just to see the report on the

ABC Temporaries
Personnel Register   2/08/88
                                      20:34:09

Last name	First name	Phone	Date hired	Social security
Westman	Andrea	301-555-5682	7/04/86	121-33-9876
Robinson	Shirley	301-555-4582	11/17/87	121-90-5432
Morse	Marcia	301-555-9876	7/25/85	123-44-8976
Jackson	David	703-555-2345	9/05/85	232-55-1234
Robinson	Wanda	202-555-9876	9/17/87	343-55-9821
Abernathy	Sandra	703-555-7337	2/17/88	495-00-3456
Morse	William	301-555-9876	2/02/88	805-34-6789
Hart	Edward	703-555-7834	10/19/86	876-54-3210
Mitchell	Mary Jo	703-555-7654	12/01/87	901-77-3456
Jones	Judi	703-555-2638	8/12/86	909-88-7654

Last name	Salary	Hourly Rate
Westman	15.00	24.00
Robinson	7.50	12.00
Morse	8.50	15.00
Jackson	7.50	12.00
Robinson	7.50	12.00
Abernathy	10.00	18.00
Morse	7.50	12.00
Hart	8.50	14.00
Mitchell	7.50	12.00
Jones	12.00	17.50

FIGURE 7-8.   Resulting custom report

screen). Within a moment, your custom report will be printed or appear on your screen. It should look like the report shown in Figure 7-8.

Remember   You can preview any report on-screen before you save it, by choosing OUT-PUT/SCREEN while designing the report.

USING THE GROUP
MENU OPTIONS

You can use the Group option of the Report Design menu to work with groupings of records within a report. Most likely, you will need to arrange reports broken down by groups. As an example, you might want to see all employees divided into groups by state of residence or by the name of the assignment. By utilizing the Group menu options, you can define up to 16 levels of groupings.

While 16 levels may seem like overkill, it is nice to know that Paradox will not limit you when you must base a complex report on a large number of subgroups. Multiple groupings can be quite common in many business applications. In something as simple as a national mailing list, for example, you might need to see records by groups of states, and within each state group by city, and within each city group by ZIP code. That represents three levels of grouping alone. Cut the data in the table more specifically, by other categories like income levels, and you will quickly come to appreciate Paradox's ability to perform groupings so effectively.

When you select Group from the Report Design menu while designing a report, the following menu options will be displayed:

Insert Delete Headings SortDirection Regroup
Insert a new group based on a field, range, or a number of records.

The Insert option lets you insert new groups into the report, while the Delete option lets you delete existing groups from the report. The Headings option is used to control where headings appear within the group. The SortDirection option is used to control whether groups should be sorted in ascending or descending order. Finally, using the Regroup option changes the ways existing groups are defined.

To add a new group to the report, choose Insert from the Group option of the Report Design menu. The next menu that appears will display the following options:

Field Range NumberRecords
Group together records with the same field value.

If you want to establish the group by field (for example, groups of records from the same state or with the same assignment), choose Field. You can also group records by a range of values in a field; choose Range if you desire this kind of grouping. Finally, Paradox lets you establish groups by a set number of records. You could set the report's design to isolate records into groups of 10, 15, or any set number of records per group. Choose NumberRecords to select grouping by such quantities as records.

When you have selected the desired type of grouping, Paradox will ask you to indicate the location for the group. You now move the cursor to the desired location,

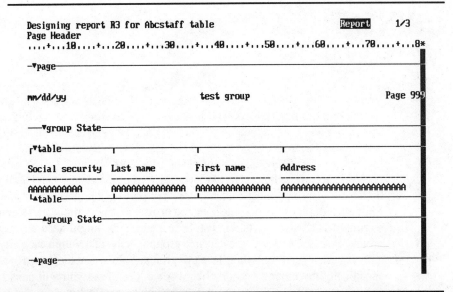

FIGURE 7-9.   Report Specification with single level of grouping

and you press RETURN to place the new group band. Group bands must fall outside of table bands (or outside of form bands in the case of free-form reports) and inside the page band. Figure 7-9 shows a Report Specification for the ABCSTAFF Personnel Report, which includes a group band for employees grouped by state.

Once you have placed the desired group, you can check to see if the results are what you desire by pressing F10 for the menu and choosing Output/Screen. The resulting report will be divided by group. When you are satisfied with the results, save the Report Specification by pressing Do-It! (F2).

Remember   You cannot add a group band inside a table band.

HANDS-ON PRACTICE: ADDING GROUPING BY ASSIGNMENT

Try adding a group by assignment name to the existing Personnel Register report you created earlier in the chapter. First, clear the workspace with ALT-F8. From the main menu, choose Report/Change, and enter **ABCSTAFF** as the table name. Select 1 as the report to modify, and press RETURN to accept the prior description. The Report Specification for the report you designed earlier will appear.

To add the group to the report, press F10 for the Report Design menu, and choose Group and then Insert to insert a new group. The report is to be grouped by assignment name (which is a field), so choose Field. The next menu shows the fields available in the table; choose Assignment from the list.

Paradox next asks you to show where the group is to be inserted. Remember that group bands must appear between the table band and the page band. Since there is only one level of grouping in this report, things are simple. Move the cursor to the blank line just above the table band. Press RETURN to place the group. Your screen should now resemble the example shown in Figure 7-10.

Remember, you do not need to save and exit the report before seeing the results. Press F10 for the menu, and choose Output/Screen or Output/Printer if you prefer to have the results printed. The report will be printed or will appear on your screen. It should resemble the one shown in Figure 7-11.

Note that the actual contents of the Assignment field do not appear with each group; to add the field, you will need to place it where you want it to appear. You can place the field used to control the group within the group band, and it will then print once for each occurrence of that group. To see how this works, press F10 for the Report Design menu. Choose the Field/Place/Regular option, and select Assignment from the menu of fields as the field to place in the report. Place the cursor in the blank line between the group band and the table band (directly underneath the designation,

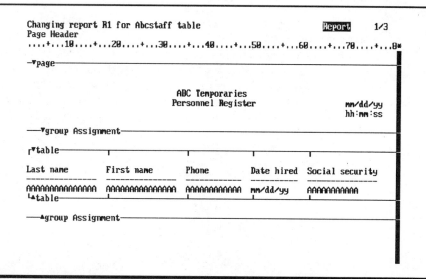

FIGURE 7-10.   Report Specification with group added

```
                          ABC Temporaries
                          Personnel Registry            2/20/88
                                                        13:43:48


        Last name    First name    Phone            Date hired    Social security
        -----------  -----------   ------------     ----------    ---------------
        Jackson      David         703-555-2345      9/05/85      232-55-1234
        Robinson     Wanda         202-555-9876      9/17/87      343-55-9821
        Abernathy    Sandra        703-555-7337      2/17/88      495-00-3456


        Westman      Andrea        301-555-5682      7/04/86      121-33-9876
        Robinson     Shirley       301-555-4582     11/17/87      121-90-5432
        Morse        Marcia        301-555-9876      7/25/85      123-44-8976
        Jones        Judi          703-555-2638      8/12/86      909-88-7654


        Morse        William       301-555-9876      2/02/88      805-34-6789
        Hart         Edward        703-555-7834     10/19/86      876-54-3210
        Mitchell     Mary Jo       703-555-7654     12/01/87      901-77-345
```

FIGURE 7-11.   Example of report with grouping

"Group Assignment"). Press RETURN to place the field, and then press RETURN again to set the width.

To see the results, press F10 for the menu and choose Output/Screen or Output/Printer if you prefer having the results printed. The report will be printed or will appear on your screen, and this time the contents for the Assignment field will appear along with each group. (Note that CTRL-BREAK can be used to stop the report at any time.) Save the report and return to the main menu by pressing Do-It! (F2).

HANDS-ON PRACTICE: CREATING A REPORT WITH MULTIPLE GROUPS

You can add as many groups as are needed (up to the Paradox limit of 16) to further define your groups. As an example, consider the HOURS table, which contains records of the employee hours worked at different assignments. If what is needed is a report grouped by assignment and by "week ending" date within each assignment group, you must create a report containing more than one group.

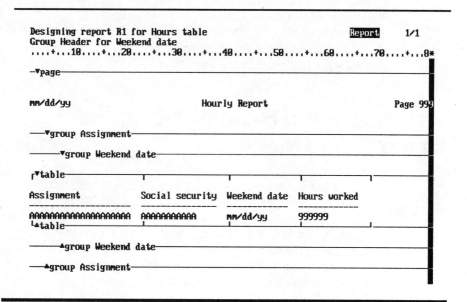

FIGURE 7-12.   Report Specification containing multiple groups

From the main menu, choose Report/Design, and enter **HOURS** as the table name for this example. Choose 1 as the report name, and enter **HOURLY REPORT** as a description. Choose Tabular for the desired type of report, and the standard Report Specification for the HOURS table will appear.

In this case, you want a report grouped by assignment name, and within each assignment name, by groups of "week ending" dates. Press F10 for the Report Specification menu, and choose Group/Insert to insert a new group. Then choose Field to base the new group on a field.

From the list of field names, choose Assignment. Place the cursor just below the line in the page band containing the date, report heading, and page number. Press RETURN to place the group based on the Assignment field. To add the second group, press F10 for the menu and choose Group/Insert and then Field. From the list of fields, choose Weekend date.

Place the cursor just underneath the Assignment group band and press RETURN. Your screen should resemble the one shown in Figure 7-12.

To test the results, press F10 for the menu and choose Output/Screen. The results should be similar to those shown in Figure 7-13. Finally, press Do-It! (F2) to save the finished report, and return to the main menu.

The Delete and Headings Options Of the Group Menu

You can delete unwanted groups with the Delete option of the Group menu. To delete an existing grouping, press F10 for the menu and choose Group/Delete. Paradox will ask you to select the group that is to be removed. Place the cursor anywhere inside of the group band that is to be deleted, and press RETURN. Paradox will require confirmation of the deletion by displaying the choices of Cancel and OK. You must choose OK to delete the group. Remember, when you delete a group band, any fields or literal text contained within that group band will also be deleted.

To control where your headings appear, use the Headings option of the Group menu. Headings normally appear at the start of each group containing the heading, and at the start of "spillover" pages, which are the pages of a report in which a group cannot fit on one page and spills over onto the next page. You can decide whether or not these headings will appear. From the Report Specification menu, choose Group/Headings. Place the cursor anywhere in the group band, and press RETURN. Paradox will display the following menu:

Page Group
Print group headings once per group and at the top of spillover pages.

2/22/88   HOURLY REPORT   Page 1

Assignment	Social security	Weekend date	Hours worked
City Revenue Dept.	232-55-1234	1/16/88	30
City Revenue Dept.	343-55-9821	1/16/88	35
City Revenue Dept.	495-00-3456	1/16/88	28
City Revenue Dept.	232-55-1234	1/23/88	30
City Revenue Dept.	343-55-9821	1/23/88	32
City Revenue Dept.	495-00-3456	1/23/88	32
National Oil Co.	121-33-9876	1/16/88	30
National Oil Co.	121-90-5432	1/16/88	27
National Oil Co.	123-44-8976	1/16/88	32
National Oil Co.	909-88-7654	1/16/88	35
National Oil Co.	121-33-9876	1/23/88	35
National Oil Co.	909-88-7654	1/23/88	33
Smith Builders	805-34-6789	1/23/88	35
Smith Builders	876-54-3210	1/23/88	30
Smith Builders	901-77-3456	1/23/88	28

FIGURE 7-13.   Results of report based on multiple groups

If you choose the Page option, group headers will appear at the start of each group and at the top of every spillover page. If you choose the Group option, group headers will print at the start of each group but not at the top of the spillover pages.

In some cases, you may want to define groups solely to implement a particular sorting order. In such cases, you would just delete all the extra lines in the group band, so no lines appear between groups.

CHANGING THE SORT DIRECTION OF A REPORT

On occasion, you may want to change the sort direction for a group of records. When you add a group band to a report, Paradox automatically handles the sorting necessary to generate the report, in the order of the groups you have specified. However, Paradox assumes that it should sort the data in *ascending* order to arrange the groups. If, for example, you group a report by a date field, the groups appear in the report by ascending order of dates, earliest to latest. If you want to change this to *descending* order (or change any other direction of any other group), you will need to use the SortDirection option of the Group menu.

To change the sort direction, choose Group/SortDirection from the Report Specification menu. Paradox will ask you to select the desired group; move the cursor anywhere in the desired group, and press RETURN. The next menu to appear displays the following options:

Ascending Descending
Values in the group will be sorted from low to high.

If you desire the group's sort direction to be ascending (letters alphabetically, numbers from least to greatest, and dates from earliest to latest), choose Ascending from this menu. If you want descending order (letters in reverse alphabetical order, numbers from greatest to least, and dates from latest to earliest), choose Descending from the menu. There will be no visible change in the Report Specification (other than the momentary appearance of the message "Settings changed"). But when the report is generated, any changes to the sort direction will take effect. Note that if you reverse the sort direction within an inner group without changing the sort direction of the outer group, the outer group's sort order will override that of the inner group.

USING SETPRINTER FOR SPECIALIZED PRINTING NEEDS

You can use the SetPrinter option of the Report Design menu to select printer ports or to choose printer setup strings for taking advantage of your printer's specialized features. Selecting Setting/Setup from the Report Specification menu reveals the Predefined and Custom options.

If you choose Predefined, Paradox lets you choose from among the following options for producing condensed or otherwise specialized print on some of the most common types of printers:

STANDARDPRINTER
SMALL-IBMGRAPHICS
REG-IBMGRAPHICS
SMALL-EPSON-MX/FX
SMALL-OKI-92/93
SMALL-OKI-82/83
SMALL-OKI-192
HPLASERJET
HPLANDSCAPE-NORMAL
HP-PORTRAIT-66LINES
HP-COMPRESSED
HP-LANDSCAPE-COMPRESSED
INTL-IBM-COMPATIBLE
INTL-IBM-CONDENSED

Select the desired choice, and it will be recorded as a part of the report.

By choosing Setting/Setup from the Report Design menu and selecting Custom from the next menu, you can enter custom setup strings or printer ports. When you select Setting/Setup/Custom, the first menu to appear offers the following choice of printer ports:

Printer port:
LPT1 LPT2 LPT3 COM1 COM2 AUX

Select the desired printer port from the menu. (Most systems use the LPT1 as the printer port. Many serial printers, including earlier versions of the Hewlett-Packard LaserJet, use COM1 as the printer port.) The next prompt that appears displays the following:

Setup string:
Enter the setup string to be sent to the printer by printing the report.

Setup strings can be up to 175 characters in length. You can enter codes, such as the escape codes commonly used to select printer fonts, by entering a backslash (\ ) followed by the three-digit ASCII code representing that escape code. For example, to turn on compressed printing with an Epson MX/FX or Epson-compatible printer, you would enter \ **015** as a setup string. You should consult your printer manual for the list of escape codes appropriate to your printer. Before resorting to these, however, try the predefined list available from the Predefined option first to see if the desired mode of printing is available without resorting to a custom string.

Keep in mind that the custom setup string that you enter will apply to the entire report. Save the completed report with Do-It! (F2), and the setup string, along with any custom printer port settings you have chosen, will be automatically placed in effect when you print the report.

Note that the Custom Configuration Program (CCP) can be used to define printer setups globally and to add custom printer setups to the list. Refer to Appendix B for details on this topic.

HINTS FOR REPORT DESIGN

Before you start to design your custom reports, you should plan the design of the report. This may mean asking the other users of the database what information will actually be needed from the report.

In many cases you will find it advantageous to outline the report contents and format on paper. Once the report has been designed on paper, your outline should resemble the actual report that is produced by Paradox. You may also find it helpful to print a list of fields from the table structure, particularly if you are designing a report that contains a large number of fields. This can be done by choosing Tools/Info/Structure from the main menu, entering the name of the table, and using ALT- F7 to print the table.

QUICK SUMMARY

To generate an instant report   Display the desired table with View or by processing a query, and press Instant Report (ALT-F7).

To design a custom report   From the menu, choose Report/Design. Enter the name of the table on which the report will be based. Choose a number for the report from the next menu to appear, and enter a description for the report. Select a tabular or free-form report, then modify the report specification that appears on the screen, as desired. Finally, press Do-It! (F2) to save the report.

To add groups to a report   When designing the report, press F10 for the Report Design Menu, and choose Group/Insert. Next, choose Field to establish the grouping based on a field, and then select the field to be used from the list of fields that appears. Place the cursor above the Table Band where the group is to be inserted, and press RETURN to place the new group.

To change the sort direction of a report   When designing the report, press F10 for the Report Design Menu, and choose Group/SortDirection. Place the cursor anywhere within the desired group, and press RETURN. Choose Ascending or Descending as desired, from the next menu.

PRESENTATION GRAPHICS

Paradox offers powerful capabilities for displaying and printing graphs. Graphs can be prepared for data analysis or for presentation-quality reports. You can use the wide variety of styling features and options offered by Paradox to enhance the appearance of your graphs.

TYPICAL GRAPHS

Some typical graphs you can create with Paradox are shown in Figure 8-1. Paradox lets you create any of the following types of graphs:

- Stacked bar

- Standard bar

- Rotated bar

- 3-D (three-dimensional) bar

- X-Y graph

- Area graph

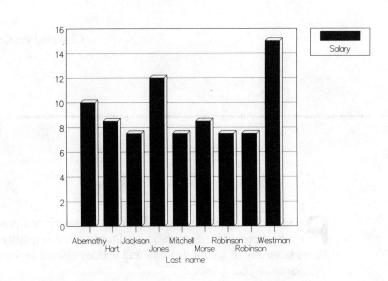

FIGURE 8-1.   Types of graphs created with Paradox

ADVERTIS

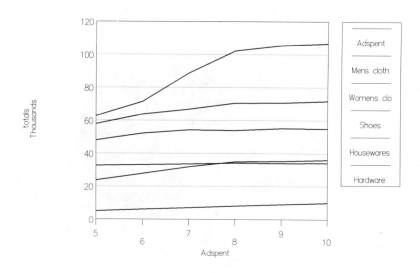

CROSSTAB

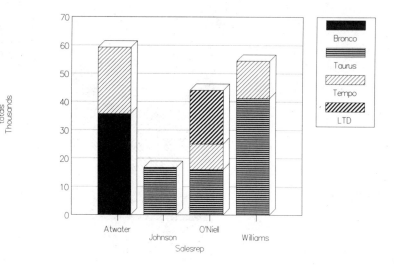

FIGURE 8-1.   Types of graphs created with Paradox (*continued*)

CARSALES

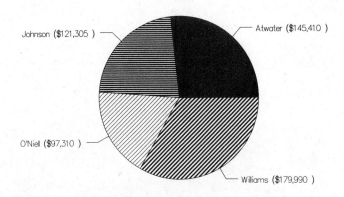

CARSALES

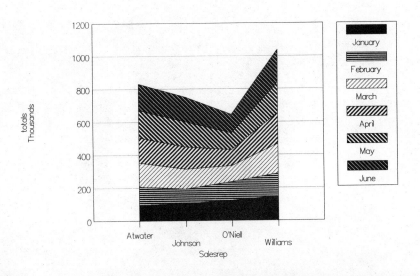

FIGURE 8-1. Types of graphs created with Paradox (*continued*)

- Line graph

- Pie chart

- Marker graph

- Combined lines and markers graph

The graphs consist primarily of elements representing the data contained within the table. The appearance of the elements vary, depending on the type of graph you select. In a bar or rotated bar graph, the data is illustrated with bars; in a line graph, the data appears as thin lines. An area graph combines a line graph with shadings underneath the lines to represent trends. In a marker graph, the data appears as small markers, and in a pie graph, data is represented as wedges of the pie. All graphs except for pie graphs have two axes: a horizontal axis, called the *X-axis* or *category axis,* and a vertical axis, called the *Y-axis* or *value axis*.

Some graphs in Paradox are combinations or variations of the types just described. The stacked bar, rotated bar, and 3-D bar are all variations of a bar graph. An X-Y graph is a line graph that displays values along both the X- and the Y-axes. X-Y graphs are used to show a corresponding relationship between two sets of numbers. Finally, a combined lines and markers graph combines a line graph with markers.

MAKING A
SIMPLE GRAPH

Paradox has some built-in features that make it very easy to produce a graph. The basic steps are as follows:

1. Place the cursor in a numeric field of a table containing the data to be graphed. (It does not matter which record the cursor is at.)

2. Press the Graph key (CTRL-F7).

At first glance, you might think that producing a graph must be more complicated, and it can be. The graphs themselves may be as simple or as complex as you care to make them. Thanks to the flexible options provided in Paradox, you can experiment with different types of graphs, customized text and legends, and fancy formatting. If all you need is a basic graph, however, the two steps just outlined can produce a complete graph for you.

Two points can help get the results you want when you use this quick technique. First, with unkeyed tables (or tables with only one field) Paradox uses the far left column of the table for names along the X-axis by default. With keyed tables, Paradox uses the rightmost key field. If the names you want to see along the X-axis are in a different field, you can perform a quick query-by-example operation and place the first checkmark in the column that contains the desired names. Include additional checkmarks in the column or columns containing the numeric data to be graphed, press Do-It!, and then use the ANSWER table that results to draw the graph. The values shown in the first series in the graph are taken from the field containing the cursor. The next numeric field (if there are any more fields) provides the second series values, the third numeric field provides the third series values, and so on.

Second, you'll often want to graph just a subset of data from a particular database. Again, use the query-by-example techniques described in Chapter 6 to build an ANSWER table containing the desired subset of your data. Then draw the graph, based on the ANSWER table, by placing the cursor anywhere in the numeric field of the ANSWER table and pressing Graph (CTRL-F7).

 You can use CTRL-R to rotate the columns. In some cases, this can make queries unnecessary.

HANDS-ON PRACTICE: CREATING AN INSTANT GRAPH

You can try the techniques just described with the ABCSTAFF table created earlier in this text. As you will see, you can quickly create a bar graph showing the salaries of the employees. To get the names of the employees to appear as names along the X-axis of the graph, you'll need to have the employee names in the first column of the table. Since that is not the way the table was originally designed, you can perform a query that will extract the contents of the Last name and Salary fields.

First, press F10 to get to the main menu, choose Ask, and enter **ABCSTAFF** as the table name. Use F6 to place checkmarks in the Last name and Salary fields. Press Do-It! (F2) to process the query and display the ANSWER table. Next, move the cursor to the Salary field of the ANSWER table, and press Graph (CTRL-F7). The resultant bar graph shows the salaries represented by bars. If you see something other than a bar graph, the default settings in your version of Paradox have been changed. Don't be concerned, as you'll soon learn how to select different graph types for display.

The default type of graph created by Paradox is a stacked bar graph. Each of the patterns in the bar represent up to six numeric fields, starting from the field where the cursor is located. In the case of the ABCSTAFF table, there is only one numeric field, so Paradox displays a bar graph with only one bar pattern. Later in this chapter you

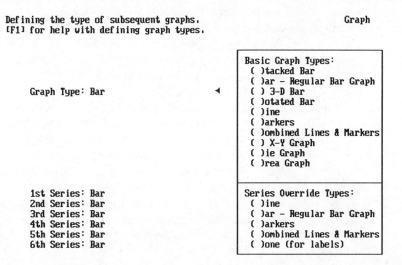

```
Defining the type of subsequent graphs.                      Graph
[F1] for help with defining graph types.


                                          ┌──────────────────────────────┐
                                          │ Basic Graph Types:           │
                                          │   ( )tacked Bar              │
                                          │   ( )ar - Regular Bar Graph   │
  Graph Type: Bar                    ◄     │   ( ) 3-D Bar                │
                                          │   ( )otated Bar              │
                                          │   ( )ine                     │
                                          │   ( )arkers                  │
                                          │   ( )ombined Lines & Markers  │
                                          │   ( ) X-Y Graph              │
                                          │   ( )ie Graph                │
                                          │   ( )rea Graph               │
                                          │                              │
                                          ├──────────────────────────────┤
  1st Series: Bar                          │ Series Override Types:       │
  2nd Series: Bar                          │   ( )ine                     │
  3rd Series: Bar                          │   ( )ar - Regular Bar Graph   │
  4th Series: Bar                          │   ( )arkers                  │
  5th Series: Bar                          │   ( )ombined Lines & Markers  │
  6th Series: Bar                          │   ( )one (for labels)        │
                                          └──────────────────────────────┘
```

FIGURE 8-2.   Customize Graph Type screen

will see examples of a table that supplies more numeric fields and the resulting default graphs displayed.

Changing the Graph Type

If the graph is still displayed, press any key to clear the graph and get back to the ANSWER table. While you still have the cursor placed in the Salary field of the table, you may wish to try creating other types of graphs. You can easily change the setting for the type of graph created with Image/Graph/Modify. Press F10 for the menu and choose Image. Then choose Graph. You will see the following menu:

Modify   Load   Save   Reset   CrossTab   ViewGraph
Modify the current graph specification.

The Graph menu offers various options pertaining to graphs. You'll use Modify shortly to change the type of graph displayed. The Load and Save options are used to load or save the specifications for a graph. ("Save" in this case means the graph settings are saved, and not an image of the graph itself.) The Reset option resets the graph to the default display specifications. CrossTab generates a crosstab of the current image, a topic covered in detail later in this chapter. Finally, ViewGraph reveals another menu with three choices: Screen (to display the graph on the screen), Printer (to print the graph), or File (to save the graph image as a disk file). Note that before printing a graph, your copy of Paradox should be configured to match your printer. If this has not been done, you'll find tips on selecting printers with the Custom Configuration Program in Appendix B of this text.

With the Graph menu still visible, select Modify. The Customize Graph Type screen shown in Figure 8-2 appears. This screen contains two areas. The upper area has one entry for Graph Type. In this box, you can enter a letter that represents the desired graph type. A help screen to the right shows the available graph types and the corresponding letters. For example, typing **S** causes "Stacked bar" to appear in the Graph Type entry, and typing **P** causes "Pie" to appear in the entry.

The bottom area of the screen contains entries for series override graph types. You use these entries to create a mixed graph, such as a stacked bar graph or a combination line and markers graph. The Series Override Graph Type options will be covered later in this chapter.

For now, you may want to try choosing one or two other graph types. After typing the letter of the desired graph type, press Do-It! (F2), and then press Graph (CTRL-F7) to draw the corresponding graph. You can get back to the Customize Graph Type screen by pressing any key to clear the graph, pressing F10 for the menu, and choosing Image/Graph/Modify.

 The default type of graph displayed or printed is a bar graph. To change the graph types, press F10 and choose Image/Graph/Modify.

Printing a Graph

To print a graph, with the cursor still in the desired field of the table and the desired graph-type settings chosen, press F10 for the menu and choose Image/Graph/View-Graph. You will see the following menu:

```
Screen    Printer    File
Display the graph on the screen.
```

The Screen option is equivalent to pressing the Graph key; it causes the graph to be displayed on the screen. The File option saves the image of the graph to a print file that is useable with other programs such as Lotus 1-2-3 or most desktop publishing software. Use the Printer choice to print the graph on your printer.

Make sure your printer is ready, and choose Printer now. The screen will clear, and in a moment you will see a message similar to this:

Graph Printer: HP Printers - HP LaserJet Plus (150 dpi)
Mode: 150 x 150 dpi Med.
Press <ESC> to cancel printing

(Your message will probably differ, depending on the type of printer you have installed with your system.) Because graphs contain large amounts of graphic data, it will take some time for the graph to print. If you have a dot-matrix printer, the graph will probably print at slow to moderate speeds, line by line. With most laser printers, there will probably be no activity for a minute or two, and then the graph will be printed. Laser printers must receive and compose the entire page in memory before any printing begins.

PARTS OF A GRAPH

Before considering the options that Paradox offers for creating graphs, you should know the parts of a graph, discussed here and shown in Figure 8-3.

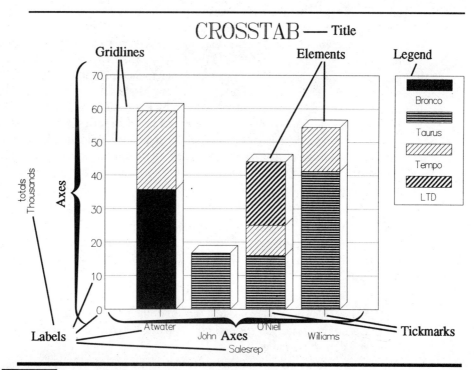

FIGURE 8-3. Parts of a graph

AXES   The axes are the horizontal and vertical frames of reference, and they appear in all types of graphs except pie charts. The horizontal axis (or X-axis) is called the category axis because categories of data are normally plotted along this line. The vertical axis (or Y-axis) is called the value axis because values are normally shown along this line. A variation on this rule is the rotated bar graph, where the axes are reversed, with the category axis vertical and the value axis horizontal. An exception to the rule is the X-Y graph, which shows values along both axes.

TICKMARKS   Tickmarks are reference marks that separate the scales of the value axis and the categories of the category axis.

LABELS   Labels describe the categories or values. By default, Paradox adds labels to the X-axis of a graph based on the contents of the leftmost column of the table. You can change these labels or omit them by using options described later in this chapter.

GRIDLINES   Gridlines are reference lines that extend across the entire area of the graph.

ELEMENTS   Elements are the bars, lines, markers, shaded areas, or pie wedges that represent the actual data in the graph. The form of the elements depends on the type of graph you choose. In a pie chart, the markers are wedges, or slices, of the pie. In a line graph, the markers are solid lines. (At some sharp angles, the lines in a line graph may appear jagged or broken; this is due to the limitations of the screen.) In a bar graph, the elements appear as bars. Each set of elements in a graph represents a field within the table. The field represented by the element is referred to as a *data series*. If a graph displays data from more than one data series, each data series will be represented by a different pattern or symbol. In Figure 8-4, for example, the January sales data make up one data series, and the February sales data comprise another data series. The data series are further differentiated by the pattern or shadings of the columns.

LEGEND   A legend defines the patterns (shadings) in the graph. The legend displays the pattern, followed by the label assigned to that pattern. Paradox uses the field names as default names within the legend, but this can also be changed, as described later in this chapter.

TITLES   Titles normally appear at the top of the graph, although you can change the title position or omit the title entirely. If no title is assigned, Paradox uses the table name as a default for the title.

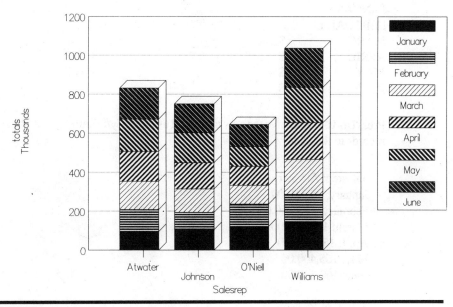

FIGURE 8-4.   Stacked bar graph

HANDS-ON PRACTICE: CREATING DIFFERENT GRAPH TYPES

To try creating different graph types, you can quickly build a table of sales figures from four sales representatives. The table will contain data for the months of January through June.

To build the table, first use ALT-F8 to clear all existing tables. Then press F10 for the menu, choose Create, and call the new table **CARSALES**. Give the following specifications for the fields:

Field name	Type
SALESREP	A20
JANUARY	$
FEBRUARY	$
MARCH	$
APRIL	$
MAY	$
JUNE	$

Press Do-It! (F2) to save the new table, and use Modify/DataEntry to add the following records to the table:

Salesrep: Atwater
January: 95,240.00
February: 112,350.00
March: 145,410.00
April: 152,800.00
May: 165,400.00
June: 160,390.00

Salesrep: Johnson
January: 103,700.00
February: 89,250.00
March: 121,305.00
April: 134,680.00
May: 152,112.00
June: 148,900.00

Salesrep: O'Niell
January: 121,500.00
February: 114,250.00
March: 97,310.00
April: 96,520.00
May: 101,280.00
June: 112,395.00

Salesrep: Williams
January: 146,200.00
February: 138,850.00

March: 179,990.00
April: 187,500.00
May: 184,350.00
June: 201,280.00

Once the table exists, place the cursor in the first numeric column, which represents the sales figures for January. Press F10 for the menu, and choose Image/Graph/Modify. For the graph type, enter S to choose Stacked Bar. (Unless your copy of Paradox has been modified, "S" will be the default choice.) Press Do-It! (F2), then press the Graph key (CTRL-F7). You will see a stacked bar graph (Figure 8-4), with a different pattern representing each of the six months of sales figures. Because the Salesrep names are in the leftmost column of the table, Paradox automatically uses them as category names along the X-axis.

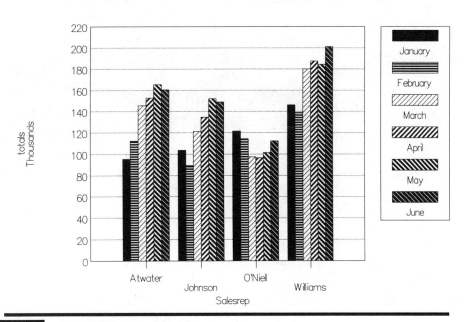

FIGURE 8-5. Multiple bar graph

Press any key to exit the graph, and then press F10 for the menu. Choose Image/Graph/Modify, and select Bar by entering **B** at the Customize Graph Type screen. Press Do-It! (F2), and then press Graph (CTRL-F7). The bar graph that appears should show a different bar for each of the sales months, as in Figure 8-5. (The 3-D bar graph provides a similar representation, but with a slight depth to the bars; you may want to try it to see the effect.)

Press any key to exit the graph, and then press F10 for the menu. Choose Image/Graph/Modify, and select Rotated Bar by typing **R** at the Customize Graph Type screen. Press Do-It! (F2), and then press Graph (CTRL-F7). Notice that the graph now takes on a horizontal orientation, as shown in Figure 8-6.

Press any key to exit the graph, and then press F10 for the menu. Choose Image/Graph/Modify, and select Line by typing **L** at the Customize Graph Type screen. Press Do-It! (F2), and then press Graph (CTRL-F7). The result shown in Figure 8-7 uses lines to represent the sales.

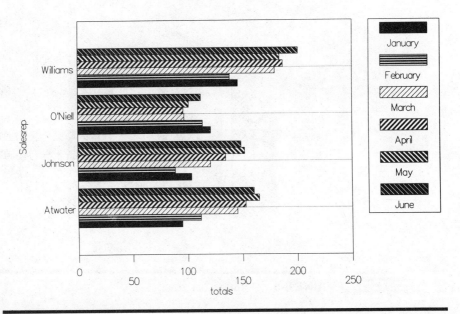

FIGURE 8-6.   Horizontal bar graph

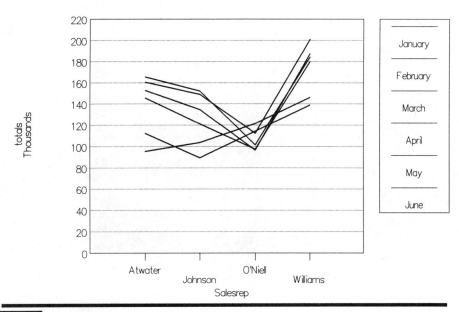

CARSALES

FIGURE 8-7. Line graph

Try repeating the procedure outlined in the previous paragraph, displaying the table as a marker graph, a combined lines and markers graph, and an area graph. An area graph, illustrated in Figure 8-8, can be very useful when you want to show the combined effects of a group of numbers.

USING SERIES OVERRIDE TO CREATE MIXED GRAPHS

Paradox lets you present your data graphically in yet another manner—as mixed graphs, which combine one type of graph with another. As an example, you could highlight the sales for a particular month by showing those sales with a different

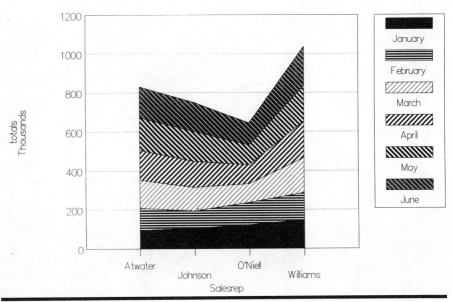

FIGURE 8-8.   Area graph

indicator than the other months. You can create mixed graphs by filling in the Series Override Graph Type options that appear when you choose Image/Graph/Modify.

Whenever Image/Graph/Modify is selected from the menu, the Customize Graph Type screen that appears contains six entries at the bottom of the screen (Figure 8-9). These entries are for up to six possible series overrides; any entries you make here will tell Paradox to override the basic graph type (selected in the top half of the screen) for that particular data series. For example, if the chosen graph type was a bar graph and you wanted to represent the third numeric column with a line graph, you would change 3rd Series under Series Override Graph Type to Line.

To try this, with the cursor still in the first numeric field of the CARSALES table, press F10 for the menu and choose Image/Graph/Modify. Select Bar as the graph type. Then press RETURN until the cursor moves down to 3rd Series in the Series Override Graph Type entry. Type **L** to change the third series to a line graph. Press Do-It! (F2), and then press Graph (CTRL-F7). The results should resemble those shown in Figure 8-10; all months are represented with bars except for March, the third column or "series," which is represented with a line.

```
Defining the type of subsequent graphs.                    Graph
[F1] for help with defining graph types.


                                                  ┌─────────────────────────────┐
                                                  │ Basic Graph Types:          │
                                                  │   ( )tacked Bar             │
                                                  │   ( )ar - Regular Bar Graph │
         Graph Type: Bar              ◄           │   ( ) 3-D Bar               │
                                                  │   ( )otated Bar             │
                                                  │   ( )ine                    │
                                                  │   ( )arkers                 │
                                                  │   ( )ombined Lines & Markers│
                                                  │   ( ) X-Y Graph             │
                                                  │   ( )ie Graph               │
                                                  │   ( )rea Graph              │
                                                  │                             │
                                                  ├─────────────────────────────┤
         1st Series: Bar                          │ Series Override Types:      │
         2nd Series: Bar                          │   ( )ine                    │
         3rd Series: Bar                          │   ( )ar - Regular Bar Graph │
         4th Series: Bar                          │   ( )arkers                 │
         5th Series: Bar                          │   ( )ombined Lines & Markers│
         6th Series: Bar                          │   ( )one (for labels)       │
                                                  └─────────────────────────────┘
```

FIGURE 8-9.   Six graph type override lines on screen

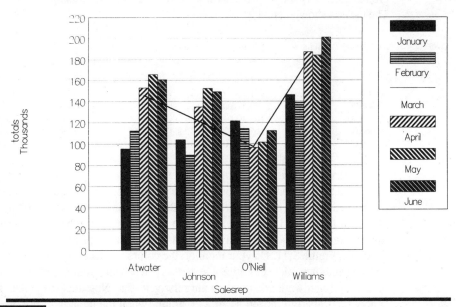

FIGURE 8-10.   Mixed bar and line graph

When you create your graphs, you should examine your data to consider whether mixed graphs can be effectively used. Experimenting with the entries in the Series Override Graph Type box will provide you with some ideas as to how you can design your own mixed graphs.

WORKING WITH X-Y GRAPHS

X-Y graphs display sets of values along both the X-axis and the Y-axis. When you select this type of graph as the graph type, Paradox uses the contents of the first numeric field within the table as the X-axis. The current field (wherever the cursor is located) and the next five fields in succession are used as the Y-axis values. Since an X-Y graph shows the relationship between one set of values and another, the entire graph must be based on numeric or currency fields. Any alphanumeric fields containing text are ignored by Paradox when you plot an X-Y graph.

As an example of when an X-Y graph would prove useful, consider a department store manager's attempt to find out where advertising dollars are spent most effectively. Increases in advertising costs appear more effective with some items than with others. Storing sales figures for different departments in a table and creating an X-Y graph will clearly show the places in which increases in advertising are most effective. The table is shown here:

Ads spent	Mens clothes	Womens clothes	Shoes	House- wares	Hard- ware	Toys
5,000.00	57,800.00	62,650.00	23,700.00	48,000.00	32,600.00	19,700.00
6,000.00	63,800.00	71,350.00	27,850.00	52,220.00	33,100.00	18,950.00
7,000.00	66,750.00	88,570.00	31,780.00	54,200.00	33,520.00	19,400.00
8,000.00	70,450.00	102,300.003	34,900.00	53,950.00	34,200.00	19,550.00
9,000.00	70,600.00	105,560.003	35,250.00	55,100.00	33,980.00	19,700.00
10,000.00	71,700.00	106,600.00	36,120.00	54,980.00	34,150.00	19,650.00

The first column, Ads spent, indicates the amount of newspaper advertising purchased by the department store during a given week. The remaining columns show the sales figures for each department of the store during that week. If the cursor is placed in the second column of the table and the X-Y graph type is chosen using Image/Graph/Modify, the graph that appears when the Graph key is pressed resembles the one in Figure 8-11. On your monitor, the colors or shadings of the lines show that clothing and shoe sales see noticeable increases when advertising costs increase, while the sales of hardware and toys remain relatively flat. Note that if the data in a table cannot be properly graphed as an X-Y graph (when the table has only one numeric field, for example), the graph will be blank.

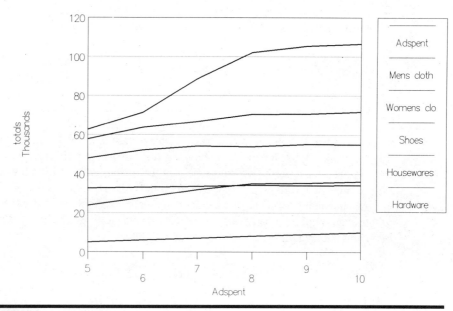

ADVERTIS

FIGURE 8-11.   X-Y graph

GRAPHING CROSSTABS

Paradox offers a CrossTab option on the Graph menu that allows you to create cross-tabulations of numeric data for graphing. A *cross-tabulation,* or *crosstab* for short, is another way of looking at your data. Crosstabs summarize the data in chosen categories. Using crosstabs, you can perform spreadsheet-like numeric analysis on the data within a table.

Paradox lets you base a crosstab on one of four possible operations: sum, count, minimum, or maximum. If you choose Image/Graph/CrossTab from the main menu, Paradox presents the choices for sum, minimum, maximum, or count in a menu. Once you choose the desired type of cross-tabulation, Paradox asks for the following three items:

- The column containing the data to be used as row labels in the crosstab (the data in this column will be used as X-axis labels when you generate a graph)

- The column containing the data to be used as column labels in the crosstab (the data in this column will define the series to be graphed)

- The column that contains the crosstab values (the values to be summarized for the graph)

If you know that you want a summary type of crosstab, you can also use the ALT-X key combination in place of choosing Image/Graph/CrossTab. However, the use of ALT-X assumes that the fields are arranged in a certain order. With ALT-X, the field for the row labels must be the one containing the cursor; the field for the values to be crosstabbed must be the rightmost field in the image; and the field for the column labels must be just to the left of the field for the crosstab values.

As an example of a use of a crosstab in creating a graph, consider the following table of automobile sales for a group of sales representatives. Each record in the table contains data regarding the sale of one automobile.

Salesrep	Model name	Price	Date sold
Atwater	Bronco	17,250.00	3/14/89
Johnson	Taurus	16,750.00	3/10/89
O'Niell	Tempo	9,085.00	3/15/89
Williams	Taurus	15,750.00	3/14/89
Atwater	Bronco	18,490.00	3/11/89
Atwater	Tempo	11,290.00	3/14/89
Atwater	Tempo	12,220.00	3/10/89
O'Niell	LTD	18,950.00	3/11/89
O'Niell	Taurus	15,990.00	3/12/89
Williams	Taurus	12,210.00	3/14/89
Williams	Tempo	13,212.00	3/11/89
Williams	Taurus	13,255.00	3/15/89

Perhaps what you need is a graph indicating the sales of each model for each sales representative. After you choose Image/Graph/CrossTab from the main menu and type 1 to select Sum, Paradox asks for the cursor to be placed in the row containing the crosstab row labels. In this example, the Salesrep name is the desired column.

After the cursor has been placed and RETURN pressed, Paradox next asks for the cursor to be placed in the column containing the crosstab column labels. The cursor is moved to the Model name column in this example, and RETURN is pressed.

```
Viewing Crosstab table: Record 1 of 4                              Main
┌CARMODEL┬───────Salesrep────────┬───────Model name──────┬───────Price───────┬───────Date so─┐
│    1   ║  Atwater               │  Bronco                │       17,250.00   ║  3/14/8
│    2   ║  Johnson               │  Taurus                │       16,750.00   ║  3/10/8
│    3   ║  O'Niell               │  Tempo                 │        9,005.00   ║  3/15/8
│    4   ║  Williams              │  Taurus                │       15,750.00   ║  3/14/8
│    5   ║  Atwater               │  Bronco                │       18,490.00   ║  3/11/8
│    6   ║  Atwater               │  Tempo                 │       11,290.00   ║  3/14/8
│    7   ║  Atwater               │  Tempo                 │       12,220.00   ║  3/10/8
│    8   ║  O'Niell               │  LTD                   │       18,950.00   ║  3/11/8
│    9   ║  O'Niell               │  Taurus                │       15,990.00   ║  3/12/8
│   10   ║  Williams              │  Taurus                │       12,210.00   ║  3/14/8
│   11   ║  Williams              │  Tempo                 │       13,212.00   ║  3/11/8
│   12   ║  Williams              │  Taurus                │       13,255.00   ║  3/15/8


     1      Atwater          35,740.00            0.00         23,510.00
     2      Johnson              0.00        16,750.00             0.00
     3      O'Niell              0.00        15,990.00          9,005.00
     4      Williams             0.00        41,215.00         13,212.00
```

FIGURE 8-12.   Table with crosstabs

Paradox next asks that the cursor be moved to the column containing the values to be cross-tabulated. In this example, the cursor is placed in the Price column and RETURN is pressed. Paradox then creates the crosstab, as shown in Figure 8-12.

All that remains to create the graph is to press Graph (CTRL-F7). Since the cursor now resides in the crosstab table, the graph reflects the data contained in the crosstab. A stacked bar graph showing the crosstab is shown in Figure 8-13. Note that if the Date sold column did not exist in this example, the table could be crosstabbed with the ALT-X key combination.

WORKING WITH PIE CHARTS

Because of their design, pie charts are a different type of graph. Pie charts show the relationship between parts and a whole, so you can plot only a single data series in a pie chart. When you select Pie as the graph type, Paradox uses the data in the column in which the cursor is located. Data in adjacent columns is ignored.

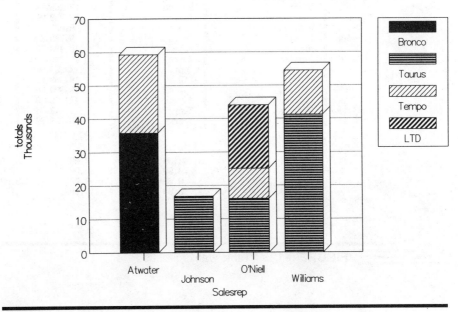

FIGURE 8-13.   Stacked bar graph with crosstabs

As an example, if you place the cursor in the March column of the CARSALES table, choose Image/Graph/Modify, select Pie as the graph type, press F2, and then press CTRL-F7, you will see a pie chart representing sales specifically for March. (The numbers may not be visible because the chart is not formatted for currency. You'll learn how to change the graph format settings in the next portion of this chapter.) Pie charts are generally for illustrating any relationship between the component parts and the whole.

CHANGING THE GRAPH FORMAT SETTINGS

Paradox also offers complete control over the colors, legends, markers, and similar parts with the Graph Design menu. This menu appears when you are at the Customize

Graph Type screen and you press F10. As an example, get to the main menu with F10 and choose Image/Graph/Modify. When the Customize Graph Type screen appears, press F10 again. At the top of the screen, the Graph Design menu appears:

Type   Overall   Series   Pies   ViewGraph   Help   DO-IT!   Cancel
Change the currently specified graph type.

The Type Option

The Type option is equivalent to filling in the desired type in the Graph Type option box of the same screen; you can select from among any of the ten valid types of Paradox graphs. Note that Paradox also displays the graph type as soon as you choose Image/Graph/Modify from the main menu.

The Overall Option

The Overall option provides a menu used to specify titles, colors, axis scale and format, gridlines, printer page layout, output device (printer or file), and whether a waiting

```
Defining titles for subsequent graphing.                           Graph
[F1] for help with defining graph titles.

                                                     ┌──────────────────┐
                                                     │ Fonts:           │
                                                     │  . Default       │
                                                     │  . Bold          │
                                                     │  . Triplex       │
                                                     │  . Sans Serif    │
                                                     │  . Small         │
                                                     │  . Simplex       │
                                                     │  . Triplex Script│
        1st Line:                          ◄         │  . Script        │
           Size: Autosize                            │  . Euro Style    │
        2nd Line:                                    │  . Complex       │
           Size: Autosize                            │  . Gothic        │
           Font: A. Default                          │                  │
                                                     ├──────────────────┤
        X-Axis:                                      │ Sizes:           │
        Y-Axis:                                      │  ( )utosize      │
           Size: Autosize                            │  ( )mall         │
                                                     │  ( )edium        │
                                                     │  ( )arge         │
                                                     └──────────────────┘
```

FIGURE 8-14.   Title Settings screen

period should occur before the graph is displayed. If you select Overall, the following menu appears:

Titles Colors Axes Grids PrinterLayout Device Wait
Specify titles for the graph.

Choosing Titles displays a screen in which you can enter titles for a graph, as shown in Figure 8-14. (If you do not enter a title, Paradox defaults to the name of the table as the title.) Note that when you choose Titles, options are also provided for changing font styles and font sizes. The possible font sizes are Small, Medium, Large, and Autosize; when you select Autosize, Paradox automatically selects a size for the fonts.

Choosing Colors reveals a menu with choices of Screen, Printer, and Copy. Use the Screen option to specify the colors to be used when the graph is displayed; use the Printer option to specify the colors to be used when the graph is printed. The Copy option lets you copy the screen colors to the printer settings, or copy the printer colors to the screen settings.

Selecting either the Screen option or the Printer option reveals the settings screen shown in Figure 8-15. Here, you can change the colors used for the background, frame, and grid of the graph; for the first and second title lines; for the X-axis and Y-axis titles; and for each of the six possible data series. The colors on the screen that correspond to choices B through H can be chosen for the background color, while any

```
Customizing screen colors for graphs.                    Graph
[F1] for help with customizing screen colors.

                                              Back-   Full
                                              ground  Color
                                              Choices Palette
                                              ___     Bckgrd

        Background: H  ◄

             Frame: B
              Grid: B


   First Title Line: B
  Second Title Line: B
       X-axis Title: B
       Y-axis Title: B

         1st Series: B
         2nd Series: C
         3rd Series: D
         4th Series: E
         5th Series: F
         6th Series: G
```

FIGURE 8-15. Color Settings screen

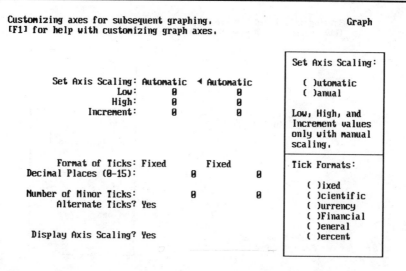

FIGURE 8-16.   Axes Settings screen

of the possible color choices on the screen can be used for the other elements of the graph. (Note that colors for pie charts are selected elsewhere, from the Pies option of the Graph Design menu.)

Choosing Axes reveals the settings screen shown in Figure 8-16. It lets you change the scale used for the X-axis or the Y-axis. In a graph, the *scale* is the incremental values displayed along the axes (or the "range" of values displayed along the axes). You can also change the format used to place the *tickmarks* (the short lines that cross the axis at regular intervals to denote a change in value). You can set Axis Scaling to Automatic or Manual. When you choose Automatic, Paradox starts the scale at zero and ends it at a value slightly above the highest value plotted on the graph. When you choose Manual, you can set the minimum and maximum values for the scale. For some applications, you may want to change the minimum and maximum scale, especially if all the values you are grouping fall within a small range. Tickmark formats will control how the tickmark labels appear. These can be set to Fixed (with two decimal places), Scientific (as scientific notation), Currency (decimal places and a dollar sign), Financial (commas between thousands and negative numbers in parentheses), General (the original format displayed in the table), or Percent (as percentages).

Choosing Grids reveals the settings screen for control of the graph gridlines, shown in Figure 8-17. You can select the types of lines used as gridlines in the graphs. You can also change the colors of the gridlines with this option, and you can turn off or on the frame that appears around the edge of the graph.

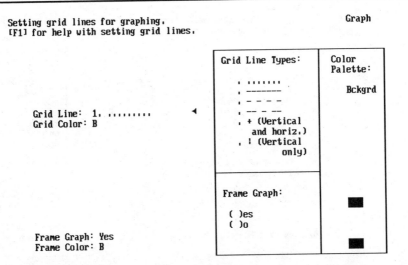

FIGURE 8-17.   Gridline Settings screen

Choosing PrinterLayout reveals the settings screen shown in Figure 8-18, with settings for left and top margins, the height and width of the graph, and orientation (landscape or portrait). Measurements with this option can be expressed in inches or in centimeters by changing the Measurement Units option while at this screen. You can also set the Break Page option to Yes, which tells Paradox to move to the top of the next page after printing the graph. (If you are printing a series of graphs, set this option to Yes if you want each graph on a separate page.) And you can set plotter speeds from a low of 0 (representing the slowest speed) to 9 (the fastest speed).

Choosing Device reveals another menu with two choices, Printer and File. You can use the Printer option to select one of four possible printers that have been previously installed for use with Paradox. (See Appendix B for tips on using the Custom Configuration Program to install printers.) You can also choose File to select one of three possible file formats for storing print images to disk files. The three possible formats are Current Printer (which creates a disk file with the same print image format as your installed printer), EPS (Encapsulated Post Script, compatible with Borland's Sprint and some desktop publishing packages), and PIC (compatible with Lotus 1-2-3 release 2.0 graphs).

Choosing Wait reveals an additional menu with two choices: Keystroke and Duration. Selecting Keystroke tells Paradox to display each graph until any key is pressed. Selecting Duration lets you enter the length of time (in seconds) that Paradox

```
Defining the layout of the graph for printing.                    Graph
[F1] for help with defining the layout of the graph printing.


        Units:  Inches      ◄      ┌─────────────────────────────────┐
                                   │ Measurement Units:              │
        Left Margin:  0            │   ( )nches                      │
         Top Margin:  0            │   ( )entimeters                 │
                                   └─────────────────────────────────┘
      Graph Height:  0
       Graph Width:  0            ┌─────────────────────────────────┐
                                  │ Orientation Options:             │
                                  │   ( )andscape (Horizontal)       │
                                  │   ( )ortrait  (Vertical)         │
                                  ├─────────────────────────────────┤
                                  │ Break Page Options:              │
                                  │   ( )es - Move to the top of the next │
                                  │            page after printing the graph. │
      Orientation: Landscape      │   ( )o                           │
                                  ├─────────────────────────────────┤
       Break Page: No             │ Plotter Speed Options:           │
                                  │   through                        │
      Plotter Speed:  0           │   uses the fastest or current speed │
                                  └─────────────────────────────────┘
```

FIGURE 8-18.   Printer layout screen

will display the graph before clearing the screen. The Duration option can be useful for creating a slide show, where various graphs are displayed by a script you create.

The Series Option

The Series option of the Graph Design menu lets you specify legends, labels, markers, fills, and colors used for a graph series. Selecting this option causes the following menu to be displayed:

LegendsAndLabels   MarkersAndFills   Colors
Specify legends and labels for graph series.

Choosing LegendsAndLabels reveals the settings screen shown in Figure 8-19. From this screen, you can select the legends or labels used for each series or data element of the graph. You can turn the legend on or off, and you can enter optional names for each data series that appears within the legend. (You'll often want to turn

```
Defining legends for subsequent graphing.                    Graph
[F1] for help with defining graph legends.


    Use a Legend?  ( / ): Yes ◄
        1st Series Legend:                          ┌──────────────┐
        2nd Series Legend:                          │ The interior │
        3rd Series Legend:                          │ label location│
        4th Series Legend:                          │ places the value│
        5th Series Legend:                          │ for each point │
        6th Series Legend:                          │ in the graph. │
                                                    │              │
                                                    │ Label Placement:│
                                                    │  ( )enter    │
        1st Series Label: None                      │  ( )bove     │
        2nd Series Label: None                      │  ( )elow     │
        3rd Series Label: None                      │  ( )ight     │
        4th Series Label: None                      │  ( )eft      │
        5th Series Label: None                      │  ( )one      │
        6th Series Label: None                      │    - to reset│
                                                    └──────────────┘
```

FIGURE 8-19.   LegendsAndLabels screen

the legend off when graphing a single series of values.) If you make no entries in the names for the legends, Paradox uses the field names as defaults for the legends. You are also provided with options for the placement of the labels; you can have labels centered (in the middle of the graph element), above the element, below the element, or to the right of the element. Finally, the None option of labels placement lets you tell Paradox to dispense with labels entirely.

Choosing MarkersAndFills reveals the settings screen shown in Figure 8-20. This screen provides the options needed to change the appearance of each of the data series in your graph. As the figure shows, you can choose from a wide variety of fill patterns and marker symbols. Marker symbols apply to marker graphs and combined graphs, while fill patterns apply to area charts and bar charts. To change the patterns used in pie charts, you must use the Pies option of the Graph Design menu.

Choosing Colors reveals another menu, with choices of Screen, Printer, and Copy. Use the Screen option to specify the colors used when the graph is displayed; use the Printer option to specify the colors used when the graph is printed. The Copy option lets you copy the screen colors to the printer settings, or copy the printer colors to the screen settings. Selecting either the Screen option or the Printer option reveals the settings screen shown previously in Figure 8-15. In operation, this screen is identical to the Overall/Colors option described earlier.

```
Customizing markers and fills for subsequent graphing.          Graph
[F1] for help with customizing markers and fills.
```

```
        Fill Pattern

        B - Filled      ◄
        C - ------
        D - Lt ///              ┌─────────────────┬──────────────────────┐
        E - Hvy //             │ Fill Patterns:  │ Marker Symbols:       │
        F - Lt \\\             │                 │                        │
        G - Hvy \\             │  - Empty        │  - Filled Square       │
                              │  - Filled       │  - Plus                │
                              │  - ------       │  - 8 Point Star        │
                              │  - Lt ///       │  - Empty Square        │
                              │  - Hvy ///      │  - X                   │
        Marker Symbol         │  - Lt \\\       │  - $                   │
                              │  - Hvy \\\      │  - Filled Triangle     │
        A - Filled Square     │  - +++++++++    │  - Hourglass           │
        A - Filled Square     │  - Crosshatch   │  - 6 Point Star        │
        A - Filled Square     │  - Hatch        │  - Box with X inside   │
        A - Filled Square     │  - Light Dots   │  - Shadowed Cross      │
        A - Filled Square     │  - Heavy Dots   │  - Vertical Line       │
        A - Filled Square     │                 │  - Horizontal Line     │
                              └─────────────────┴──────────────────────┘
```

FIGURE 8-20.   MarkersAndFills screen

The Pies Option

The Pies option pertains only to pie charts. When you select Pies, the settings screen shown in Figure 8-21 appears. From this screen you can explode pie slices (pull them out from other slices), choose fill patterns and colors for the slices, and choose a format for the labels. In the Label Format entry box, you can enter V (for value), P (for percent), C (for currency), or N (for no labels).

You can choose colors and fill patterns for up to nine slices of a pie chart. If a pie chart contains more than nine slices, the color and fill choices are repeated in order. In the Fill Pattern entry boxes, you can enter the letter that corresponds to your choice of fill type, as shown in the help screen on the right. Note that under the Colors entries, you can choose colors for both screen display and for printing. Enter Yes or No in the Explode Slice? boxes to tell Paradox whether a particular pie slice should be exploded.

As an example of the use of the options that apply to pie charts, consider the problem of displaying the dollar values in the pie chart earlier. If the Graph Design menu is not still on your screen, choose Image/Graph/Modify from the main menu and press F10 again to display it. Choose Pies from the menu. The next screen to appear, shown in Figure 8-21, offers options for customizing pie charts.

With the cursor in the Label Format option, type C to enter Currency. Press RETURN once to move to the 1st Pie Slice entry, and enter Y to change the Explode Pie Slice

```
Customizing pie charts for graphs.                                    Graph
[F1] for help with customizing pie charts.
```

Label Format: Currency ◄				Label Formats:	Color Palette:
				( )alue	
				( )ercent	BckGrd
Explode				( )urrency	
Slice?	Fill	──Colors──		( )one	
(✓)	Pattern	Screen	Print	Fill Patterns:	
No	B – Filled	B	B	– Filled	
No	C – ───────	C	C	– ───────	
No	D – Lt ///	D	D	– Lt ///	
				– Hvy //	
No	E – Hvy //	E	E	– Lt \\\	
No	F – Lt \\\	F	F	– Hvy \\	
No	G – Hvy \\	G	G	– ++++++	■
				– Crosshatch	
No	H – +++++++	H	H	– Hatch	
No	I–Crosshatch	I	I	– Light Dots	
No	J – Hatch	J	J	– Heavy Dots	■

──────── **FIGURE 8-21.**   Pie Settings screen

option from No to Yes. You may also want to experiment with changing some of the colors and fill patterns to suit your tastes; the help screen at the right shows the characters used to select the desired fill patterns or slice colors. When you are done, press Do-It! (F2) followed by Graph (CTRL-F7) to see the results.

The ViewGraph Option

The ViewGraph option presents a menu that lets you display the graph on the screen, print the graph, or store a print image in a disk file. Note that all the ViewGraph options are also available from the main menu by choosing Image/Graph/ViewGraph. The options work in the same manner as described earlier in this text. Finally, the Help, DO-IT!, and Cancel options of the Graph Design menu perform the same tasks as they do elsewhere in Paradox.

Experimenting with all of the graph options in Paradox will be time well spent. If you've examined the options described in the latter half of this chapter, it is probably evident that a detailed discussion of Paradox graphics could fill a book of its own. Try some of these options in combination with your own tables to become proficient at creating Paradox graphs.

QUICK SUMMARY

To create a graph   Place the cursor in the numeric field that is to be graphed, and press Graph (CTRL-F7).

To print a graph   Place the cursor in the numeric field that is to be graphed, press F10 for the menu, and choose Image/Graph/ViewGraph. Make sure your printer is ready, then select Printer from the next menu to print the graph.

To change the graph type   Press F10 for the menu, and then choose Image/Graph/Modify. When the Customize Graph Type screen appears, make the desired changes to the graph type, or to the series types. Press Do-It! (F2) to store the changes, then use Graph (CTRL-F7) to display the graph.

USING THE
RELATIONAL
POWERS
OF PARADOX

As you learned in Chapter 1, Paradox is a relational database manager. Its relational capabilities allow you to define relationships between two or more tables. This chapter will describe a number of ways you can take advantage of the relational capabilities of Paradox. By using example elements within Query Forms, you can link multiple tables by means of a common field that exists in each table.

The hands-on practice examples in this chapter will make extensive use of the ABCSTAFF and HOURS tables that were created in Chapters 3 and 4. Therefore, if you did not create those tables as outlined earlier, you should do so now before proceeding.

Consider the ABCSTAFF and HOURS tables. The HOURS table contains records of the hours worked by each employee, and the client for whom (or assignment at which) the employee performed the work. However, the HOURS table does not contain the names of the employees. The ABCSTAFF table, on the other hand, contains the full names of each employee, but no record of the hours worked.

The payroll coordinator at ABC Temporaries now needs a report in the format illustrated by Figure 9-1. This report will be used by the payroll department to handle check requests when the payroll is processed.

A report with this kind of information is a relational report because it draws its information from more than one table. The ABCSTAFF table contains the Last name and First name fields. The HOURS table contains the Assignment and Hours worked fields. In order to produce a report based on these fields, you must design a query that will retrieve data from both tables and link them into a single table. That table can then be used to produce the desired report.

The key to retrieving data from a relational database is to link records on some sort of matching, or common, field. In this context, the term "common field" is used to indicate a field that is common to both tables. Consider an example of two tables containing records of computer parts and of purchasers who have ordered certain parts. These tables (called PARTS and ORDERS in this example) are examples of tables

Last name	First name	Assignment	Hours Worked
Westman	Andres	National Oil Co.	37
Smith	William	Smith Builders	40
Jones	Judi	City Revenue Dept.	35
Abernathy	Frank	City Revenue Dept.	35
Mmm Mm m	*vLmm*	*mm mmm*	*m*
mmmm Mm	*mmm mm*	*mmm mm*	*mmm*
Mmm m	*mm mmm*	*m Mmm M*	*mmm*

FIGURE 9-1.   Desired relational report

that benefit from the use of relational commands. The PARTS table, which is shown by the table structure listed here, contains part numbers, descriptions, and the costs of each part:

Name of Field	Type
PARTNO	numeric
DESCRIPT	alphanumeric
COST	dollar

The ORDERS table, on the other hand, contains the names and customer numbers of the customers who order computer parts, as well as the part numbers and quantities of the parts that have been ordered.

Name of Field	Type
CUSTNO	numeric
CUSTNAME	alphanumeric
PARTNO	numeric
QUANTITY	numeric

Using two separate tables is a better solution than using a single table in this case, because a single table would require unneeded duplication of information. If you had a single table with all of the fields present in these two tables, each time one customer ordered a part number that had been previously ordered by another customer, you would have to duplicate the part description and part cost. To avoid such duplication, you can use two tables and link the tables together based on the contents of the common part number field, PARTNO, as illustrated in Figure 9-2. With all relational databases, you can establish a link between common fields to match a particular record in one table with a corresponding record in another table.

Take ABC Temporaries' problem of the payroll again. If you needed to know how many hours Andrea Westman worked, you could find out by looking at the data from the two tables, as shown in Figure 9-3. You would first look at the listing from the ABCSTAFF table and find the social security number for Ms. Westman, which is 121-33-9876. You would then refer to the listing of the HOURS table and look for all of the records with a matching social security number. The Hours worked fields from these records could be used to calculate the salary for Ms. Westman. The process of matching social security numbers between the tables could be repeated for every employee in the company.

An important point to realize is that without a field that contains matching data in each of the tables, such a relational link is not possible. This is one reason that the design of complex, relational databases is not a process to be taken lightly. If an important field is not included in a table, you may find it difficult or impossible to

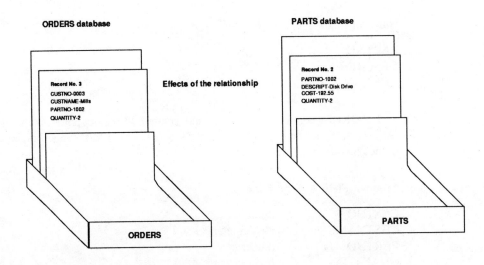

FIGURE 9-2.   Concept of relational database

HOURS	Assignment	Social security	Weekend date	Hours worked
1	National Oil Co.	909-88-7654	1/16/88	35
2	National Oil Co.	121-33-9876	1/16/88	30
3	National Oil Co.	121-90-5432	1/16/88	27
4	National Oil Co.	123-44-8976	1/16/88	32
5	City Revenue Dept.	343-55-9821	1/16/88	35
6	City Revenue Dept.	495-00-3456	1/16/88	28
7	City Revenue Dept.	232-55-1234	1/16/88	30
8	Smith Builders	876-54-3210	1/23/88	30
9	Smith Builders	901-77-3456	1/23/88	28
10	Smith Builders	805-34-6789	1/23/88	35
11	City Revenue Dept.	232-55-1234	1/23/88	30
12	City Revenue Dept.	495-00-3456	1/23/88	32
13	City Revenue Dept.	343-55-9821	1/23/88	32
14	National Oil Co.	121-33-9876	1/23/88	35
15	National Oil Co.	909-88-7654	1/23/88	33

ABCSTAFF	Social security	Last name	First name	Address
1	121-33-9876	Westman	Andrea	4007 East Avenu
2	121-90-5432	Robinson	Shirley	267 Browning Av
3	123-44-8976	Morse	Marcia	4260 Park Avenu
4	232-55-1234	Jackson	David	4102 Valley Lan

FIGURE 9-3.   HOURS, ABCSTAFF tables

access multiple tables in the desired manner. As Figure 9-3 illustrates, the Social security field makes it possible to access data simultaneously from both tables.

To link multiple tables in Paradox, you use a Query Form in a manner similar to that for nonrelational queries, which you performed in Chapter 6. The one notable difference is that you use example elements in the common fields of the Query Forms. These example elements tell Paradox which fields are used to provide the links between tables.

QUERYING FROM TWO TABLES

To query from two tables, use Clear All (ALT-F8) if necessary to clear the workspace. From the main menu, choose Ask, enter the name for the first table, and choose the fields for inclusion in the answer in the normal manner, by using F6 to place checkmarks in those fields. You can also set any selection criteria that the records must meet by entering these criteria in the fields of the Query Form, as described in Chapter 6.

When the first Query Form contains the desired checkmarks and criteria, choose Ask from the main menu and enter the name for the second table. Paradox places a Query Form for the second table below the first. You can again proceed to choose the fields to be included in the answer and enter any desired selection criteria. Figure 9-4 shows a workspace containing two Query Forms from the ABCSTAFF and HOURS tables, with selected fields of Last name and First name from the ABCSTAFF table and Weekend date and Hours worked from the HOURS table.

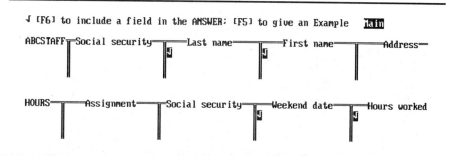

FIGURE 9-4.   Example of partially filled-in queries for two tables

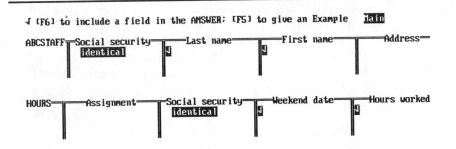

FIGURE 9-5.   Example of partially filled-in queries for two tables

Finally, enter the example element that is used to link the tables that have the common field. To enter an example element, place the cursor in the common field, press Example (F5), and enter an example element.

An example element is not some arbitrary value that you must always use. Paradox is only concerned about what the examples represent—that is, the same value in two separate tables. As you can see in Figure 9-5, the data entered as "identical" in both Social security fields could have been entered as 12345, or as the word "nonsense." You can enter any set of letters or numbers (but no spaces or punctuation marks) as an example element; what is important is that the example elements entered into the fields of the two tables are the same.

The example element appears highlighted as you enter it, which visually identifies it as an example element and not just criteria for the field. Next, move the cursor to the common field in the second table, press Example (F5) again, and fill in the same example element used in the common field of the first table. Figure 9-5 shows the queries with the same example element entered into the Social security fields of both tables.

PERFORMING THE QUERY

Once you have entered the example elements, chosen the desired fields, and supplied any record selection criteria, you are ready to perform the query. Press Do-It! (F2) or choose Do-It! from the main menu, and an answer based on the query will appear, as shown in Figure 9-6.

Viewing Answer table: Record 1 of 15   Main ▲━

HOURS	Assignment	Social security identical	Weekend date N	Hours worked N

ANSWER	Last name	First name	Weekend date	Hours worked
1	Abernathy	Sandra	1/16/88	28
2	Abernathy	Sandra	1/23/88	32
3	Hart	Edward	1/23/88	30
4	Jackson	David	1/16/88	30
5	Jackson	David	1/23/88	30
6	Jones	Judi	1/16/88	35
7	Jones	Judi	1/23/88	33
8	Mitchell	Mary Jo	1/23/88	28
9	Morse	Marcia	1/16/88	32
10	Morse	William	1/23/88	35
11	Robinson	Shirley	1/16/88	27
12	Robinson	Wanda	1/16/88	35
13	Robinson	Wanda	1/23/88	32
14	Westman	Andrea	1/16/88	30
15	Westman	Andrea	1/23/88	35

FIGURE 9-6.   Answer to relational query

One important point to remember is that the order you follow in supplying the data does not matter. You could first fill in the example elements, then pick the fields to be included in the answer, and then provide any record selection criteria. Or you could perform all of the necessary steps for one table, proceed to perform all of the steps for the second table, and then choose Do-It! to process the query. Regardless of the order, once you process the query, the answer appears. (Note that the order of the fields in the query will determine the order that fields appear in the answer.) If you need a printed report at this point, the easiest way to get one would be to press ALT-F7 for an instant report.

HANDS-ON PRACTICE: QUERYING FROM TWO TABLES

To get a listing containing the employee's last name, assignment, "week ending" date, and the number of hours worked with both tables linked through the common (Social

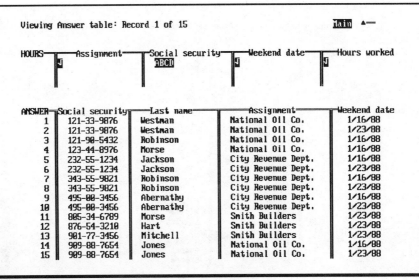

FIGURE 9-7.   Result of first practice query

security) field, try the following steps. Press Clear All (ALT-F8) to clear the workspace. From the main menu, choose Ask and enter **ABCSTAFF** as the table name. Use F6 to choose the Social security and Last name fields for inclusion in the answer. Move the cursor to the Social security field and press F5 to start an example element. Enter

ABCD

as the example. Press F10 for the menu, choose Ask, and this time enter **HOURS** as the name of the table.

When the Query Form for the second table appears, use the F6 key to place checkmarks in the Assignment, Weekend date, and Hours worked fields. Then move the cursor to the Social security field, press F5 to start an example element, and enter

ABCD

as the example element. Finally, press Do-It! (F2). The result of the relational query should appear on the screen, as shown in Figure 9-7.

Selection criteria can be used in either table to limit the records available in a relational query. As an example, perhaps you only want to see records for National Oil so that you can bill that particular client for services rendered by the staff of ABC Temporaries. Press F3 once to move the cursor from the ANSWER table back up to

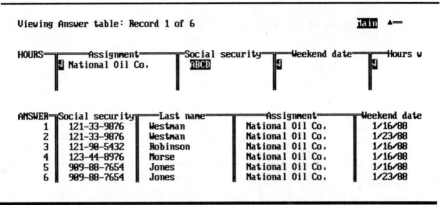

FIGURE 9-8.   Results of practice query for National Oil Co.

the Query Form for the HOURS table. Then move the cursor to the Assignment field, and enter

National Oil Co.

as the selection criteria. Press Do-It! (F2). The old ANSWER table will be rewritten, and the ANSWER table (Figure 9-8) will display only those employees who put in time for National Oil.

Paradox allows you to add a selection criterion in the same query field as the example element; just use a comma to separate the example element and the selection criterion. As an example, perhaps you wish to retrieve records using the fields you have already checked for inclusion in the answer, but you only want to see records for Ms. Andrea Westman. Press F3 to move the cursor back up to the Assignment field of the second Query Form, and use CTRL-BACKSPACE to delete the selection criterion from the field.

Move the cursor to the Social security field, add a comma after the example element, and then enter

121-33-9876

Press F2 to process the query. The results will show the records for Ms. Westman, as shown in Figure 9-9.

Remember   If you often use the same query to link multiple tables, save the query with Scripts/QuerySave. See Chapter 10 for more details on scripts.

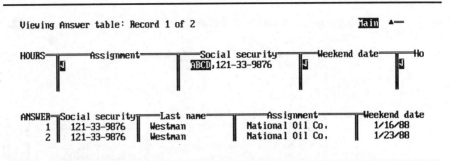

FIGURE 9-9.   Relational query for a single name

Using Linked Tables
With AND Selection Criteria

Paradox does not limit the way you use selection criteria: you have the same flexibility as you do in queries performed on a single table. As an example, perhaps you need a listing of employees who worked for the City Revenue Department during the week ending 1/23/88.

Press F3 to move back to the Query Form for the HOURS table, and remove the social security number and the comma with BACKSPACE (but leave the example element) in the Social security field.

Move the cursor to the Weekend date field and enter

1/23/88

Next, move the cursor to the Assignment field and enter

City Revenue Dept.

Press F2 to process the query. The results, shown in Figure 9-10, show all employees who worked for the City Revenue Department *and* worked on the "week ending" date of 1/23/88.

The conditions do not need to be in the same table. For example, you might need a listing of all employees assigned to National Oil who are earning more than $10.00 an hour. The fields you are using to limit the records, Salary and Assignment, are in two different tables.

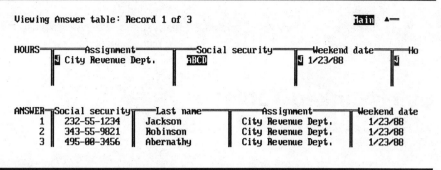

FIGURE 9-10.   Query of linked tables with AND condition

Press F3 twice to get back to the Query Form for the ABCSTAFF table. In the Salary field of this form, enter

>10

Then move to the second Query Form with F4. In the Assignment field, use CTRL-BACKSPACE to delete the "City Revenue Dept." entry. Enter

National Oil Co.

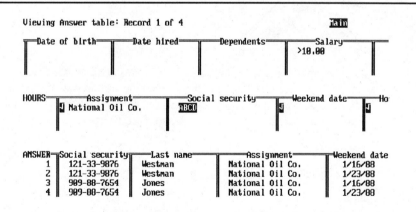

FIGURE 9-11.   Query of linked tables with conditions in separate tables

as the condition, and then move to the Weekend date field and use CTRL-BACKSPACE to delete the prior entry in this field. Finally, press F2 to process the query. The result, as shown in Figure 9-11, shows that four records meet the two conditions.

Using Linked Tables
With OR Selection Criteria

You can enter additional criteria in the additional rows of the Query Forms to specify OR conditions, in which records are selected when one *or* another condition is met. As an example, perhaps you want to see all of the employees who are assigned to National Oil or to Smith Builders.

First press ALT-F8 to clear the workspace. You will need to use something a little different for queries of multiple tables using OR conditions. You must enter example elements that will link either of the conditions on each line of the Query Form.

From the main menu, choose Ask, and enter **ABCSTAFF** for the table name. Place checkmarks in the Social security and Last name fields with F6. Move to the Social security field, press F5 to begin the example, and enter

FIRST

as the example element. Move the cursor down one line, and press F6 to add a checkmark. Then press F5 to begin another example. Enter

SECOND

as the name for the second example. Move the cursor over to the Last name field, and press F6 to add a checkmark in the field on the second row of the Query Form.

Press F10 for the menu, choose Ask, and enter **HOURS** as the name for the second table to be queried. Move to the Assignment field, enter a checkmark with F6, and enter

National Oil Co.

as the selection criterion. Place the cursor in the Social security field and press F5 to begin the example element. Then enter

FIRST

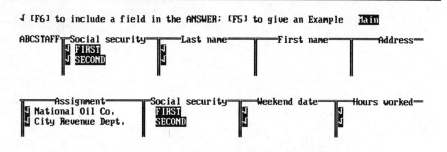

FIGURE 9-12.   Filled-in query forms for OR conditionals

as the matching example element for linking the tables. To complete this line of the query, move the cursor to the Weekend date and Hours worked fields, and press F6 while in those fields to include them in the ANSWER table.

Move the cursor down one line and back to the Assignment field. Add a checkmark with F6, and then enter

City Revenue Dept.

as the selection criterion for this row of the query. Move the cursor over to the Social security field. Press F5 to begin the example element, and enter

SECOND

as the matching example element for linking the tables. Finally, move the cursor to the Weekend date and Hours worked fields, and press F6 while in those fields to include them in the ANSWER table. At this point, your query should resemble the example illustrated in Figure 9-12.

Before you process this query, take a moment to think about how it is structured. The first line of the Query Form for HOURS, which will select records that contain "National Oil Co." in the Assignment field, is linked to the ABCSTAFF table through the example element called FIRST. The second line of the Query Form for HOURS, which selects records with "City Revenue Dept." in the Assignment field, is linked to the ABCSTAFF table through the example element called SECOND. In the case of OR conditionals like this one, Paradox is performing two separate queries at the same time: one to link records having "National Oil Co." in a field, and the other to link records having "City Revenue Dept." in the field. To see the results, press F2, and the ANSWER table will appear, as shown in Figure 9-13.

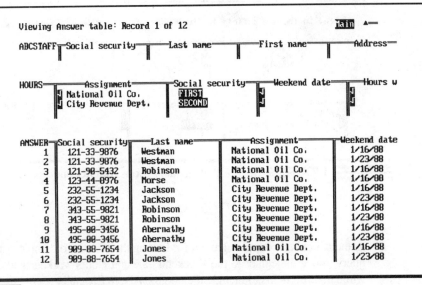

FIGURE 9-13.   Answer from OR query based on two tables

Note that in versions of Paradox from 3.0 and above, you can also use the OR operator in a field, to specify OR conditions. For example, you could enter "National Oil Co. OR Smith Builders" on a single line of a query in the ASSIGNMENT field.

LINKING MORE THAN TWO TABLES

In theory, you can link as many tables as you need (up to the limits of possible open files that your operating system can handle at one time) to provide you with the answers you need while you are using Paradox. (In practice, more than six linked tables may cause an out-of-memory condition.) You can see an example of linked tables by creating one more table, CLIENTS, which will contain the addresses of the clients for whom ABC Temporaries performs work.

Use ALT-F8 to clear the screen. Get to the main menu with F10 and choose Create. Call the new table CLIENTS. Define the following fields:

Field Name	Field Type
Client name	A25
Address	A25
City	A15
State	A2
ZIP Code	A5

After defining the structure, save the table by pressing F2. Then choose Modify/Edit from the main menu, enter **CLIENTS** for the table name, and add the three records shown here to the new table:

Client name: National Oil Co.
Address: 1201 Germantown Road
City: Fairfax
State: VA
Zip: 20305

Client name: City Revenue Dept.
Address: 2000 Town Hall Square
City: Alexandria
State: VA
Zip: 22045

Client name: Smith Builders
Address: 2370 Rockville Pike
City: Rockville
State: MD
Zip: 30504

Press Do-It! (F2) to save the edits, and then clear the workspace with ALT-F8.

Perhaps you need a listing of assignments, the city of each assignment, the name of each employee, and "week ending" dates so that you can track the validity of expense reports handed in by your staff for car mileage. The fields you need are in three different tables, so you will need to fill in three Query Forms to get the answer you need.

From the main menu, choose Ask and enter **ABCSTAFF** for the table name. When the Query Form appears, move the cursor to the Social security field and press F5 to begin an example. Enter **1234** as the example. Then move the cursor to the Last name field and place a checkmark with F6 to include this field in the answer.

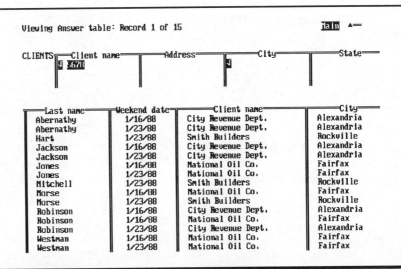

Viewing Answer table: Record 1 of 15   Main ▲═

CLIENTS	Client name	Address	City	State
	√ 5678		√	

Last name	Weekend date	Client name	City
Abernathy	1/16/88	City Revenue Dept.	Alexandria
Abernathy	1/23/88	City Revenue Dept.	Alexandria
Hart	1/23/88	Smith Builders	Rockville
Jackson	1/16/88	City Revenue Dept.	Alexandria
Jackson	1/23/88	City Revenue Dept.	Alexandria
Jones	1/16/88	National Oil Co.	Fairfax
Jones	1/23/88	National Oil Co.	Fairfax
Mitchell	1/23/88	Smith Builders	Rockville
Morse	1/16/88	National Oil Co.	Fairfax
Morse	1/23/88	Smith Builders	Rockville
Robinson	1/16/88	City Revenue Dept.	Alexandria
Robinson	1/16/88	National Oil Co.	Fairfax
Robinson	1/23/88	City Revenue Dept.	Alexandria
Westman	1/16/88	National Oil Co.	Fairfax
Westman	1/23/88	National Oil Co.	Fairfax

FIGURE 9-14.   Results of query on three tables

Press F10 for the menu, choose Ask, and enter **HOURS** for the table name. When the Query Form appears, move the cursor to the Social security field and press F5 to begin an example. Enter **1234** as the example. Then move the cursor to the Weekend date field and place a checkmark in this field with F6 to include this field in the answer.

Move the cursor to the Assignment field, and press F5 to begin the example element that will provide the link to the third table. Enter **5678** as the example. Then press F10 for the menu, choose Ask, and enter **CLIENTS** as the desired table to display another Query Form. Move the cursor to the Client name field, press F5 to begin the example, and enter **5678** as the example element that tells Paradox to match the data found in the Assignment field of the HOURS table.

To complete the query, first press F6 so that a checkmark will tell Paradox to include the name of the client in the answer. Then move to the City field and press F6 again to add a checkmark in this field. Press F2 to process the query. The result, shown in Figure 9-14, includes the desired fields selected from the ABCSTAFF, HOURS, and CLIENTS tables.

One additional point can be noted from this example. The example element used to link the second and third tables was placed in two fields that had different field names. (The HOURS table stored the name of the client in a field called Assignment, while the CLIENTS table stored the name of the clients in a field called Client name.) Unlike some relational database managers, Paradox does not require you to name the fields with identical field names before you can draw links between different tables, nor must the fields have identical widths. The only requirement is that the *data* contained in the linked fields can be matched. It would make no sense, for example, to try to draw a link between two fields containing dissimilar data, such as a phone-number field and a date-of-birth field.

CREATING AND USING MULTITABLE FORMS

Paradox version 3.0 lets you create multitable forms, which let you view or edit data from more than one table at a time. Multitable forms can be very useful with sales or billing applications, where you often want to display a number of records (such as those for purchases) that are linked to a single record (such as that of a customer). This section will show how a multitable form can be used for the personnel needs of ABC Temporaries. The form in the following example will use the ABCSTAFF table to show data for any employee of ABC Temporaries and will use the HOURS table to show all hours worked for that employee.

You can use multitable forms any time you want to display data from two or more tables at the same time. While a relational link between the tables is common, such a link is *not* a requirement. You can have multitable forms with linked tables, or you can have multitable forms with unlinked tables. When the tables are unlinked, each table on the form is accessed independently of the others; think of it as moving between tables, but in a form view instead of the usual table view. On the other hand, if the tables are linked, then the records on one table will depend on the records in another. In our example, the records that appear in the hours portion of the form will be linked to a particular employee.

> **Note** Multitable forms are very useful for displaying orders associated with a given customer in sales applications.

Whenever you design a multitable form, you are actually placing several forms (one for each table) on the screen. One form must be the *master form*, while the remaining forms are *embedded forms*. When tables are linked, the master form controls what records appear in the embedded forms; in effect, the master form "owns" any embedded forms. When tables are unlinked, it does not matter which table is used as the basis of the master form. In these cases, you may want to use the table that logically should be at the top of the form as the master form. In our example, each employee will "own" a series of one or more records for hours worked during a week. Therefore, the form based on the employees' table (ABCSTAFF) becomes the master form, while the form based on the hours worked (HOURS) becomes the embedded form.

Keep in mind that if the tables are linked, both tables must have a matching key field. If the relationship is a "one-to-many" relationship (as in this example, with one employee having many records of hours worked), then the detail table (in this case, HOURS) must have a secondary key. To meet this requirement in the example, you will later use Modify/Restructure to add keys to the Social security and Weekend date fields of the HOURS table.

The basic steps involved in creating a multitable form are to first decide which table is to be the basis of the master form, and then design and save the forms to be used as embedded forms by using the usual methods of form design covered in Chapter 5. Finally, you begin designing the form for the master table, and choose Multi/Tables from the Forms menu. You use this menu option to place the embedded form or forms onto the master form and to specify the link (if any) between your master form and the embedded forms.

Note the following limitations regarding multitable forms:

- A master form can be a multipage form, but it cannot be a multirecord form.

- An embedded form can be a multirecord form, but it cannot be a multipage form.

- Nesting of embedded forms is not permitted; that is, you cannot embed a form on another embedded form.

- A maximum of nine embedded tables are permitted (five if you are using a version of Paradox older than version 3.5.)

HANDS-ON PRACTICE: CREATING A MULTITABLE FORM

You've already determined that the ABCSTAFF table is to be the basis of the master form for the form you wish to create for ABC Temporaries. The next step is to design and save the form that will serve as the embedded form. The managers at ABC Temporaries have suggested a form with a listing of the "week ending" date, hours worked, and assignment name for each employee. The conceptual design of such a form is shown in Figure 9-15.

Press F10 for the menu, and choose Modify/Restructure. For the table name, enter **HOURS**. When the table structure appears add an asterisk after the A11 field designation beside the Social security field. Also, add an asterisk after the D field designation beside the Weekend date field. Then press Do-It! (F2) to save the changes.

Name: *illegible handwriting*
Soc. Security: XXX-XX-XXXX

Weekend Date	Hours Worked	Assignment
1-16-91	37	*illegible*
1-23-91	30	*illegible*
1-30-91	35	*illegible*
2-6-91	42	*illegible*

FIGURE 9-15. Sample multitable form

Adding the asterisks will make these fields into key fields so they can be properly linked within the multitable form.

If any tables are on the workspace, clear them with ALT- F8. Press F10 for the menu, and choose Forms/Design. Enter **HOURS** as the name for the table. Select 1 from the menu of form names, and enter **Multirecord of Hours Worked** as a form description.

With the cursor at row 1 column 1, press F10 for the Forms menu, and choose Multi/Records to place the multirecord region on the new form. From the next menu, choose Define. Next, press RETURN to begin the selection at the upper-left corner.

Move the cursor 50 spaces to the right, and press RETURN to define the region. Paradox will now ask you to add (or delete) the repeating rows for the additional records. Press the down arrow key nine times, and then press RETURN. (This will allow for a total of ten hourly records visible in the form at a time.)

Move the cursor back to row 1, column 1. Press F10 for the Forms menu, and choose Field/Place/Regular. Select Weekend date from the list of fields, and press RETURN twice to place the field.

Move the cursor two spaces to the right, press F10 for the Forms menu, and choose Field/Place/Regular. Select Hours worked from the list of fields and press RETURN; then press the left arrow key ten times to narrow the field's width, and press RETURN again to place the field.

Move the cursor two spaces to the right. Press F10 for the Forms menu, and choose Field/Place/Regular. Select Assignment from the list of fields, and press RETURN twice to place the field.

This is all you need for the hourly portion of the multitable form. You can add headings later, after embedding this form onto the master form. First, however, you must save this form. Press Do-It! (F2) to save the form and return to the menu.

The final step in the process is to design the master form and to use the Multi/Tables option to place the embedded form and to specify the link. From the menu, choose Forms/Design, and enter **ABCSTAFF** as the name of the table. Select 3 as the name for the new form, and enter **Multitable with Hours** as a description.

Move the cursor to row 5, column 10, and enter

Name:

as a label. Add one space, press F10 for the Forms menu, and choose Field/Place/Regular. Select First name from the list of available fields, and press RETURN twice to place the field.

Press the spacebar once, press F10 for the Forms menu, and choose Field/Place/Regular. Select Last name from the list of available fields, and press RETURN twice to place the field.

Move the cursor to row 7, column 10, and enter

Soc. Security:

as a label. Add one space, press F10 for the Forms menu, and choose Field/Place/Regular. Select Social security from the list of available fields, and press RETURN twice to place the field. This is all the data that will be needed for the master form, so you are ready to embed the other form and establish the link between the two tables.

Press F10 for the menu, and choose Multi. (You use this option whenever you want to design or remove a multitable form.) The next menu to appear offers two choices: Tables and Records. In this case, Tables is the proper choice because it is used to place, remove, or move a form from another table. (The other choice, Records, is used with multirecord forms as described in Chapter 5.)

Choose Tables from the menu. When you do so, the following menu appears:

Place   Remove   Move   DisplayOnly
Place another table's form on the current form.

The Place option is used to embed another form. The Remove option removes an existing embedded form. The Move option lets you move an existing embedded form to another location, and the DisplayOnly option lets you specify whether a form will be used only for display or for editing.

Since you wish to place the hourly form, choose Place. The next menu to appear offers the choice of Linked or Unlinked. Since the records in the HOURS table will be linked to each respective employee when displayed in this form, choose Linked.

Paradox will now ask you for the name of the table to link. Enter **HOURS** as the table name. The list of forms available for the HOURS table will next appear; choose 1, which corresponds to the multirecord form you created earlier. Next, this menu appears:

Select ABCSTAFF field to match Social Security in HOURS.
Social security   Last name   First name   Address   City   State   ZIP Code

Choose Social security from the menu, which tells Paradox to match records in the HOURS table with a record in the ABCSTAFF table based on matching social security numbers. A shaded box representing the multirecord form for HOURS you created earlier will appear on the screen.

Use the arrow keys to roughly center the shaded box in the lower portion of the screen, and then press RETURN to place the box. Move the cursor until it is immediately above the upper left corner of the shaded box. Enter **Weekend Date** and then press the right arrow key four times. Enter **Hours worked** and then press the right arrow key ten times. Finally, enter **Assignment**.

With the hourly form embedded on the master form and the labels added, the form is complete. Press Do-It! (F2) to save the form and return to the menu. Choose View, and enter **ABCSTAFF** as the table to view. The form can be chosen like any other form with the Image/PickForm option. Once you are viewing the table, press F10 for the menu and choose Image/PickForm. From the menu of available forms, choose number 3. You should see a record displayed in the multitable form.

Try using the PGUP and PGDN keys to move around the ABCSTAFF table. Note that as you move from employee to employee, the appropriate hourly records appear in the lower portion of the form. Also, try using the F3 and F4 keys to move between the master and embedded portions of the form.

Referential Integrity:
A Note and a Warning

When you link tables while designing a multitable form, Paradox automatically establishes certain rules regarding *referential integrity*. This means that Paradox protects you by imposing certain rules on what kinds of edits and deletions can be made when you use the form. For example, Paradox would not let you change a social security number or delete an employee in the ABCSTAFF table as long as there were records for that social security number in the HOURS table. To make such an edit or a deletion would break the logical link between the tables. You could, on the other hand, delete all the records for a given social security number in the HOURS table, and then delete the employee from the ABCSTAFF table.

Paradox provides the benefit of referential integrity only as long as you are adding or editing through the multitable form that establishes the link. Once this link has been established, Paradox won't let you edit the tables on an individual basis in that editing session. But once you leave the current editing session, you are unprotected if you decide not to use the form. If you design and use linked multitable forms, it is a wise idea to avoid any editing of the tables on an individual basis. Sticking with the forms will maintain the referential integrity provided by Paradox.

A NOTE ABOUT REPORTS

Generating reports from a relational database is no different than generating reports from a nonrelational database. You design your reports in the same manner as with other tables, as outlined earlier in Chapter 7. One way is to simply base the report on the relational table (which is the one created as an ANSWER table as the result of your queries). Remember that if you are going to design custom reports to be used with ANSWER tables and you want to keep the reports, save the ANSWER table under a different name. To do so, choose Tools/Rename/Table/Answer from the main menu, and give the table a new name. The associated custom reports that you create for use along with the ANSWER table will be saved under the new name. Another method that gets around the limitation of using the ANSWER table is described in more detail shortly.

Of course, as your primary tables change with the addition and editing of data, you will find that each time you need an up-to-date report of a relational nature, you must perform a query to get the most recent data from the related tables into an ANSWER table to produce the report. If you are using custom reports, this creates a new problem: each time you generate an answer and rename that ANSWER table to a new name, it overwrites the old name if you use the same name. In the process, your custom report also gets overwritten, since it was associated with the old ANSWER table that you named earlier.

One way around this is to copy the structure from the ANSWER table to a dummy table and create the custom report while using the dummy table. You can then empty the dummy table of any records, transfer the results of your most recent queries into the dummy table, and then generate the desired custom report.

To create a dummy table based on the structure of the ANSWER table, go to the main menu and choose Tools/Copy/Table. When prompted for the name of the table to copy, enter **ANSWER**. Paradox will ask for a new table; enter any name you desire for the new "dummy" table. Once you supply the name, Paradox will copy the ANSWER table into the new table under your assigned name. If you have not yet created the desired report, you can design it while you are using the dummy table and save it (by pressing F2 when you are finished with the Report Specification) along with the dummy table.

Next, empty the dummy table of all records. To do this, choose Tools/More/Empty from the main menu, and enter the name of your dummy table. Confirm the action by selecting OK from the next menu that appears, and the dummy table will be emptied of records.

Whenever you need to generate the report based on the relational data, structure your queries to provide the answer you want; then, from the main menu, choose Tools/More/Add to add records to the dummy table. When Paradox prompts you for the source table name, use ANSWER; for the target table, use the name of your dummy table. Paradox will copy the records to the dummy table, and you can generate the report. Be sure to remember to empty all records from the dummy table after each use with Tools/More/Empty from the main menu, or you may accidentally generate a report with more records in the dummy table than you actually want.

Another way to create multitable reports is to use Field/Lookup when designing the report and to create calculated fields within the report's design, which will access the fields in the other tables. This method has the advantage of not using the ANSWER table, so you need not worry about copying the records in the ANSWER table to another file. The basic steps in this method are as follows:

1. Begin designing the report, using the table that is the primary source of your data. (For example, if you wanted a listing of hours worked, you would design the report around the HOURS table.) The table with the most key fields is normally the master table.

2. Press F10 for the menu, and choose Field/Lookup. This option lets you set, remove, or change links to the records in another table.

3. From the next menu, choose Link. Then enter the name of the table to be linked.

4. From the next menu, select the field by name that will provide the match.

5. Use Field/Place/Calculated to place the calculated fields that will provide the data from the other tables. You use a format like

   [ABCSTAFF->LAST NAME]

   with the calculated field enclosed in brackets and the field name preceded by the other table name, a hyphen, and a greater- than symbol. This tells Paradox where to look to find the matching data.

Follow the normal methods of report design (detailed in Chapter 7 and Chapter 12) to place the fields where desired. When you generate the report, Paradox will automatically establish the link between tables and produce the desired data.

HANDS-ON PRACTICE: CREATING A MULTITABLE REPORT

To try the method just described, get to the menu with F10 and choose Report/Design. This example will provide a report of hours worked that includes "week ending" dates and the last name of the employee. For the table name, enter **HOURS**. Then select 2 as a report name (or some other number if you have already used 2 as a name). For a description, enter **Multitable sample**. For the type of report, choose Tabular.

The Report Specification will appear, with fields automatically inserted for the fields in the HOURS table. Press F10 for the Report Design menu, and choose Field/Erase. Move the cursor to the Social security field and press RETURN to remove the field.

Press F10, and choose Field/Lookup/Link. Enter **ABCSTAFF** as the table to be linked to this report. You will now see this prompt:

Select HOURS field to match Social security in ABCSTAFF.
Social security   Weekend date   Hours worked   Assignment

The Social security field should be highlighted. This is the field that will provide the link, so press RETURN to select it.

Now that you've linked this report to the other table, you can proceed to add calculated fields that refer to the other table.

Press F10 for the menu. With the cursor still at the start of the old location of the Social security field, choose Field/Place/Calculated. For the expression, enter

[ABCSTAFF->LAST NAME]

Be sure to include the surrounding brackets, and the hyphen and greater-than symbol between the table name and the field name. Then press RETURN twice to place the field.

Replace the heading above the field, "Social security," with **Last Name**. For simplicity's sake, this will be the only field referenced from the other table. In practice,

5/12/89	Multitable sample	Page 1	
Last Name	Weekend date	Hours worked	Assignment
---------------	----------- ------	-------------------	-----------------
Westman	1/16/88	30	National Oil Co.
Westman	1/23/88	35	National Oil Co.
Robinson	1/16/88	27	National Oil Co.
Morse	1/16/88	32	National Oil Co.
Jackson	1/16/88	30	City Revenue Dept.
Jackson	1/23/88	30	City Revenue Dept.
Robinson	1/16/88	35	City Revenue Dept.
Robinson	1/23/88	32	City Revenue Dept.
Abernathy	1/16/88	28	City Revenue Dept.
Abernathy	1/23/88	32	City Revenue Dept.
Morse	1/23/88	35	Smith Builders
Hart	1/23/88	30	Smith Builders
Mitchell	1/23/88	28	Smith Builders
Jones	1/16/88	35	National Oil Co.
Jones	1/23/88	33	National Oil Co.

FIGURE 9-16.   Sample multitable report

you could add other fields by using the same type of expression in additional calculated fields.

To see the results, press F10 for the menu, and choose Output/Screen (or choose Output/Printer if you prefer a printed copy). The report should resemble the sample shown in Figure 9-16. Press F10 for the menu again, and choose Do-It! or press F2. The report will be saved, and you will be returned to the main menu.

When you have created a multitable report with this method, you can use the report at any time along with the existing tables; there is no need to perform a relational query beforehand, since the relational link is designed into the report. This type of report takes a little longer to design, but once stored you can produce reports very quickly.

QUICK SUMMARY

To query from two tables   Clear the workspace if necessary, with Clear All (ALT-F8). Press F10 for the menu, and choose Ask. Enter the name for the first table, and choose the fields for inclusion with the Check (F6) key. Place any desired selection criteria in the fields of the Query Form. When the first query form is filled in, press

F10 for the menu, choose Ask, and enter the name of the second table. Again, choose fields for inclusion with the Check (F6) key, and place any desired selection criteria in the fields of the Query Form. Finally, enter the example element used to link the common field, by moving the cursor to the common field in each query form, pressing Example (F5), and entering an example element. Press Do-It! (F2) to process the query.

To use linked tables with AND selection criteria   Add as many conditions as are needed, in the different fields of either of the query forms.

To use linked tables with OR selection criteria   In each query form, use the down arrow key as necessary, to add additional lines for more criteria to the Query Form, or include the OR operator between multiple query criteria.

To generate relational reports   Build and process a query that performs the relational link. Then design (if necessary) and generate the report based on the ANSWER table provided by the relational query.

chapter 10

THE POWER
OF SCRIPTS

Hands-on Practice: Recording and Playing an Instant Script
Recording and Playing Scripts
Hands-on Practice: Creating a Custom Script
Using Play and QuerySave
Using ShowPlay
Using RepeatPlay
The Init Script
Managing Your Scripts
Editing Scripts with the Editor
Quick Summary

Paradox allows you to define combinations of keystrokes called *scripts* that can automate many of the tasks you normally perform when you are using Paradox. The script capability is similar in function to the macro capabilities presented in some other popular software. Scripts let you record a sequence of characters in a single key combination or as a named file. You can save the script and later use it to play back those key sequences by pressing the same single key combination, or you can use a menu option to retrieve the script file by name. When the script is played back, Paradox works as if you had manually performed the operations contained within the script.

You can use a feature of Paradox called *instant scripts* to quickly assign a sequence of operations to a key combination. By using scripts, you can literally save hundreds of keystrokes you must use regularly to print daily reports, fill in complex Query Forms, or perform similar repetitive tasks.

If you use commercially available keyboard enhancers like Superkey and ProKey, you are familiar with the advantages of automating your work with scripts. Other keyboard-enhancer users may wonder whether they should simply continue to use such products instead of using Paradox's script capability. The advantage of using the script capability within Paradox is twofold. First, you will not consume additional memory because you have loaded a memory resident keyboard enhancer. Second, you will avoid any possible conflict between the operation of Paradox and the memory resident keyboard enhancer. Memory resident programs have, in the past, been known to conflict with other software packages. Borland's Sidekick and Superkey are both compatible with Paradox; however, there is no guarantee that you will not encounter any problems using other memory resident packages with Paradox. Another advantage of scripts is that they can be incorporated into larger PAL scripts; keyboard macros cannot.

Note ≡ Scripts are ideal for automating repetitive tasks performed through the Paradox menus.

The easiest way to use a script is to record and/or play back an instant script. With the ALT-F3 (Instant Script Record) key combination, you can start and end the recording of an instant script. You can play back that script at any time with ALT-F4 (Instant Script Play). When you record an instant script, it is saved to disk automatically before you exit Paradox. You can replay the script at any time, and the script will remain available until you create another instant script. Each instant script you record overwrites the previous instant script.

To create an instant script, perform the following steps:

1. Press ALT-F3. The message "Beginning recording of INSTANT" will momentarily appear at the bottom of the screen.

2. Perform whatever Paradox operations you wish recorded in the script.

3. Press ALT-F3. The message "Ending recording of instant" will momentarily appear at the bottom of the screen.

To play back the instant script, press ALT-F4. The Paradox operations that were performed when the script was recorded will be carried out as if those menu options had been entered by hand.

Remember Instant scripts are always saved under the name INSTANT.SC. So any instant script you record will overwrite a previous one.

HANDS-ON PRACTICE: RECORDING AND PLAYING AN INSTANT SCRIPT

Perhaps you regularly need to print a report of employees' hours worked, including the names of the employees. In the case of ABC Temporaries, this requires the use of the relational database based on two tables, ABCSTAFF and HOURS, so you need to fill out a Query Form with example elements each week when you need the report. This is a perfect task for a script.

Press ALT-F3 to start recording the instant script. Clear the workspace with ALT-F8. Then, from the main menu, choose Ask and enter **ABCSTAFF** as the name of the table. In the Social security field, press F5 to begin an example, and enter **SAME**. Then use F6 to place checkmarks in the Last name and First name fields.

Press F10 for the menu, choose Ask, and enter **HOURS** as the table name. Move to the Social security field, press F5 to begin an example, and enter **SAME**. Then use the F6 key to place checkmarks in the Weekend date and the Hours worked fields. Finally, press Do-It! (F2) to process the query. If you have a printer attached, turn it on and press ALT-F7 for an instant report.

Finally, press ALT-F3 to end the recording of the script. Now that the script exists, you can use a single key combination to ask about the tables, fill in the Query Form,

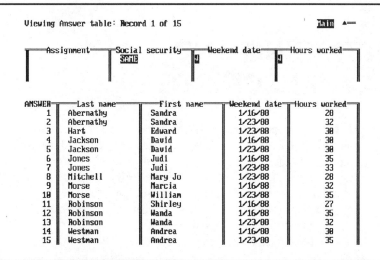

FIGURE 10-1.   Results of instant script

and generate the report. To see how this is done, first clear the workspace with ALT-F8. Then press ALT-F4 to play the instant script. Depending on your PC's speed, it may take a few moments to see the results, but Paradox is performing the work in the background.

When Paradox is done performing the steps recorded within the script, the AN-SWER table based on the query will appear along with the Query Forms, resembling the example shown in Figure 10-1. If you chose to print an instant report while you were recording the script, that report would again be printed.

Saving an Instant Script
Under Another Name

Any instant script you create is stored as a script with the name INSTANT. If you want to keep that script and not overwrite it the next time you create an instant script, you can do so by changing the script's name. Simply go to the main menu with F10 and choose Tools/Rename/Script. Paradox will ask you for the name of the script; enter **INSTANT**. You will then be asked to enter a new name for the script. Enter any valid DOS name of eight characters or less (and no spaces), and the script will be renamed.

Once you have renamed the script, you cannot replay it with ALT-F4, but you can replay it at any time by choosing the script by name through the Script menu. This is discussed in the following section.

RECORDING AND
PLAYING SCRIPTS

If you use scripts regularly, you will need to be able to store and play more than a single script. Paradox allows you to create a virtually unlimited number of scripts by letting you store custom scripts. Each custom script is assigned a name, which must again follow the standards of DOS files (eight characters or less, and no spaces). Paradox stores these scripts as files with an .SC extension. You cannot add any extensions of your own when providing a name for your scripts; the program will add the .SC extension automatically.

The basic steps for creating a script are as follows:

1. From the main menu, choose Scripts/BeginRecord (or use ALT-F3 for an instant script).

2. Enter a name for the new script.

3. Perform the operations that are to be recorded in the script.

4. Press F10 (if necessary) to display the main menu, and choose Scripts/End-Record.

Once the script has been recorded, you can play it at any time by choosing Scripts/Play from the main menu and entering the name for that script.

HANDS-ON PRACTICE: CREATING A CUSTOM SCRIPT

Perhaps you need a script that will isolate all employees assigned to the National Oil Company and produce the custom report you designed earlier showing those employees. The first step is to begin recording the script. Clear the workspace with ALT-F8. Then choose Scripts from the main menu.

The next menu to appear shows the following options:

Play BeginRecord QuerySave ShowPlay RepeatPlay Editor
Play a script.

The BeginRecord option is used to start recording the script, while the Play option is used to play an existing script. The remaining options will be discussed shortly.

Choose BeginRecord from the menu. Paradox will now display the following prompt:

Script:
Enter name for new script.

For this example, enter **MYFIRST** as the name. Paradox will momentarily display a message in the lower-right corner, indicating it is beginning a script called MYFIRST, and then the main menu will reappear. Also, once you perform the first action that will be recorded, the letter "R" will appear in the upper-right corner of the screen, indicating that Paradox is "recording" a script. You are now ready to perform the options that will be recorded within the script.

Since you want only the employees for National Oil, you will need a query. Press F10 for the menu. Although the menu should be visible, it's a good idea to get into the habit of starting menu tasks within scripts with F10 (or with ALT-F8). That way, whenever you play back the script, you'll start from a common point (the menu). Choose Ask from the menu and enter **ABCSTAFF** as the table name. With the cursor still at the far left side of the table, press F6 to place checkmarks in all fields. Then move the cursor to the Assignment field and enter the criterion:

National Oil Co.

Then press Do-It! (F2) to process the query. The ANSWER table that appears will contain only those employees assigned to National Oil.

Press F10 for the main menu, and choose Report/Output. For the name of the table, choose ANSWER. From the next menu of possible reports to choose, select R for standard report. Then select Printer (or, if you do not have a printer attached or simply prefer not to use paper, choose Screen). Finally, clear the workspace with ALT-F8. This is not a requirement, but it is done in this case for aesthetic reasons. Choose Scripts from the main menu.

You will notice that the Script menu now has slightly different choices than it did when you began. It now shows the following options:

Cancel End-Record Play QuerySave RepeatPlay
Stop recording script without keeping it.

The Cancel option lets you cancel the recording of the script, while the End-Record option will stop recording and save the script. (The remaining options will be discussed later in this chapter.)

Choose End-Record to end the recording of your script. The script will be stored under the name MYFIRST, which you assigned earlier, and the main menu will reappear.

Playing the Custom Script

To play the script, choose Scripts from the main menu, and then choose Play. Paradox will ask for the name of the script; enter **MYFIRST**, and the script will be played. The resulting report will appear on the screen or will be printed.

USING PLAY AND QUERYSAVE

While you were recording the script, two new options appeared in the Script menu: Play and QuerySave. These are options that you may find useful as you begin working regularly with scripts.

The Play option lets you play an existing script while you are in the midst of recording a new script. In this manner, you can combine existing scripts to perform more complex tasks.

The QuerySave option can also be useful. While you could store the steps necessary for a query in any script, just as you did in the example earlier, the QuerySave option of the Script menu offers the advantage of storing only the query. To save a query, while the Query Form is present in the workspace, press F10 for the menu and choose Scripts/QuerySave. Paradox will ask you for a name for the script. Enter the desired name, and Paradox will save the present Query Form in that script. Whenever you wish to reuse that query, simply choose Scripts/Play from the menu and enter the name of the script that contains the query. The query will reappear, and you can then press Do-It! (F2) to process it and obtain up-to-date results.

The advantage of saving a query as a script in itself, using the QuerySave option, is that when the script is played, the query appears but is not immediately executed (as may be the case with a query you save with BeginRecord). With this method, you can make changes to the query if you wish before pressing F2 to process the query.

USING SHOWPLAY

Another way to play a script, but at a speed sufficiently slow to observe the results, is with the ShowPlay option of the Script menu. To use this option, choose Scripts/Showplay from the main menu, and enter the name of the script to be played. Paradox will then offer the choice of Fast or Slow as the playback speeds for the script. You select your desired choice of speeds, and the script is played at that speed.

To see an example, press F10 (if necessary) to display the main menu, and choose Scripts/ShowPlay. For the name of the script, enter **MYFIRST**. Paradox will display the following choices:

Fast Slow
Play script rapidly.

Choose Slow from the menu. The script will be replayed at a slow speed. When it has finished, you may want to repeat this process but choose Fast from the menu to observe the difference in playback speeds.

USING REPEATPLAY

You can repeat a script a selected number of times with the RepeatPlay option of the Script menu. To use this option, choose Scripts/RepeatPlay from the main menu, and then enter the name of the script to be played. Paradox next asks for the number of times you want the script played. You can enter a number up to 99,999, or you can enter the letter "c" in which case the script gets played continuously. If you need to interrupt a script while it is repeating, press CTRL-BREAK and select Cancel from the menu that appears.

THE INIT SCRIPT

If there is a set of tasks that you normally perform each time you start using Paradox, you can record the tasks in a script and assign the script the name INIT. If a script named INIT is found, it will be run by Paradox as soon as the program is started. Note that the INIT script must be stored in the default directory unless you are on a network, in which case the INIT script must be stored in a private directory. (Use the Custom Configuration Program, described in Appendix B, to change the default directory.)

MANAGING YOUR SCRIPTS

Because scripts can save so much time, they tend to collect quickly in your subdirectory. Before you know it, you will have dozens of scripts for various tasks, some of which you may no longer be using. You can keep things organized with the various options of the Tools menu for deleting scripts, renaming scripts, or displaying lists of scripts.

To delete unwanted scripts, choose Tools/Delete/Scripts from the main menu. Paradox will ask you for the name of the script to delete; if you are unsure of the spelling, you can press RETURN alone to see a menu of all available scripts. Enter the

```
Viewing List table: Record 1 of 6                              Main

LIST                             Name                          Date
      1   Custom                                               7/14/87
      2   Debugtst                                             4/15/87
      3   Instant                                              2/20/88
      4   Keybind                                              5/19/87
      5   Myfirst                                              2/20/88
      6   Ordercli                                             4/15/87
```

FIGURE 10-2. List of scripts

script name or choose it by name from the menu, and Paradox will ask for confirmation by displaying the following:

Cancel OK
Do not delete script.

You must choose OK to delete the script. You can use a similar menu choice to rename a script. From the main menu, choose Tools/Rename/Script, enter the current name, and then enter the new name for the script.

To see a list of your scripts, choose Tools/Info/Inventory/Scripts from the main menu. Press RETURN to choose the default directory (or enter an optional directory name), and the scripts contained in that directory will appear in a temporary table called LIST, similar to the example in Figure 10-2. The dates displayed indicate the date each script was created or last modified.

EDITING SCRIPTS WITH THE EDITOR

Paradox contains an editor that can be used to edit scripts. Scripts are written in PAL, a powerful programming language that Paradox provides for advanced users and developers. If you plan to build sophisticated scripts (including custom applications) yourself, you will find the editor useful for changing scripts, rather than re-recording them from scratch.

If programming does not interest you, rest assured that such in-depth involvement is purely optional. You can continue to create and save complex scripts that make your data management tasks easy with the Paradox features you have already explored. You can also use the Paradox Personal Programmer, a development tool that writes

```
Changing script C:\paradox2\myfirst                                  Script
....+...10....+...20....+...30....+...40....+...50....+...60....+...70....+...80
{Ask} {abcstaff} Check Right Right Right Right Right Right Right
Right Right Right Right Right "National Oil Co."
Do_It! Menu {Report} {Output} {Answer} {R} {Screen} ClearAll
{Scripts} {End-Record}
```

FIGURE 10-3.   Script within the script editor

sophisticated custom applications in Paradox for you, without knowing any programming. (The Personal Programmer is covered in more detail in Chapter 13.) If you are willing to explore the flexible language that is PAL, however, the editor is a tool that will assist you.

To edit an existing script, choose Scripts/Editor/Edit from the main menu and enter the name of the desired script. Once you enter the script name, the script will appear within the editor. As an example, press F10 for the main menu, and choose Scripts/Editor/Edit. Enter **MYFIRST** as a script name. The script you created earlier appears on the screen, similar to the example shown in Figure 10-3.

The editor works much like a word processor. You can add additional valid PAL commands or read other scripts into the existing script. You can use the cursor keys or any of the keys listed in Table 10-1 to edit a script while you are in the editor.

Key	Effect
↑	Cursor up one line
↓	Cursor down one line
←	Cursor left one character
→	Cursor right one character
BACKSPACE	Delete character to left of cursor
DELETE	Delete character at cursor location
HOME	Cursor to first line of script
END	Cursor to last line of script
PGUP	Cursor up half screen
PGDN	Cursor down half screen
CTRL-HOME	Cursor to start of current line
CTRL-END	Cursor to end of current line
CTRL-Y	Delete from cursor to end of line

TABLE 10-1.   Editing Keys for Scripts

While you are in the editor, pressing F10 displays the Editor menu, which offers the following options:

Read Go Print Help Do-It! Cancel

The Read option lets you read the contents of another script into the script that you are editing. Use this option to combine numerous small scripts into one large script. When you choose Read and enter a script name, that script is read into the current script at the cursor position. The Go option saves the script, leaves the editor, and plays the script. The Print option prints the script, using the default printer port, while the Do-It! option saves any changes to the script and returns you to the workspace. The Help and Cancel options perform the same tasks as they do elsewhere in Paradox.

How Scripts Are Recorded

Whether you use Instant Script Record (ALT-F3), BeginRecord, or QuerySave, Paradox will always store your script in the PAL programming language. The scripts you create will contain any one of these four items:

- Menu choices

- Quoted strings

- Special Paradox keys

- Query images

Menu choices appear within braces. In the example in Figure 10-3, menu choices such as Ask, Abcstaff, Report, and Answer are enclosed in braces. Paradox special keys are spelled out; in Figure 10-3, Do_It! and ClearAll represent Paradox special keys pressed during the recording of the script. Quoted strings contain characters enclosed in quotation marks; in Figure 10-3, "National Oil Co." represents the string of text entered in response to the query during the recording of the script. Queries that are saved with the QuerySave option of the Scripts menu resemble the actual query, with columns containing the selected fields, the word "Check" to indicate the presence of a checkmark, and any conditions of the query. As an example, if a Query Form for the HOURS table is displayed, all fields checked, and >40 entered in the Hours worked field, the resulting script (when saved with Scripts/QuerySave) is similar to the following:

```
Query
Hours    | Social security  |Weekend date  | Hours worked  | Assignment |
         | Check            | Check         | Check >40     | Check      |
         |                  |               |               |            |
         |                  |               |               |            |
Endquery
```

While you can create a script with a query by duplicating this overall design, it is usually easiest to fill in the Query Form and then choose Scripts/QuerySave to save the query as a script.

If you create scripts with the editor (as opposed to recording them as keystrokes), keep in mind the following. Function keys are represented by the Paradox key name (such as Do_It!), rather than by the function key name (such as F10). Responses to any prompts and quoted strings are entered exactly as you would type them in response to Paradox prompts.

Saving the Edited Script

To save the edited script, press Do-It! (F2) or choose Do-It! from the menu. The changes are saved, and the workspace reappears. You can then play the script with the usual options. If you are still in the editor now, press Do-It! (F2) to get back to the workspace.

Although you know how to use the editor to edit a script in Paradox, you may not yet know how to write your own scripts with the PAL language. Chapter 14 provides an introduction to programming in PAL. The intent of this portion of the chapter has been to make you aware that these facilities exist within Paradox. Whether or not you wish to make use of this advanced capability is up to you.

If you want to find out more about programming with PAL, consider Chapter 14, along with other resources that delve specifically into programming and applications development. The *PAL User's Guide* supplied with your Paradox documentation is an excellent resource.

QUICK SUMMARY

To record an instant script   Press ALT-F3, then perform the desired actions to be recorded. When done, press ALT-F3 again.

To play an instant script   Press ALT-F4.

To record a custom script   Press F10 for the menu, and then choose Scripts/BeginRecord. Enter a name for the script. Perform the desired actions to be recorded. Press F10 for the menu, and choose Scripts/EndRecord.

To play a custom script   Press F10 for the menu, and choose Scripts/Play. Enter the name of the desired script.

To save a query as a script   With the query form(s) visible on the screen, press F10 for the menu, and choose Scripts/QuerySave. Enter the desired name for the script.

To delete unwanted scripts   Press F10 for the menu, and choose Tools/Delete/Script. Enter the name of the script to delete, or press RETURN and choose the desired script from the list which appears.

chapter 11
MANAGING FILES

Once you have created a table, you will probably need to make changes to the design of it. Despite your best-laid plans, the need for additional fields or for changes to existing fields will arise. With Paradox, no database design is cast in stone. You can readily add new fields or change the design of an existing field.

In addition to helping you manage the characteristics of your tables, Paradox also lets you manage files by doing tasks usually achieved through DOS—tasks such as erasing and renaming files. Modifications to the structure of a table are performed through the Modify option of the main menu. Tasks such as erasing and renaming files can be performed from the Tools option of the main menu.

PARADOX OBJECTS

To effectively manage your files, you will need to know how Paradox stores those files. To handle database work, Paradox stores your records in tables. The table is a separate disk file with a default extension of .DB. A table, however, is just one of many types of *objects* that Paradox regularly deals with. Paradox objects include tables and various family members associated with tables, including forms and reports. Reports are saved with a default extension of .R, while forms are saved with an .F extension.

The custom forms and reports that you create have numbers added to the .F or .R extensions. For example, a custom report given the name of 2 from the menu would be stored with the same name as the table, but with an extension of .R2, while a form assigned the number 5 for its name would be stored with the same name as the table, but with an .F5 extension. Also included as objects within Paradox are any temporary tables, such as ANSWER or LIST. Of course, since these are temporary, they are overwritten by successive operations.

You can view the members of a Paradox family at any time. Just choose Tools/Info/Family from the main menu, and enter the name of the desired table.

Remember   When you delete a table, the associated family members are also deleted.

CHANGING THE TABLE DESIGN

To change the design (or structure) of a table, go to the main menu, and choose Modify and then Restructure. Paradox will prompt you for the name of the table to be changed, so enter the table name. The table structure will then appear, as shown in Figure 11-1.

Make the desired changes to the field names and field types. Once you have completed the changes to the structure, press Do-It! (F2) or press F10 and choose Do-It!

```
Restructuring Abcstaff table                              Restructure

STRUCT         Field Name        Field Type
      1   Social security       A11*      ┌──── FIELD TYPES ────
      2   Last name             A15       │ A_: Alphanumeric (ex: A25)
      3   First name            A15       │  Any combination of
      4   Address               A25       │  characters and spaces
      5   City                  A15       │  up to specified width.
      6   State                 A2        │  Maximum width is 255
      7   ZIP Code              A10       │
      8   Date of birth         D         │ N: Numbers with or without
      9   Date hired            D         │  decimal digits.
     10   Dependents            N         │
     11   Salary                $         │ $: Currency amounts.
     12   Assignment            A20       │
     13   Hourly Rate           $         │ D: Dates in the form
     14   Phone                 A12       │  mm/dd/yy, dd-mon-yy,
                                          │  or dd.mm.yy
                                          │
                                          │ Use 'x' after field type to
                                          │ show a key field (ex: A4x).
```

FIGURE 11-1. Table structure for existing table

from the menu to complete the redesign of the table. (As an alternative, you can choose Cancel from the menu, and any changes made to the table will not be saved.)

RENAMING FILES

You can rename Paradox objects from within Paradox by using the Rename command, available from the Tools choice of the main menu. Paradox lets you rename tables and associated objects, or just the forms, reports, or scripts. To rename a Paradox object, go to the main menu and choose Tools. From the Tools menu, which appears next, choose Rename.

The next menu displays these choices:

Table Form Report Script Graph
Rename a table and its family of forms, reports, and indexes.

This menu provides you with the options of renaming a table, a form, a report, a Paradox script, or a graph. You can also rename the forms and reports associated with a table. Choose the desired item to rename (a table, form, report, script, or graph), and Paradox will prompt you for the name of the item.

Use the Rename option from the Paradox menus to rename tables, so the associated family objects will also be renamed. If you use DOS commands to rename tables, the associated objects won't be renamed automatically.

Enter or select the item, and Paradox will ask you for a new name. Supply the name of your choice, and Paradox will rename the object.

DELETING FILES

The Delete option of the Tools menu also aids in the maintenance of Paradox objects. It can be used to delete tables, reports, forms, scripts, query speedups (which are explained later in this chapter), KeepSets, and graphs. Also on this menu is a ValCheck option, which lets you delete ValCheck files (created with the Modify/ValCheck option).

To delete a Paradox object, select Tools from the main menu, and then choose Delete from the next menu that appears. Select the object to be deleted, and Paradox will prompt you for the name of the object. Choose the object, and Paradox will next display a menu offering the choices of Cancel and OK. You must confirm the deletion by selecting OK before Paradox will delete the object. Remember: if you delete a table, its family of associated objects (such as custom reports and forms) is also deleted.

CHANGING A DIRECTORY

Although you should never need to change directories if you leave all of your data in a single Paradox subdirectory, some PC users use so many subdirectories that the ability to switch directories from within a program becomes critical. The Directory command, available from the More command on the Tools menu, can perform this important task. To change a directory, choose Tools from the main menu, and choose More from the next menu that appears. You will see additional choices that would not fit on the first menu.

Once you select More, another menu appears. The Directory choice from this menu is used to change directories. Choose this command, and Paradox will prompt you for a directory name. Enter the name of a valid subdirectory, and Paradox will switch to that subdirectory. Note that Paradox will always clear the workspace when you change directories. You can permanently reset your directory with the Defaults/SetDirectory option of the Custom Configuration Program. See Appendix B for details.

Remember   When you change directories, Paradox clears the workspace.

ACCESSING DOS

If you want to erase, rename, or copy files that are not Paradox files or objects, you can resort to the use of such DOS commands as ERASE, RENAME, and COPY to perform basic housekeeping. Paradox's ToDOS menu choice, available from the More choice of the Tools menu, can be a handy option for performing such DOS functions as formatting or copying a disk without leaving Paradox. Selecting ToDOS from the Tools/More choices of the main menu results in the appearance of a DOS prompt. (The CTRL-O key combination can be used for the same purpose.) Perform the desired DOS functions, or run another program (see the warning that follows). When you are done, type **EXIT** at the DOS prompt to return to Paradox.

To see how this works, get to the main menu and choose Tools/More. Choose ToDOS from the next menu that appears, and you will see something similar to the following on the screen:

```
Warning! Do not delete or edit Paradox objects
or load RAM-resident programs.
To return to Paradox, type EXIT
```

```
The IBM Personal Computer DOS
Version 3.20 (C)Copyright International Business Machines Corp 1981, 1986
Copyright Microsoft Corp. 1981, 1986
```

You are now back in DOS, but Paradox remains in a portion of your computer's memory. Try entering the following command:

```
COPY ABCSTAFF.R TEST.TMP
```

The message "(1) files copied" shows that the file has been copied with the DOS COPY command. If you prefer, try running another program, but be forewarned that the program must be very small to run in a standard (640K RAM) computer along with Paradox. Do *not* try to load memory resident programs. A later section, "A Warning about Accessing DOS," will explain why.

The fact that Paradox remains in memory while you use the ToDOS option severely limits what programs you can run. Paradox requires 512K of memory. Subtract this figure from the amount of your computer's *available* memory (what is left after DOS has loaded), and then subtract the amount of memory consumed by any memory resident software that you may be using. The figure that remains is the amount of memory currently available for use by other programs.

Most desktop computers will not be able to load and run additional programs of significant size, but you can use most DOS functions like COPY and FORMAT because these functions use very little memory. Note also that you should *not* use the

DOS PRINT and MODE commands through the Paradox ToDOS option, because these commands may alter memory, causing problems when Paradox is reloaded.

At the DOS prompt, type **EXIT** and press RETURN. In a moment, the Paradox workspace appears, and you are again ready to work in Paradox.

Using Big-DOS

If you are desperate for additional memory, you can use the special ALT-O key combination within Paradox to access DOS. The ALT-O key combination (as opposed to CTRL-O) is referred to as the *Big-DOS key,* and it accesses DOS just as CTRL-O or the ToDOS menu option does. However, with ALT-O, Paradox saves much more of its own environment to disk. The end result is that it takes longer to get to DOS with ALT-O, but you are left with roughly 500K of available memory on a 640K machine.

A WARNING ABOUT ACCESSING DOS

Do *not* use the ToDOS option to load any software that is memory resident. These programs are also known as TSRs, which stands for "terminate and stay resident." Memory resident programs are those that "pop up" at the touch of a key combination that contains SHIFT, CTRL, or ALT. If you load a memory resident program from ToDOS, the TSR will probably overwrite portions of Paradox that are temporarily stored in the memory of your computer. When you try to return to Paradox by typing EXIT, you may be in for an unpleasant surprise. Your computer will probably freeze, requiring a complete reboot of the system.

If you do not know whether a program is a TSR, do not try to load the program through the DOS window supplied by ToDOS. Instead, save your changes with Do-It!, and exit from Paradox before trying to load the program in question.

Also, while at DOS you should not copy Paradox objects for other uses in Paradox, because corruption of files may occur. Use the Paradox menu options under Tools to make copies of Paradox objects.

BOOSTING PERFORMANCE WITH QUERYSPEED

To reduce the processing time needed by Paradox to perform often-used queries, you may want to make use of the QuerySpeed option of the Tools menu. (In earlier versions of Paradox, this was called Query Speedup.) For queries that you perform on a regular basis, this can be a very useful option. The QuerySpeed option, when selected while a particular query is visible on the screen, tells Paradox to build secondary index files for all non-key fields that contain a selection criterion. Once these index files have been built, Paradox uses them to quickly process your query. You do not need to do anything out of the ordinary to maintain these indexes; they are automatically updated each time you perform the query.

To use QuerySpeed, you must first have the Query Form you use regularly in the workspace. With the Query Form visible, get to the main menu with F10 and choose Tools/QuerySpeed. Paradox will display the message "Processing query speedup" as it creates the indexes. (Note that if there are no non-key fields used in the query, Paradox will instead display the message "No speedup possible," as key fields are already indexed.) Once the operation is complete, you can proceed to perform your query whenever you wish in the usual manner. The indexes are built through the query and are then available to speed up zooms as well as other queries.

While the QuerySpeed option can noticeably improve performance, there is a tradeoff involved: the building of the necessary index files will consume disk space. Keep in mind that you can use Tools/Delete to erase the index files created by QuerySpeed, so you may want to compare system performance versus available disk space with and without the advantages of this option.

EXPORTING AND IMPORTING DATA

No PC is an island. You may need to use other programs along with Paradox, or others in your office may use other popular programs like Lotus 1-2-3 or WordStar with its

MailMerge option. The ExportImport option, located on the Tools menu, allows you to import files from other programs into Paradox, and to export data from Paradox tables for use by the other programs.

To export or import files, go to the main menu with F10 and choose Tools/Export-Import. The next menu that appears provides two choices: Export, which is used to move data from Paradox to other programs, and Import, which is used to move data from other programs into Paradox.

Exporting Data

To export data from Paradox, choose Export from the menu. Paradox will next display the following choices in the form of a menu:

Quattro /PRO 1-2-3 Symphony Dbase Pfs Reflex VisiCalc ASCII
Export to a .WKQ file.

You can export from Paradox to one of eight possible formats, as indicated by the choices in this menu. The choices are Quattro/PRO worksheet format (.WKQ or .WQ1), Lotus worksheet format (.WKS or .WK1), Symphony worksheet format (.WR1), dBASE format (.DBF), PFS:File format (no extension), Reflex format (.RXD), VisiCalc format (DIF), and ASCII text format. As a general rule, most word processors will read information stored as ASCII text. Many spreadsheets will transfer data that follows the Lotus 1-2-3 file format, and most database managers will transfer files using the popular dBASE file format. If it is not obvious which format your software package uses, check your user's manual.

If you choose Dbase from the available menu options, Paradox will ask which version of dBASE you are using (dBASE II, dBASE III, or dBASE IV). If you select Quattro/PRO, Lotus 1-2-3, or Symphony, Paradox will ask which version of the spreadsheet you are using. If you select ASCII, Paradox will ask whether or not the data should be delimited with some type of field marker (such as quotation marks). The ASCII format, with a quotation mark as a delimiter, is frequently used with merge files (such as WordStar/MailMerge). When exporting to a word processor, in some cases you get better results using Report/Output/File from the menu. You may want to try both methods to see which works best for you.

After you have selected the type of file to be exported to, Paradox will display the following prompt:

Name:
Enter name of table to export, or press ↵ to see a list of tables.

Enter the name of the table that will supply the records. Paradox will next ask for a valid filename to export the records to. You can add an extension, if desired, to the exported file. (Note that if you choose Quattro, Reflex, Lotus 1-2-3, or dBASE and omit the extension, Paradox will supply the proper extension automatically.)

Once you have entered a valid filename, Paradox will export the table you chose into the new file. If a file with the same name you selected for the exported file exists, Paradox will not automatically overwrite the existing file; it will present you with a menu with Cancel and Replace options, and you must choose Replace to overwrite the file.

Importing Data

To import data from Paradox, select Tools/ExportImport from the main menu and then choose Import from the next menu that appears. Paradox will display the following choices in the form of a menu:

Quattro /PRO 1-2-3 Symphony Dbase Pfs Reflex VisiCalc ASCII
Import a .WKQ or .WQ1 file.

Paradox imports data from foreign files, using any one of the same eight possible formats used for exporting files. The choices are Quattro or Quattro Pro worksheet format (.WKQ or .WQ1), Lotus worksheet format (.WKS or .WK1), Symphony worksheet format (.WR1), dBASE format (.DBF), PFS:File format (no extension), Reflex format (.RXD), VisiCalc format (DIF), and ASCII text format.

If you select Quattro/PRO, Lotus 1-2-3, or Symphony, Paradox will ask which version of the spreadsheet you are using. If you select ASCII, Paradox will ask whether or not the data is delimited with some type of field marker (such as quotation marks). Imported dBASE files are analyzed by Paradox automatically, and the program determines which version of dBASE was used to create the file.

Warning: If you are using a dBASE IV file with memo fields and a version of Paradox prior to version 3.5, you will get an "Invalid dBASE file" error when trying to import the file. You must use the COPY TO *<filename>* TYPE DBMEMO3 command within dBASE IV first, to convert the dBASE IV file to dBASE III Plus file format.

After you have selected the type of file for import, Paradox will display the following prompt:

File name:
Enter name of file to import, or press ↵ to see a list of files.

Enter the name of the foreign file that will supply the records. Paradox will next ask for a name for the new table into which the records will be imported. Enter a table name of your choice, and Paradox will perform the conversion. During this process, it will display a progress report on the screen.

Some Notes On Importing Data

Paradox makes certain assumptions as it imports data from other programs into a Paradox table. When importing ASCII text that is delimited, Paradox assumes that the delimiters used are the double quotation marks around the fields and the comma as a separator between fields. If the delimiters are any other characters, you must use the Custom Configuration Program (detailed in Appendix B) to change the default delimiters.

Paradox must convert the data in different fields to its own field formats. Depending on the other program, the results will usually be what you want, but you may in rare cases need to do some fine-tuning. Paradox tries to determine the precise field names and best field types to use, based on the contents of the foreign file you are importing.

If Paradox cannot determine the field name, it will name the new field as FIELD-n, where n represents the number of the field in the order of the structure. Paradox also maintains a temporary table called PROBLEMS. If any records cannot be successfully converted during the conversion process, they will be stored in the PROBLEMS table. Finally, note that field types may or may not come across as the exact type of field you would prefer in Paradox. Table 11-1 shows how types of data from various program files will be imported into Paradox.

PARADOX AND QUATTRO PRO

If you must work with both databases and spreadsheets, the most effective way to use Paradox along with a spreadsheet is to make use of Borland's Quattro Pro. Paradox and Quattro Pro are designed to work well together. And in addition to Quattro Pro's being fully compatible with the Lotus 1-2-3 file format (up to version 2.2), Quattro Pro and Paradox can reside concurrently in memory. This is possible with a feature called Paradox Access. With Paradox Access, you can run Quattro Pro from within

Field Type	Type Within Paradox
dBASE character	Alphanumeric
dBASE number	Number
dBASE number with 2 decimal places	Currency
dBASE logical	Alphanumeric with 1-character width
dBASE date	Date
dBASE memo	Alphanumeric (only first 255 characters will import)
PFS field, nonnumeric	Alphanumeric
PFS field, numbers	Number
PFS field, numbers with 2 decimal places	Currency
PFS field, using dd/mm/yy format	Date
DIF field, text	Alphanumeric
DIF field, numbers	Number
DIF field, numbers with 2 decimal places	Currency
DIF field, text in a dd/mm/yy format	Date
1-2-3 labels	Alphanumeric
1-2-3 numbers	Numeric
1-2-3 numbers with 2 decimal places	Currency
1-2-3 numbers, formatted as mm/dd/yy	Date
Symphony	See 1-2-3 above

TABLE 11-1.   How Types of Fields Are Imported into Paradox

Paradox, automatically load a table into a Quattro Pro spreadsheet, work with the table while in Quattro Pro, and return to Paradox at the touch of a single key combination.

To use Paradox Access, you must have Paradox version 3.5 or above, and you must have Quattro Pro version 2.0 or above. You must also have two megabytes or more of installed memory. And, if you want to access data that is stored on a SQL Server on a network, you will also need to have Paradox SQL Link installed (Paradox SQL Link is available separately from Borland). If you do not have sufficient memory to use Paradox Access, you can still share files between Paradox and Quattro Pro; you can also use the menu options in Quattro Pro to directly view, query, or edit Paradox tables.

Note that before you can use Paradox Access, you must do the following:

1. Change the FILES setting in your computer's CONFIG.SYS file to read FILES = 40. (If the FILES setting in your CONFIG.SYS file is already greater than 40, you can leave it as-is.)

2. Run the SHARE command from DOS. (You may need to change to your DOS subdirectory to run the SHARE command.) If you get a "bad command or filename" error message when trying to run SHARE, copy the program, SHARE.EXE from your DOS Supplemental Diskette into your Paradox directory, or into a directory named in your PATH statement.

3. Use the PXACCESS batch file to start Paradox. PXACCESS.BAT can be found on your Quattro Pro disks. This is a batch file that will start Paradox with various memory options that optimize it for simultaneous use with Quattro Pro.

4. Make sure that your Paradox working directory and your private directory are different directories. While in Paradox, choose Tools/Net/SetPrivate, and change your private directory to something other than the directory that holds your working database files.

Once you have started Paradox with the PXACCESS batch file, you can use the CTRL-F10 key combination to switch back and forth between Paradox and Quattro Pro. Whenever you switch to Quattro Pro, Quattro Pro loads the ANSWER table by default. You can load any Paradox table (memory permitting) while in Quattro Pro with Quattro Pro's Load File command.

When you have finished working in Quattro Pro, press CTRL- F10 again, and you will be back in Paradox. With Paradox Access, there is no need to close spreadsheet files, or exit Quattro Pro as you normally would. You can later go from Paradox back to Quattro Pro again with CTRL-F10, and the workspace in Quattro Pro will be intact.

HANDS-ON PRACTICE: MOVING FROM PARADOX TO 1-2-3

As mentioned earlier, with Quattro Pro you can directly work with Paradox tables. With Lotus 1-2-3 and many other earlier spreadsheets, you must resort to importing and exporting files. For users of such products, this portion of the chapter demonstrates examples of importing and exporting 1-2-3 worksheets with Paradox. If you make use of Lotus 1-2-3 or a compatible spreadsheet, you may want to consider duplicating the examples by using your copy of the Lotus 1-2-3 program.

Exporting a Paradox table to a 1-2-3 worksheet is a simple matter. Go to the main menu and choose Tools/ExportImport. From the next menu that appears, choose Export. Paradox will display a menu of available file formats:

Quattro /PRO 1-2-3 Symphony DBase Pfs Reflex VisiCalc ASCII
Export to a .WKQ or .WQ1 file.

Choose 1-2-3 from the menu. Paradox will ask you whether you want to export the file in 1-2-3 Release 1a format or in 1-2-3 Release 2 format. Choose the format that matches your copy of 1-2-3.

Paradox next asks for a table to export. Enter **ABCSTAFF** as a table name. Finally, Paradox will ask for the filename to be assigned to the converted 1-2-3 file.

As you enter the filename, you can save time by including a drive and subdirectory specifier so that the resulting 1-2-3 file will be copied to the disk or subdirectory that you normally use along with 1-2-3. As an example, if your 1-2-3 files are stored on drive C in a subdirectory named LOTUS, and you want to name the worksheet file ABC, you could enter

C:\LOTUS\ABC

```
E1: [W16] 'City                                                      READY

         E           F    G          H           I          J
1  City             State ZIP Code   Date of birth Date hired Dependents
2  Silver Spring    MD    20910-0124   29-May-61   04-Jul-86      2
3  Takoma Park      MD    20912        02-Nov-64   17-Nov-87      1
4  Chevy Chase      MD    20815-0988   01-Mar-54   25-Jul-85      2
5  Falls Church     VA    22044        22-Dec-55   05-Sep-85      1
6  Washington       DC    20009        22-Jun-66   17-Sep-87      0
7  Herndon          VA    22071        02-Oct-59   17-Feb-88      1
8  Chevy Chase      MD    20815-0988   17-Aug-52   02-Feb-88      1
9  Fairfax          VA    22025        20-Dec-55   19-Oct-86      3
10 Arlington        VA    22203        17-Aug-58   01-Dec-87      1
11 Reston           VA    22090        18-Sep-61   12-Aug-86      1
12
13
14
15
16
17
18
19
20
10-Feb-88  10:36 PM
```

FIGURE 11-2.   The ABCSTAFF table in the Lotus 1-2-3 worksheet

in response to Paradox's request for a filename. Note that you need not include an extension; Paradox will provide the proper extension automatically as it creates the 1-2-3 file.

Enter the desired filename for the 1-2-3 file, and Paradox will proceed to convert the ABCSTAFF table to a worksheet compatible with 1-2-3. During the conversion process, a progress message will appear briefly near the bottom of the screen. When the workspace reappears, the conversion process is complete.

Once you have stored or copied the 1-2-3 file to the appropriate disk or subdirectory, you can load Lotus 1-2-3 in the usual manner and get into the 1-2-3 worksheet. Use the / File Retrieve command to display the directory of 1-2-3 files. From the directory, highlight the desired file (in this case, ABC.WK1 or ABC.WKS) and press RETURN. The spreadsheet will then be loaded; it will look similar to the example that is shown in Figure 11-2.

HANDS-ON PRACTICE: MOVING FROM 1-2-3 TO PARADOX

As an example of a worksheet that can be imported into Paradox, consider the worksheet shown in Figure 11-3. This sample worksheet is typical of a 1-2-3

A1:   READY

	A	B	C	D	E	F
1			ABC Trading Company			
2			Stock Transactions			
3						
4	Stock	Shares	Per Share	Amount	Commission	Buyer
5						
6	IBM	290	125.625	$36,431.25	$3,643.13	Johnson, William
7	JJR	100	30.250	$3,025.00	$302.50	Atkins, Charles
8	DCD	300	56.700	$17,010.00	$1,701.00	Bennington, Sue
9	CVB	450	43.000	$19,350.00	$1,935.00	Robertson, Nancy
10	ZAX	400	38.780	$15,512.00	$1,551.20	Boyer, James
11	CGC	100	39.000	$3,900.00	$390.00	Thompson, Linda
12	THM	300	80.500	$24,150.00	$2,415.00	Rowe, Mike
13	QRT	700	37.725	$26,407.50	$2,640.75	Williams, Yvonne
14	KDK	200	55.000	$11,000.00	$1,100.00	Robertson, Nancy
15	ZDD	180	42.100	$7,578.00	$757.80	Johnson, William
16						
17						
18	Totals	3020	N/A	$164,363.75	$16,436.38	
19						
20	Averages	302	54.868	$16,570.14	$1,657.01	

10-Feb-88 10:37 PM

FIGURE 11-3. Sample 1-2-3 worksheet

worksheet in that certain fields (or columns, as they are referred to when in spreadsheet form) contain headings in the form of labels, numeric data, and formulas that result in the display of numeric data. In the example, the figures in columns B and C are actual values, but the figures in columns D and E are calculated from formulas entered in those columns. Columns A and F contain labels or text entries. The totals and averages at the bottom of the worksheet are also based on formulas stored in cells at the bottom of the worksheet.

When Paradox converts the worksheet to a Paradox table, the necessary calculations stored in the worksheet formulas are performed for the existing data within the worksheet. The Paradox table that results from the conversion does not contain 1-2-3 formulas; instead, it contains the numbers that appear as a result of those formulas.

Since Paradox can deal with multiple versions of Lotus 1-2-3 and Symphony, you do not need to perform any special preparation for the 1-2-3 or Symphony worksheet file. To make the file easier to locate, you may want to copy the file from your 1-2-3 data disk or 1-2-3 subdirectory into the PARADOX3 subdirectory.

Go to the main menu and choose Tools/ExportImport. From the next menu that appears, choose Import. You will see a menu like this:

Quattro 1-2-3 Symphony DBase Pfs Reflex VisiCalc ASCII
Import a .WKQ file.

Choose 1-2-3 from the menu, and Paradox will ask whether you wish to import a file from 1-2-3 Release 1a or Release 2. Choose the appropriate option for your version of 1-2-3.

Paradox will next display the following prompt:

File name:
Enter name of file to import.

Enter the name of your 1-2-3 worksheet (in this example, STOCKS). If you are unsure of the spelling of the filename, you can press RETURN without entering a name, and Paradox will display all files with a Lotus 1-2-3 extension.

Once you enter the name of the 1-2-3 file, you will see this prompt:

Table:
Enter name to be given to new Paradox table.

Enter a name for a new Paradox table. Once you supply the name, Paradox will analyze the worksheet and convert its contents to records in a table. When this process is complete, the new table will appear within the workspace, as shown in Figure 11-4.

Once the data is in Paradox, you may want to make changes to some records or to the structure of the table in order to take better advantage of the capabilities of Paradox.

```
Viewing Stocks table: Record 1 of 14                          Main
STOCKS──Field-1────────────Field-2────────Abc trading company──
    1                                      Stock Transactions
    2     Stock       Shares               Per Share
    3     IBM         290                  125.6250000000
    4     JJR         100                  30.2500000000
    5     DCD         300                  56.7000000000
    6     CUB         450                  43
    7     ZQX         400                  38.7000000000
    8     CGG         100                  39
    9     THM         300                  88.5000000000
   10     QRT         700                  37.7250000000
   11     KDK         200                  55
   12     ZDD         100                  42.1000000000
   13     Totals      3020.0000000000      N/A
   14     Averages    302.0000000000       54.8600000000
```

14 records converted

FIGURE 11-4.   STOCKS worksheet imported into Paradox table

```
Viewing Struct table: Record 1 of 6                          Main  ◄═

STOCKS┬─Field-1────────┬────────Field-2────────┬─Abc trading company═══┬─
     2 ║ Stock          │ Shares                │ Per Share
     3 ║ IBM            │ 290                   │ 125.6250000000
     4 ║ JJR            │ 100                   │ 30.2500000000
     5 ║ DCD            │ 300                   │ 56.7000000000
     6 ║ CUB            │ 450                   │ 43
     7 ║ ZQX            │ 400                   │ 38.7000000000
     8 ║ CGG            │ 100                   │ 39
     9 ║ THM            │ 300                   │ 80.5000000000
    10 ║ QRT            │ 700                   │ 37.7250000000
    11 ║ KDK            │ 200                   │ 55
    12 ║ ZDD            │ 100                   │ 42.1000000000
    13 ║ Totals         │ 3020.0000000000       │ N/A
    14 ║ Averages       │ 302.0000000000        │ 54.8680000000

STRUCT┬─────────Field Name─────────┬Field Type┐
     1 ║ Field-1                    │ A10
     2 ║ Field-2                    │ A24
     3 ║ Abc trading company        │ A24
     4 ║ Field-4                    │ A24
     5 ║ Field-5                    │ A24
     6 ║ Field-6                    │ A10    ┌──────────────────────────┐
                                            │ Stocks table has 14 records│
                                            └──────────────────────────┘
```

FIGURE 11-5.   Structure table for an imported Lotus 1-2-3 file

The field names within the new database are Field-1, Field-2, and so on (with the exception of the third field) because Paradox uses any labels in the first row of the imported spreadsheet as field names. If cells in those rows happen to be blank (as in this example), Paradox will substitute default field names. You can modify the structure of the table, changing the field names to ones you may prefer.

A more serious problem occurs if you attempt to use the math capabilities of Paradox to obtain totals and averages for the numbers. If your imported Lotus 1-2-3 file has a design like the one in Figure 11-4, you cannot obtain any totals, because the fields are all alphanumeric fields.

Consider the structure table shown in Figure 11-5, which appears when you choose Tools/Info/Structure to display the structure of the new table. Although the 1-2-3 fields containing the number of shares, stock prices, and commission amounts are clearly numeric, Paradox designated the fields as text fields. It did so because the labels near the top of the 1-2-3 worksheet were entered as text; in the translation process, the new fields were designated as text to maintain the labels. Since you want to use the numbers as values, you can delete the row containing the labels, modify the structure of the table with Modify/Restructure, and make the necessary changes to the Field Type designations to change the field types to numeric fields.

Also change the field names so they indicate the purpose of each field. If this is done, the 1-2-3 labels are no longer necessary and can be deleted from the Paradox database. In our example, the field names assigned during the translation process are

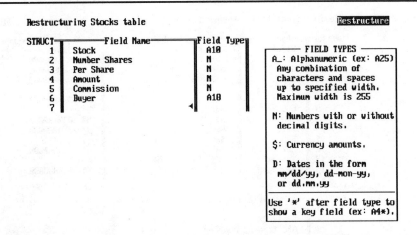

Restructuring Stocks table   Restructure

STRUCT——————Field Name——————Field Type
    1 │ Stock   │ A10   │   ┌──── FIELD TYPES ────┐
    2 │ Number Shares   │ N   │   │ A_: Alphanumeric (ex: A25)│
    3 │ Per Share   │ N   │   │ Any combination of   │
    4 │ Amount   │ N   │   │ characters and spaces   │
    5 │ Commission   │ N   │   │ up to specified width.   │
    6 │ Buyer   │ A10   │   │ Maximum width is 255   │
    7 │   │   │◀   │   │
                                                      │ N: Numbers with or without│
                                                      │ decimal digits.   │
                                                      │   │
                                                      │ $: Currency amounts.   │
                                                      │   │
                                                      │ D: Dates in the form   │
                                                      │ mm/dd/yy, dd-mon-yy,   │
                                                      │ or dd.mm.yy   │
                                                      │   │
                                                      │ Use '*' after field type to│
                                                      │ show a key field (ex: A4*).│

FIGURE 11-6.   Modified table structure

replaced with more descriptive names for the actual fields, and the field types for the Shares, Per Share, Amount, and Commission fields have been changed to numeric fields, as shown in Figure 11-6.

You may also want to delete certain records from the Paradox database. Any rows in the 1-2-3 worksheet that contained other descriptive text for the columns will appear as unwanted records in the Paradox database. You can easily delete these records by getting into Edit mode with F9 and then pressing the DEL key while the cursor is at an unwanted record. When these changes are made to the table in Figure 11-6, the result looks like Figure 11-7.

Helpful Hints For Importing 1-2-3 Files

You can save some cleanup work on the Paradox database by doing preparation work within the worksheet before leaving 1-2-3. Any Lotus 1-2-3 macros, for example, will clutter your table, appearing as fields of text. Headers entered as labels above the columns of worksheet data can present the same problem, as shown earlier. You may want to specify a range of data that contains only the information you will need while you are in the 1-2-3 worksheet, and export that range of data to a separate worksheet

```
Editing Stocks table: Record 10 of 10                          Edit
STOCKS        Stock      Number Shares    Per Share       Amount      Commissi
   1          IBM            290            125.63        36431.25     3643.13
   2          JJR            100             30.25          3025         302.5
   3          DCD            300             56.7          17010        1701
   4          CUB            450             43            19350        1935
   5          ZQX            400             38.78         15512        1551.2
   6          CGG            100             39             3900         390
   7          THM            300             80.5          24150        2415
   8          QRT            700             37.72         26407.5      2640.75
   9          KDK            200             55            11000        1100
  10          ZDD            100             42.1           7578         757.8
```

FIGURE 11-7.   Paradox table after changes are completed

file. Then translate that file to Paradox format and add the necessary field names to the database.

To export a range from a 1-2-3 worksheet as a separate worksheet file, you use the / File Xtract command of 1-2-3. Simply get into your worksheet in the usual manner, and enter the 1-2-3 command / File Xtract. Select Values from the next menu, and then enter a name for the new worksheet. Finally, place the cursor at the start of the range of cells to be stored in the new worksheet, press the period key to anchor the range, and move the cursor to the end of the range of cells; then press RETURN. The new worksheet will be created, and you can use it within Paradox.

One major advantage of performing this type of preparation before you leave the 1-2-3 environment is that if you transfer columns of numbers that do not contain any headings to Paradox, they will be imported into the new database as numeric fields. Thus, you will not need to modify the table structure to change fields from text to numeric in order to obtain proper totals.

Users of Symphony should also keep in mind that they cannot translate Symphony files that are password protected to Paradox format without unprotecting them first. If you are using a password-protected Symphony worksheet, extract the range of data to another worksheet that is not password protected. Then import the file into Paradox in the manner just described.

PROTECTING TABLES

To ensure security, Paradox lets you protect your tables from unauthorized access. Perhaps you are storing salary records, medical histories, or something else that contains sensitive information, and you do not want any savvy computer user to be able to browse through your files at will. Paradox provides tools for protecting your files with passwords. These tools are available from the More option of the Tools menu.

To protect a table, choose Tools/More/Protect from the main menu. The next menu that appears will provide the following three options:

Password ClearPasswords Write-protect
Set or remove passwords for a table or script.

Note ≡ The passwords that you assign to tables or scripts should be written down in a secure but safe place. If you assign a password to a table and later forget the password, **there is no way to access that table without the password**. In short, do not lose your passwords. Also, it might be a wise idea to store an unprotected copy of the table in a safe place, such as a locked file cabinet.

To protect a table from unauthorized access, choose Password from the menu. Paradox will next ask you whether you wish to protect a table or a script. Choose Table, and enter the name of the table that is to be protected.

Tip ≡ Passwords are case-sensitive.

Once you have supplied the name, Paradox will ask you to supply a password:

Password:
Enter new owner password or press ↵ to remove all passwords.

Enter the desired password, which can be up to 15 characters long. For your protection, Paradox will ask you to repeat the password. Once you have entered it twice identically, Paradox will display a table for the addition of any optional auxiliary passwords.

If you are not using Paradox on a network, you can omit the addition of any auxiliary passwords. Just press Do-It! (F2), and Paradox will assign the password to the table. From then on, any attempts to view or manipulate the table will require the entry of the password. Paradox automatically prompts the user for the password as he or she chooses commands that would require access to the protected table.

Removing a Password

To remove password protection from a table, follow the same steps you use to add a password. When Paradox prompts you for the master password, press RETURN without entering any name, and Paradox will "decrypt" the table, removing the password protection.

Using ClearPasswords

Also available from the Protect menu is the ClearPasswords option. This choice does not remove password protection (to do that, see the previous paragraph), but it can be useful in maintaining security. When you access a table with a password, Paradox remembers that you have been granted access, and the program will let you manipulate the data in that table for the remainder of the session. However, in some cases you might want Paradox to reinstate the protection of your tables—for example, when you leave for lunch but want to leave your computer turned on and in Paradox.

You can use the ClearPasswords option to restore the protection of your password-protected tables after you have entered a password. In effect, this command negates the effect of your previous action of supplying the passwords, so any access of protected tables will again require the entry of the passwords.

To clear your passwords, choose Tools/More/Protect from the main menu. From the next menu that appears, choose ClearPasswords. Paradox will request confirmation of this action by displaying a menu with Cancel and OK as choices. Select OK to proceed, and Paradox will clear its memory of any passwords you have entered since you started your session.

QUICK SUMMARY

To restructure a table Press F10 for the menu, and choose Modify/Restructure. Make the desired changes to the table structure, then press Do-It! (F2).

To rename a Paradox object Press F10 for the menu, and choose Tools/Rename, then choose the desired object (a table, form, report, script, or graph). Enter the name of the object, then enter the new name desired.

To delete a Paradox object Press F10 for the menu, and choose Tools/Delete, then choose the desired object (a table, form, report, script, queryspeed, keepset, valcheck, or graph). Enter the name of the object, then confirm your choice by choosing OK.

To access DOS from within Paradox   Press F10 for the menu, and choose Tools/More/To Dos (or, press CTRL-O). When done with DOS, enter **EXIT** at the DOS prompt to return to Paradox. To access DOS with a maximum amount of free memory while at DOS, press ALT-O.

To export a Paradox table for use with other software   Press F10 for the menu, and choose Export/Import, then choose Export. From the next menu, select the desired file format (Quattro/PRO, 1-2-3, Symphony, Dbase, Pfs, Reflex, VisiCalc, or ASCII). If asked, choose a version for the file format. Enter the name of the table to export when asked, then enter the name for the new file. (Remember, you can include a drive identifier and/or pathname along with the new filename.)

To import files created by other software programs for use in Paradox   Press F10 for the menu, and choose Export/Import, then choose Import. From the next menu, select the desired file format (Quattro/PRO, 1-2-3, Symphony, Dbase, Pfs, Reflex, VisiCalc, or ASCII). If asked, choose a version for the file format. Enter the name of the file to import when asked. (Remember, you can include a drive identifier and/or pathname along with the filename.) Finally, enter the name for the new table into which the records will be imported.

To password-protect a table   Press F10 for the menu, and then choose Tools/More/Protect and Password. From the next menu, choose Table, and enter the name of the table to be password-protected. Finally, enter the desired password twice, then press Do-It! (F2).

ADVANCED REPORT TOPICS

Chapter 7 began the process of presenting how Paradox can meet your reporting needs through standard and custom reports. This chapter continues with that topic, describing the use of free-form reports in detail.

You can create free-form reports in Paradox from the Report Specification screen. Unlike tabular reports, free-form reports are not limited to a columnar format. In a free-form report, you can place the fields wherever they need to appear. Perhaps the most well-known example of a free-form report is a sheet of mailing labels. Mailing labels do not appear in columnar (or tabular) form; instead, the name, address, city, state, and ZIP code fields are placed in a desired location to fit a printed label. Besides mailing labels, free-form reports can also be used for common tasks like printing checks, generating invoices, and creating reports that contain large amounts of textual material.

Although you cannot create a free-form report as quickly as you can generate a tabular report with the Instant Report key, a default free-form report can be created almost as quickly by choosing the appropriate options and saving the report immediately. To quickly create a free-form report that uses the default format, simply perform these steps:

1. Choose Report/Design from the main menu, and enter the name for the table.

2. Choose a name, and enter a description for the report.

3. Select Free-Form from the next menu that appears. The default Report Specification for a free-form report will appear on the screen.

4. Press Do-It! (F2) to store the default free-form report.

Once you have created a default free-form report, you can generate the report by choosing Report from the main menu, and then choosing Output followed by the name of the table. Then choose the stored report by name from the menu that appears, and select Printer, Screen, or File as desired. Figure 12-1 shows a portion of the report produced from the ABCSTAFF table, using the steps just outlined.

Note that the report illustrates the design of a default free-form report. The date appears at the top left of each page; a report heading, which uses the description you entered when you named the report, appears at the top center of the page. A page number appears at the top right of the page. The names of the fields appear as field headings, and the contents of each field appear to the right of the field name. Each record in the table used to print the report appears with all of the fields in the record.

If you would like to use a free-form report as the default report, you can replace the Standard Report (called R) with a free-form report that you design for the appropriate table. Then, pressing ALT-F7 will print that report.

HANDS-ON PRACTICE: PRODUCING A SELECTIVE FREE-FORM REPORT

As with tabular reports, you can use temporary tables to generate free-form reports that meet your precise needs. You can often save time by limiting the fields produced in an ANSWER table and basing a free-form report that uses the default Report

1/21/88   Freeform Test   Page 1

Social security: 232-55-1234
Last name: Jackson
First name: David
Address: 4102 Valley Lane
City: Arlington
State: VA
ZIP Code: 22044
Date of birth: 12/22/55
Date hired: 9/05/85
Dependents: 1
Salary: 7.50
Assignment: City Revenue Dept.
Hourly Rate: 12.00
Phone: 703-555-2345

Social security: 495-00-3456
Last name: Abernathy
First name: Sandra
Address: 1512 Redskins Park Drive
City: Herndon
State: VA
ZIP Code: 22071
Date of birth: 10/02/59
Date hired: 2/17/88
Dependents: 1
Salary: 10.00
Assignment: City Revenue Dept.
Hourly Rate: 18.00
Phone: 703-555-7337

Social security: 876-54-3210
Last name: Hart
First name: Edward
Address: 6200 Germantown Road
City: Fairfax
State: VA
ZIP Code: 22025
Date of birth: 12/20/55

FIGURE 12-1. Example of default free-form report

Date hired: 10/19/86
Dependents: 3
Salary: 8.50
Assignment: Smith Builders
Hourly Rate: 14.00
Phone: 703-555-7834

FIGURE 12-1. Example of default free-form report (*continued*)

Specification on that temporary (ANSWER) table. As an example, perhaps you need a quick mailing list. You only need the names and addresses of the employees, and for this example, you only need those employees who live in Maryland.

First clear the workspace, if necessary, with ALT-F8. From the main menu, choose Ask, and enter **ABCSTAFF** for the table name. Use the F6 key to place checkmarks in the Last name, First name, Address, City, State, and ZIP Code fields. In the State field, enter **MD**. Then press Do-It! (F2) to process the query. The fields you selected with checkmarks in the ANSWER table should appear along with only those records for employees with "MD" in the State field.

Press F10 for the main menu, choose Report/Design, and enter **ANSWER** for the table name. From the next menu that appears, choose 1 as a name and enter **TEST1** as a description for the report. Select Free-Form from the next menu that appears, press ENTER and then press Do-It! (F2) to store the default free-form report.

Press F10 for the main menu, choose Report/Output, and enter **ANSWER** as the table name. Choose 1 for the name of the report from the menu that appears, and select Printer or Screen as desired. The report should resemble the one shown in Figure 12-2.

This technique of using default free-form reports along with ANSWER tables can prove quite useful when you need free-form listings such as address or telephone directories, or similar listings based on selective data. Keep in mind that if you want to generate such a report regularly, rename the ANSWER table so that the report will not be erased the next time you perform a query.

Before proceeding, press ALT-F8 to clear the workspace.

DESIGNING A CUSTOM FREE-FORM REPORT

You will probably want to change the default design of the free-form report to meet your own needs. As with tabular reports, Paradox provides extreme flexibility for free-form report design. You can rearrange the location of fields, delete unwanted

1/21/88   Test1   Page 1

Last name: Morse
First name: Marcia
Address: 4260 Park Avenue
City: Chevy Chase
State: MD
ZIP Code: 20815-0988

Last name: Morse
First name: William
Address: 4260 Park Avenue
City: Chevy Chase
State: MD
ZIP Code: 20815-0988

Last name: Robinson
First name: Shirley
Address: 267 Browning Ave #2A
City: Takoma Park
State: MD
ZIP Code: 20912

Last name: Westman
First name: Andrea
Address: 4807 East Avenue
City: Silver Spring
State: MD
ZIP Code: 20910-0124

FIGURE 12-2.   Example of report based on ANSWER table

fields, or add calculated or summary fields. You can also change margins and use grouping options to generate free-form reports with records divided into specific groups.

The basic steps involved in designing a custom free-form report are as follows:

1. Choose a table for the report.

2. Select a name (numeric designator) and enter a report description.

3. From the next menu that appears, choose Free-Form as the report type.
4. Modify the Report Specification that appears on the screen. By pressing F10, you can choose any of the available options that apply to free-form reports from the Report Design menu.
5. Press Do-It! (F2) or choose DO-IT! from the menu to save the report.

The Report Specification

The Report Specification is made up of several parts, as illustrated in Figure 12-3. The most significant part of a free-form report is the form band, which contains most fields that appear in the report. (Fields can appear in other bands, as in group bands, to identify the group.) Form bands are used in free-form reports, while table bands are used in columnar reports.

All items (table fields, calculated or summary fields, or literal text) that are placed within the form band appear once for each record in the table. Within the form band, you include the information (usually fields) that is needed in the body of the report. Since free-form reports do not limit you to placing the fields within specific columns, you can place them anywhere on the screen that they are needed. The values in the form band appear as *field masks*, with letters (such as AAAAA) indicating alphanu-

```
Field  Group  Output  Setting  Help  DO-IT!  Cancel              Report     1/1
Place, erase, reformat, justify, or wrap fields.
....+...10....+...20....+...30....+...40....+...50....+...60....+...70....+...8*

-▼page-----------------------------------------------------------------------

mm/dd/yy                          Test Report                        Page 999

 ——▼group State--------------------------------------------------------------

-▼form-----------------------------------------------------------------------

Last name: AAAAAAAAAAAAAAA
First name: AAAAAAAAAAAAAAA
Address: AAAAAAAAAAAAAAAAAAAAAAAAA
City: AAAAAAAAAAAAAAA
State: AA
ZIP Code: AAAAAAAAAA

-▲form-----------------------------------------------------------------------

 ——▲group State--------------------------------------------------------------

-▲page-----------------------------------------------------------------------
```

FIGURE 12-3. Parts of a Report Specification for free-form reports

meric fields, numbers (such as 999999) representing number fields, and mm/dd/yy designations representing date fields. Literal text can be placed anywhere to describe field contents or to provide other information within the report.

Free-form reports bear some similarities to tabular reports. Both make use of a page band, which appears once for each page of the report. Page bands can contain any page headers or footers you specify, along with dates, times, or page-number fields. Free-form reports can also contain group bands, which serve the same purpose as they do with tabular reports. Group bands are optional and are printed once for each group of records in the report. As an example of a group, you might prefer to print a free-form report of employees divided into groups by assignment. A single report can contain up to 16 group bands.

To modify the report, you will need the various options provided by the menu that appears when you press F10 while you are designing a free-form report. The menu provides the following options:

- *Field:* Use the Field option to place fields, change the format of fields, justify or wordwrap fields, include fields from linked tables (as detailed in Chapter 9), and delete unwanted fields.

- *Group:* Use the Group option to add, remove, or change the format for groupings within the report.

- *Output:* Use the Output option to generate a report (to the printer, screen, or file) while you are in the process of designing the report. This can be very helpful when you want to see if a report's format is satisfactory before you save the report.

- *Setting:* Use the Setting option to trim unwanted blank lines or spaces, change page layout dimensions, set margins, format for mailing labels, or enter setup strings and printer port configurations.

The Help, DO-IT!, and Cancel options perform the same tasks as they do elsewhere in Paradox.

The precise options that you choose from the menus while designing a free-form report will, of course, vary with your desired final design. The hands-on practice sessions in this chapter will demonstrate the more commonly used options that Paradox provides. For your reference, the common tasks you can perform while designing free-form reports are further outlined here:

- To place new fields, choose Field/Place from the Design menu, and then choose the type of field desired from the next menu that appears. If you select Regular as the field type, Paradox will display a menu of the available fields. If you select Summary or Calculated, you can enter an expression that will calculate the field.

If you select the Date or Time field, you can choose from among the available date or time formats.

- To remove fields, choose Field/Erase from the Design menu. Then place the cursor on the desired field and press RETURN to erase it. You can use CTRL-Y to delete an entire line.

- To edit headers or footers in the page band, place the cursor in the desired portion of the page band. Enter the desired heading or edit the existing headings. The page number and system date are fields, not literal text. You can remove or add these by selecting Field from the Design menu and using the Place option to place the fields or the Erase option to erase unwanted fields.

- To reformat fields, choose Field/Reformat from the Design menu. Then place the cursor in the field you want to reformat, and press RETURN to select the field. Enter a width, or select from the menu the desired format for the field.

- To add literal text (such as field titles), place the cursor at the desired location and type the desired text.

- To link the report to another table, choose Field/Lookup/Link. Enter the name of the other table, and then choose the key field from the list of fields that appears. (See Chapter 9 for more details on this topic.)

Saving the Report

After the desired changes have been made to the Report Specification, press Do-It! (F2) or choose DO-IT! from the menu to save the report.

HANDS-ON PRACTICE: CREATING A CUSTOM PERSONNEL LIST

In the case of ABC Temporaries, the managers want a custom personnel list that will resemble the format shown here:

(date)   Personnel List   (page no.)

Name: XXXXXXXXXXX XXXXXXXXXXXX Soc. Sec: 999-99-9999
Address: XXXXXXXXXXXXXXXXXXXXXXXXXXXXXXXXX
City: XXXXXXXXXXXXXXXX State: XX Zip Code: 99999

Date Born: MM/DD/YY   Date Hired: MM/DD/YY

Press F10, if necessary, for the main menu, and choose Report/Design. Enter **ABCSTAFF** as the table name. For the name of the report, choose 3 (or select another unused name if you have already used 3 for a different report). For a description, enter **PERSONNEL LIST**. Paradox now displays the following menu:

Tabular Free-Form
Print the information in rows and columns

Select Free-Form, and the Report Specification will appear.

Use the DEL key to delete the word "Last" from the Last name heading. Also delete the First name heading. Place the cursor at the start of the Social security heading. Press CTRL-Y to delete the line containing the Social security field. Next, place the cursor at the start of the First name field, press the INS key to get into Insert mode, and then press BACKSPACE (to pull the field up onto the prior line). Add a space between the last name and first name fields.

Move the cursor three spaces to the right of the First name field, and enter the following:

Soc. Sec:

Then press F10 for the menu, and choose Field/Place/Regular. Choose Social security from the list of fields, and then press RETURN twice, once to place the field and once to set the field width.

Place the cursor two spaces to the right of the City field, and enter the following:

State:

Then press F10, choose Field/Place/Regular, and select State. Press RETURN twice, once to place the field and once to set the field width.

Place the cursor two spaces to the right of the State field, and enter the following:

Zip Code:

Then press F10, choose Field/Place/Regular, and select Zip Code. Press RETURN twice, once to place the field and once to set the field width.

---Remember   Whenever you use CTRL-Y to delete a line, any field present on that line is also deleted.

Place the cursor at the start of the now unneeded State heading on the line below. Press CTRL-Y twice to delete the next two lines, and then press RETURN once to add an extra blank line. Move the cursor four spaces to the right of the end of the Date of birth field. Enter the following:

Date Hired:

Press F10, choose Field/Place/Regular, and select Date Hired. Choose the first date format from the next menu that appears. Press RETURN to place the field. Place the cursor at the start of the next line. Use the CTRL-Y key combination to delete the lines containing the extra unneeded Date hired field, along with the Dependents, Salary, Assignment, Hourly Rate, and Phone fields. Press RETURN again to add another blank line in the form band. This will add more blank space between records when the report is printed. When done, your Report Specification should resemble the example shown in Figure 12-4.

```
Designing report R3 for Abcstaff table                    Report Ins 1/1
Form Band
....+...10....+...20....+...30....+...40....+...50....+...60....+...70....+...8*

 -▼page─────────────────────────────────────────────────────────────────


 mm/dd/yy                         Personnel List                    Page 999

 -▼form─────────────────────────────────────────────────────────────────

 name: AAAAAAAAAAAAAAA AAAAAAAAAAAAAAA  Soc. Sec:AAAAAAAAAA
 Address: AAAAAAAAAAAAAAAAAAAAAAAAAA
 City: AAAAAAAAAAAAAAA  State:AA  Zip Code:AAAAAAAAA

 Date of birth: mm/dd/yy     Date Hired:mm/dd/yy

 -▲form─────────────────────────────────────────────────────────────────



 -▲page─────────────────────────────────────────────────────────────────
```

FIGURE 12-4.   Completed Report Specification

To test the design before saving the report, press F10 for the menu, and choose Output/Screen. When you have finished previewing the report, press Do-It! (F2) to save the report, and return to the workspace.

DESIGNING MAILING LABELS

You can use the free-form reports available within Paradox to generate mailing labels. The basic steps in this process involve designing a form band of the report to contain the fields desired in the label; removing all extra lines from the report bands and page bands; setting the page length to Continuous to avoid the usual page breaks that occur with normal printer paper; and using the LineSqueeze and FieldSqueeze options of the RemoveBlanks menu option to suppress blank lines and unwanted spaces. To generate more than one label per row of the page, simply add as many page widths as you need, and choose Labels from the Design menu to continue the printing.

Consider the example of creating mailing labels for ABC Temporaries in the "two-across" format. From the main menu, choose Report/Design, and choose ABCSTAFF as the table name. Select 4 as the report name, and enter **MAILING LABELS** as the description. Then choose Free-Form from the next menu, and the Report Specification will be displayed.

Place the cursor just below the page-band border, and press the Report Delete Line key (CTRL-Y) six times to remove the lines in the page heading. Move the cursor to the blank line above the Social security field and press CTRL-Y twice, once to delete the blank line and once to delete the line containing the Social security field.

Use the DEL key to delete the Last name heading. Move the cursor to the start of the First name heading. Go into Insert mode by pressing the INS key until "Ins" appears at the upper-right corner of the screen. Then press BACKSPACE once to backspace the existing carriage return and move the First name field onto the same line as the last name. Press the spacebar once to add a space, and then use the DEL key to delete the First name heading. Also use the DEL key to delete the headings for the Address and City fields, while leaving the fields intact.

Move the cursor down to the start of the State heading, and press CTRL-Y nine times to delete all of the remaining fields. Then press RETURN four times to add four extra blank lines. These will serve as spacing between the labels. In your own applications, you can add as many lines as are necessary to fit your particular labels.

Place the cursor two spaces to the right of the City field, press F10 for the menu, and choose Field/Place/Regular. Select State from the list of fields, and press RETURN twice to place the field and set the width.

Next, move the cursor two spaces to the right of the end of the State field, press F10 for the menu, and choose Field/Place/Regular. Select Zip Code from the list of fields, and press RETURN twice to place the field and set the width.

```
Designing report R4 for Abcstaff table                    Report Ins 1/1
Page Footer
....+...10....+...20....+...30....+...40....+...50....+...60....+...70....+...8*
                                                                             █
  —▼page—————————————————————————————————————————————————————————————————   █
  —▼form—————————————————————————————————————————————————————————————————   █
AAAAAAAAAAAAAAA AAAAAAAAAAAAAAA                                               █
AAAAAAAAAAAAAAAAAAAAAAAAAAA                                                   █
AAAAAAAAAAAAAAA AA AAAAAAAAA                                                  █
                                                                             █
                                                                             █
                                                                             █
  —▲form—————————————————————————————————————————————————————————————————   █
  —▲page—————————————————————————————————————————————————————————————————   █
                                                                             █
```

FIGURE 12-5.   Report Specification for mailing labels

Move the cursor below the form band and into the page band, and place the cursor at the left edge. Then press CTRL-Y four times to remove the extra blank lines. (Since this report will be used with mailing labels, no extra space, headers, or footers are necessary.)

At this point, your screen should resemble the example shown in Figure 12-5. You can visually check the results while still designing the report by using the Output option of the Report Specification menu. Press F10 for the menu, and choose Output. Select Screen from the next menu that appears, and you should see a report that resembles this:

```
Westman      Andrea
4807 East Avenue
Silver Spring   MD         20910-0124


Robinson     Shirley
267 Browning Ave #2A
Takoma Park    MD          20912


Morse        Marcia
4260 Park Avenue
Chevy Chase    MD          20815-0988
```

This report approximates the appearance of mailing labels, but there are obviously a few problems. The names have too much space between them, as do the City and State fields. This is because Paradox is using the default lengths of the fields.

The RemoveBlanks menu option can be used to solve this problem. Finish previewing the report, press F10 for the menu, and choose Setting. The following menu options will appear:

RemoveBlanks PageLayout Margin Setup Wait Labels
Specify removing blank lines or field positions.

The RemoveBlanks option lets you tell Paradox to trim extra leading or trailing blank spaces, or to suppress the printing of blank lines when a field is empty.

Choose RemoveBlanks from the menu. The next menu offers the following options:

LineSqueeze FieldSqueeze
Suppress printing of lines which have all fields blank.

The LineSqueeze option tells Paradox to suppress the printing of lines when all of the fields in that line are blank. The FieldSqueeze option suppresses extra spaces between fields. Choose FieldSqueeze from the menu, and then choose Yes from the next menu to confirm the action.

This will put the names closer together, but the labels will still print last name first. However, a more pleasant appearance would be to show the first name, followed by the last name. To accomplish this, the name fields must be moved. Place the cursor at the start of the Last name field, and make sure you are in Insert mode (press the INS key until "Ins" appears at the upper-right corner of the screen). Press the spacebar once to push the Last name field to the right one space.

Press F10 for the menu, and choose Field/Erase. Place the cursor within the Firstname field, and press RETURN to remove the field. Then move the cursor back to the far left, to the space you inserted beside the Last name field. Press F10 for the menu, choose Field/Place/Regular, and choose First name from the list of fields that appears. Then, press RETURN twice to complete the placement of the field.

For one last aesthetic touch, move the cursor to the space immediately following the City field, and insert a comma. This will cause a comma to appear between each city and state when the report is printed.

You can immediately see the results by using the Output option of the Report Specification menu. Press F10 for the menu, and choose Output. Select Screen from the next menu that appears, and this time you should see a report with names and addresses in a format resembling this:

Andrea Westman
4807 East Avenue
Silver Spring, MD 20910-0124

Shirley Robinson
267 Browning Ave #2A
Takoma Park, MD 20912

Marcia Morse
4260 Park Avenue
Chevy Chase, MD 20815-0988

All that remains is to provide the labels in the "two-across" format, which prints two names across the label. To perform this task, you will add a page width for each additional label you need across the page, and you will use the Labels option of the menu to tell Paradox to use a "print-across" format.

You will need to adjust the width of the pages, since labels are not normally 80 characters wide each. Press F10 for the menu, and choose Setting/PageLayout/Width. Backspace through the default width of 80, and enter **40** as the new width for the mailing labels. Press F10 for the menu again, and choose Setting. From the next menu that appears, select PageLayout. Choose Insert to add the second page width.

Finally, press F10 for the menu once more, and choose Setting/Labels. Then select Yes to confirm the use of the mailing-label format. If you again test your design by pressing F10 and choosing Output/Screen, you should see an example similar in format to the one shown here (your names may be in a different order):

Andrea Westman   Shirley Robinson
4807 East Avenue   267 Browning Ave #2A
Silver Spring, MD 20910-0124   Takoma Park, MD 20912

Wanda Robinson   Sandra Abernathy
1607 21st Street, NW   1512 Redskins Park Drive
Washington, DC 20009   Herndon, VA 22071

Mary Jo Mitchell   Judi Jones
617 North Oakland Street   5203 North Shore Drive
Arlington, VA 22203   Reston, VA 22090

This looks fine on-screen, but when you print the labels you'll also want the page length set to Continuous to match continuous-form labels. Press F10 and choose Setting/PageLayout/Length. Backspace the existing value, and enter C to set the page length to Continuous.

> **Note** If you use sheet labels with a laser printer, leave the Setting/PageLayout/Length value at 66 or less. With Hewlett- Packard LaserJet printers, a value of 60 often works well.

Finally, press Do-It! (F2) to save the report. You can generate the report at any time with the usual menu options of Report/Output followed by the name of the table and of the report, and then the choice of output destinations (Printer, Screen, or File).

When dealing with mailing labels, remember that they can be difficult to align in the printer. You may want to experiment with sheets of ordinary paper first, before trying to print on the actual labels.

You can make changes as needed to fit your preferred size of labels. For example, if less space is desired between labels, remove blank lines with CTRL-Y; if more space is needed, make sure you are in Insert mode (press the INS key until the letters "Ins" appear in the upper-right corner of the screen), and then press RETURN where you want to add new blank lines. You can use the various options displayed when you choose Settings/PageLayout to change your page widths, lengths, or the number of labels that appear across a page. Be sure to choose the Labels option from the menu when you are designing a report that will provide mailing labels, so Paradox will print across in the proper format.

FORM LETTERS

You can also generate form letters with a free-form report. Since literal text can be entered anywhere you wish within the form band of the free-form report, you can simply type the text of the form letter into the report's form band. Insert the fields at the desired locations; use the FieldSqueeze option (from the menu, you choose Setting/RemoveBlanks/FieldSqueeze) to close up any excess space between the contents of fields and the literal text that makes up the letter. An example of a free-form report designed as a form letter appears in Figure 12-6.

Note the presence of the reserved word "PAGEBREAK" in this report form. Use this reserved word to tell Paradox to start a new page. The word "PAGEBREAK" must appear on a line by itself, flush at the left margin, and it must be in uppercase letters.

Depending on where you place "PAGEBREAK," you will get different results. For example, if you place the word at the header or footer of a group, Paradox will start a

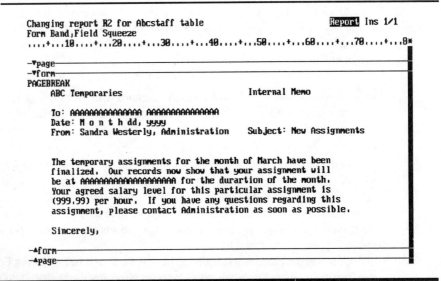

```
Changing report R2 for Abcstaff table                    Report  Ins 1/1
Form Band,Field Squeeze
....+...10....+...20....+...30....+...40....+...50....+...60....+...70....+...8*
 -▼page─────────────────────────────────────────────────────────────────
 -▼form─────────────────────────────────────────────────────────────────
PAGEBREAK
    ABC Temporaries                         Internal Memo

    To: AAAAAAAAAAAAAA AAAAAAAAAAAAAA
    Date: M o n t h dd, yyyy
    From: Sandra Westerly, Administration   Subject: New Assignments


    The temporary assignments for the month of March have been
    finalized.  Our records now show that your assignment will
    be at AAAAAAAAAAAAAAAAAAAA for the durartion of the month.
    Your agreed salary level for this particular assignment is
    (999.99) per hour.  If you have any questions regarding this
    assignment, please contact Administration as soon as possible.

    Sincerely,

 -▲form─────────────────────────────────────────────────────────────────
 -▲page─────────────────────────────────────────────────────────────────
```

FIGURE 12-6. Example of form letter

new page for each group. If you place it at the start of a form band, each record will occupy a separate page.

CREATING INVOICES

You can generate invoices by designing free-form reports to contain calculated fields or summary fields. Consider the ABC Temporaries billing task. Each client needs an invoice that shows the hours worked and a total amount due for the employees who worked for that client. The Report Specification shown in Figure 12-7 could handle this need.

This particular report is based on an ANSWER table that draws data from the ABCSTAFF and HOURS tables. The tables are linked through an example element in the Social security field. The Assignment, Weekend date, and Hours worked fields from the HOURS table are selected for inclusion in the ANSWER table, as are the Last name, First name, and Hourly Rate fields from the ABCSTAFF table. The calculated field shown next to the total heading for each employee is a result of the expression

[Hours worked] * [Hourly Rate]

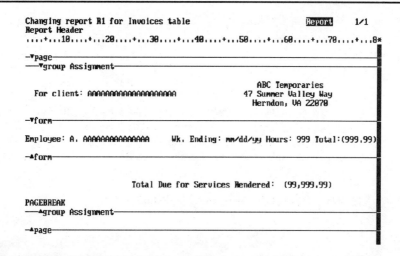

```
Changing report R1 for Invoices table                    Report    1/1
Report Header
....+...10....+...20....+...30....+...40....+...50....+...60....+...70....+...8*
 ─▼page───────────────────────────────────────────────────────────────────
 ───▼group Assignment──────────────────────────────────────────────────────

                                                 ABC Temporaries
       For client: AAAAAAAAAAAAAAAAAA           47 Summer Valley Way
                                                 Herndon, VA 22070

 ─▼form────────────────────────────────────────────────────────────────────

 Employee: A. AAAAAAAAAAAAAA     Wk. Ending: mm/dd/yy Hours: 999 Total:(999.99)
 ─▲form────────────────────────────────────────────────────────────────────


                    Total Due for Services Rendered:  (99,999.99)

 PAGEBREAK
 ───▲group Assignment──────────────────────────────────────────────────────
 ─▲page───────────────────────────────────────────────────────────────────
```

FIGURE 12-7.   Report Specification for invoices

and the summary field shown next to the "Total Due for Services Rendered" heading
is a summary field based upon a calculated field (with the same expression).

To create the summary field, select Field/Place/Summary/Calculated. Then the
expression just given is entered. The Sum option is chosen from the next menu that
appears, and PerGroup is selected to indicate that the field will show a summary total
for each group (or client). Finally, the field is placed in the desired location. The results
of a report following this design are shown in Figure 12-8.

Without the addition of the reserved word "PAGEBREAK" in the Report Specification shown in Figure 12-7, the billings would print in a continous format. The
PAGEBREAK notation causes each assignment group to print on a separate page.

FINAL ADVICE

The majority of operations you will perform when designing reports are the same with
tabular reports as with free-form reports. The main differences are that with tabular
reports, the Setting menu includes the options Formats and GroupRepeats. With
free-form reports, however, these options are not available. Instead, two new options
are offered, Labels and RemoveBlanks. All other options are the same between the
two types of reports, and you can perform similar steps to design your tabular or

For client: City Revenue Dept.

ABC Temporaries
47 Summer Valley Way
Herndon, VA 22071

Employee: S. Abernathy   Wk Ending: 1/16/88 Hours: 28 Total: 504.00
Employee: S. Abernathy   Wk Ending: 1/23/88 Hours: 32 Total: 576.00
Employee: D. Jackson   Wk Ending: 1/16/88 Hours: 30 Total: 360.00
Employee: D. Jackson   Wk Ending: 1/23/88 Hours: 30 Total: 360.00
Employee: W. Robinson   Wk Ending: 1/16/88 Hours: 35 Total: 420.00
Employee: W. Robinson   Wk Ending: 1/23/88 Hours: 32 Total: 384.00

Total Due for Services Rendered: 2,604.00

For client: National Oil Co.

ABC Temporaries
47 Summer Valley Way
Herndon, VA 22071

Employee: J. Jones   Wk Ending: 1/16/88 Hours: 35 Total: 612.50
Employee: J. Jones   Wk Ending: 1/23/88 Hours: 33 Total: 577.50
Employee: M. Morse   Wk Ending: 1/16/88 Hours: 32 Total: 480.00
Employee: S. Robinson   Wk Ending: 1/16/88 Hours: 27 Total: 324.00
Employee: A. Westman   Wk Ending: 1/16/88 Hours: 30 Total: 720.00
Employee: A. Westman   Wk Ending: 1/23/88 Hours: 35 Total: 840.00

Total Due for Services Rendered: 3,554.00

For client: Smith Builders

ABC Temporaries
47 Summer Valley Way
Herndon, VA 22071

Employee: E. Hart   Wk Ending: 1/23/88 Hours: 30 Total: 420.00
Employee: M. Mitchell   Wk Ending: 1/23/88 Hours: 28 Total: 336.00
Employee: W. Morse   Wk Ending: 1/23/88 Hours: 35 Total: 420.00

Total Due for Services Rendered: 1,176.00

FIGURE 12-8.   Example of an invoice

free-form reports. See Chapter 7 (if you have not already read it) for additional important details on report design.

QUICK SUMMARY

To quickly create a default free-form report   Press F10 for the menu, and choose Report/Design. Enter the name for the table on which to base the report. Choose a name and enter a description for the report when prompted. Select Free-Form from the next menu, then press Do-It! (F2) to store the default report.

To create a custom free-form report   Press F10 for the menu, and choose Report/Design. Enter the name for the table on which to base the report. Choose a name and enter a description for the report when prompted. Select Free-Form from the next menu. Modify the Report Specification that appears on the screen. (Press F10 to use the available menu options for placing and moving fields, adding group bands, and changing settings.) When done with the report's design, press Do-It! (F2) to store the report.

chapter **13**

USING
THE PERSONAL
PROGRAMMER

If you have followed this text closely, you have a good understanding of how you can put Paradox to work. You have created different tables, used the menu choices for getting information from those tables, designed custom reports, and used scripts to automate your work. However, what may for many people be the most advanced feature of Paradox has been saved for this chapter.

The Paradox Personal Programmer is a complete development tool that you can use to create complete applications, with custom menus and help screens, for the users of your tables, reports, and forms. And you need not learn to program to create these applications; you can create them by choosing from a series of menu selections.

Note that the Paradox Personal Programmer does require a hard disk with at least 3.5MB of free space and 640K of memory (595K of free RAM; use the DOS CHKDSK command to check available memory). You *cannot* run the Paradox Personal Programmer on a machine that lacks a hard disk.

AN APPLICATION, DEFINED

Why are applications so important to database users? In a nutshell, an application makes things easier on the average user by combining a series of "building blocks" (such as tables, forms, reports, and scripts) into a complete system. An application is what makes an accounts receivable database different from an accounts payable database. Both systems may deal with the same kinds of information—dollar amounts and the bills, addressed to recipients, that contain breakdowns of those amounts. However, the accounts receivable database is designed to deal with outsiders sending money to the company, while the accounts payable database deals with the company sending money to outsiders.

The fields used in the tables for both systems could be quite similar in nature, but the job handled by the systems would be noticeably different. Paradox provides the tools necessary to handle either task; but it is the application that makes the systems perform differently.

Besides helping you meet the needs of a specific task, an application binds together the building blocks of a database. If you consider the parts of a Paradox database—one or more tables, the forms, and the reports—to be building blocks of a sort, the application can be thought of as the frame that holds these blocks together, making them a complete operating unit. An application is a customized menu system that helps organize and automate the operations involved in managing the database.

Applications are nothing new in the computer world, and there is a good chance that you have already used some types of specialized applications with a database of some sort. Programs to handle mailing lists, inventory, sales tracking, and accounting are all specialized applications that make use of databases. But to use these types of applications, you had to buy a software package designed for the application (or pay a programmer to write it), and then you were often stuck with something that did most—but not all—of what you wanted. With the Paradox Personal Programmer, you can build custom applications designed to do precisely what you want, without learning programming and without hiring a programmer.

Much of what you need to know in order to use the Paradox Personal Programmer is already familiar to you if you read through the rest of this book. The Paradox Personal Programmer uses the same kinds of menus as you have seen throughout Paradox. In addition, a series of help screens are displayed the entire time you use the Paradox Personal Programmer, explaining your options each step of the way.

THE DESIGN OF A TYPICAL APPLICATION

To further illustrate how an application can make things easier for you, consider the work you have done throughout this book (if you have followed the examples) to create a usable system for ABC Temporaries. You have tables for tracking both employees and the time worked for clients, and you have custom forms and custom reports. With your familiarity with Paradox, if you want to add or edit data or generate reports, you can load Paradox and use the various menu options to accomplish the desired results.

What happens, however, when you want to show someone else in the office how to add or edit data, or how to produce reports? That person must go through the same kind of learning process to become familiar with the Paradox menus in order to accomplish the same kind of results that you can manage. If your office has a moderate-to-high staff turnover, which is common in today's business world, you might have to show people how to use Paradox over and over, for the same application, year in and year out.

The answer to this sort of dilemma, as proven by thousands of programmers year after year, is to build custom applications with menu choices that casual users will need no specialized training to understand. While the act of filling in a Query Form may now seem like child's play to you, to someone who has never seen a Query Form before, it will seem like mastering a foreign language. Rather than present a Query Form to the casual user, a custom application will display a custom prompt asking for a value. The Paradox Personal Programmer lets you design the application to communicate in terms that people in your office will understand.

As an example, the employees of ABC Temporaries commonly need to perform the following tasks:

- Add employees to the ABCSTAFF table

- Edit employees in the ABCSTAFF table

- Add client time to the HOURS table

- Edit client time in the HOURS table

- Display a list of employees on the screen

- Print a list of employees

- Display a list of client time records

- Print a list of client time records

You can automate these tasks by using the Paradox Personal Programmer to create an application. The application will provide a menu choice for each task. If you were to try to sketch out the design of such an application on paper, it might resemble the chart shown in Figure 13-1. The example design makes use of two menus, a main menu and secondary menu, or submenu. The secondary menu contains all of the choices for generating reports. As you design your own applications, you may find the use of secondary menus for specific areas, such as working with a particular table or generating reports, to be a wise idea. If you try to place too many menu choices on a single menu, the application can become visually confusing.

When designing any application, it is usually helpful to sketch out a preliminary design on paper before you start to use the Paradox Personal Programmer. Having the design outlined in this manner can give you a reference point to work from when you are actually building the application.

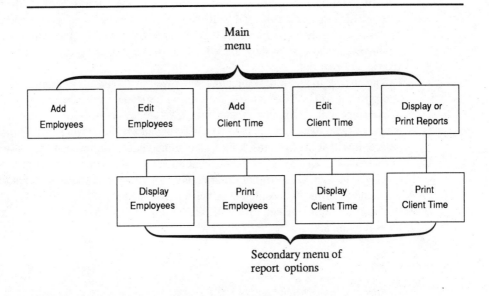

FIGURE 13-1.   Design of application for ABC Temporaries

INSTALLING THE PARADOX PERSONAL PROGRAMMER

Before using the Paradox Personal Programmer, you must install it. The Paradox Personal Programmer is *not* automatically installed as a part of the normal Paradox installation procedure, although you can select a menu option to install it during the installation process. The installation process differs with your version of Paradox (DOS or OS/2), so in all cases you should refer to the chapter on installation in the *Guide to the Paradox Personal Programmer* (contained with your Paradox documentation).

If you are using Paradox with DOS, you can switch to the C:\PDOX35 subdirectory, insert the Installation Disk in drive A, and then enter

A:INSTALL

From the menu that appears, choose Optional Software Installation to begin the installation of the Paradox Personal Programmer. Refer to your Paradox documentation for additional details on the installation, and follow the prompts that appear on the screen to complete the installation process.

An Important Note For DOS Users

As indicated in the installation section of the *Guide to the Paradox Personal Programmer*, you should update your PATH command for the Paradox Personal Programmer to operate with DOS while you are using other subdirectories. The Paradox Personal Programmer installation process normally places the Paradox Personal Programmer files in a subdirectory named \PDOX35\PPROG. The PATH command contained in your AUTOEXEC.BAT file should set a path to this subdirectory.

You can update your AUTOEXEC.BAT file with any word processor that can load and save files as ASCII text, or with the DOS COPY command (see your DOS manual for details on this command). As an example, a typical AUTOEXEC.BAT file that provides a path to both the PDOX35 and the PPROG subdirectories might resemble the following:

```
date
path=c:\perfect;c:\;c:\fastback;c:\pdox35;c:\pdox35\pprog
prompt $p$g
cls
type menu
```

If you prefer not to change your AUTOEXEC.BAT file, you can put a PATH command into effect just before starting the Paradox Personal Programmer by typing the command at that time. For example, assuming your hard disk was on drive C, you could enter

PATH=C:\PDOX35;C:\PDOX35\PPROG

at the DOS prompt to set the needed path. Doing this (or updating your AU-TOEXEC.BAT file) will allow you to store your applications in different subdirectories of your choice and run the Paradox Personal Programmer from any of those subdirectories. Another option is to include a command like the previous one in a batch file to be run when you want to use the Personal Programmer. An example would be

```
path=\dos;\pdox35;\pdox35\pprog
pprog
path=\dos;\fastback
```

Note that you should include the DOS directory in the path if you want to use the ToDos option.

USING THE PARADOX PERSONAL PROGRAMMER

Once you have established the proper path, switch to the subdirectory that contains the tables, reports, and forms you will be using in the application. (You can create the tables, forms, and reports from within the Paradox Personal Programmer, but building the application will take considerably less time if the building blocks already exist when you start the Personal Programmer.)

From the DOS prompt, enter **PPROG**. In a moment, you will see the main menu for the Paradox Personal Programmer. It resembles the example shown in Figure 13-2. The bottom half of the screen displays various help messages, which provide additional details about the steps you are performing. At the top of the screen are the following menu options:

Create Modify Summarize Review Play Tools Exit
Create a new application.

The Create option lets you create a new application, while the Modify option lets you change an existing application. The Summarize option is used to print a summary of an existing application, and the Review option lets you review the menu selections for an application. Use the Play option to play an application (or to play any Paradox script). The Tools option lets you copy, delete, and rename applications, change settings, and change the default directory. Finally, the Exit choice lets you leave the Paradox Personal Programmer and return to the operating system.

Because the Paradox Personal Programmer is a very flexible tool that can be molded to fit your specific needs, the process of designing an application will vary significantly from application to application. However, the basic steps involved in each case do not differ. These steps include the following:

1. Choose Create from the Paradox Personal Programmer main menu.

2. Select the tables that the application will work with. An application can have up to 15 tables; they can be used on an individual basis or can be used in combination to produce relational reports or multitable forms.

3. Build the menu structure for the application by defining the main menu and any submenus.

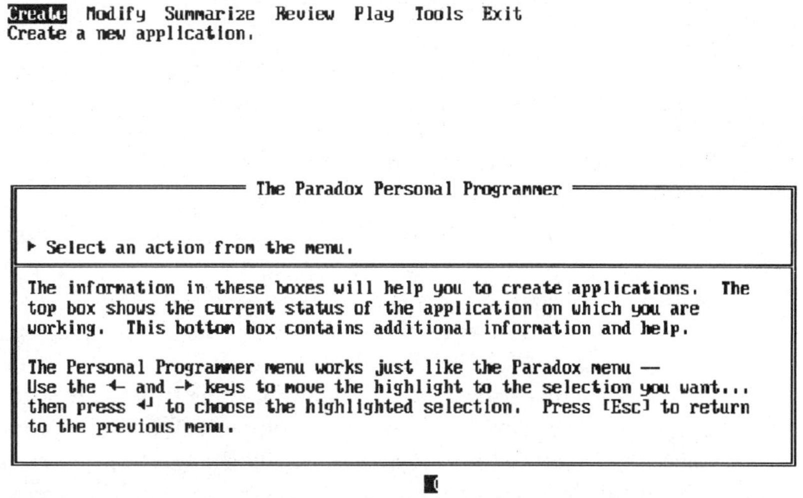

Create Modify Summarize Review Play Tools Exit
Create a new application.

```
================= The Paradox Personal Programmer =================

 ▸ Select an action from the menu.
-------------------------------------------------------------------
The information in these boxes will help you to create applications.  The
top box shows the current status of the application on which you are
working.  This bottom box contains additional information and help.

The Personal Programmer menu works just like the Paradox menu —
Use the ← and → keys to move the highlight to the selection you want...
then press ◄┘ to choose the highlighted selection.  Press [Esc] to return
to the previous menu.
```

FIGURE 13-2. Main menu for Paradox Personal Programmer

4. Define each menu option by telling the Paradox Personal Programmer which actions it should take when the option is selected by the user at run time.

5. As an option, design a *splash screen* for the application, which is an introductory screen containing text of your choosing. This screen is seen by the user each time the application is started.

6. Press Do-It! (F2) to tell the Personal Programmer to write the application.

7. Exit from the Paradox Personal Programmer. You can then run the application just as you would run any other Paradox script.

HANDS-ON PRACTICE: USING THE PERSONAL PROGRAMMER

To provide an actual example you can follow, the next portion of this chapter will demonstrate how you can use the Paradox Personal Programmer to create an application for the ABC Temporaries database you have constructed throughout this book. The application will need the following tables, forms, and reports:

- The ABCSTAFF table created in Chapter 3

- The HOURS table created in Chapter 4

- The custom form for the ABCSTAFF table created in Chapter 5

- The custom report for the ABCSTAFF table created in Chapter 7

If you have not yet created any of these items, you should refer back to the appropriate chapters and do so before proceeding. Also, if you have not yet installed the Paradox Personal Programmer, do so before you proceed.

Switch to the directory containing the ABC Temporaries tables and other Paradox objects (probably C:\PDOX35, unless you are using a different directory by choice). Start the Paradox Personal Programmer by entering **PPROG** from the DOS prompt. (If you see the response "Bad command or file name," you have not properly modified your PATH command; see the previous installation section in this chapter for details.)

As the Paradox Personal Programmer loads, you will briefly see an introductory screen. Then the main menu for the Paradox Personal Programmer will appear, as shown in Figure 13-2. At the top of the screen are the menu options. The bottom half of the screen displays the help messages that provide additional details about the steps you are performing.

In this case, you want to create a new application for ABC Temporaries, so choose Create from the main menu. The Paradox Personal Programmer will next display the following prompt:

Application name:
Enter a name for the new application.

Names for your applications can be one to five characters long; they must not include spaces. In this case, enter **STAFF** as the application name. In a moment, the Paradox Personal Programmer will display the following menu:

ExistingTable NewTable RemoveTable DO-IT! Cancel
Choose an existing table to use in the application.

At this point, you must tell the Personal Programmer which tables you want to use in the application. You can use up to 15 tables in an application, but you cannot select temporary tables (you would not want to anyway, since you never know for sure whether they will be present or not).

Choose ExistingTable from the menu. Enter **ABCSTAFF** as the desired table name. The table name ABCSTAFF will appear under the "Selected tables" heading below the menu.

Choose ExistingTable again from the menu. This time, enter **HOURS** as the desired table. Then choose DO-IT! from the menu (or press F2) to tell the Personal Programmer that these are all the tables you will use in your application.

The next menu prompt will display the names of your tables, and you will be asked to enter a description of each of them. For ABCSTAFF, enter **Personnel Listing**, and for the HOURS table, enter **Client Time Records**.

When you have entered the descriptions, the Personal Programmer will save the information, and then the screen shown in Figure 13-3 will appear. From this screen, you design the main menu of the application. You may recall from earlier in the chapter that the choices for the ABC Temporaries main menu would be as follows:

1. Add employees

2. Edit employees

3. Add client time

4. Edit client time

5. Display or print reports

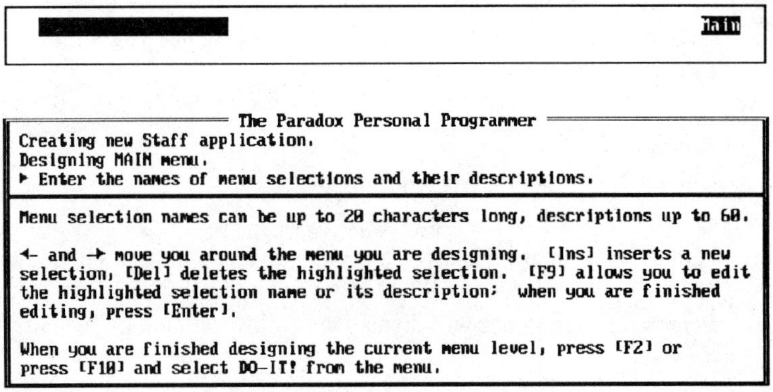

```
┌──────────────────────────────────────────────────────────────────────┐
│ ██████████████████████                                          Main  │
└──────────────────────────────────────────────────────────────────────┘
```

```
┌════════════════════ The Paradox Personal Programmer ═════════════════┐
│ Creating new Staff application.                                       │
│ Designing MAIN menu.                                                  │
│ ▶ Enter the names of menu selections and their descriptions.          │
├───────────────────────────────────────────────────────────────────────┤
│ Menu selection names can be up to 28 characters long, descriptions up to 60. │
│                                                                       │
│ ←- and -→ move you around the menu you are designing.  [Ins] inserts a new │
│ selection; [Del] deletes the highlighted selection.  [F9] allows you to edit │
│ the highlighted selection name or its description;  when you are finished │
│ editing, press [Enter].                                               │
│                                                                       │
│ When you are finished designing the current menu level, press [F2] or │
│ press [F10] and select DO-IT! from the menu.                          │
└───────────────────────────────────────────────────────────────────────┘
```

FIGURE 13-3.   Main menu design screen

For the first menu choice, enter

Add Employees

Once you enter the menu choice, the cursor will move to a longer field below, and you can enter a description for the choice. This description will appear when the menu choice is highlighted while the application is in use. Therefore, it is a wise idea to think carefully about what you put in this field when you are designing your own applications. Clear, friendly explanations can make things much easier for the users of your applications.

In this case, enter

Add new employees to personnel list

as the description. Finish the entry with RETURN, and the cursor moves to the right, highlighting what will become the second menu choice from your application's main menu. Enter

Edit Employees

for the second menu choice. For the description below, enter

Edit existing records for personnel

For the third menu choice, enter

Add Weekly Time

For the accompanying description, enter

Add week ending timesheet data from an employee

For the fourth menu choice, enter

Edit/Delete Time

as the choice. As an accompanying description, enter

Edit or delete a timesheet record

The next option of the main menu will provide access to another menu, for a choice of different reports. Enter

Reports

as the menu choice, and enter

Display or print reports

as an accompanying description.

You have now finished defining the options for the application's main menu, so press Do-It! (F2). Within a moment, a new screen will appear, similar to the one shown in Figure 13-4. From this screen (and others like it), you will tell the Personal Programmer what actions to take when certain menu selections are chosen in your application. Also, note that the Add Employees menu action you entered earlier is flashing; this indicates that you must now specify an action for this particular menu choice.

Choose SpecifyAction from the menu to specify the action for your menu choices. The next menu to appear shows the following options:

Menu View Report DataEntry Edit Script Help NotDefined Cancel
Attach a submenu to the current menu selection.

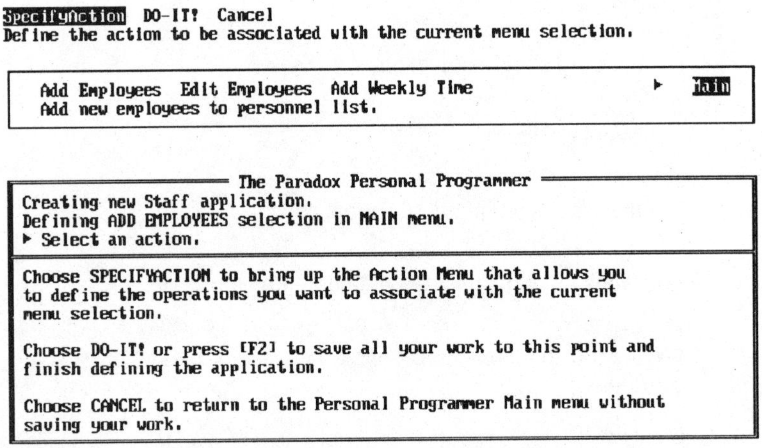

```
Specifyaction DO-IT! Cancel
Define the action to be associated with the current menu selection.

┌─────────────────────────────────────────────────────────────────────┐
│ Add Employees  Edit Employees  Add Weekly Time              ►   Main  │
│ Add new employees to personnel list.                                  │
└─────────────────────────────────────────────────────────────────────┘


┌══════════════ The Paradox Personal Programmer ═══════════════┐
│ Creating new Staff application.                                │
│ Defining ADD EMPLOYEES selection in MAIN menu.                 │
│ ► Select an action.                                            │
├────────────────────────────────────────────────────────────────┤
│ Choose SPECIFYACTION to bring up the Action Menu that allows you │
│ to define the operations you want to associate with the current │
│ menu selection.                                                  │
│                                                                  │
│ Choose DO-IT! or press [F2] to save all your work to this point and │
│ finish defining the application.                                 │
│                                                                  │
│ Choose CANCEL to return to the Personal Programmer Main menu without │
│ saving your work.                                                │
└──────────────────────────────────────────────────────────────────┘
```

FIGURE 13-4.   Screen used to define selections

You can select the appropriate choice for the action that you want your application to take when the user selects this item from the menu.

Since you will need to add employees in response to this item, select DataEntry as your choice. In a moment, another menu appears.

SelectTable AllTables DO-IT! Cancel
Select a table to use in the current operation.

You can choose whether the DataEntry operation is to apply to all tables simultaneously or to selected tables. Choose SelectTable to add to a single table. From the next menu that appears, choose ABCSTAFF as the table to add records to.

Choose DO-IT! or press F2. The Personal Programmer now asks if you want to display the information in a form view, a table view, or if you want to allow users to toggle between both views. For this example, choose FormView from the menu.

The next menu to appear shows these choices:

Design Borrow StandardForm
Design a new form to use in the current operation.

You could create the form from scratch with Design, use an existing form with Borrow, or choose StandardForm to accept a default form. Since you already created a custom form in Chapter 5 for this table, you can take advantage of that form. Choose Borrow from the menu. From the menu of available forms that next appears, choose 1 (your Personnel Updates custom form). After making your selection, you will see this menu:

Settings DO-IT! Cancel
Create validity checks and image settings.

You can add validity checks and image settings to the form if you wish. In this case, none are wanted, so choose DO-IT! or press F2, and the definitions for your first menu choice will be stored.

The Edit Employees option appears next, and you must perform similar steps to pick an action in response to this menu choice. Choose Edit as your desired action. From the next menu that appears, choose SelectTable, and then enter **ABCSTAFF** as the table to edit. Choose DO-IT! or press F2. You will now see the following menu:

SelectRecords AllRecords
Use a query to specify the records to be shown in this operation.

In the case of an edit, you can allow all records to be edited, or you can design the application so that a specific record is edited. For practice, you will design the application to allow this table to be edited, based on a specific record. Choose SelectRecords from the menu. A Query Form will soon appear.

Before you try to enter checkmarks or examples, be warned that entering data into this Query Form is slightly different from what you are used to in Paradox. You cannot use checkmarks or example elements here. However, you can provide application users with the ability to provide the selection criteria while the application is running. You do this by entering *tilde variables* in place of actual values in the Query Form. Tilde variables are variables preceded by a tilde character (~). When the Personal Programmer sees a tilde variable in the Query Form, it will ask you to supply a prompt. The user will see this prompt and respond to it with the data that finds its way into the actual query.

In this case, you need to allow the application user to enter a social security number in the Social security field. Since social security numbers are unique for each employee, this method of editing will ensure selection of the desired record. Move the cursor to the Social security field, and enter the following:

~ZRESPONSE

Note that the word "ZRESPONSE" is simply a variable in which Paradox will store the user's response when the application runs. The actual word used here is not important—but the tilde symbol is.

Press F2, and the message "Scanning query" will momentarily appear in the lower-right corner. In a moment, you will see the following:

Prompt:
Enter the prompt for variable "ZRESPONSE".

The Personal Programmer needs to know what prompt (or message) it should display to the user when the editing operation is performed. The Query Form needs to have a valid social security number entered, so you should supply the following prompt:

Enter the social security number:

Press RETURN when you have finished entering the prompt. The Personal Programmer will now display the following:

Data type: A11
Enter the data type for variable "ZRESPONSE"

The Personal Programmer is assuming that a data type that is the same as the Social security field type (alphanumeric, 11 characters) should be used for the variable. This is a correct assumption, so press RETURN to accept the data type. If you perform complex work with queries based on dates, numbers, or calculations, these kinds of assumptions that the Personal Programmer makes may not always be correct, and you may have to change them. Your PAL user's guide offers additional information on the advanced topics of using variables in applications.

The next menu to appear asks which type of view is to be used to edit the records. You can again use the same custom form you used for data entry, so choose FormView and then Borrow. Choose 1 from the menu of available forms to use the Personnel Updates form. In a moment, the following menu appears:

Settings InsertDelete DO-IT! Cancel
Create validity checks and image settings.

Again, validity check settings are not needed. However, the InsertDelete option of this menu is worth noting. If you want your users to be able to add or delete records while editing a table, you can choose Insert/Delete and then Yes to provide this capability. For now, choose DO-IT! or press F2 to save the definitions for the Edit Employees choice of the main menu.

The next choice, Add Weekly Time, must allow the addition of records to the HOURS table. Choose DataEntry from the menu. From the next menu, choose SelectTable, and enter **HOURS** as the desired table. Then choose DO-IT! or press F2.

For the desired form, choose FormView from the next menu to appear. Choose StandardForm to accept the default form for the HOURS table. Then choose DO-IT! or press F2 to save the definitions.

The next choice to appear is Edit/Delete Time. For the sake of this example, you will use a different approach here—you will allow users to edit all records in a table view, rather than selecting a single record in a form view. Choose Edit from the menu. From the next menu that appears, choose SelectTable, and then choose HOURS as the desired table. Choose DO-IT! or press F2.

For the type of display, choose TableView from the next menu. When the menu for choosing settings and insert/delete options next appears, choose Insert/Delete, then Delete, and then Yes to permit the deletion of records during editing. Finally, choose DO-IT! or press F2 to save the definitions for this menu choice. Note that key fields should not be edited when using the Personal Programmer. To change a key field in a Personal Programmer application, you should delete and re-enter the record.

The Reports option is now flashing on the screen, and the Personal Programmer asks you to define the actions for that menu option. This menu choice must lead to yet another menu, because you want to offer four different report choices. To do so on the main menu would clutter the screen, so choose Menu as your next action to define an additional menu.

Within a moment, a screen for new menu choices will appear. These choices will appear on the secondary menu of the application, whenever the user selects Reports as a main menu choice.

In the case of ABC Temporaries, you may recall the following desires for the report choices, as shown in Figure 13-1:

1. Display the employee list

2. Print the employee list

3. Display the client time records

4. Print the client time records

For the first option, enter

Display Employees

As a description, enter

Display the employee list on screen

For the second option, enter

Print Employees

As a description, enter

Print the employee list

For the third option, enter

Display Client Time

As a description, enter

Display the client time records on screen

For the fourth option, enter

Print Client Time

As a description, enter

Print the client time records

As a last menu option, enter

Cancel Reports

As a description, enter

Return to prior menu

Press F2 to complete the secondary menu design. In a moment, the Display Employees option begins flashing, and you must define an action for this option. Choose SpecifyAction, and then select Report. From the next menu, choose SelectTable, and then choose ABCSTAFF as the table to produce the report. Press F2, or choose DO-IT! from the menu.

From the next menu, choose AllRecords so that all records will be included in the report. When the next menu appears, choose Borrow, which will allow you to use the report you created back in Chapter 7. From the list of available reports that appears, choose 1 (Personnel Register).

The next menu to appear looks familiar:

Printer Screen File
Send the report to the printer.

Since the Display Employee option of the application will display the report, choose Screen. The definitions for the menu option will be saved, and the next menu option, Print Employees, will begin flashing.

Choose Report and SelectTable, and then choose ABCSTAFF as the desired table. Press F2 or choose DO-IT!. From the next menu to appear, choose AllRecords to include all records in the printed version of the report. Choose Borrow from the next menu, and then choose 1 (Personnel Register) to use the existing report again. Choose Printer from the next menu, and the definition will be saved.

The third submenu option, Display Client Time, is now flashing, awaiting a definition. Choose Report and SelectTable, and then choose HOURS as the table to supply this report. Press F2 or choose DO-IT! from the menu. Choose AllRecords from the next menu, and then choose StandardReport to accept the default report for the HOURS table. Finally, choose Screen to indicate the report's destination for this menu choice.

For the Print Client Time option, which is now flashing, choose Report, and then SelectTable, and again choose HOURS as the table to supply this report. Press F2 or choose DO-IT! to complete the selection. Choose AllRecords from the next menu, and again choose StandardReport to accept the default report for the HOURS table. In this case, choose Printer to indicate the report's destination for this menu choice.

One more option, and your work with the Paradox Personal Programmer is nearly complete. You need to tell the Personal Programmer that the Cancel Reports option, which is now flashing, can be used to exit from the secondary menu and return to the main menu. Choose Cancel from the menu.

With all of the options defined, the Paradox Personal Programmer now presents the following menu:

SplashScreen NoSplashScreen
Design a splash screen for the application.

You can decide whether you want to include a splash screen, which is an introductory screen, with the text of your choice. The splash screen, if used, will greet the user each time the application is started.

For the sake of example, choose SplashScreen now. In a moment, a Form Design screen will appear. You can use the techniques you learned earlier for designing custom forms to "paint" a splash screen.

As an example, press F10 for the menu; choose Border, then Place, and then Double-Line. Move the cursor approximately to row 4, column 4, and press RETURN to start the border. Then move the cursor down 15 lines and across 65 characters to draw a large box. You press RETURN to complete your border.

Next, place the cursor just inside the upper-left corner of the box. Press F10 for the menu, and choose Border/Place/Other to place another border that consists of a character of your choice. The Personal Programmer will next ask you for the character you want to use in the border. Hold down the ALT key on your keyboard, and while you are holding it down, use the numeric keypad keys (*not* the other number keys) to type the number **176**, then release the ALT key. A checkerboard block character should appear next to the "Character:" prompt.

Press RETURN, and with the cursor just inside the left corner of the border, press RETURN again to start the border. Move the cursor down one line and to the right until it is just inside the righthand border. Then press RETURN to draw a border composed of the graphics character.

Move the cursor to position 8,22 (you can tell the position from the numbers shown at the upper-left corner when the menu does not appear). Add the following text at this position:

ABC Temporaries Personnel System

and at position 12,25 add the following text:

designed by (your name here)

If you feel particularly creative, you may want to spend a few moments adding more text or special effects. When you are done, press F2 to save the splash screen.

After you have responded to the SplashScreen/NoSplashScreen menu, the Paradox Personal Programmer presents you with one final question in the form of the following menu:

DO-IT! Cancel
Generate and save the script files and libraries for the current application.

In this case, choose DO-IT! or press F2 to tell the Personal Programmer to write the application. The remaining option, Cancel, lets you cancel all additions or changes you made during this session with the Personal Programmer. You should not normally choose Cancel with a new application, even if you made a choice somewhere along the line that you would like to do over. If you are creating an application for the first time, choosing Cancel may result in the loss of all design work. It is much easier to modify an existing application with the Paradox Personal Programmer than to create the application all over again.

After you choose DO-IT!, the Paradox Personal Programmer will proceed to write the application for you. Dozens of lines of PAL code will scroll up the screen during this process. When it has finished, the Paradox Personal Programmer will return to its main menu.

To see the results, choose Play from the menu and enter **STAFF** as the name of the application to play. You will see your splash screen (if you created one) along with a request for a password. Press RETURN alone, since none of the tables involved in this application are password protected. The main menu you defined while in the Paradox Personal Programmer will appear, resembling the following:

Add Employees Edit Employees Add Weekly Time Edit/Delete Time Reports
Add new employees to personnel list.

Try adding and editing records or printing reports with the various choices of the application. When you have finished testing the system, choose Leave from the main menu to leave the application, and then confirm this with Yes. You will be returned to the Paradox Personal Programmer's main menu.

RUNNING THE APPLICATION

The Personal Programmer automatically adds an option called Leave to the main menu, allowing you to exit the application. You do not need to enter the Paradox Personal Programmer to run your application; there are a number of ways in which an application created with the Paradox Personal Programmer can be run. Probably the easiest method for other Paradox users is to run the application from within Paradox. Because the application is a sophisticated series of PAL scripts, you can run the application as you would run other PAL scripts, from the Scripts menu choice of the main menu in Paradox. If you choose to store your applications in separate subdirectories (a good idea for helping to keep your hard disk manageable), you will want first to change to the proper subdirectory after starting Paradox. You can do this by choosing Tools/More/Directory from the main menu and entering the name for the directory. Once in the directory, choose Scripts/Play from the main menu and then enter the name of the application to run it. If the Paradox program directory is included in the path set by your AUTOEXEC.BAT file, you can load Paradox from the directory that contains the application.

You can also run an application from DOS by starting Paradox with the program name, followed by the name of the application. As an example, you could get to the subdirectory that contains the application with the normal DOS CD\commands. Then you could enter **PARADOX STAFF** to load Paradox and run the application.

MODIFYING AN APPLICATION

"Nothing is constant except change," the old saying goes. For changing your applications, you can use the Modify option from the main menu of the Personal Programmer. When you choose this option and enter the name of the application, you are offered a new menu. It contains options for changing the tables, menu options and actions, and the splash screen used in your application. You are also given the ability to move to the first undefined menu action (to add an action for it), and you have the usual DO-IT! and Cancel options available.

You make changes by choosing your desired selections from the various menus. As in designing an application, help screens explain in detail what you are doing at any given time. Once your changes are complete, use F2 to save the modifications. If you make some modifications to an application and then decide that you do not want those modifications, you can choose Cancel to exit the modification process without saving the changes.

To modify the ABC Temporaries application, choose Modify from the main menu of the Paradox Personal Programmer. In response to the prompt for the application name, enter **STAFF**. The Personal Programmer will load the application, and in a moment, the following menu will appear:

Tables MenuAction NotDefined SplashScreen DO-IT! Cancel
Select one or more tables to add to or remove from the application.

The Tables option of this menu lets you add tables to or remove tables from the existing application. The MenuAction option lets you modify the selections or the actions of a menu option. The NotDefined option automatically moves you to the first undefined choice in the application, where you can proceed to define a choice for that menu selection. The SplashScreen option lets you change the splash screen used with the application. The DO-IT! and Cancel options perform the same tasks as they do elsewhere in Paradox.

In this case, you want to add a menu action to your reports menu in order to generate a relational report based on two tables, ABCSTAFF and HOURS. Choose MenuAction from the menu. In a moment, you will see the menu choices for the main menu of the application. Select Reports from this menu. The secondary menu, containing all of your report choices, will then appear.

Highlight Print Client Time and press F10 to modify this menu option. A new menu with the following options will appear:

Menu Action DO-IT! Cancel
Modify the current menu level by adding, deleting, or editing selections.

Choose Menu to add an additional option to the current menu. Note that when you make this choice, the help screen informs you that you can use the INS key to insert new selections, or the DEL key to delete selections. Press the INS key once to add a new selection to the menu.

For the new menu selection, enter

Print Bills

For a description, enter

Print bills for clients

Then press Do-It! (F2). You do not want to modify any other selections at this time, so press Do-It! (F2) again. The menu used to modify applications will appear again.

This time, choose NotDefined from the menu. In a moment, the Personal Programmer will move to the menu option you just added, Print Bills, because there is no definition for this new menu option. Press F10 for the menu, and choose Action to define an action. From the next menu that appears, choose Define. In a moment, the following menu appears:

Menu View Report DataEntry Edit Script Help NotDefined Cancel
Allow users to send a report to the printer, screen, or file.

You want to assign a new report to the menu option, so choose Report from this menu. Choose SelectTable and then ABCSTAFF from the list of tables. Choose SelectTable once more, and choose HOURS from the table list. Keep in mind that you can always modify the objects incorporated in the application (such as reports and form view) through Paradox itself. Those changes will be reflected in the application.

Creating a Multitable View

Because you chose more than one table, the next menu asks if you want to create a new multitable view, or borrow an existing one. You can use multitable views to generate reports based on the data in more than one table. You have not yet defined any multitable views, so choose Create to define one. A Query Form soon appears, similar to the example shown in Figure 13-5.

Place the cursor in the Social security field of the ABCSTAFF table, press F5 to begin an example, and then enter **SAME** in the field. Use the F6 key to place checkmarks in the Last name and Hourly Rate fields.

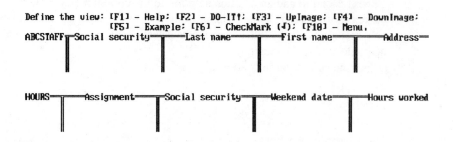

FIGURE 13-5.   Query Form for use with multiple tables

Press F4 to move down to the HOURS table. Move over to the Social security field, press F5 to start an example, and enter **SAME** in the field. Then move to the Hours column (the far left column) and use F6 to place checkmarks in all fields. Finally, press Do- It! (F2).

The next menu to appear offers you the option of including selected records or all records. If this were an actual application for your use, you might prefer to select records based on a range of dates; by selecting only those records for the current month, for example, you could generate a billing appropriate to that month. For the sake of this example, you will use all records, so choose AllRecords from the menu.

The next menu option provides you with a choice of reports; choose StandardReport. (If you feel adventuresome, you may want to come back later and modify this report, adding groups for the assignment names.) Finally, choose Printer from the next menu to send the report's output to the printer.

The menu that appears after the definition has been saved lets you continue with your modifications to other menu actions. In this example, no other modifications of the actions are needed, so press Do-It! (F2), and you will be returned to the Modify menu. Choose DO-IT! from this menu or press F2 and the Paradox Personal Programmer will rewrite the PAL code for the application. When this process is complete, the main menu of the Paradox Personal Programmer will appear. You can try the new menu choice by running the application with the Play option of the Personal Programmer main menu.

SUMMARIZING AN APPLICATION

You can use the Summarize option of the Personal Programmer main menu to generate a summary of the menus, files, or the structure of an application. To do this, choose

Summarize from the menu, and enter the name for the application. You will then see the following menu:

Menu File Tree All
Output listing of the menu structure and the definition of each selection.

Use Menu to generate a report that describes each menu selection; File to generate a list of all of the files used by the application; Tree to display the application's design as a tree structure; or All to generate all of these. The results can be sent to the printer, screen, or to a disk file.

Figure 13-6 shows an example of all three types of summaries, generated for the application described throughout this chapter. Generating such reports is highly recommended; an experienced Paradox user who wishes to modify your application later will find these reports useful.

REVIEWING AN APPLICATION

To review the structure of an application, choose Review from the main menu of the Personal Programmer, and then enter the name of the application. You can then use the cursor keys to move along the various menus; the RETURN key can be used to move down by a level, and the ESCAPE key can be used to move up by a level. When you are done reviewing the application, press Do-It! (F2) to return to the main menu of the Personal Programmer.

ABOUT THE TOOLS

The options that are available from the Tools menu of the Personal Programmer operate similarly to those of the Paradox Tools menu. You can use Copy to copy an application to another directory, Delete to delete an application, or Rename to rename an application. The Settings option provides options for the control of printer settings, the amount of help displayed while the Personal Programmer is being used, and some advanced options for using procedure libraries. (The topic of procedure libraries is beyond the scope of this book, although you can find more details on that subject in your Paradox documentation.) Finally, the Directory option lets you change the default directory.

2/26/88   Staff Menu Structure   Page 1

Menu Path:
/Main/

Script containing this menu: Staff1
Library containing the procedures for this menu: Staff1

Selection Name	Selection Action	Source Table	Map Table	Tables Used	Query, Help, or User Script
Add Employees	DataEntry			Abcstaff	
Edit Employees	Edit			Abcstaff	Staffq1
Add Weekly Time	DataEntry			Hours	
Edit/Delete Time	Edit			Hours	
Reports	Menu				
Leave	Leave				

Menu Path:
/Main/Reports/

Script containing this menu: Staff2
Library containing the procedures for this menu: Staff1

Selection Name	Selection Action	Source Table	Map Table	Tables Used	Query, Help, or User Script
Display Employees	Report			Abcstaff	
Print Employees	Report			Abcstaff	
Display Client Time	Report			Hours	
Print Bills	Report	Staffs1	Staffm1	Abcstaff Hours	Staffq2
Print Client Time	Report			Hours	
Cancel Reports	Cancel				

FIGURE 13-6.   Sample summaries

You may want to create your reports, images, and validity checks (valchecks) in
Paradox, then use the Borrow option to use them in the Paradox Personal Programmer.
By doing so, you can thoroughly debug and refine your reports, forms, and similar
documents before building the complete application.

2/26/88   Application Scripts and Tables   Page 1

Libs:

    Name

    Staff1

Scripts:

    Name

    Staff
    Staff1
    Staff2
    Staffcp
    Staffg
    Staffq1
    Staffq2
    Staffutl

Tables:

    Name

    Abcstaff
    Hours
    Staffm1
    Staffs1

FIGURE 13-6.   Sample summaries (*continued*)

JUST THE BEGINNING...

This chapter has given you some idea of the power and ease of use that a professional application, written with the help of the Paradox Personal Programmer, can provide. Chapter 15, "Sample Applications," provides additional examples of how the Personal Programmer can be used to design and implement applications. If your job can be made easier by means of applications, take the time to explore all of the features of

---

2/26/88   Application Menu Tree: Page 1.1
                     =================

Main
:--- Add Employees [DataEntry]
:--- Edit Employees [Edit]
:--- Add Weekly Time [DataEntry]
:--- Edit/Delete Time [Edit]
:--- Reports

:   :--- Display Employees [Report]
:   :--- Print Employees [Report]
:   :--- Display Client Time [Report]
:   :--- Print Bills [Report]
:   :--- Print Client Time [Report]
:   :--- Cancel Reports [Cancel]
---- Leave [Leave]

Note: "...<Menu Selection> Selection" means that <Menu Selection>Selection is
not defined.

FIGURE 13-6.   Sample summaries (*continued*)

the Personal Programmer. The applications that result will be well worth the time you spend.

QUICK SUMMARY

To create an application using the Paradox Personal Programmer, perform the following steps:

1. Enter **PPROG** from the DOS prompt to load the Personal Programmer. If you get a "Bad command or file name" message, you need to install the Personal Programmer on your system.

2. Choose CREATE from the Paradox Personal Programmer main menu.

3. Select the tables with which the application will work.

4. Build the menu structure for the application, by defining the main menu and any submenus.

5. Define the menu selections, by telling the Paradox Personal Programmer which actions it should take in response to each menu selection.

6. As an option, design a splash screen for the application, which is an introductory screen containing text of your choosing. This screen is seen by the user each time the application is started.

7. Choose Do-It! (F2) which will tell the Paradox Personal Programmer to write the application.

8. Exit from the Paradox Personal Programmer. You can then run the application, by choosing Scripts/Play from the menu, and entering the name of the application.

chapter 14

INTRODUCTION TO PAL PROGRAMMING

While you may not have purchased Paradox with the intention of becoming a computer programmer, you will find that programming with Paradox is not as difficult as you might expect. As you will see in this chapter, you program in Paradox through the use of PAL commands. PAL is an abbreviation for Paradox Application Language, the programming language that is built into Paradox. Using programs that automate the way Paradox works for you is well worth the effort spent in designing and writing the programs. While you can create applications with the Personal Programmer, as detailed in the previous chapter, a knowledge of PAL programming adds flexibility to what you can do with Paradox. Armed with such knowledge, you can create applications based on your own program design. It is not recommended that you attempt to modify applications built with the Personal Programmer, because they are highly modular in nature. However, you can learn much about good programming style by studying the applications created by the Personal Programmer.

Any computer program is simply a series of instructions to a computer. These instructions are commands that cause the computer to perform specific tasks. The commands are written in a file contained on a disk, and they are performed each time the file is retrieved from the disk.

In a way, you are already familiar with PAL programs, because scripts (detailed in Chapter 10) are stored in PAL. To create your PAL programs, you will probably use a combination of the keystrokes stored in scripts and various commands that are a part of PAL.

CREATING AND SAVING A PAL PROGRAM

You can create PAL programs with the Editor built into Paradox or with any word processor that can save text as ASCII files. The Paradox Editor normally assigns a file extension of .SC to all programs you write; if you use a word processor outside of Paradox to write programs, you should add an .SC extension to the program when you save it.

To create a program in the Paradox Editor, you choose Scripts/Editor/Write from the Paradox menu. Next, you enter the filename for the script when prompted, and the blank screen of the PAL Editor appears. At this point, you can type the desired lines of the program. You can correct mistakes with the BACKSPACE or DEL keys, and the usual cursor keys. One handy shortcut key to remember for major modifications is the CTRL-Y key combination, which deletes the line that the cursor is on. Once the program is completed, press Do-It! (F2) to save the program.

Running any PAL program is the same as running any script recorded in PAL; from the Paradox main menu, choose Scripts/Play and enter the name of the program. If there are no errors in your program, the program performs as planned. If there are any bugs in the program, Paradox stops running and presents you with a menu with two options: Cancel and Debug. Selecting Cancel returns you to the Paradox main menu, while selecting Debug displays the line where the error was detected, along with a description of the problem.

To edit an existing PAL program, choose Scripts/Editor/Edit from the Paradox main menu and enter the name of the program. The existing program appears within the Paradox Editor. You can make the desired changes and press Do-It! (F2) to save the edited program.

YOUR FIRST PAL PROGRAM

You can try creating and running a simple program in PAL now. Press F10 for the menu, and choose Scripts/Editor/Write. Enter **PROGRAM1** as the name for the script. When the Editor appears, type the following lines, pressing RETURN at the end of each line:

```
? "Enter your name:"
ACCEPT "A15" TO TheName
? "The name that you entered was: "
?? TheName
SLEEP 5000
```

Once you've entered the program, press Do-It! (F2) to save the completed program. From the menu, choose Scripts/Play, then enter **PROGRAM1** when prompted for the name of the script. You should see the prompt "Enter your name" appear on the screen. Type your name and press RETURN, and you'll see the response provided by the program.

Some common commands used in PAL will be explained later in this chapter. For now, here's an explanation of the program you just created. The ? command on the first line displays the "Enter your name" message on the screen. Whenever Paradox sees the question mark as a starting command, it places whatever follows the question mark on the screen at the current cursor location.

The second line of the program reads

```
ACCEPT "A15" TO TheName
```

In this line, the ACCEPT command tells Paradox to accept a value typed at the keyboard, and to store that value to an area in memory. Such areas in memory are called *memory variables,* and each memory variable must have its own name so that it can be identified by the different parts of your program. In this case, "TheName" is the name of the memory variable. The designation "A15" indicates that the variable will contain alphanumeric data, and will store a maximum of 15 characters. (You can use the same type designations for memory variables that you use when naming fields of a table.)

The third and fourth lines of the program,

```
? "The name that you entered was: "
?? TheName
```

use the ? and ?? commands to display the response. The ?? command is similar to the ? command explained earlier. The only difference is that the ?? command displays the information on the same line, without moving the cursor to a new line. The ? command always moves the cursor to a new line before displaying the information.

The SLEEP command that begins the last line of the program is used to provide time to view the response before the Paradox menu reappears. The number indicates approximately the number of milliseconds that the program should pause; hence, there is roughly a five-second delay after the name is displayed by the program before the Paradox menu reappears.

USING PAL SCRIPTS IN LARGER APPLICATIONS

One of the most useful traits of Paradox in regards to programming is that scripts in Paradox are normally stored in PAL. As a result, it is a simple matter to store a series of actions in Paradox to a script, and use the text of that script as part of a more complex PAL program. This is commonly done for tasks like placing a particular table in use, choosing a sort order, printing stored reports, and so on. For example, the ABCSTAFF table contains the names and addresses of the employees for ABC Temporaries. On a monthly basis, a report sorted by last name is required. The report is a default Paradox report. To first sort the table, you can choose Modify/Sort from the main menu, and enter the name of the table (in this example, ABCSTAFF) at the prompt. Next, you choose Same from the menu (to place the results of the sort in the same table). When the Sort Order screen appears, you place a 1 for first sort field beside the desired field name (in this example, Last Name). You then press Do-It! (F2), and the sorted table appears. To print the table, you press F10 to reveal the main menu, and choose Report/Output, followed by the name of the table. You choose the default report form from the next menu, and then choose either Printer or Screen, and the desired report is produced.

If you've followed the exercises in this book, these kinds of actions are already familiar to you. With PAL programming, before beginning the actions described to sort the table and print the report, you can press ALT-F3 to begin recording an instant script. Once the last action is completed, you press ALT-F3 again, and recording of the script stops. As noted in Chapter 10, instant scripts are stored under the name INSTANT.SC in the default directory. The contents of the script just described would resemble the following:

```
{Modify} {Sort} {ABCSTAFF} {Same} Down "1" Do_It!
Menu {Report} {Output} {ABCSTAFF} {R} {Screen}
```

The Paradox Editor has a Read option for reading other script files into an existing file. Hence, the easiest way to write portions of programs for selecting tables, printing reports, and so on is to perform the actions while recording a script, then use the Read menu option when in the Editor to read the contents of the script into the larger program. You can tie together the various tasks by means of menu choices implemented with the SHOWMENU...TO command, described later in this chapter.

Remember that menu choices in PAL always appear within braces. In the prior example, {Sort}, {Report}, and {Output} were menu selections chosen during the recording of the script. Paradox function keys are always spelled out, as are cursor keys and the RETURN key. In the example, Do_It! and Menu represent the Do-It! (F2) and Menu (F10) keys, while Down and Up represent the cursor down and cursor up keys. Any text entered in response to a Paradox prompt will be surrounded by quotation marks.

INTERACTING WITH USERS

Much of PAL programming involves interaction with the user of the program. Various commands are provided for displaying information on the screen and for getting replies from the user. For example, the ? and ?? commands display data on the screen, the @ command places the cursor at a specific position, and the ACCEPT command gets a value from the user. Here is a brief list and explanation of some of the more common PAL commands:

Command	Explanation
? <*expression*>	Writes the contents of *expression* at the beginning of a line below the current cursor position.
?? <*expression*>	Writes the contents of *expression* at the current location of the cursor.
@ <*row*>,<*col*>	Positions the cursor at the selected row and column location.
ACCEPT <*data type*> TO <*variable name*>	Accepts a value from the keyboard and stores it to the named memory variable.
BEEP	Sounds a beep.
CLEAR	Clears the PAL canvas.
MESSAGE <*expression*>	Displays a message at the lower-right corner of the screen.
MOVE TO [*field name*]	Moves the cursor to the named field of the active table.
PRINT <*expression*>	Sends values to the printer.

PRINTER ON/OFF	Turns on (or off) echoing of screen output to the printer.
SHOWMENU <*menu item list*> TO <*variable name*>	Creates and displays a Paradox menu. The item selected is stored as <*variable name*>.
STYLE ATTRIBUTE *n*	Sets the display attributes for text shown on the screen.
SLEEP *n*	Pauses the program for *n* milliseconds.
TEXT <*text to be shown*> ENDTEXT	Displays all text between TEXT and ENDTEXT on the screen.
VIEW <*table name*>	Displays a table in the Paradox workspace; equivalent to choosing View from the menu.

Note that there are many additional commands you can use to manipulate data in PAL; the previous list is a brief introduction. You can refer to your *PAL User's Guide* for a complete list of all commands and functions that you can use when programming in PAL.

As an example that includes more of the commands just described, you can write a simple program in PAL to ask for the name and age of a user, and then display that information on the screen using a different screen color. The program is shown below; to create it, choose Scripts/Editor/Write from the main menu, and call the program PROGRAM2. As the first line of the program demonstrates, you can add comments to a PAL program by starting the line with a semicolon. Whenever a line begins with a semicolon, PAL does not act on what is contained in the line. Hence, you can include programming comments, which are usually notes that help you understand parts of the program, by writing text after a semicolon.

```
; --This is a simple test of PAL programming
CLEAR
STYLE ATTRIBUTE 20
@ 5,15
?? "Type your name, and press RETURN: "
ACCEPT "A20" TO TheName
STYLE ATTRIBUTE 45
@ 8,15
?? "Enter your age: "
ACCEPT "N" PICTURE "##" TO TheAge
STYLE ATTRIBUTE 12
@ 12,10
?? "Your name is ", TheName, " and you are ", TheAge, " years old."
SLEEP 5000
BEEP BEEP BEEP
```

When done, save the program with Do-It! (F2), and run it by choosing Scripts/Play from the main menu and entering **PROGRAM2** as the name of the script to be played. The program prompts for a name and age (using red characters on blue background for the name prompt and magenta characters on green background for the age). Finally, the response containing the name and age is displayed, using red characters on a black background.

Since much of your work in Paradox involves working with tables, you will need to access those tables and the data contained in various fields within a PAL application. As mentioned in the list of commands earlier, you can use the VIEW *<table name>* command to display a table on the screen, and you can use the MOVETO [*field name*] command to move to a particular field. In scripts, you can use field names from the currently active table by placing square brackets around the name of the field. In the following script, the VIEW "Abcstaff" statement places the ABCSTAFF table on the workspace, the MOVETO [SALARY] statement moves the cursor to the SALARY field of the table, and the EDITKEY command, equivalent to pressing Edit-(F9) places the user in an editing mode. The next three statements, WAIT TABLE, MESSAGE, and UNTIL, cause the table to remain visible until editing is completed; the WAIT TABLE and UNTIL commands are described in detail near the end of this chapter.

```
VIEW "Abcstaff"
MOVETO [SALARY]
EDITKEY
WAIT TABLE
        MESSAGE "Press F2 when done."
UNTIL "F2"
DO_IT!
```

DECISION-MAKING WITHIN A PROGRAM

In many PAL programs, Paradox will need to perform different operations depending on the user's response to a menu option or depending on different values encountered in a table. For example, if the user has a choice of editing or printing a record based on choices shown in a main menu, the program must be able to perform the chosen operation. Paradox uses the IF, ELSE, and ENDIF commands to branch to the part of the program where the chosen operation is performed. The IF and ENDIF commands are used as a matched pair enclosing a number of other PAL commands. The ELSE command is optional and is used within the body of IF-ENDIF as another decision step. The IF-ENDIF command can be used to decide between actions in a program. The format of the command is

```
IF <condition exists> THEN
      <desired commands here >
ELSE
      <more desired commands here >
ENDIF
```

This decision-making command must always start with IF and end with ENDIF. The commands that you place between the IF and ENDIF commands determine exactly what will occur if the condition is true, unless an ELSE is encountered. If an ELSE is encountered and the condition specified by ELSE is true, the commands that follow ELSE are carried out. A good way to write these commands is to write them in "pseudocode" first and then compare them.

Pseudocode	Paradox

If last name is Cooke, then display last name.	IF LASTNAME = "Cooke" THEN
	   ? LASTNAME
	ENDIF

If monthly rent is less than $300, then display "Reasonably priced."	IF RENT < 300 THEN
	   ? "Reasonably priced"
	ENDIF

Using IF and ENDIF alone will work fine for making a single decision. But if you wish to add an alternative choice, you'll need the ELSE statement.

Pseudocode	Paradox

If last name is Cooke, then print last name; or else print "There is no one by that name in this database."	IF LASTNAME = "Cooke" THEN
	   ? LASTNAME
	ELSE
	   ? "There is no one by
	   that name in this
	   database."
	ENDIF

Paradox will evaluate the condition following the IF command to see if any action should be taken. If no action is necessary, Paradox will simply move on to the next command after the ENDIF command. As an example of the use of the IF and ENDIF commands, the following PAL program asks a user for his or her age, and then displays an appropriate message depending on the response.

```
CLEAR
@ 5,10
?? "Enter your age. "
ACCEPT "N" TO TheAge
;---act on the response.
IF TheAge > 20 THEN
    @ 10,10
    ?? "Of legal drinking age."
ELSE
    @ 10,10
    ?? "Sorry. No alcohol served to minors."
ENDIF
SLEEP 5000
```

In this simple example, the program displays one of two messages depending upon the response given. The SLEEP 5000 command is added after the IF...ENDIF command to provide time for the user to view the response before the Paradox menu reappears.

EVALUATING MULTIPLE CHOICES WITH SWITCH, CASE, AND ENDSWITCH

Your program may need to make more than two or three decisions from a single response. A series of IF-ENDIF commands could do the job, but using more than three IF-ENDIF's to test the value of one field or memory variable is unwieldy. An easier way is to use the SWITCH, CASE, and ENDSWITCH commands. With the CASE statement, the IF-ENDIF tests are made into cases, and Paradox then chooses the first case, second case, or another case. These cases are grouped between a SWITCH command and an ENDSWITCH command. The OTHERWISE command works exactly like the ELSE in an IF-ENDIF statement. The basic syntax for these commands is as follows:

```
SWITCH
    CASE <first condition >:
        <perform these commands>
    CASE <second condition >:
        <perform these commands>
    CASE <third condition >:
        <perform these commands>
    OTHERWISE:
        <perform these commands>
ENDSWITCH
```

Again, note that the OTHERWISE statement (and any commands that follow it) is optional. Note also that there is no limit to the number of CASE statements; while this example shows three, you could have ten, twenty, or more CASE statements between a SWITCH and ENDSWITCH statement.

With the SWITCH...ENDSWITCH statements, the first CASE statement that meets a specified condition will be acted on, and the rest will be ignored. If no condition for any of the CASE statements is met and an OTHERWISE statement is included, the commands following the OTHERWISE statement are carried out. If no condition for any of the CASE statements is met and an OTHERWISE statement is not included, control of the program proceeds to the next statement after the END-SWITCH command. The following program demonstrates the use of the SWITCH...ENDSWITCH commands:

```
CLEAR
TEXT
    Enter 1 to view the ABCSTAFF table.
    Enter 2 to view the HOURS table.
    Enter 3 to view the CLIENTS table.
ENDTEXT
ACCEPT "N" PICTURE "#" TO Choosy
;---respond to the answer.
SWITCH
    CASE Choosy = 1:
        ClearAll {View} {ABCSTAFF}
    CASE Choosy = 2:
        ClearAll {View} {HOURS}
    CASE Choosy = 3:
        ClearAll {View} {CLIENTS}
```

```
OTHERWISE:
    @ 5,5
    ?? "Invalid choice!  Enter a number from 1 to 3."
    BEEP BEEP BEEP
    SLEEP 5000
ENDSWITCH
```

In this program, a series of options is first displayed using the TEXT...ENDTEXT commands. The TEXT...ENDTEXT commands cause everything between them to appear on the screen. Next, the ACCEPT statement is used to get the response, in the form of a single-digit numeric value, from the user. Finally, the CASE statements between SWITCH and ENDSWITCH take the appropriate action, depending on the response; if the user enters 1, the ABCSTAFF table appears; if the user enters 2, the HOURS table appears; and, if the user enters 3, the CLIENTS table appears.

One important point to remember is that all CASE and OTHERWISE statements must end with a colon, or the program will crash with a "colon expected" error message.

GOING IN CIRCLES

There will be many times when your program will need to perform the same task repeatedly. Paradox has two commands, WHILE and ENDWHILE, that are used as a matched pair to repeat a series of commands for as long as is necessary. You enclose the commands that you wish to repeat between the WHILE and the ENDWHILE commands. The WHILE command always begins the loop, and the ENDWHILE command normally ends the loop. The series of commands contained within the WHILE loop will continue to execute until the condition, specified immediately next to the WHILE command, is no longer true. You determine when the loop should stop by specifying the condition; otherwise, the loop could go on indefinitely. The WHILE...ENDWHILE commands use the following syntax:

```
WHILE <condition exists>
   <commands to be repeated>
ENDWHILE
```

The following simple program demonstrates the use of WHILE...ENDWHILE by counting to 10, and displaying the value after each increase in a memory variable called CountIt:

```
CLEAR
CountIt = 0
WHILE CountIt < 11
    ? "The value of CountIt is now ", CountIt
    SLEEP 500
    CountIt = CountIt + 1
ENDWHILE
SLEEP 1000
```

In this program, after the screen is erased with the CLEAR command, a memory variable called CountIt is created, and a numeric value of zero is stored to that variable. The next line,

WHILE CountIt < 11

indicates the start of the WHILE...ENDWHILE loop. The specified condition is "CountIt < 11," so the loop will repeat for as long as the value of the memory variable, CountIt, is less than 11. The lines between the WHILE and the ENDWHILE commands display the value of the variable, pause the program (giving the user time to read the screen), and increase the value of the variable by one. Once the value of CountIt reaches 11, control of the program passes beyond the ENDWHILE command to the command that follows.

CREATING MENUS IN PAL PROGRAMS

You can create menu options that tie together various portions of a PAL program with the SHOWMENU TO command. This command lets you display menu options complete with help text in a style that imitates the Paradox menus. The syntax for the SHOWMENU TO command is as follows:

```
SHOWMENU
    <first option >    : <help text >,
    <second option > : <help text >,
    <last option>      : <help text >
TO <variable name>
```

When the program runs, Paradox automatically places the named options as menu items at the top of the screen. (Again, there is no limit to the number of options you can include; although for readability, you should design your systems so that all the options for a menu will fit on the screen.) As each item is highlighted, the help text appears beneath the menu items. Once a choice is made, a text string containing the name of that menu item is stored to the memory variable. Your program can then act on that variable as desired, usually through the use of the SWITCH...ENDSWITCH command. The following example demonstrates the use of the SHOWMENU TO command in a rewrite of the program shown earlier to view different tables. Instead of using TEXT and ENDTEXT to display choices, this program uses SHOWMENU TO to provide the options as menu choices.

```
CLEAR
SHOWMENU
   "ABCSTAFF"    : "View the Abcstaff table",
   "HOURS"       : "View the Hours table",
   "CLIENTS"     : "View the Clients table"
TO Choosy
;---respond to the answer.
SWITCH
   CASE Choosy = "ABCSTAFF":
       ClearAll {View} {ABCSTAFF}
   CASE Choosy = "HOURS":
       ClearAll {View} {HOURS}
   CASE Choosy = "CLIENTS":
       ClearAll {View} {CLIENTS}
ENDSWITCH
```

Notice that in this example the CASE statements test for text strings that are the names of the menu items, such as "ABCSTAFF" and "HOURS." You must enclose the menu items in quotes, and you must add commas at the end of all but the last statement in a group of SHOWMENU statements. Omission of the commas is a common cause of program bugs when developing PAL applications.

PUTTING IT ALL TOGETHER IN A COMPLETE PAL APPLICATION

You can use any or all of the techniques discussed in this chapter to develop a complete application in PAL. The following simple application provides options for adding new records to the ABCSTAFF table, editing the table, sorting the table, and printing the default report for the table.

The application consists of two programs; both can be created and saved separately using the Editor. The first program displays the menu, acts on the appropriate choices, and includes the necessary commands or Paradox keystrokes to add and edit data, and to print a default report. The second program, named SortIt.SC, is a routine for sorting the table. Note that the fourth option of the application's main menu calls the sorting routine by using the PLAY "SortIt" statement. In PAL, the PLAY command calls another program. When the second program completes its execution, control returns to the main program. You can use the PLAY command to easily implement "modular programming techniques" (the use of many small programs to build a large application) as your PAL programs grow more complex.

Two commands in the program that have not yet been described are the WAIT TABLE...UNTIL and the SORT commands. You use WAIT TABLE...UNTIL *<condition>* to cause a table to remain on the screen until the user does something (specified by the condition) to clear the table. The SORT command lets you sort a table, and it uses the syntax SORT *"table-name"* ON *"field1"*,...*"field2"*,...*"fieldN"*. The same sort could be stored in a program by recording an instant script and choosing the sort options from the Paradox menu, but the SORT command is faster to include in a program once you know the syntax of the command.

```
;---ABC.SC is Abcstaff table application.
Choosy = " "
WHILE Choosy <> "Exit"
    CLEAR
    SHOWMENU
        "Add"    : "Add new records to the ABCSTAFF table",
        "Edit"   : "Edit records in the ABCSTAFF table",
        "Sort"   : "Sort the ABCSTAFF table by last name or ZIP",
        "Print"  : "Print the standard report",
        "Exit"   : "Return to Paradox main menu"
    TO Choosy
    ;---respond to the answer.
    SWITCH
        CASE Choosy = "Add":
            ClearAll {Modify} {DataEntry} {abcstaff}
            Menu {Image} {PickForm} {F}
            ;---in data entry mode until user hits do-it key.
            WAIT TABLE
                    MESSAGE "--Press Do-It! (F2) when finished."
            UNTIL "F2"
            DO_IT!
            ClearAll
        CASE Choosy = "Edit":
            ClearAll {Modify} {Edit} {abcstaff}
            ;---in table mode until user completes edits.
            WAIT TABLE
                    MESSAGE "--Press Do-It! (F2) when finished."
```

```
                UNTIL "F2"
                DO_IT!
                ClearAll
            CASE Choosy = "Sort":
                ClearAll
                Play "SortIt"
            CASE Choosy = "Print":
                ClearAll Menu {Report} {Output}
                {ABCSTAFF} {R} {Printer}
        ENDSWITCH
ENDWHILE
CLEARALL
CLEAR


;---this program is stored as SortIt.SC---
CLEAR
TEXT
  Enter 1 to sort by last name.
  Enter 2 to sort by ZIP code.
ENDTEXT
ACCEPT "N" PICTURE "#" TO WHICHWAY
;---respond to the answer.
IF WHICHWAY = 1 THEN
    SORT "Abcstaff" ON "Last Name"
ELSE
    SORT "Abcstaff" ON "ZIP"
ENDIF
CLEAR
```

Because it is such a rich programming language, all of the commands and functions in PAL could not be covered in this brief introduction. The *PAL Users' Guide* provided with your Paradox documentation provides more detail on all the commands and functions in PAL. Also, keep in mind that you can learn a great deal about programming in PAL by studying the programs created by the Personal Programmer, detailed in the previous chapter.

chapter 15

NETWORKING
WITH PARADOX

This chapter provides information that you will find useful if you intend to use the network version of Paradox. Included in this chapter are an overview of local area networks, requirements and instructions for using Paradox on a network, and general hints for effective network use.

The complexity of local area networks requires this chapter to be a bit more technical than most other chapters in this book. It is assumed that the reader is already familiar with the use of Paradox, basic DOS commands (including the use of DOS subdirectories), and the network commands for the particular network on which Paradox is installed. Refer to the appropriate manuals for network operation to answer any questions you have about the use of your network's operating system commands.

PARADOX AND NETWORKS

A *local area network,* or *LAN,* is a system of computer communications that links together a number of personal computers, usually within a single building, for the transfer of information between computer users. In its minimal configuration, a local area network consists of two PCs connected by some type of wire that allows information to be transferred between the two machines. A local area network allows the sharing of printers, modems, hard disks, and other devices that may be attached to computers on the network. Files (such as Paradox tables) and commonly used software can also be shared. Figure 15-1 illustrates how computers can be linked together by means of a local area network.

There are different designs for local area networks, but all LANs are made up of the same basic components: servers, work stations, and the physical cable that links the components together. Servers are computers that provide devices that can be used by all users of the network. Most servers are one of three types: file servers, which provide shared hard disks; print servers, which provide shared printers; and communications servers, which provide shared modems. Servers can simultaneously provide more than one of these functions; a single server, for example, may have a hard disk and a printer attached, making that server both a file server and a print server.

Work stations are the computers attached to a network that do not normally provide shared resources for other users. These stations are used by the individual users of the network to run software that may be present on a work station or on the file server. Some types of networks allow the simultaneous use of the same computer for a file server and a work station, although this practice is not recommended—network performance suffers as a result. Paradox version 3.5 can be installed on a network's file servers, work stations, or both. The Paradox Multi Pack must be installed on a file server.

Under the terms of the license agreement, network users are limited to one active user of Paradox per copy of Paradox 3.5 and five users per copy of the Paradox Multi Pack. It is possible to have a mix of Paradox versions on a single network. As an example, you could have three copies of Paradox version 3.5 (two installed on a file server and one installed on a work station) along with one Paradox Multi Pack (installed on the file server). Such a combination would allow up to eight users to access Paradox at the same time. It is also possible to have different versions of Paradox on the same LAN, although for consistency, you should upgrade all your copies of Paradox to the latest version.

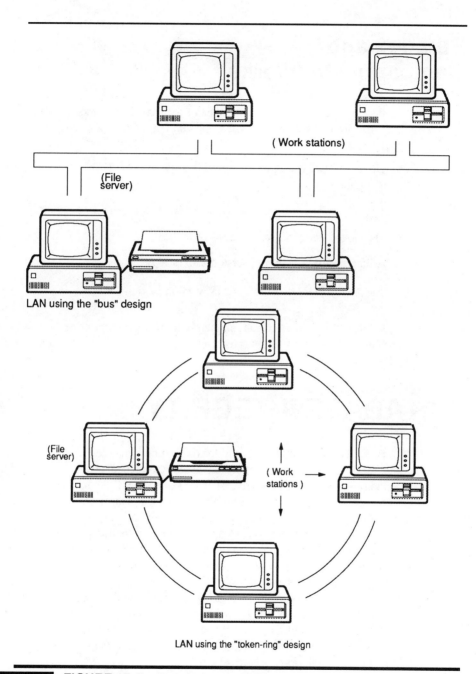

FIGURE 15-1.   Local area network

Paradox and Compatible Networks

At the time of this writing, a number of local area networks are compatible with Paradox. Some networks that will work with Paradox include the following:

- The IBM Token Ring or PC Network with IBM PC LAN program, version 1.12 or higher

- The 3COM 3+ network or 3+ Open Network, version 1.0 or higher

- The Novell network, version 2.0A or higher

- A Banyon Vines network, version 2.10 or higher

- The AT&T Star GROUP for DOS, version 3 or higher

In addition, any network that is completely compatible with any of these networks can use Paradox. The network must use DOS 3.1 or above, or OS/2 version 1.0 or above.

DATABASE INTEGRITY

Users of database software on any local area network face the problem of *database integrity*. The completeness of the database is threatened whenever two users attempt to modify the same database record at the same time. If the software is not designed to operate on a network, serious problems can occur. One user may write over another user's changes, or in more extreme cases, the network operating software may crash and bring the entire network down. In network lingo, such a potential disaster is known as a *collision*. Another common problem, aptly described as a *deadly embrace,* can occur when applications execute endless loops, trying to provide exclusive use of the same file to more than one user on the network.

To prevent such problems, Paradox performs automatic *family* and *record locking*, and it also lets users specifically lock files when desired. Family locking causes a table and its associated objects in use by one user to be restricted or made unavailable to other users on the network. Record locking performs the same type of safeguard, but does so for an individual record within a file.

Paradox will automatically perform the most advantageous type of locking on any table that you use. In addition to the locking that is set automatically by Paradox, you can use specific menu options to designate files as locked or as available by means of a "prevent-lock" menu option.

REQUIREMENTS FOR NETWORK USE

To run Paradox on a network, you will need certain minimum hardware configurations in your file servers or work stations. The computers can be any IBM PC, XT, or AT, PS/2 model 25, 30, 50, 60, or 80; or completely IBM-compatible computers, with any combination of disk drives. The computer must be equipped with 640K of memory and with DOS 3.1 or above (DOS 3.2 or above if you are using the IBM Token Ring network).

Some network operating systems use relatively large amounts of conventional memory. As a result, Paradox cannot be loaded into conventional memory while you are working in such a network. In such cases, you must use an expanded memory board that meets the EMS or EEMS specification. The expanded memory board must contain a minimum of 512K of RAM.

 Network requirements for Paradox with SQL Link are different than those stated here. Refer to your SQL Link *Users' Guide* for additional information.

A NOTE ON INSTALLATION

The actual installation process will not be detailed in this book, as it varies greatly according to the brand of network hardware and software you are using. For specific instructions on the installation of Paradox on your particular network, you should consult the Paradox *Network Administrator's Guide* contained in your Paradox documentation. The remainder of this chapter assumes that your network administrator (the person who manages the network) has already installed Paradox on your network for your use.

If you are faced with the task of installing Paradox on a network, you should thoroughly study the "Installation Overview" chapter of the *Network Administrator's Guide* and then proceed to the chapter that provides details for your brand of network.

HINTS ON GETTING STARTED ON A NETWORK

The precise method used to start Paradox varies from network to network. Some networks use their own custom menus, which will display Paradox, along with other available programs on the network, as a series of menu choices. Other networks use batch files to start programs. In all cases, do not start Paradox from the shared data directory or from the Paradox system directory.

If the copy of Paradox you will use is installed on the file server, you want to be sure you are linked to the file server directory in order to access those files. You should contact your network administrator to determine the proper command or menu choice to start Paradox on your network.

If you attempt to load Paradox on a network and you are unsuccessful, the reason could be indicated by one of the following four common error messages:

- *Can't start Paradox: total number of authorized users has been reached.* This message means that the limit for the number of authorized users on your network has been reached. You must wait for someone who is currently using Paradox on the network to quit using Paradox before you can use the program. To avoid this kind of problem on a long-term basis, you may want to purchase an additional copy of Paradox. If you install that copy on your work station, you will have access to it at all times. (Other network users will not be able to use your copy of Paradox, even when you are not using it.)

- *Can't start Paradox: can't get private directory.* This message means that Paradox was unable to reserve the private directory that is used for your temporary tables. This message usually indicates a problem with the way Paradox was installed on the network. Contact your network administrator for assistance with this problem.

- *Can't start Paradox: invalid PARADOX.CFG file.* This message indicates a problem with the way Paradox was installed, a problem with your DOS path, the presence of more than one configuration file on the same physical drive, or a problem with the path set by the network operating system software. Contact your network administrator for assistance with this problem.

- *Unable to record lock/unlock Paradox net file.* This message can occur for a number of reasons. Either the map to the logical drive specified for the PARA-DOX.NET file is not properly set up, or you do not have proper access rights to the PDOXDATA directory, or there are garbage PARADOX.LCK files left behind because of an abnormal exit from Paradox (in which case you can delete the files and restart Paradox). Contact your network administrator, if necessary, for assistance.

USING PARADOX ON A NETWORK

Paradox's built-in sophistication lets you use it on a network much like you would in a computer not attached to a network. As mentioned earlier, Paradox will automatically lock (prevent other users from having full access to) tables, reports, and forms when necessary. To share tables, forms, and reports with other users, no special precautions need to be taken, other than storing the tables and associated objects in a shared directory on the network.

As you use Paradox on the network, certain operations that you perform will cause Paradox to place limitations, in the form of locks, on what other users can simultaneously do with the data that you are using. This prevents damage to a table or an associated object when two or more users are working with the same data. As an example, if you restructure a table, Paradox automatically places a *full lock* on that table so that no other user can add or edit data while you are changing the table's structure. Also, if another user is viewing a table, Paradox will not let you restructure that table until that user finishes with the table. If a table that you want to use is restricted in some way by some type of lock, Paradox will display a message telling you which network user is using that table.

Network Locks

To prevent the damage that could result from concurrent access, Paradox places restrictions on your data when necessary. These restrictions are described here.

FULL LOCK   This is the most restrictive type of lock that can be placed on a table or object. A full lock prevents another user from accessing that table or object for any reason. Operations that involve major changes to the data, such as sorting to the same table, restructuring a table, emptying a table, and protecting (encrypting) a table, often require full locks.

WRITE LOCK   This type of lock lets other users access a table or object, but they cannot make any changes to it while the write lock remains in place.

PREVENT WRITE LOCK   This restriction prevents other users from placing a write lock on a table or object while you are using it.

Command	Type of Lock
Ask	Prevent full lock
Create	Full lock on table being created
Forms/Design	Full lock on form, prevent full lock on table
Forms/Change	Full lock on form, prevent full lock on table
Modify/Edit	Full lock
Modify/CoEdit	Prevent full lock; prevent write lock while a record is locked
Modify/DataEntry	Prevent full lock on source table; prevent write lock on source when Do-It! is used to add entries to source
Modify/Restructure	Full lock
Modify/Sort	Full lock if sort is to same table; write lock on source, full lock on target if sort is to new table
Report/Output	Prevent full lock
Report/RangeOutput	Prevent full lock
Report/Design	Prevent full lock on table; full lock on report
Report/Change	Prevent full lock on table; full lock on report
Tools/Rename	Full lock on source and target
Tools/ExportImport/Export	Write lock on source
Tools/ExportImport/Import	Full lock on target
Tools/Copy/Table	Write lock on source, full lock on target
Tools/Copy/Form	Write lock on source form, full lock on target form, prevent lock on table
Tools/Copy/Report	Write lock on source report, full lock on target report, prevent lock on table
Tools/Copy/Script	Write lock on source script, full lock on target script, prevent lock on table
Tools/Copy/JustFamily	Full lock on target table and objects, write lock on source table objects, prevent full lock on source table
Tools/Delete/Table	Full lock on table
Tools/Delete/Form	Full lock on form, prevent full lock on table
Tools/Delete/Report	Full lock on report, prevent full lock on table
Tools/Delete/Keepset	Full lock on both table and object
Tools/Delete/ValCheck	Full lock on both table and object
Tools/More/Add	Write lock on source, prevent write lock on target

TABLE 15-1.   Automatic Locks Resulting from Commonly Used Menu Options

Command	Type of Lock
Tools/More/Empty	Full lock
Tools/More/Protect	Full lock
View	Prevent full lock
ValCheck/Define	Full lock on table during editing or data entry session
ValCheck/Clear	Full lock on table during editing or data entry session

TABLE 15-1.   Automatic Locks Resulting from Commonly Used Menu Options (*continued*)

PREVENT FULL LOCK   This restriction prevents other users from placing a full lock on a table or an object. Other users will be able to perform any operation with the object simultaneously, except for an operation that requires a full lock. In Paradox, this is the least restrictive type of lock you can place on an object or a table.

While Paradox handles locking in the background to protect your data, you will find it helpful to know which menu options result in certain types of locks. This may help you plan your own operations so as to minimize inconvenience for fellow users. Table 15-1 shows the types of locks Paradox places on tables and associated objects automatically as a result of your choosing menu options. The table includes the most commonly used Paradox options; for a full list of all menu options, see your Paradox documentation.

Placing Explicit Locks

Although Paradox does an excellent job of placing locks automatically, there may be times when you prefer to place a certain type of lock manually, to ensure that you will be able to access an object when you need to. As an example, imagine you have a request on your desk to restructure a table as soon as possible, and you are on your way out the door to lunch. Past habit tells you that it is difficult (or impossible) to get full control over that shared table in the busy hours following lunch. You may decide to place a full lock on the table now so that you can restructure it when you return from lunch.

To place explicit locks, use Tools/Net/Lock from the main menu. To place explicit prevent locks, choose Tools/Net/PreventLock from the menu. When you choose either of these options, Paradox will ask if you wish to place (or prevent) a full lock or a write lock. Choose FullLock or WriteLock from the menu to place or prevent the desired type of lock.

Using CoEdit

Paradox offers a special editing mode that allows multiple users maximum access to a shared table. If you want to edit a shared table on the network, use the Modify/CoEdit option rather than the Modify/Edit option. The important difference between these two options is that CoEdit is designed to allow concurrent access to the table. By comparison, Edit will force a full lock on the table, making it impossible for anyone else to use the table while you are editing records.

To use the CoEdit option, simply choose Modify/CoEdit from the main menu, and then enter the name of the table to edit. This option will place a prevent full lock on the table being edited. It will also place a prevent write lock whenever you lock a single record (see the next section).

Record Locking
On Demand with ALT-L

You can lock a single record, allowing other users to modify other records while preventing your chosen record from being modified by anyone else. This can be very useful if you know in advance that you are going to edit a series of records, and you want to lock the records so that they remain available.

Paradox automatically locks a record whenever you are in CoEdit mode and you begin to change a record. You can also lock a record explicitly by placing the cursor anywhere in the record and pressing ALT-L. (The ALT-L key is a toggle, so pressing it repeatedly locks and unlocks the current record.)

When you press ALT-L or when you begin changing a record while in CoEdit mode, the status line at the top of the screen will indicate that the record has been locked. Other users will be able to view the record, but they will not be able to modify or delete the record until you unlock it by pressing ALT-L again or by moving the cursor away from the record.

Who Has the Lock?

On a busy network, you may try to gain exclusive access to a particular table, and see an error message similar to "Table has been locked by Mary and 2 others." To find out who is responsible for tying up the table in this kind of situation, use the Lock option of the Tools/Info menu.

From the main menu, choose Tools/Info/Lock, and then enter the name of the table you are attempting to use. Paradox will respond with the names of the users who have placed locks on the table. Unfortunately, Paradox cannot kick those users off the network for you; you will have to solve this problem yourself.

Dealing with the "Lockout After Data Entry" Syndrome

When adding data into a shared table on a busy network, you may often find yourself running into the "lockout syndrome," where you are locked out of a table at the end of a data entry process. What happens is this. You choose Modify/DataEntry to begin adding records, and Paradox places a prevent full lock on the table. The new records get placed in the temporary ENTRY table, where Paradox normally puts the new records you add while using the DataEntry mode of operation.

An hour later, you are done adding data and you press Do-It! (F2), which normally causes Paradox to place a prevent write lock on the original table, and you proceed to add the records to that table. In the last two minutes, however, someone else on the network has begun sorting the table to another table, so that person now has a write lock on the original table. You cannot complete your data entry process until the write lock is released. The table being sorted contains 40 fields and 39,000 records, which means it will be locked for a while yet.

There are two ways to deal with this type of problem. One method is to place an explicit lock on the table with Tools/Net/Lock from the menu before starting the data entry. This will ensure that the table remains available for your use, although it will not win you any friends on the network. A second method, less obtrusive to other users, is to proceed with the data entry without placing any explicit locks beforehand. If you find the table locked upon completion of the data entry, press F10 while you are still in DataEntry mode and choose KeepEntry to save the table under the temporary table name ENTRY. Later, when the original table is available, you can use Tools/Add to add the new records in the ENTRY table to another table. A recommended alternative is to use CoEdit for data entry on a network, as CoEdit is designed to allow simultaneous data entry by multiple users.

Be sure to either add the records to the original table or to rename the ENTRY table before you exit from Paradox. Since ENTRY is a temporary table, it will be lost if you exit without renaming it.

Changing Your Private Directory or User Name

While running on a network, Paradox maintains a private directory and user name for you. The private directory is where your temporary tables are stored. You can change the private directory with the SetDirectory option, available from the Net menu.

To change your private directory, choose Tools/Net/SetPrivate from the main menu, and then enter the new directory (including the drive identifier and path, if desired). To change your user name, choose Tools/Net/Username from the main menu, and enter the desired new user name. Note that selecting either of these options will cause Paradox to clear the workspace and to delete any temporary tables.

Refreshing Your Screen

Whenever you are working with shared tables, your screen image may not necessarily reflect reality at a given instant. It is possible that you will view a table and someone will modify a record five seconds after you have used the View option to bring the table onto your screen. Until your screen is "refreshed" (updated) with the most current information in the table, you will be viewing slightly inaccurate data. You can change the interval of time at which Paradox automatically refreshes your screen by choosing Tools/Net/AutoRefresh and entering a desired value (in seconds) for the refresh time. You can also manually refresh the screen at any time by pressing ALT-R.

Listing Users

You can obtain a list of the users who are currently running Paradox on the network at any time. From the main menu, choose Tools/Info/Who, and a table will appear, listing all network users who are currently running Paradox.

IF YOU HAVE SQL LINK...

Network users of Paradox version 3.5 can take advantage of Paradox SQL Link, an optional product from Borland that allows Paradox to access SQL databases stored on SQL servers. Paradox 3.5 works with Paradox SQL Link to let users access remote

SQL data without learning complex SQL commands. SQL (Structured Query Language) is an industry-standard data language for relational databases residing on minicomputers, mainframes, and PC database servers. If Paradox SQL Link is installed on your network, the menu commands shown below offer the additional options described. Note that all of the commands may not provide all the options shown, depending on the type of server used, and your access rights to the SQL tables on the network.

ASK: You can use Ask to query a remote table stored on the SQL Server. Note that not all Paradox query options are available when querying remote SQL tables.

REPORT: You can use Report to design and print reports based on the remote tables.

CREATE: You can use Create to create remote tables. When you choose this option, Paradox will ask whether you want to create a local table or a table on the SQL Server.

MODIFY/DATAENTRY: You can use Modify/DataEntry to add new records to a table on the SQL Server.

FORMS: You can use Forms to create a data entry form for a table on the SQL Server.

TOOLS/DELETE: You can use Tools/Delete to delete a table on the SQL Server.

TOOLS/MORE/ADD: You can use this option to specify the name of a table on the SQL Server as a source or destination table for adding records.

TOOLS/MORE/EMPTY: You can use this option to specify the name of a table on the SQL Server to empty.

Also, note that when Paradox SQL Link has been installed, the Tools menu displays the additional SQL command. When you choose SQL from the Tools menu, another menu provides you with options related specifically to SQL: Connection, Transaction, ReplicaTools, SQLSave, and Preferences. You can gain additional information about these commands from the SQL Link *Users Guide* supplied with Paradox SQL Link.

GENERAL NETWORK HINTS

To make the most effective use of Paradox on a network, you should keep a few points in mind. In any multiuser environment, large numbers of files tend to clutter the working space on the file servers. To hold such clutter to a minimum, heavy users who do not need to share table access should be provided with individual subdirectories on each file server or on local hard disks if available. If some users will be creating smaller files that will not be used by other network users, encourage them to store such files at their work stations rather than on the file server. This will leave the server more available for its intended purpose: providing shared files.

Back up all tables and associated objects regularly to floppy disks or a tape backup. Create new applications at a work station, and thoroughly test those applications before placing the files in shared space on the file server. A multiuser environment is not the best place to finalize an application's design.

QUICK SUMMARY

To list users on the network   Press F10 for the menu, and choose Tools/Info/Who.

To list locks placed on a table   Press F10 for the menu, and then choose Tools/Info/Lock, then enter the name of the desired table.

To place a lock on a table   Press F10 for the menu, and then choose Tools/Net/Lock. From the next menu, choose FullLock to place a full lock on the table, or choose WriteLock to place a write lock on the table.

To prevent a lock on a table   Press F10 for the menu, and then choose Tools/Net/PreventLock. From the next menu, choose FullLock to prevent others from setting a full lock on the table, or choose WriteLock to prevent others from setting a write lock on the table.

To edit a table on a network while allowing shared access   Press F10 for the menu, and choose Modify/CoEdit (or press ALT-F9).

To lock or unlock a single record while in CoEdit mode   Press the ALT-L key.

To change your private directory or user name   Press F10 for the menu, and choose Tools/Net/SetPrivate (to change your private directory), or choose Tools/Net/User-Name (to change your user name). Enter the desired new directory name or user name.

chapter 16

SAMPLE
APPLICATIONS

A Mailing List
A Sales-Tracking Database

This chapter contains step-by-step details for building two sample Paradox applications. To greatly speed the development process, the applications are developed by using the Paradox Personal Programmer. If you have not yet installed the Personal Programmer on your system, you must do so, as detailed in Chapter 13, before building any of these applications. You will want to try these applications and then modify and expand them to fill your own needs.

A MAILING LIST

The mailing-list application maintains a mailing list. Menu options are used to add names to the list, edit existing names, or delete names that are no longer needed. The printer options offered by the application allow the printing of names in the form of a registry or as mailing labels selected by state.

First create a table for the application. Call the table MAILLIST, and specify the fields and their characteristics as shown here:

Field Name	Field Type
Last name	A20
First name	A20
Company	A20
Address	A30
City	A20
State	A2
ZIP Code	A5

Load the Paradox Personal Programmer, and use the Tools/Directory choice to change to the directory that contains the MAILLIST table.

Choose Create, call the application MAILS, select ExistingTable, enter **MAIL-LIST** as the table name, and then select DO-IT! or press F2. For a table description, enter **Mailing List**.

For the first main menu choice, enter

Add Names

For the description, enter **Add new names to mailing list**. For the second menu choice, enter

Edit/Delete Names

For the description, enter **Edit or delete names in the mailing list**.

For the third menu choice, enter

Print Registry

For the description, enter **Print Registry of Names**. For the fourth menu choice, enter

Print Labels

For the description, enter **Print mailing labels for a given State**.

Press F2 to save the menu choices. Then choose SpecifyAction from the next menu that appears. For Add Names, choose DataEntry from the menu. Choose SelectTable, and then choose MAILLIST from the list. Choose FormView from the next menu, and then choose StandardForm.

Choose Settings from the next menu, and when the form appears, place the cursor in the State field and press F10. Choose ValCheck/Define/Picture. Enter && (which tells Paradox to limit all entries in this field to two letters that will be converted to uppercase).

Move the cursor to the ZIP Code field, press F10, and choose ValCheck/Define/Picture. Enter ##### as the picture. Then, press Do-It! (F2). From the next menu that appears, choose DO-IT! or press F2 again.

For the Edit/Delete Names menu option, choose Edit from the main menu. Choose SelectTable and then MAILLIST. From the next menu, choose TableView. Then choose Insert/Delete, Delete, and then Yes to allow deletions from the editing option. Finally, press F2 to save the menu definition.

For the Print Registry option, choose Report from the main menu. Choose SelectTable and then MAILLIST. From the next menu, choose AllRecords. Then choose StandardReport, and choose Printer from the next menu to appear.

For the Print Labels option, you will need a custom report for the mailing labels. From the menu, choose Report, then SelectTable, then MAILLIST, and then SelectRecords. In the Query Form that appears, place the cursor in the State field and enter the following:

~tellme

Then press Do-It! (F2). In a moment, Paradox will ask for a prompt to be entered by the user before printing the mailing labels. Enter

Enter the two-letter abbreviation of the State:

as a prompt. Then press RETURN to accept A2 as a data type for the variable.

From the next menu to appear, choose Design. Select 1 as a report name, and then enter **LABELS** as a description and choose FreeForm. In a moment, a free-form report that uses the default Report Specification will appear on the screen.

Move the cursor down two lines and press CTRL-Y six times to delete all of the lines between the start of the page and the form bands. Using the techniques for report design covered in Chapter 12, move the First name field to the same line as the Last name field, and delete all of the headings, leaving just the data fields. Then place the State and ZIP Code fields on the same line as the City field.

Move the cursor to the left edge of the screen, and use CTRL-Y to remove the blank line at the top of the form band. Then add two blank lines at the bottom of the form band. Move to the start of the line immediately below the bottom of the form band, and press CTRL-Y four times to remove the blanks.

Press F10, and choose Setting/RemoveBlanks/FieldSqueeze/Yes. Then press F10 again, and choose Setting/RemoveBlanks/ LineSqueeze/Yes/Fixed. (These two steps will trim blank spaces between fields and will trim lines that would otherwise be blank when no data occupies a field.) Press F10 once more, and choose Setting/PageLayout/Length. Enter C to set the new page length to Continous. Finally, press F2 to store the form for the mailing labels.

From the next menu to appear, choose Printer to direct the mailing labels to the printer. Finally, choose No in response to the question that asks if you want to create a splash screen, and press Do-It! (F2) to generate the application.

Use the Play option of the Personal Programmer main menu to test the application. You may want to try adding some features of your own with the menu's Modify choice.

A SALES-TRACKING DATABASE

For an example of a more complex—and fully relational—application, consider the problems involved in tracking sales of items. The transactions themselves must be recorded in a transactions table; listings of customers who purchase the items are kept in a customers table; and products (or the inventory of items to be sold) are kept in an inventory table. The application must be able to query the related tables as necessary to produce the necessary bills and reports.

Before starting, you may want to create a directory from DOS; you cannot create new directories from the Personal Programmer. This directory will be used to store all of the sales files used in the application. You could use commands like

```
CD\
MD\SALES
```

from DOS to create a new subdirectory called SALES. Then you could get into the Personal Programmer in the usual manner and use the Tools/Directory menu option to change to the SALES directory.

Choose Create, and enter **SALES** as the application name. From the next menu, choose NewTable. Call the table TRANSACT (for "transactions"), and enter the structure shown here:

Field Name	Field Type
Customer Code	A4
Product Code	A4
Quantity Sold	N
Date of Sale	D

After pressing Do-It! to save the structure, choose NewTable again, and call the next table CUSTOM (for "customers"). Enter the table structure shown here:

Field Name	Field Type
Customer Code	A4
Customer Name	A30
Address	A30
City	A15
State	A2
ZIP Code	A5

After pressing Do-It! to save the structure, choose NewTable again, and call the next table PRODUCTS. Enter the table structure shown here:

Field Name	Field Type
Product Code	A4
Description	A30
Cost	$
Supplier	A30

Save the new table's structure with Do-It! (F2), and then press Do-It! (F2) again to save the list of tables for the application. Paradox will next prompt you for descriptions for the new tables.

For the TRANSACT table, enter **Sales transactions** as a description. For the CUSTOM table, enter **Customer list** as a description. For the PRODUCTS table, enter **Inventory of products** as a description.

After you enter the descriptions, the first option for the application's main menu will appear. For the first menu choice, enter

Sales Transactions

As a description, enter **Add or edit sales transactions**. For the second menu choice, enter

Maintain Customers

As a description, enter **Add or edit customer list**.
For the third menu choice, enter

Maintain Inventory

As a description, enter **Add, edit, delete inventory items**. For the fourth menu choice, enter

Print Reports

As a description, enter **Print reports of sales, inventory, or customers**.

When you have finished defining the main menu names and descriptions, press Do-It! (F2). From the next menu that appears, choose SpecifyAction.

For the SALES TRANSACTIONS menu choice, choose Menu. For the first option of the submenu that appears, enter

Enter a Sale

For the description, enter **Enter a new sales transaction**. For the second option of the submenu, enter

Edit/Delete Sales

For the description, enter **Edit or delete sales transactions**. Then press F2, and choose SpecifyAction from the next menu that appears.

For Enter a Sale, choose DataEntry, then SelectTable, and then TRANSACT as the table name. Press Do-It! (F2). From the next menu, choose TableView and then select DO-IT!

For Edit/Delete Sales, choose Edit, then SelectTable, and then TRANSACT as the table name. Press Do-It! (F2). From the next menu, choose TableView, then Insert-Delete, then Delete, then Yes, and then DO-IT!

The next menu option that needs defining is the Maintain Customers menu option. For this choice, choose Menu. For the first option of the submenu that appears, enter

Enter New Customer

For the description, enter **Enter a new customer name and address**.

For the second option of the submenu, enter

Edit/Delete Customer

For the description, enter **Edit or delete an existing customer**. Then press F2, and choose SpecifyAction from the next menu that appears. For Enter New Customer, choose DataEntry, then SelectTable, and then CUSTOM as the table name. Press

Do-It! (F2). From the next menu, choose FormView, then StandardForm, and then select DO-IT!

For Edit/Delete Customer, choose Edit, then SelectTable, and then CUSTOM as the table name. Press Do-It! (F2). From the next menu, choose TableView, then InsertDelete, then Delete, then Yes, and then DO-IT!

The next menu option that will need a definition is the Maintain Inventory option. As a choice, choose Menu. For the first option of the submenu that appears, enter

Enter New Product

For the description, enter **Enter a new inventory item, with product code**. For the second option of the submenu, enter

Edit/Delete Product

For the description, enter **Edit or delete an existing inventory item**. Then press F2, and choose SpecifyAction from the next menu that appears.

For Enter New Product, choose DataEntry, then SelectTable, and then PROD-UCTS as the table name. Press Do-It! (F2). From the next menu, choose FormView, then StandardForm, and then DO-IT! For Edit/Delete Product, choose Edit, then Select-Table, and then PRODUCTS as the table name. Press Do-It! (F2). From the next menu, choose TableView, then InsertDelete, then Delete, then Yes, and then DO-IT!

The next menu that needs defining is the Print Reports menu. For this choice, select Menu. When the first submenu choice appears, enter

Print Transactions

As a description, enter **Print Sales Transactions**. For the second submenu choice, enter

Print Customers

As a description, enter **Print the Customer List**. For the third submenu choice, enter

Print Products

As a description, enter **Print the Inventory (Product) List**.

Press Do-It! (F2) to save the menu names and descriptions, and then choose SpecifyAction from the next menu to appear. For the Print Transactions option, choose

Report and then choose AllTables. From the next menu to appear, choose Create (to create a new multitable view). A Query Form will appear.

In the TRANSACT query, with the cursor at the far left, press F6 to place a checkmark in all the fields. Then move to the Customer Code field, press F5 to begin an example, and enter the following:

link1

Move the cursor to the Product Code field, press F5 to begin another example, and enter the following:

link2

Then press F4 to move the cursor down to the Query Form for CUSTOM. Place the cursor in the Customer Code field, press F5 to begin an example, and enter the following:

link1

Then move the cursor to the Customer Name field, and press F6 to place a checkmark.

Press F4 to move down to the query for PRODUCTS. Move the cursor to the Product Code field, press the F5 key to begin an example, and enter the following:

link2

Place the cursor in the Description field and press F6 to add a checkmark. Move the cursor to the Cost field, and press F6 again to add a checkmark. Finally, press Do-It! (F2) to store the completed query.

From the next menu to appear, choose AllRecords. Then choose Design to design a new report. Select 1 as a name for the report, and enter **Transaction Report** as a description.

From the next menu to appear, choose FreeForm for the type of report. In a moment, the default free-form report containing the selected columns from the three tables will appear on the screen.

Move the cursor down six lines. Press F10 for the Report Design menu, and choose Group/Insert/Field to add a group to the report based on a field. Select Customer Code as the desired field from the list that appears. With the cursor appearing anywhere on the line just below the report date, page number, and heading, press RETURN to place the group in this location.

Move the cursor down until it is located just below the bottom of the form band and just above the bottom of the group band. Enter

Total for Customer

and press the spacebar once to add a space. Press F10 for the Report Design menu. Choose Field/Place/Summary/Regular. From the list of fields that appears, choose Cost. From the next menu to appear, choose Sum and then choose PerGroup. With the cursor between the end of the form band and the end of the group band and just to the right of the heading you just added, press RETURN three times—once to set the field, once to set the width, and once to set the number of decimal places. Finally, press F2 to save the Report Specification. From the next menu, choose Printer to direct the report's output to the default printer.

The next menu action to require defining is the PRINT CUSTOMERS option. For this choice, choose Report, then SelectTable, then Custom, and then DO-IT! From the next menu to appear, choose AllRecords. Then choose StandardReport followed by Printer.

Now define the PRINT PRODUCTS option. For this choice, choose Report, then SelectTable, then Products, and then DO-IT! From the next menu to appear, choose AllRecords. Then choose StandardReport and Printer.

Choose SplashScreen and follow the procedures covered in Chapter 13 if you desire a splash screen, or choose NoSplashScreen if you do not want to use a splash screen. Then choose DO-IT! (or press F2) to write the application.

Use the Play option of the Personal Programmer main menu to test the application. You may want to try adding some additional features to the application. As a starting point, you might want to add validity checking to the TRANSACT table, using the related tables as lookup tables. You could use the ValCheck/Define/TableLookup options to check that a customer number entered into a new transaction actually exists in the Customer Code field of the CUSTOMER table, and that a product code entered into a new transaction actually exists in the Product Code field of the PRODUCTS table.

Another option you might want to add would use a free-form report to generate bills to each customer. You could design the bill as a form letter, with a summary field containing the total amount owed by the customer. You could also limit the records included in the bill to a specific range of dates so that you could, for example, produce on a monthly basis the bills that apply only to purchases made during that month. This chapter has provided you with the ideas to get you started on developing your own applications.

PARADOX
MENU OPTIONS

This appendix provides a summary of the Paradox menu options. Use it to jog your memory—it will quickly show you which options are available for Paradox operations. Included with each menu option is a listing of the steps needed to perform the operation. Note that all options are selected from the main menu unless otherwise indicated.

1-2-3

Sequence:
Tools/ExportImport/Import/1-2-3
Tools/ExportImport/Export/1-2-3

Use the 1-2-3 option to exchange files between Paradox and 1-2-3. To import a 1-2-3 file into Paradox, choose Tools/ExportImport/Import/1-2-3 from the main menu. From the next menu, choose Release 1a or Release 2 as desired. Enter a filename for the 1-2-3 worksheet, and then enter the name of the new Paradox table that will receive the 1-2-3 data. Paradox will proceed to convert your 1-2-3 worksheet into a Paradox table and will display the table in the workspace.

To export a file from Paradox to 1-2-3, choose Tools/ExportImport/Export/1-2-3 from the main menu. From the next menu, choose Release 1a or Release 2 as desired. Enter the name of the table that is to be exported to the 1-2-3 program, and then enter a filename for the resulting 1-2-3 worksheet. Alphanumeric fields will become labels within cells; number fields will become numbers in cells with a general format; currency fields will become numbers within cells with a 1-2-3 format; and date fields will become numbers with a date format.

Add

Sequence:
Tools/More/Add

The Add option lets you add records from one table to another table. Use Add to merge a single table into another table. Choose Tools/More/Add, and Paradox prompts you for the name of the source table (which will supply the records to be added) and the target table (which will receive the records). The fields in the two tables must be of compatible types and must be arranged in the same order.

Note that if the target table contains a key field, two additional menu options will appear. NewEntries adds records to the end of the target table (and places any records with a matching key field in a temporary table called KEYVIOL). The Update option updates records in the target table based on matching key field values. If the target table is not keyed, no such option is provided, and the records from the source table are added to the end of the target table.

All

Sequence (from the Edit Menu):
ValCheck/Clear/All

The All option lets you clear, from the table in use, all validity checks previously established with ValCheck. While in Edit mode, press F10 for the Edit menu, then choose ValCheck/Clear/All to clear the validity checks.

AppendDelimited

Sequence:
Tools/ExportImport/Import/ASCII/AppendDelimited

Use the AppendDelimited option to append data from a foreign file that uses delimited ASCII format into an existing Paradox table. Fields in such a foreign file are usually separated by commas, and may optionally be enclosed in single or double quotes; the ASCII text file should have an extension of .TXT. Choose Tools/ExportImport/Import/ASCII/AppendDelimited, and supply the name of the foreign file. Then supply the name of the table to which the data should be appended.

   Note that if the target table contains a key field, two additional menu options will appear. NewEntries adds records to the end of the target table (and places any records with a matching key field in a temporary table called KEYVIOL). The Update option updates records in the target table based on matching key field values. If the target table is not keyed, no such option is provided, and the records from the source table are added to the end of the target table.

Area

Sequence (from the Form Design Menu):
Area/Erase
Area/Move

Use the Area option to move or erase portions of a form. To move an area, choose Area/Move from the Form Design menu. Place the cursor at one corner of the area to be moved and press RETURN; move the cursor to the diagonal corner of the area and press RETURN again; finally, use the cursor keys to drag the area to its new location and press RETURN.

   To erase an area, from the Form Design menu, choose Area/Erase. Place the cursor at one corner of the area to be erased and press RETURN; then move the cursor to the diagonal corner of the area, and press RETURN again to erase the area.

ASCII

Sequence:
Tools/ExportImport/Export/ASCII
Tools/ExportImport/Import/ASCII

Use the ASCII option to transfer data in ASCII format to and from Paradox tables. To export data as ASCII, choose Tools/ExportImport/Export/ASCII, and choose Delimited or Text as the format. Enter a name for the table that is to be exported, and then enter a filename for the ASCII file.

To import an ASCII file into a Paradox table, choose Tools/ExportImport/Import/ASCII, and choose Delimited, AppendDelimited, or Text as the format. Enter the name of the foreign file, and then supply the name of the table to which the data should be imported. Note that if you do not specify an extension, the default extension is .TXT. You can only use the Text option when exporting single-field files. When importing, use the Text option for fixed-length, non-delimited files.

Ask

Sequence:
Ask

Use the Ask option to compose a query that will let you select a subset of records based on various criteria and establish relationships between multiple tables. Choose Ask and enter the name of the appropriate table to display a Query Form containing the fields for that table. Place the cursor in any desired field, and press F6 to include the fields in the answer. (To include every field in the answer, place the cursor at the extreme left and press F6 for all fields or ALT-F6 for all fields with duplicate records included). To select certain records, enter the matching criteria in the fields.

To compose queries that depend on information in multiple tables, repeat this process for as many tables as necessary. Link the common fields in the multiple tables by pressing F5 to place example elements in the common fields. When the Query Form is completed, press Do-It! (F2) to produce the results, which are stored in a temporary ANSWER table. Use the Tools/Rename/Table option to rename the ANSWER table if a permanent record of the query results is desired.

AutoRefresh

Sequence:
Modify/CoEdit/*tablename*F10/AutoRefresh
Tools/Net/AutoRefresh

Use the AutoRefresh option to change the time interval (in seconds) that Paradox waits before refreshing the screen when you are in CoEdit mode. From the CoEdit menu, choose AutoRefresh. Enter a number for the desired value, from 1 to 3600 seconds (1 hour). The default value is 3 seconds.

Average

Sequence (from the Report Design Menu):
Field/Place/Summary/Calculated/*<expression>*/Average
Field/Place/Calculated/*<expression>*/Average

Use the Average option to average the values in a numeric field on a custom free-form or tabular report. From the Report Design menu, choose Field/Place/Summary/Calculated/Average if the field to be averaged in the report is a summary field. Then select PerGroup (if you want a summary each time the group changes) or Overall (if you only desire an overall summary). Use the cursor to place the field in its desired band, and press RETURN. Next, adjust the number of digits displayed with the left and right cursor keys, and press RETURN. Finally, adjust the number of decimal points displayed with the cursor keys, and press RETURN to complete the placement of the field.

BeginRecord

Sequence:
Scripts/BeginRecord

Use the BeginRecord option to begin recording a new script. Choose Scripts/Begin-Record, and enter a name for the new script. Paradox will record all further actions until you end the recording with Scripts/EndRecord. Use Scripts/Play or Scripts/ShowPlay to play back a recorded script.

Blink

Sequence (from the Form Design Menu):
Style/Blink (Version 2.0 only)
Style/Monochrome/Blink (Version 3.5 and 3.0)

Use the Blink option to turn on or off the blinking of text and borders on a form. From the Form Design menu, choose Style/Blink/Blink, and then enter the text or borders that are to have a blinking format. Choose Style/Blink/NoBlink before entering the text or borders to turn off the blinking.

Border (to Add or
Erase Borders in a Form)

Sequence (from the Form Design Menu):
Border

Use this Border option to add or erase borders in a form. To add a border, choose Border/Place from the Form Design menu. From the next menu, choose SingleLine, DoubleLine, or Other for the type of border. Place the cursor at one corner of the border and press RETURN; move the cursor to the diagonal corner and press RETURN again to draw the border.

To remove a border, choose Border/Erase from the Form Design menu. Place the cursor at one corner of the border and press RETURN to select it. Then move the cursor to the diagonal corner and press RETURN again to erase the border.

Border (to Add or Change
Colors of Existing Border)

Sequence (from the Form Design Menu):
Style/Color/Border

Use this Border option to add or change colors of an existing border. From the Form Design menu, choose Style/Color/Border. Place the cursor at one corner of the border and press RETURN to select it. Then move the cursor to the diagonal corner of the border and press RETURN. Finally, use the arrow keys followed by RETURN to select the desired colors from the color palette that appears.

Borrow

Sequence:
Create/Borrow
Modify/Restructure/Borrow

Use the Borrow option to "borrow" the structure of an existing table while you are designing or restructuring another table. To borrow a table's structure, choose Create and enter the name of the table; then press F10, choose Borrow, and enter the name of the table to borrow the structure from. While restructuring, press F10, choose Borrow, and enter the name of the table from which to borrow the structure.

Note that fields borrowed from the other table will be inserted into the current table structure, above the present cursor location.

CalcEdit

Sequence (from the Form Design or Report Specification Menu):
Field/CalcEdit

Use the CalcEdit option to edit an expression used in the calculated field of a form or report. From either the Form Design menu or the Report Specification menu, choose Field/CalcEdit. Place the cursor at the desired field, and press RETURN to select the field. The existing expression will appear at the top of the screen, and you can edit the expression as desired.

Cancel

Sequence:
Cancel

Use the Cancel option to cancel the current Paradox operation. In most cases, Paradox will request confirmation by displaying an additional menu with Yes and No options. You must choose Yes to confirm the cancellation of the option.

Change

Sequence:
Forms/Change
Report/Change

Use the Change option to change existing forms or reports. To change a form, choose Forms/Change and enter a name for the table. Select an identifier for the form, and change the description or press RETURN to accept the existing description. Then make the desired changes to the form itself and press Do-It! (F2).

To change a Report Specification, choose Report/Change and enter a name for the table. Select a designator for the report, and the report description will appear. Make any desired changes to the report description and press RETURN to display the Report Specification. Make the desired changes, and press Do-It! (F2).

Clear

Sequence (from the Edit Menu):
ValCheck/Clear

Use the Clear option to clear validity check settings from a single field or from an entire table. To clear the validity check settings, press F10 while editing, and then select ValCheck/Clear. To clear the validity settings from all fields, choose All from the next menu. To clear the validity settings from a single field, choose Field, move the cursor to the desired field, and press RETURN to select the field.

Note that if you are using Paradox on a network, you may need to use a password to modify any validity checks if the table's owner has restricted access to that table.

ClearPasswords

Sequence:
Tools/More/Protect/ClearPasswords

Use the ClearPasswords option to clear all passwords entered during a session from memory. Choose Tools/More/Protect/ClearPasswords. The passwords you entered to access protected objects will be cleared from memory, and any further use of those objects will again require the entry of the passwords.

CoEdit

Sequence:
Modify/CoEdit
ALT-F9

Use the CoEdit option to edit a table while other users may also be editing that table on a network. Choose Modify/CoEdit, and enter the name of the table to be coedited. When done editing, press Do-It! (F2). Note that you cannot cancel a CoEdit session. The records must be deleted while in CoEdit mode, or emptied when in main mode.

Color

Sequence (from the Form Design Menu):
Style/Color

Use this option to choose foreground or background colors for an area or border in a form. From the Form Design menu, choose Style/Color. From the next menu to appear, choose Area (to color an area of the form), or choose Border (to color a border). Place the cursor in one corner of the area or border and press RETURN; then move the cursor to the diagonal corner of the area or border and press RETURN again. Finally, use the arrow keys followed by RETURN to select the desired colors from the color palette that appears.

ColumnSize

Sequence:
Image/ColumnSize

Use the ColumnSize option to change the width of a column in a table. To change the column size, choose Image/ColumnSize and then move the cursor to the column that is to be resized. Press RETURN, and use the left and right arrow keys to adjust the column size. Then press RETURN to set the new column width.

Copy

Sequence:
Tools/Copy

Use this Copy option to copy Paradox objects, including tables, along with associated forms and reports or scripts. From the menu, choose Tools/Copy, and Paradox offers an additional menu with options of Table, Form, Report, Script, and JustFamily. Choose Form, Report, or Script to copy any of these specific objects; choose Just-Family to copy all associated objects except the table; and choose Table to copy the table and its family. Finally, enter the names of the source table and target table if prompted.

Note that if you choose Tools/Copy/JustFamily, the target table that will receive the copied objects must exist and have the same structure.

Copy (for Reports)

Sequence (from the Report Specification Menu):
TableBand/Copy

Use this Copy option to copy columns from one location in a tabular report to another. From the Report Specification menu, choose TableBand/Copy. Place the cursor in the desired column of the table band, and press RETURN to select the column. Then place the cursor in the desired location for the copy, and press RETURN again.

Count

Sequence (from the Report Design Menu):
Field/Place/Summary/Calculated/*<expression>*/Count

Use the Count option to count the number of values in a field on a custom free-form or tabular report. From the Report Design menu, choose Field/Place/Summary/Calculated/Count if the field to be counted is a summary field. Then select PerGroup (for a count of the number of values in a field for each group) or Overall (for an overall count). Use the cursor to place the field in the desired location and press RETURN. Next, adjust the number of digits displayed with the left and right arrow keys, and then press RETURN. Finally, adjust the number of decimal points displayed with the cursor keys, and press RETURN to complete the placement of the field.

Create

Sequence:
Create

Use the Create option to create a new Paradox table. Choose Create from the menu, and enter a name for the new table. Paradox displays a table structure image, with entries for field names and corresponding field types. Fill in the desired fields and field types. Add an asterisk beside the field type to indicate a key field. (Key fields must be the first fields in a table.) After defining the fields, press Do-It! (F2) to store the completed table definition.

CrossTab

Sequence:
Image/Graph/CrossTab

Use the CrossTab option to build a crosstab table based on the current table. A crosstab is a cross-tabulation, or spreadsheet-like numeric analysis of data within a table. With the desired table to be cross-tabulated on the screen, choose Image/Graph/CrossTab. A new table named CROSSTAB will appear, containing the summary values in crosstab form.

DataEntry

Sequence:
Modify/DataEntry

Use the DataEntry option to add records to a table without displaying existing records on the screen. Choose Modify/DataEntry, and enter the table name. A new temporary table called ENTRY will appear, and you can proceed to add the necessary records.

When done with the data entry, press Do-It! (F2) to store the records in the original table.

Date

Sequence (from the Report Design Menu):
Field/Place/Date

Use the Date option to place a field containing the current date in a custom free-form or tabular report. From the Report Design menu, choose Field/Place/Date. Select one of 11 possible date formats that appear as a menu. Move the cursor to the location on the report at which the date is to appear, and press RETURN to place the date field.

dBASE

Sequence:
Tools/ExportImport/Import/dBASE
Tools/ExportImport/Export/dBASE

Use the dBASE option to exchange files between Paradox and dBASE. To import a dBASE file into Paradox, from the menu choose Tools/ExportImport/Import/dBASE and enter the name of the file to import; then enter a name for the new Paradox table that will receive the dBASE data. Paradox will automatically analyze the type of dBASE file and convert it into a Paradox table. Note that only the first 255 characters of a dBASE memo field will be imported into a Paradox table.

To export a file from Paradox to dBASE, from the menu choose Tools/ExportImport/Export/dBASE. Select dBASE II, dBASE III, or dBASE IV from the next menu that appears. Enter the name of the table that is to be exported to dBASE, and then enter a filename for the resulting dBASE file. Alphanumeric fields will become dBASE character fields; number fields will become dBASE numeric fields; currency fields will become dBASE numeric fields with two decimal places; and date fields will become dBASE date fields (if exported to dBASE III, III PLUS, or IV) or character fields (if exported to dBASE II).

Default

Sequence (from the Edit Menu):
ValCheck/Define/Default

Use the Default option to set the default value for a field in the table. While in DataEntry or Edit mode, press F10 for the menu, and then choose ValCheck/Define. Place the cursor in the field for which you want to set the default value, and press RETURN. From the next menu, choose Default, and enter the value that Paradox is to insert if the field is left blank.

Default (for Forms, Version 2.0 Only)

Sequence (from the Form Design Menu):
Style/Default

Use this Default option to set the attributes used in a form (such as blinking, reverse video, and intensity) to the default values while you are designing the form. From the Form Design menu, choose Style/Default to set the text and borders to the default attributes of normal intensity, no blinking, no reversal, and no field names displayed during editing. After making this choice, any text or borders that you add to the form will possess the default attributes.

Delete (for Paradox Objects)

Sequence:
Tools/Delete

Use the Delete option to delete Paradox objects, including tables, forms, reports, scripts, query speedup files, image settings, or validity checks. From the menu, choose

Tools/Delete, and Paradox offers an additional menu with options of Table, Form, Report, Script, QuerySpeedup, KeepSet, ValCheck, and Graph. Select the object that is to be deleted. If you select Table, both the table and all its associated objects will be deleted.

Delete (for Bands in a Custom Report)

Sequence (from the Report Design Menu):
Group/Delete
Setting/PageLayout/Delete

When designing reports, you can use the Delete option to delete group bands or to delete the last page-width setting. To delete a group, press F10 for the Report Design menu and choose Group/Delete. Place the cursor at the group to be deleted, and press RETURN.

To delete the last page width, press F10 for the Report Design menu and choose Setting/PageLayout/Delete. Then choose OK from the next menu to confirm the operation.

Delete (for Pages in a Form)

Sequence:
Page/Delete

Use this Delete option to delete any page of a form. While designing or changing the form, with the cursor at the desired page, press F10 for the Form Design menu. Choose Page/Delete to delete the unwanted page.

Design

Sequence:
Forms/Design
Report/Design

Use the Design option to design new forms or custom reports. To design a form, choose Forms/Design and enter a name for the table. Select an identifier for the form, and enter a description; then design the form as desired. When done with the design, press Do-It! (F2).

To design a report, choose Report/Design and enter a name for the table. Select a designator for the report, and then enter a description. Choose Tabular or Free-Form for the desired type of report, and then design the report as desired. When done with the Report Specification, press Do-It! (F2).

Directory

Sequence:
Tools/More/Directory

Use the Directory option to change the default directory being used by Paradox. Choose Tools/More/Directory, and enter the directory name that you desire. The name may be preceded by a disk drive identifier such as B:\FILES. Note that when you change directories, the workspace is cleared and any temporary tables are discarded.

DisplayOnly

Sequence (from the Form Design Menu):
Field/Place/DisplayOnly

Use the DisplayOnly option to place a display-only field at the desired location on a form. From the Form Design menu, choose Field/Place/DisplayOnly. Select the desired field from the list of fields that appears, and then place the cursor at the desired location for the display-only field. Press RETURN to anchor the starting location for the field. Adjust the field's width with the left and right cursor keys, and then press RETURN again to complete the placement of the field.

DO-IT!

Sequence:
DO-IT!

Use the Do-It! option to complete the current Paradox operation. Selecting DO-IT! from a menu is functionally equivalent to pressing the Do-It! (F2) key.

Double-Line

Sequence (from the Form Design Menu):
Border/Place/Double-Line

Use the Double-Line option to add a double-line border in a form. To add the border, choose Border/Place/Double-Line from the Form Design menu. Place the cursor at one corner of the border and press RETURN; move the cursor to the diagonal corner and press RETURN again to draw the border.

Edit (for Modifying A Table)

Sequence:
Modify/Edit

Use this Edit option to edit an existing table. Choose Modify/Edit, and enter the name of the table you wish to edit. The cursor will appear in the first record of that table, and you can use the editing keys in Paradox to help you edit the desired records. To edit in a form layout, press the Form Toggle (F7) key. When done editing records, press Do-It! (F2).

Edit (for Modifying A Script)

Sequence:
Scripts/Editor/Edit

Use this Edit option to edit an existing script. Choose Scripts/Editor/Edit, and enter the name of the script you wish to modify. The script editor will appear, and you can make the desired changes to the existing script. When done editing the script, press Do-It! (F2).

Editor

Sequence:
Scripts/Editor

See Scripts/Editor/Edit or Scripts/Editor/Write.

Empty

Sequence:
Tools/More/Empty

Use the Empty option to empty an entire table of all records. Choose Tools/More /Empty, and enter the name for the desired table. As a safeguard, Paradox will require confirmation by displaying a menu with Cancel and OK options. You must select OK to empty the table.

End-Record

Sequence:
Scripts/End-Record

Use this option to end the recording of a script. When you are done recording a script, press F10. From the menu that appears, choose Scripts/End-Record. Use Scripts/Play or Scripts/ShowPlay to play back a recorded script.

Entry

Sequence:
Modify/Multientry/Entry

Use the Entry option to enter records into a single source table for storage in several target tables. Choose Modify/Multientry/Entry. Enter the name of the source table and then supply the name of the map table (created with Modify/Multientry/Setup). You can then enter data into the source table. When you complete the data entry with Do-It! (F2), the data will be added to the appropriate fields in the target tables, as defined by the map table.

Erase (for Forms)

Sequence (from the Form Design Menu):
Field/Erase
Area/Erase

Use this Erase option to erase portions of a form. To erase a field, choose Field/Erase from the Form Design menu. Place the cursor anywhere in the desired field, and press RETURN to erase the field.

To erase an area, choose Area/Erase from the Form Design menu. Place the cursor at one corner of the area to be erased and press RETURN; then move the cursor to the diagonal corner and press RETURN again to erase the area.

Erase (for Reports)

Sequence (from the Report Specification Menu):
Field/Erase
TableBand/Erase

Use this Erase option to erase fields or columns from a tabular report. To erase a field within the report, choose Field/Erase from the Report Specification menu. Place the cursor on the desired field, and press RETURN to erase the field. To erase a table band, choose TableBand/Erase from the Report Specification menu. Place the cursor on the desired column, and press RETURN to erase the table band.

Exit

Sequence:
Exit

Use the Exit option to exit Paradox and return to the operating system. When you exit from Paradox, any data in temporary tables (such as ANSWER, ENTRY, and

KEYVIOL) is discarded. When you select Exit, Paradox will confirm that you want to leave the program. Select Yes to proceed or No to cancel the command.

Export

Sequence:
Tools/ExportImport/Export

Use the Export option to export files from a Paradox table to other software. To export a file from Paradox, choose Tools/ExportImport/Export from the menu. Select the desired file format from the available choices. Paradox lets you export files to Lotus 1-2-3, Quattro/QuattroPro, Symphony, dBASE, PFS, VisiCalc (DIF), and ASCII formats.

After selecting the desired format (and in the case of 1-2-3, Quattro or Quattro Pro, Symphony, and dBASE, the desired version), you must enter the table name, and supply a filename for the resulting file. Extensions are optional, but in the case of 1-2-3, Quattro or Quattro Pro, Symphony, and dBASE files, Paradox will automatically supply the proper extension if you omit it.

ExportImport

Sequence:
Tools/ExportImport

See Tools/ExportImport/Export or Tools/ExportImport/Import.

Family

Sequence:
Tools/Info/Family

Use the Family option to list all forms and reports associated with a table. Choose Tools/Info/Family and enter a name for the desired table. Paradox will display a table named FAMILY, which contains the name and creation date of all reports and forms, along with the table name.

Fast

Sequence:
Scripts/ShowPlay/Fast

Use the Fast option to play back each step in a recorded script so that you can watch it at fast speed. Choose Scripts/ShowPlay, and enter the name of the desired script. Then select Fast to play the script rapidly.

See also Slow.

Field (to Clear Validity Checks)

Sequence (from the Edit Menu):
ValCheck/Clear/Field

Use this Field option to clear validity check settings from a single field. Press F10 while in DataEntry or Edit mode and then select ValCheck/Clear/Field. Move the cursor to the desired field, and press RETURN to select the field.

Note that if you are using Paradox on a network, and if the table's owner has restricted access to that table, you may need to use a password to modify any validity checks.

Field (to Change Field Attributes in Forms or Reports)

Sequence (from the Form Design or Report Specification Menu):
Field

Use this Field option to place, erase, reformat, justify, recalculate, or wordwrap fields while designing forms or reports. From the Form Design or Report Specification menu, choose Field. From the next menu that appears, select the appropriate option from the menu, and then place the cursor on the field and press RETURN to carry out the desired operation. For more specifics on an option, see the option by name in this appendix.

Field (to Group Records
In a Report Field)

Sequence (from the Report Specification Menu):
Group/Insert/Field

Use this Field option to group together records that have the same field value within a report. From the Report Specification menu, choose Group/Insert/Field. From the list of fields that next appears, choose a field to group on. Place the cursor at the desired location for the group, and press RETURN.

Field (in DataEntry
Or Edit Mode)

Sequence (from the Edit Menu):
Image/Goto/Field

Use this Field option to locate the cursor at a specific field while adding or editing records. Press F10 to display the Edit menu, and then choose Image/Goto/Field. Select the desired field from the list of fields that appears. The cursor will move to that field.

FieldNames

Sequence (from the Form Design Menu):
Style/FieldNames

Use the FieldNames option to display or hide the names of fields while you are placing the fields during the form design process. From the Form Design menu, choose Style/FieldNames. From the next menu that appears, choose Show to show the names of fields during the design process or Hide to hide them.

FieldSqueeze

Sequence (from the Report Specification Menu):
Setting/RemoveBlanks/FieldSqueeze

Use the FieldSqueeze option in a free-form custom report to tell Paradox to suppress the printing of leading and trailing blank spaces contained in a field. From the Report Specification menu, choose Setting/RemoveBlanks/FieldSqueeze. From the next menu, choose Yes to confirm the suppression of blank spaces.

File (to Redirect a Finished Report to a Disk File)

Sequence:
Report/Output/File

Use this File option to redirect the output of a report to a disk file. Choose Report/Output and enter the name of the desired table. Next, choose from among the available reports. Then choose File to direct the output to a disk file, and enter a filename. If you omit an extension, Paradox will supply a default extension of .RPT to the filename.

File (to Redirect a Report In Progress to a Disk File)

Sequence (from the Report Specification Menu):
Output/File

Use this File option to redirect the output of a report to a disk file while you are in the process of creating or modifying the report. From the Report Specification menu, choose Output and then choose File to direct the output to a disk file. Paradox will prompt you for a filename. If you omit an extension, Paradox will supply a default extension of .RPT to the filename.

File (to Redirect a Select Range Of a Report to a Disk File)

Sequence:
Report/RangeOutput/File

Use this File option to redirect a portion of a report to a disk file. Choose Report/Range-Output, and enter the name of the desired table. Next, choose from among the available reports, choose File to direct the output to a disk file, and enter a filename. Finally, indicate the desired starting and ending page numbers of the report, which are to be included in the resulting file. If you omit an extension, Paradox will supply a default extension of .RPT to the filename.

Files

Sequence:
Tools/Info/Inventory/Files

Use the Files option to display the names of all files located in a directory or on a disk. Choose Tools/Info/Inventory/Files. As an option, you can enter a pattern that can include drive identifiers or DOS wild cards. Press RETURN to see a table displaying the names of the files.

Note that the pattern can also include drive identifiers. For example, you could enter B: as a pattern to tell Paradox to display all files on the disk in drive B. Or you could enter C:\LOTUS*.wk? to tell Paradox to display all files with an extension of .WKS or .WK1 (for 1-2-3 worksheet files) found in the subdirectory named C:\LOTUS.

Fixed

Sequence (from the Main or Edit Menu):
Image/Format/Fixed

Use the Fixed option to specify a fixed format for a number field. Choose Image/Format, and place the cursor in the number field you wish to reformat. Choose Fixed, and then enter the desired number of decimal places for the field.

Form (to Copy an Existing Form)

Sequence:
Tools/Copy/Form

Use this Form option to copy a form. From the menu, choose the option called Tools/Copy/Form. Choose SameTable to copy the form to the same table, or choose DifferentTable to copy the form to a different table. Then enter the names for the associated table. From the list of form designators that appears, select a form to copy; then, from the next list that appears, select another form designator to which you can copy the form.

Form (to Delete an Existing Form)

Sequence:
Tools/Delete/Form

Use this Form option to delete a form. From the menu, choose Tools/Delete/Form. Enter the name of the table associated with the desired form, and then, from the list of form designators that appears, choose the form that is to be deleted.

Form (to Rename an Existing Form)

Sequence:
Tools/Rename/Form

Use this Form option to rename a form. From the menu, choose Tools/Rename/Form. Enter the name of the table associated with the desired form. From the list of form designators that appears, select the form to be renamed; then, from the next list that appears, select another form designator, which will serve as the new form name.

Format (to Change the Display Format of a Field)

Sequence (from the Main or Edit Menu):
Image/Format

Use this Format option to specify a format for a number, currency, or date field. Paradox permits four types of numeric or currency formats: general (all numbers justified in the column), fixed (a fixed number of decimal places), comma (with commas inserted and negative numbers in parentheses), or scientific (exponential) format. Three types of date formats are available. From the main menu, choose Image/Format, and place the cursor in the field you wish to reformat. Choose the desired format from the list of available formats. Depending on the type of field and the format chosen, Paradox may ask you for additional information, such as the number of decimal places to use.

Format (to Change the Overall Format of a Tabular Report)

Sequence (from the Report Specification Menu):
Setting/Format

Use this Format option to specify whether tabular reports should be arranged in tables of groups or in groups of tables. From the Report Specification menu, choose Setting/Format. Select GroupsOfTables or TablesOfGroups as desired. When arranged as tables of groups, the table header appears once at the top of each page, and group headers always appear under the table headers. By contrast, when arranged in groups of tables, the table header is repeated after every group header.

Forms

Sequence:
Forms

Use the Forms option of the main menu to design or change custom forms. Choose Forms, and then select Design to design a new form or Change to edit an existing form.

Enter the name of the table with which the form will be used, select a designator to identify the form and then enter a description for the form. Design or change the form as desired, and then press Do-It! (F2) to store the design. To use the form, select Image/PickForm from the main menu and identify the form by name. Note that a table must contain records before the form can be used.

Free-Form

Sequence:
Report/Design/Free-Form

Use the Free-Form option to design a free-form custom report. Choose Report/Design, and enter the name of the table. Select a designator for the report, and then enter a description. Choose Free-Form for the type of report, and the Report Specification menu will appear. Design the report as desired, and then press Do-It! (F2) to store it.

General

Sequence (from the Main or Edit Menu):
Image/Format/General

Use the General option to specify a general format for a selected number field. The general format shows only as many decimal places as necessary (trailing zeros are omitted), but aligns all decimal places so that the entire column of numbers remains easy to read. From the menu, choose Image/Format, and place the cursor in the number field you wish to reformat. Choose General, and then enter the desired number of decimal places for the field.

Go

Sequence:
Scripts/Editor/Write/Go
Scripts/Editor/Edit/Go

Use the Go option to tell Paradox to exit from the script editor and play the script. While in the script editor, press F10 for the menu and choose Go. Any changes made to the script while in the script editor will be saved, and the script will be played.

Goto (Version 2.0 Only)

Sequence:
Image/Goto

Use the Goto option to locate the cursor at a specific field, record number, or matching value. From the next menu that appears, choose Field, Record, or Value to go to a specific field, record number, or value. Note that in Paradox versions 3.5 and 3.0, this option is called Zoom (*see* Zoom).

Graph

Sequence:
Image/Graph

Use the Graph option to view graphs or to send graphs to the printer or to a file. Also use this option to change, load, or save graph settings, or to create crosstabs. The next menu that appears provides the following options:

- Modify, to modify the current graph specification

- Load, to load a stored graph specification

- Save, to save the current graph specification

- Reset, to reset the graph specifications to the default settings

- CrossTab, to create a crosstab of the current image

- ViewGraph, to view a graph of the current image

Select the desired option. For more specifics on an option, see the option by name in this appendix.

Group

Sequence (from the Report Specification Menu):
Group

Use the Group option to insert a group, delete a group, or change the formats for a group within a custom report. From the Report Specification menu, choose Group. The next menu that appears provides the following options:

- Insert, to insert a new group into a report

- Delete, to delete an existing report group

- Headings, to specify when group headings should be repeated

- SortDirection, to change the sort direction for a group

- Regroup, to change the desired type of grouping used in the report

Select the desired option. For more specifics on an option, see the option by name in this appendix.

GroupRepeats

Sequence (from the Report Specification Menu):
Setting/GroupRepeats

Use the GroupRepeats option to allow or to suppress the printing of all occurrences of repeated field values within a group. From the Report Specification menu, choose Setting/GroupRepeats. The next menu that appears will provide the choices of Retain and Suppress. Choose Retain to allow repeated field values to print within groups on the report, or choose Suppress to prevent such printings in the report.

GroupsOfTables

Sequence (from the Report Specification Menu):
Setting/Format/GroupsOfTables

Use the GroupsOfTables option to arrange reports in groups of tables. When arranged in groups of tables, the table header gets repeated after every group header. To specify this formatting, from the Report Specification menu, choose Setting/Format/Groups-OfTables.

Headings

Sequence (from the Report Specification Menu):
Group/Headings

Use the Headings option to specify when group headings should be repeated within a custom report. From the Report Specification menu, choose Group/Headings. Move the cursor to the headings within the report that are to be changed, and press RETURN to select the group. The next menu that appears will offer two choices: Page and Group. Choose Page to print the group headings once per group and at the top of all spillover pages; choose Group to print the group headings only once per group.

Help

Sequence:
Help

Use the Help option to access the on-line Help System provided with Paradox. Once in the Help System, you can use menu choices to access the various Help topics. When finished with Help, choose Paradox from the Help menu or press ESCAPE until you exit the Help System. Note that you can also get context-sensitive help at any time by pressing F1.

Hide

Sequence (from the Form Design Menu):
Style/FieldNames/Hide

Use the Hide option to cancel the display of the names of fields while you are placing them during the form design process. From the Form Design menu, choose Style/FieldNames/Hide to hide the names of the fields during the design process.
See also Show.

High (Version 2.0 Only)

Sequence (from the Form Design Menu):
Style/Intensity/High

Use the High option to set the text within a custom form to high-intensity display. From the Form Design menu, choose Style/Intensity/High.

HighValue

Sequence (from the Edit Menu):
ValCheck/Define/HighValue

Use the HighValue option to supply a maximum acceptable value when setting validity checks for a field. From the Edit menu, choose ValCheck/Define, and place the cursor in the field to which the validity check must apply. Choose HighValue and enter the highest acceptable value for the field.

Image

Sequence:
Image

Use the Image option to change the way Paradox displays the information on the screen. Choose Image. The next menu that appears provides the following options:

- TableSize, to change the size of the table (by limiting the number of records visible at one time)

- ColumnSize, to change the width of a column

- Format, to change the display format for a column

- Zoom (Goto in version 2), to go to a field, record, or value

- Move, to move a column to a new position

- PickForm, to select a form for the current image

- KeepSet, to make the current image settings permanent

- Graph, to display or print graphs

Select the desired option. For more specifics on an option, see the option by name in this appendix.

Import

Sequence:
Tools/ExportImport/Import

Use the Import option to import files from other software to a Paradox table. To import a file into Paradox, choose Tools/ExportImport/Import from the menu. Select the desired file format from the available choices. Parodox lets you import files from

1-2-3, Quattro or Quattro Pro, Symphony, dBASE, PFS, VisiCalc (DIF), and ASCII formats.

After you select the desired format (and in the case of 1-2-3, Quattro or Quattro Pro, or Symphony, the desired version), you must supply a name for the new table that is to receive the imported records. The records will be imported and converted to a Paradox table that matches the structure of the imported file. If Paradox cannot determine field names (for example, for ASCII delimited files or spreadsheets with no labels in the top row), it will name the fields in the new table FIELD-1, FIELD-2, FIELD-3, and so on.

Info

Structure:
Tools/Info

Use the Info option to display information about Paradox objects, DOS files, and network users. Choose Tools/Info. The next menu that appears provides the following options:

- Structure, to list the structure of a table

- Inventory, to list tables, scripts, or DOS files

- Family, to list forms and reports associated with a table

- Who, to list users who are running Paradox on a network

- Lock, to list locks for a table

Select the desired option. For more specifics on an option, see the option by name in this appendix.

Insert (to Insert Pages or Bands in Reports)

Sequence (from the Report Design Menu):
Group/Insert
Setting/PageLayout/Insert
TableBand/Insert

Use the Insert option to insert group bands, a new page in a report, or new table bands in a tabular report. To insert a group, press F10 for the Report Design menu and choose Group/Insert. Choose the type of group desired (by group of field values, range of field values, or specified number of records) from the next menu that appears. If you choose to group by either of the first two options, you must also supply a field name to group on. If you choose the third option, you must specify the number of records to include in each group. Finally, place the cursor at the desired location for the group and press RETURN.

To insert a new page at the end of the report, press F10 for the Report Design menu and choose Setting/PageLayout/Insert. To insert a table band into a report, press F10 for the Report Design menu and choose TableBand/Insert. Place the cursor at the location where the new table band is to appear and press RETURN.

Insert (to Insert Pages In a Form)

Sequence:
Page/Insert

Use this Insert option to insert a new page in a form. While designing or changing the form, with the cursor at the desired location, press F10 for the Form Design menu. Choose Page/Insert to insert a new page.

Intensity (Version 2.0 Only)

Sequence (from the Form Design Menu):
Style/Intensity

Use the Intensity option to set the text within a custom form to regular or high-intensity display. From the Form Design menu, choose Style/Intensity. Then select the desired style (High or Regular).

Inventory

Sequence:
Tools/Info/Inventory

Use the Inventory option to obtain information about tables, scripts, or DOS files. Choose Tools/Info/Inventory. From the next menu that appears, select Tables to list all tables, Scripts to list all scripts, or Files to list all DOS files.

JustFamily

Sequence:
Tools/Copy/JustFamily

Use the JustFamily option to copy a family of Paradox objects associated with a table to another table. From the menu, choose Tools/Copy/JustFamily. Enter the names for a source table and a target table when prompted. Note that the target table, which will receive the copied objects, must exist. Also, any objects in the target table that have the same names as objects in the source table will be overwritten.

KeepEntry

Sequence:
Modify/DataEntry/KeepEntry

Use the KeepEntry option when in DataEntry mode to keep the ENTRY table after completing the data entry. If you use KeepEntry, the added records are kept in the

ENTRY table, rather than being added to the primary table. (Rename the ENTRY table or add the records to another table before exiting Paradox to avoid loss of data.) Choose Modify/DataEntry to enter DataEntry mode, and begin adding records. Once the records have been added, to keep the ENTRY table, press F10 for the Edit menu and choose KeepEntry.

KeepSet

Sequence:
Image/KeepSet

Use the KeepSet option to make the current settings for the table image permanent. From the main menu or the Edit menu, choose Image/KeepSet. If you make the image settings permanent and later want to delete those settings, you can do so by choosing Tools/Delete/KeepSet and supplying the name of the appropriate table. Note that in Paradox version 2.0 this option is called KeepSettings.

Labels

Sequence (from the Report Specification Menu):
Setting/Labels

Use the Labels option to specify mailing-label format while you are designing a free-form report. From the Report Specification menu, choose Setting/Labels. Then confirm with Yes at the next menu that appears.

Length

Sequence (from the Report Specification Menu):
Setting/PageLayout/Length

Use the Length option to control the page length in a custom report. From the Report Specification menu, choose Setting/PageLayout/Length. Enter a length, in number of lines per page, for the page length, or enter C for continuous length (useful with mailing labels or other continuous forms). Note that while the standard for 8.5-inch by 11-inch paper is 66 lines, some laser printers may eject the paper prematurely unless you set the page length of a report at no more than 62 lines.

LineSqueeze

Sequence (from the Report Specification Menu):
Setting/RemoveBlanks/LineSqueeze

Use the LineSqueeze option in a free-form custom report to tell Paradox to suppress the printing of blank lines when a field contains no data. From the Report Specification menu, choose Setting/RemoveBlanks/LineSqueeze. From the next menu, choose Yes to confirm the suppression of blank lines. Then choose Fixed to place blank lines at the bottom of the record or Variable to delete blank lines, thereby varying the number of lines occupied by each record.

Load

Sequence:
Image/Graph/Load

Use the Load option to load graph settings from an existing graph file. Choose Image/Graph/Load. Paradox will prompt you for the name of the graph; enter the name, or press RETURN for a list of available graph names and select the desired name from the list.

Lock (to Place or Remove Network Locks)

Sequence:
Tools/Net/Lock

Use this Lock option to place an explicit lock on a table or to unlock a table while operating on a network. Choose Tools/Net/Lock. The next menu will provide choices for the type of lock desired (FullLock and WriteLock). Select the type of lock desired, and enter the name of the table to lock. Finally, choose Set to place the lock, or choose Clear to release an existing lock.

Lock (to List Network Locks)

Sequence:
Tools/Info/Lock

Use this Lock option to list all locks for a table when you are operating on a network. Choose Tools/Info/Lock, and enter the desired table.

Lookup

Sequence (from the Report Design Menu):
Field/Lookup

Use the Lookup option to establish, change, or remove a relational link from the report to another table. From the Report Design menu, choose Field/Lookup. From the next menu to appear, choose Link (to add a relational link), Unlink (to remove an existing link), or Relink (to change an existing link). Then select the desired table and the name of the field when prompted.

LowValue

Sequence (from the Edit Menu):
ValCheck/Define/LowValue

Use the LowValue option to supply a minimum acceptable value when setting validity checks for a field. From the Edit menu, choose ValCheck/Define and place the cursor in the field to which the validity check must apply. Choose LowValue, and enter the lowest acceptable value for the field.

Margin

Sequence (from the Report Specification Menu):
Setting/Margin

Use the Margin option to set the left margin in a custom report. From the Report Specification menu, choose Setting/Margin. Enter the desired value for the left margin.

Modify (to Modify Tables)

Sequence:
Modify

Use this Modify option to perform common operations that result in the modification of tables, such as sorting, adding, and editing records and restructuring a table. Choose Modify. The next menu that appears provides the following options:

- Sort, to sort or arrange records in a specific order

- Edit, to insert, delete, or change records

- CoEdit, to edit a table with other users concurrently

- DataEntry, to add new records to a table

- Multientry, to add records to a table that posts to two or more tables simultaneously

- Restructure, to change the structure of an existing table

Select the desired option. For more specifics on an option, see the option by name in this appendix.

Modify (to Modify Graphs)

Sequence:
Image/Graph/Modify

Use this Modify option to modify the settings used for the current graph. Choose Image/Graph/Modify. Then change the graph settings by typing the desired settings in the Graph Type form that appears, or press F10 to display the Graph Design menu and change the various graph settings.

Monochrome

Sequence (from the Form Design Menu):
Style/Monochrome

Use the Monochrome option to choose intensity, reverse video, blinking, or normal screen attributes for an area or border of a form. From the Form Design menu, choose Style/Monochrome. From the next menu to appear, choose Area (to change the attributes for an area) or choose Border (to change the attributes for a border). Place the cursor at one corner of the area or border and press RETURN; then move the cursor to the diagonal corner of the area or border and press RETURN. Finally, use the left or right arrow key to switch between available styles. Press RETURN when the desired style appears.

More

Sequence:
Tools/More

Use the More option to display the second line of menu choices applicable to the Tools menu. Choose Tools/More. The menu that appears provides the following options:

- Add, to add records contained in one table to the records in another table

- Multiadd, to add records to two or more tables simultaneously

- Subtract, to subtract the records of one table from those of another

- Empty, to remove all records from a table

- Protect, to password- or write-protect a table or script and to clear passwords

- Directory, to change the working directory (also clears temporary tables and the workspace)

- ToDOS, to suspend Paradox and access DOS through a DOS "shell"

Select the desired option. For more specifics on an option, see the option by name in this appendix.

Move (to Move a Column)

Sequence (from the Main or Edit Menu):
Image/Move

Use this Move option to move a column to another location. From the main or Edit menu, choose Image/Move. Paradox will display a list of columns by name; choose the column to be moved from the list, and press RETURN. Place the cursor at the new location for the column, and press RETURN again to move the column.

Move (to Move Areas Within Custom Forms)

Sequence (from the Form Design Menu):
Area/Move

Use this Move option to move an area of a form you are designing or changing to a different part of the form. From the Form Design menu, choose Area/Move. Place the cursor at one corner of the area to be moved, and press RETURN; move the cursor to the diagonal corner of the area and press RETURN again. Finally, use the cursor keys to drag the area to its new location, and press RETURN.

Move (to Move Table Bands Within a Tabular Report)

Sequence (from the Report Specification Menu):
TableBand/Move

Use this Move option to move a column from one portion of a tabular report to another. From the Report Specification menu, choose TableBand/Move. Place the cursor within the table band, in the column to be selected, and press RETURN to choose the column. Then move the cursor to the new location for the column, and press RETURN again to move the table band.

Multi

Sequence (from the Form Design Menu):
Multi

Use the Multi option to design multitable forms or multirecord forms. While designing the form, press F10 and choose Multi. From the next menu to appear, choose Tables (to place, remove, or move a form from another table) or choose Records (to place, remove, or adjust a multirecord region on the form).

MultiAdd

Sequence:
Tools/More/MultiAdd

Use the MultiAdd option to add records from a single source table to several target tables. Choose Tools/More/MultiAdd. Enter the name of the source table, and then supply the name of the map table (previously created with Modify/MultiEntry/Setup).

The existing data in the source table will then be added to the appropriate fields in the target tables, as defined by the map table.

MultiEntry

Sequence:
Modify/MultiEntry

Use the MultiEntry option to enter records into a single source table for storage in several target tables. Both the source and map tables must be created before you use this command. Choose Modify/MultiEntry/Entry. Enter the name of the source table, and then supply the name of the map table. You can then enter data into the source table. When you complete the data entry with Do-It! (F2), the data will be added to the appropriate fields in the target tables, as defined by the map table.

Net

Sequence:
Tools/Net

Use the Net option to lock or unlock tables, to prevent others from locking a table, to change your private directory or user name, or to change the AutoRefresh interval. Choose Tools/Net. The menu that appears provides the following options:

- Lock, to lock or unlock a table
- PreventLock, to prevent others from locking tables
- SetPrivate, to change your private directory
- UserName, to change your user name
- AutoRefresh, to change the delay time for automatic screen refreshing

Select the desired option. For more specifics on an option, see the option by name in this appendix.

NewEntries

Sequence:
Tools/More/Add/NewEntries

Use the NewEntries option to add records in a source table to a keyed target table without disturbing any existing records in the target table. Choose Tools/More/Add. Enter the name of the source table and the target table. If the target table maintains a key field, the next menu provides the choice of NewEntries for adding records to the target table and Update for updating the target table records based on the source table records. Choose NewEntries to add the records to the target table without changing any existing records in that table.

No

Sequence:
No

Use the No option to tell Paradox not to perform a specific type of operation.

NoBlink (Version 2.0 Only)

Sequence (from the Form Design Menu):
Style/Blink/NoBlink

Use the NoBlink option to turn off blinking for the text and borders you are adding to a form. From the Form Design menu, choose Style/Blink/NoBlink, and then add the text or borders that should not be blinking.

#Record

Sequence (from the Form Design Menu):
Field/Place/#Record

Use the #Record option to place a record number field while designing a form. From the Form Design menu, choose Field/Place/#Record. Place the cursor at the desired form location for the record number and press RETURN; then use the left and right cursor keys to adjust the width of the field, and press RETURN.

NumberRecords

Sequence (from the Report Design Menu):
Group/Insert/NumberRecords

Use the NumberRecords option to specify how many records will be contained in a report grouping. From the Report Design menu, choose Group/Insert/NumberRecords. Next, specify the number of records to be contained in each group. Finally, place the cursor at the desired location for the new group to be inserted, and press RETURN.

OK

Sequence:
OK

Use the OK option to tell Paradox to proceed with a specific type of operation.

Other

Sequence (from the Form Design Menu):
Border/Place/Other

Use the Other option to add borders, composed of characters of your own choosing, to a form. From the Form Design menu, choose the Border/Place/Other option. Next, specify a character to be used as the border character. (You can specify graphics characters by holding down the ALT key and typing three-digit numbers on the numeric keypad that represent the ASCII code for the graphics character.) Place the cursor at one corner of the border and press RETURN; move the cursor to the diagonal corner of the border and press RETURN again to draw the border.

Output (to Generate
A Report)

Sequence:
Report/Output

Use this Output option to generate a report. Choose Report/Output, and then enter a name for the appropriate table. Next, select a report from the list of report designators that appears. Choose Printer, File, or Screen from the next menu for the report's output.

Output (to Generate a Report
Being Designed or Changed)

Sequence (from the Report Specification Menu):
Output

Use this Output option to generate a report while you are in the process of designing or changing the report. This is useful for proofing the report's design before you leave the design process. From the Report Specification menu, choose Output. Then select Printer, Screen, or File as desired. The report will be produced and sent to the device you have selected.

Overall

Sequence (from the Graph Design Menu):
Overall

Use the Overall option of the Graph Design menu to customize various settings that affect graphs. From the Graph Design menu, select Overall. From the next menu to appear, select one of the six types of settings that can be changed: Titles, Colors, Axes, Grids, PrinterLayout (to define a page layout for printers or plotters), Device (to define the desired printer or plotter), and Wait (to specify a length of time that each graph will be displayed).

Page (for a Custom Report)

Sequence (from the Report Specification Menu):
Field/Place/Page

Use this Page option to place a page number field on a custom report. From the Report Specification menu, choose Field/Place/Page. Move the cursor to the location you want for the page number, and press RETURN to place the field. Note that the page number fields should be placed within the page bands. Placing page number fields elsewhere may produce bizarre results.

Page (for a Multipage Form)

Sequence (from the Form Design Menu):
Page

Use this Page option to add or remove a page from a multiple-page form. From the Form Design menu, choose Page. From the next menu to appear, choose Insert to add a page, or choose Delete to remove the current page of the form. If you choose Delete, you must confirm the deletion by choosing OK from the next menu. If you choose Insert, you will see another menu with Before and After options. Choose Before to place a new page before the current page of the form. Choose After to place the new page after the current page of the form.

PageLayout

Sequence (from the Report Specification Menu):
Setting/PageLayout

Use the PageLayout option to set the page length and page width within a custom report. From the Report Specification menu, choose Setting/PageLayout. From the next menu, choose Length, Width, Insert (to add a new page width at the end of the report), or Delete (to remove the last page width). If you choose Length or Width, Paradox will prompt you for a length value in number of lines per page, or a width value in characters. If you select Insert, Paradox will place a blank page width at the right side of the report specification. If you select Delete, Paradox will delete the last page width, along with any fields and literals contained within it.

Password

Sequence:
Tools/More/Protect/Password

Use the Password option to assign or remove a password. Choose Tools/More/Protect/Password, and then choose Table or Script. Next, enter the name of the table or script to be protected, followed by the desired password. If you are password-protecting a table, you will see an auxiliary password form after you supply the initial password. The assignment of auxiliary passwords is optional; it is generally not needed unless you are using Paradox in a multiuser environment. Press Do-It! (F2) to store the changes and assign the password.

Pfs

Sequence:
Tools/ExportImport/Import/Pfs
Tools/ExportImport/Export/Pfs

Use the Pfs option to exchange files between Paradox and PFS. To import a PFS file into Paradox, choose Tools/ExportImport/Import/Pfs from the menu and enter the name of the file you wish to import. Then enter a name for the new Paradox table that will receive the PFS data. To export a file from Paradox to PFS, choose Tools/Export-Import/Export/Pfs from the menu. Enter the name of the table that is to be exported to PFS, and then enter a filename for the resulting PFS file. Note that PFS does not use specific data types, so all fields from the Paradox table will appear as character fields within PFS.

PickForm

Sequence:
Image/PickForm

Use the PickForm option to select a form for viewing or editing records from the current table. Choose Image/PickForm, and then select a form designator from the list of forms that appears. Each time you switch to a form view with Form Toggle (F7), the form you selected will appear. After you clear the workspace or exit Paradox, the selected form is no longer in effect until you choose it again. To make the form selection permanent, save the Image settings with Image/KeepSet.

Picture

Sequence (from the Edit Menu):
ValCheck/Define/Picture

Use the Picture option to define a "picture" format, a format that data entry must follow for a specific field. From the Edit menu, choose ValCheck/Define and place the cursor in the desired field. Then choose Picture, and enter the desired format, using a valid PAL picture format. Valid format characters include the following:

#	Accept any numeric digit
?	Accept any letter
&	Accept any letter, convert to uppercase
!	Accept any character; if letter, convert to uppercase
;	Take literally
*	Repetition counts
[ ]	Optional items
{ }	Grouping operator
,	Alternative values

Pies

Sequence (from the Graph Design Menu):
Pies

Use the Pies option of the Graph Design menu to choose labels, exploding slicing, fill patterns, and colors for pie charts. From the Graph Design menu, select Pie. Then fill in the desired options within the form that appears. When you finish filling in options in the form, press Menu (F10) to continue defining other graph selections or press Do-It! (F2) to store the settings.

Place (When Designing Reports)

Sequence (from the Report Specification Menu):
Field/Place

Use this Place option to place fields while you are designing custom reports. From the Report Specification menu, choose Field/Place. From the next menu, select the desired field type (Regular, Summary, Calculated, Date, Time, Page, or #Record). Identify the field or field format from the successive menus that may appear, depending on your selection. Move the cursor to the desired location for the field, and press RETURN to place the field.

Place (When Designing Custom Forms)

Sequence (from the Form Design Menu):
Field/Place

Use this Place option to place fields while you are designing custom forms. From the Form Design menu, choose Field/Place. From the next menu that appears, select the desired field type (Regular, DisplayOnly, Calculated, or #Record). Identify the field or field format from the successive menus that may appear, depending upon your selection. Move the cursor to the desired location for the field, and press RETURN to place the field.

Place (When Designing Multitable Forms)

Sequence (from the Form Design Menu):
Multi/Tables/Place

Use this Place option to place another table's form on the current form when designing multitable forms. From the Form Design menu, choose Multi/Tables/Place. From the next menu to appear, choose Linked (if the forms are to be linked relationally) or choose Unlinked. Enter the name of the desired table at the next prompt, and place the form in the desired location with the arrow keys.

Play

Sequence:
Scripts/Play

Use the Play option to play back a script. Choose Scripts/Play, and enter the name of the script.

PreventLock

Sequence:
Tools/Net/PreventLock

Use the PreventLock option to prevent others from locking a table while you are on a network. Also use PreventLock to clear a prevent write lock or a prevent full lock. Choose Tools/Net/PreventLock. Select FullLock or WriteLock as the type of prevent lock desired, and enter the name of the table to which the prevent lock should be applied. Finally, choose Set to place the prevent lock or Clear to release an existing prevent lock. If your attempt to place or clear the prevent lock is successful, Paradox will display a message informing you of this fact.

Print

Sequence:
Scripts/Editor/Write/Print
Scripts/Editor/Edit/Print

Use the Print option to tell Paradox to print a script while you are using the script editor. While in the script editor, press F10 for the menu and choose Print to print the script.

Printer (to Direct the Report Output to the Printer)

Sequence:
Report/Output/Printer

Use this Printer option to direct the output of a report to the printer. Choose Report/Output and enter the name of the desired table. Next, choose from among the available reports, and then choose Printer to direct the output to the printer. The output is directed to your PC's default printer. In most cases this is the printer connected to LPT1, unless you have used the DOS MODE command or your network operating system software to change this setting.

Printer (to Direct a Select Report Range to the Printer)

Sequence:
Report/RangeOutput/Printer

Use this Printer option to direct a portion of a report to the printer. Choose Report/RangeOutput, and enter the name of the desired table. Next, choose from among the available reports, and then choose Printer. Enter the desired starting and ending page numbers of the report. The output is directed to your PC's default printer. In most cases this is the printer connected to LPT1, unless you have used the DOS MODE command or your network operating system software to change this setting.

Printer (to Print the Report While Designing or Modifying It)

Sequence (from the Report Specification Menu):
Output/Printer

Use this Printer option to print a report while you are in the process of creating or modifying that report. This can be useful for ensuring, before you exit from the Report Specification, that the report you are designing will meet your needs. From the Report Specification menu, choose Output and then Printer to direct the output to the printer. The output is directed to your PC's default printer. In most cases this is the printer connected to LPT1, unless you have used the DOS MODE command or your network operating system software to change this setting.

Protect

Sequence:
Tools/More/Protect

Use the Protect option to set and remove passwords for scripts or tables, temporarily clear passwords from memory, or write-protect tables. Choose Tools/More/Protect. The next menu provides you with three choices: Password, to set or remove passwords from a table or script; ClearPasswords, to clear passwords from memory; and Write-Protect, to write-protect a table. For additional details on these options, see each option by name in this appendix.

Quattro

Sequence:
Tools/ExportImport/Import/Quattro
Tools/ExportImport/Export/Quattro

Use the Quattro option to exchange files between Paradox and Quattro. To import a Quattro file into Paradox, choose Tools/ExportImport/Import/Quattro from the main menu. From the next menu, choose Quattro or Quattro Pro as desired. Enter a filename for the Quattro worksheet, and then enter the name of the new Paradox table that will receive the Quattro data. Paradox will proceed to convert your Quattro worksheet into a Paradox table and will display the table in the workspace.

To export a file from Paradox to Quattro, choose Tools/ExportImport/Export/Quattro from the main menu. From the next menu, choose Quattro or Quattro Pro as desired. Enter the name of the table that is to be exported to the Quattro program, and then enter a filename for the resulting Quattro worksheet. Alphanumeric fields will become labels within cells; number fields will become numbers in cells with a general format; currency fields will become numbers within cells with a Quattro format; and date fields will become numbers with a date format.

QuerySave

Sequence:
Scripts/QuerySave

Use the QuerySave option to save a Query Form that is currently in the workspace as a script. With a Query Form visible in the workspace, press F10 for the main menu, and choose Scripts/QuerySave. Then enter a name for the script.

QuerySpeed

Sequence:
Tools/QuerySpeed

Use the QuerySpeed option to speed the performance of regularly used queries by building internal index files on non-key fields containing selection criteria in the query. Choose Tools/Query/Speed.

Note that if the fields used in your query are key fields, no performance benefits can be gained with QuerySpeed. In such cases, Paradox will respond with a "No speedup possible" message if you try to use the QuerySpeed option.

Keep in mind that the secondary indexes maintained by Paradox consume disk space. If you are not using existing queries and you want to delete the files created by a QuerySpeed operation, choose Tools/Delete/QuerySpeed and then provide a table name to delete the index files.

Range

Sequence (from the Report Specification Menu):
Group/Insert/Range

Use the Range option to group together records that have values within a specified range within a report. From the Report Specification menu, choose Group/Insert/Range. From the list of fields that appears next, choose a field to group on, and then specify the size or scope of the range. Place the cursor at the desired location for the group, and press RETURN.

RangeOutput

Sequence:
Report/RangeOutput

Use the RangeOutput option to send specified pages of a report to the printer, the screen, or a disk file. Choose Report/RangeOutput, and then enter a name for the appropriate table. Next, select a report from the list of report designators that appears, and then choose Printer, File, or Screen as desired. If prompted, enter the starting and ending page numbers for the report.

Read

Sequence:
Scripts/Editor/Write/Read
Scripts/Editor/Edit/Read

Use the Read option to read an existing script into a script that you are creating or editing with the script editor. While in the script editor, place the cursor where the new script is to appear, press F10 for the menu, and choose Read. Enter the name of the script you wish to read into the editor.

Record

Sequence (from the Main or Edit Menu):
Image/Zoom/Record

Use the Record option to locate the cursor at a specific record number. From the main menu or the Edit menu, choose Image/Zoom/Record. Enter a record number, and the cursor will move to that record. Users of Paradox version 2.0 should note that the sequence in version 2.0 is Image/Goto/Record.

Records

Sequence (from the Form Design Menu):
Multi/Records

Use the Records option to place, remove, or adjust a multirecord region on a form. From the Form Design menu, choose Multi/Records. From the next menu to appear, choose Define (to define a multirecord region on the form), Remove (to remove an existing multirecord region), or Adjust (to adjust the size of an existing multirecord region).

Reformat

Sequence (from the Form Design or Report Specification Menu):
Field/Reformat

Use the Reformat option to reformat fields while you are designing forms or reports. From the Form Design or Report Specification menu, choose Field/Reformat. Place the cursor on the field you wish to reformat, and press RETURN to select the field. Choose the desired options from the choices that appear for reformatting the field. Note that you can change field widths only in forms.

Regroup

Sequence (from the Report Specification Menu):
Group/Regroup

Use the Regroup option to change the type of grouping used in a custom report. From the Report Specification menu, choose Group/Regroup. Place the cursor at the desired group, and press RETURN to select it. Then choose the appropriate grouping method (Field, Range, or NumberRecords) and provide the required information when prompted.

Regular (Version 2.0 only)

Sequence (from the Form Design Menu):
Style/Intensity/Regular

Use the Regular option to set the text within a custom form to regular intensity display. From the Form Design menu, choose Style/Intensity/Regular.

RemoveBlanks

Sequence (from the Report Specification Menu):
Setting/RemoveBlanks

Use the RemoveBlanks option to suppress the printing of blank lines or blank fields within the form band in a custom free-form report. From the Report Specification menu, choose Setting/RemoveBlanks. From the next menu that appears, choose LineSqueeze to suppress blank lines when fields are empty, or choose FieldSqueeze to suppress blank characters when field data contains leading or trailing blank spaces.

Rename

Sequence:
Tools/Rename

Use the Rename option to rename tables, forms, reports, or scripts. Choose Tools/Rename. From the next menu that appears, choose Table, Form, Report, or Script, and enter the old and then the new name for the object.

RepeatPlay

Sequence:
Scripts/RepeatPlay

Use this option to play a script a set number of times, or to play the script continuously. Choose Scripts/RepeatPlay. Next, enter the name of the desired script. At the next prompt, enter the number of times to play the script, or enter **C** for continuous play.

Report

Sequence:
Report

Use the Report option of the main menu to create and modify reports. Choose Report. The menu that appears provides the following options:

- Output, to send a report to the printer, screen, or disk file

- Design, to design a new Report Specification

- Change, to change an existing Report Specification

- RangeOutput, to send specified report pages to the printer, screen, or disk file

- SetPrinter, to select a printer port or enter a setup string

Select the desired option. For more specifics on an option, see the option by name in this appendix.

Required

Sequence (from the Edit Menu):
ValCheck/Define/Required

Use the Required option to tell Paradox that all new or edited records must contain an entry in a specific field. Paradox will display an error message if you press RETURN after leaving the field blank during data entry. While in DataEntry or Edit mode, press F10 for the menu, and then choose ValCheck/Define. Place the cursor in the desired field and press RETURN. From the next menu, choose Required, and then Yes. (The No option from this menu may be used later, if you want to remove the Required status from the field.) Press Do-It! (F2) to save the validity check to the table, or else it will be discarded.

Reset

Sequence:
Image/Graph/Reset

Use the Reset option to restore graph settings to their default values, as defined by the Custom Configuration Program (CCP). Choose Image/Graph/Reset, and press Do-It! (F2) to restore the graph settings to the default values.

Resize

Sequence (from the Report Specification Menu):
TableBand/Resize

Use the Resize option to change the size of a table band in a custom tabular report. From the Report Specification menu, choose TableBand/Resize. Move the cursor to the column to be resized, and press RETURN. Use the left and right arrow keys to resize the column, and then press RETURN to set the new size.

Restructure

Sequence:
Modify/Restructure

Use the Restructure option to change a table's structure. Choose the option called Modify/Restructure, and enter the name of the desired table. Make the desired changes to the field names and field types, and press Do-It! (F2) to store the changes.

Retain

Sequence (from the Report Specification Menu):
Setting/GroupRepeats/Retain

Use the Retain option to allow the printing of all occurrences of repeated field values within a group. From the Report Specification menu, choose Setting/GroupRepeats/Retain to allow repeated field values to print within groups on the report.

Reversal (Version 2.0 Only)

Sequence (from the Form Design Menu):
Style/Reversal

Use the Reversal option to select reverse video or normal text while you are designing or changing custom forms. From the Form Design menu, choose Style/Reversal. From the next menu that appears, select Reverse Video for dark text on a light background, or choose Normal for light text on a dark background.

Save

Sequence:
Image/Graph/Save

Use the Save option to save graph settings to a file. Choose Image/Graph/Save. Paradox will prompt you for the name of the file; enter the name, and the current graph settings will be saved to a settings file. Note that to save an image of the graph itself, you should use Image/ViewGraph/File.

Scientific

Sequence (from the Main or Edit Menu):
Image/Format/Scientific

Use the Scientific option to select scientific (exponential) format for the display of number fields. From the main menu or the Edit menu, choose Image/Format. Place the cursor in the number field you wish to reformat, and press RETURN to select the field. Choose Scientific from the next menu, and specify the number of decimal places you desire.

Screen (to Direct a Finished Report to the Screen)

Sequence:
Report/Output/Screen

Use this Screen option to direct the output of a report to the screen. Choose Report/Output, and enter the name of the desired table. Next, choose from among the available reports, and then choose Screen to display the report. At the end of each page, you must press a key to display additional pages.

Screen (to Direct a Report In Progress to the Screen)

Sequence (from the Report Specification Menu):
Output/Screen

Use this Screen option to display the output of a report while you are in the process of creating or modifying the report. This can be useful for ensuring, before you exit from the Report Specification menu that the report you are designing will meet your needs. From the Report Specification menu, choose Output. Then choose Screen to direct the output to the screen.

Screen (to Direct a Select Report Range to the Screen)

Sequence:
Report/RangeOutput/Screen

Use this Screen option to direct a portion of a report to the screen. Choose Report/RangeOutput, and enter the name of the desired table. Choose from among the available reports, and then choose Screen. Then indicate the desired starting and ending page numbers of the report.

Script

Sequence:
Tools/Copy/Script
Tools/Delete/Script
Tools/Rename/Script
Tools/More/Protect/Password/Script

Use these versions of the Tools options to copy, rename, or delete scripts. To copy a script, choose Tools/Copy/Script. Enter the name of the script to copy, followed by the new name for the copy. To delete a script, choose Tools/Delete/Script, enter the name for the script, and confirm the deletion by choosing OK from the next menu. To rename a script, choose Tools/Rename/Script and enter the name of the script, followed by the new name for the script.

To password-protect a script, or to clear password protection from a script, choose Tools/More/Protect/Password/Script, and enter the name of the desired script. Enter the password when prompted to do so, and enter it a second time to confirm the correct spelling (or press RETURN without entering any passwords to clear the password from a protected script).

Scripts (to Play, Record, Save, or Change)

Sequence:
Scripts

Use this Scripts option to play and record scripts; to save a query as a script; to play scripts repeatedly or at slow speeds; or to change scripts with the editor. From the menu, choose Scripts. The following menu options then become available:

- Play, to play a script

- BeginRecord, to begin recording a script

- QuerySave, to save a query as a script

- ShowPlay, to play a script slowly

- RepeatPlay, to play a script a number of times

- Editor, to edit a script

Select the desired option. For more specifics on an option, see the option by name in this appendix.

Scripts (to List Scripts)

Sequence:
Tools/Info/Inventory/Scripts

Use the Scripts option to list all available scripts in the current directory. Choose Tools/Info/Inventory/Scripts. Enter a directory name, or press RETURN without a name to list scripts in the current directory.

Series

Sequence (from the Graph Design Menu):
Series

Use the Series option of the Graph Design menu to define legends, labels, markers, fill patterns, and colors for each data series within the graph. From the Graph Design menu, select Series. From the next menu to appear, choose LegendsAndLabels, MarkersAndFills, or Colors. Use LegendsAndLabels to define whether a legend will appear and to choose the placement of labels. Use MarkersAndFills to choose the markers and fill patterns for bars or points within a graph. Use Colors to define the colors that will be displayed or printed.

SetPrinter

Sequence:
Report/SetPrinter

Use the SetPrinter option to select a setup string or a printer port for printed output. Choose Report/SetPrinter. The next menu that appears offers the choice of Regular, to use the printer port and setup string stored with the report, or Override, to override the printer port and setup string stored with the report. If you choose Override, you must either enter a setup string or choose a printer port.

SetPrivate

Sequence:
Tools/Net/SetPrivate

Use the SetPrivate option to change your private directory while you are using Paradox on a network. Choose Tools/Net/SetPrivate, and enter the directory name (including the drive identifier and path). Paradox will display a menu requiring confirmation; you must choose OK to change your private directory.

Note that Paradox must clear the workspace and delete all temporary tables as a result of this menu option. If you want to keep any data contained in temporary tables, be sure to rename the tables before you choose the SetPrivate option. Also, you cannot make a directory private if other network users are working with Paradox objects in that directory.

Setting (with Tabular Custom Reports)

Sequence (from the Report Specification Menu):
Setting

Use this Setting option to change the settings of a tabular custom report. From the Report Specification menu, choose Setting. The following menu options then become available:

- Format, to specify the overall report format

- GroupRepeats, to suppress or retain printing of repeated values in a group

- PageLayout, to set page lengths and widths, and to insert or delete page widths

- Margin, to change the left margin of the report

- Setup, to specify a setup string or set the printer port

- Wait, to pause report printing after each page

Select the desired option. For more specifics on an option, see the option by name in this appendix.

Setting (with Free-Form Custom Reports)

Sequence (from the Report Specification Menu):
Setting

Use this Setting option to change the settings of a free-form custom report. From the Report Specification menu, choose Setting. The following menu options then become available:

- RemoveBlanks, to suppress blank lines or fields

- PageLayout, to set page lengths and widths, and to insert or delete page widths

- Margin, to change the left margin of the report

- Setup, to specify a setup string or set the printer port

- Wait, to pause report printing after each page

- Labels, to specify the printing of mailing labels

Select the desired option. For more specifics on an option, see the option by name in this appendix.

Setup (When Designing Reports)

Sequence (from the Report Specification Menu):
Setting/Setup

Use this Setup option to specify, prior to printing a report, the printer port and/or setup string to be sent to the printer. From the Report Specification menu, choose Setting/Setup. Select Predefined to choose a setup string from a predefined list, or choose Custom to enter a custom printer port and setup string.

Setup (When Adding Data To Multiple Tables)

Sequence:
Modify/MultiEntry/Setup

Use this Setup option to set up the source and map tables used with the MultiEntry option. Remember that the Query Form used for each of the target tables should be in the workspace before you use the Setup option. Choose Modify/MultiEntry/Setup. Enter the name of the new source table, and then enter the name of the new map table.

Paradox will create the source and map tables, and you can then use Modify/Multi-Entry/Entry or Tools/More/MultiAdd to add records to multiple tables simultaneously.

Show

Sequence (from the Form Design Menu):
Style/FieldNames/Show

Use the Show option to show the names of fields while you are placing them during the form design process. From the Form Design menu, choose the Style/Field-Names/Show option.

ShowHighlight

Sequence (from the Form Design Menu):
Style/ShowHighlight

Use the ShowHighlight option with multirecord forms to show or hide the highlight of a multirecord region. From the Form Design menu, choose Style/ShowHighlight. From the next menu that appears, choose Show (to show the multirecord region in a highlighted intensity) or Hide (to display the mutirecord region in the same intensity as the initial record in the form).

ShowPlay

Sequence:
Scripts/ShowPlay

Use the ShowPlay option to play a script at a speed that is sufficiently slow for you to observe the effects. Choose Scripts/ShowPlay, and enter the name of the script. The next menu that appears provides the choice of Fast (to play the script rapidly) or Slow (to play the script slowly). Choose the desired speed at which to play the script.

Single-Line

Sequence (from the Form Design Menu):
Border/Place/Single-Line

Use the Single-Line option to add a single-line border in a form. To add the border, choose Border/Place/Single-Line from the Form Design menu. Place the cursor at one corner of the border, and press RETURN; move the cursor to the diagonal corner of the border, and press RETURN again in order to draw the border.

Slow

Sequence:
Scripts/ShowPlay/Slow

Use the Slow option to play a script at the slowest possible speed. Choose Scripts/ShowPlay, and enter the name of the script. Then choose Slow to play the script slowly.

Sort

Sequence:
Modify/Sort

Use the Sort option to sort the records in a table. Choose Modify/Sort, and enter the name of the table to sort. If the table is keyed, you must also enter the name for the new table that will result from the sort. Fill in the sort screen by placing numbers to indicate the priority for the sort order next to the desired fields and, if desired, placing the letter "D" (for "descending") to the right of the number. Then press Do-It! (F2) to perform the sort.

SortDirection

Sequence (from the Report Specification Menu):
Group/SortDirection

Use the SortDirection option to specify the sort direction you prefer when groups are included in a custom report. From the Report Specification menu, choose Group/Sort-Direction. Move the cursor to the group whose sort order is to be changed, and press RETURN to select that group. Then choose Ascending or Descending for the sort order.

Structure

Sequence:
Tools/Info/Structure

Use the Structure option to display the structure of a table. Choose Tools/Info/Structure, and enter the name of the desired table.

Style

Sequence (from the Form Design Menu):
Style

Use the Style option to choose the style of text when you are designing a custom form. From the Form Design menu, choose Style. The menu that appears next displays the following options:

- Intensity, for choosing between normal and high-intensity text

- Color, to select desired colors (version 3.5)

- Monochrome, to select monochrome display (version 3.5)

- Blink, to select blinking or nonblinking text

- Reversal, to choose reverse video or normal display

- ShowHighlight, to show or hide the highlight in a multirecord form

- FieldNames, to show or hide field names during form design

- Default, to restore default values for the above options

Select the desired option. For more specifics on an option, see the option by name in this appendix.

Subtract

Sequence:
Tools/More/Subtract

Use the Subtract option to remove all records in one table that match records in another table. Choose Tools/More/Subtract, and then enter the name of the source table (the table containing the records to be subtracted from the other table). Next, enter the name of the target table (the table from which to subtract the records). If the target table is not keyed, Paradox will remove all records that exactly match records in the source table. If the target table is keyed, Paradox will remove all records in which the key fields match the key fields of any record in the source table.

Sum

Sequence (from the Report Design Menu):
Field/Place/Summary/Calculated/Sum
Field/Place/Summary/Regular/Sum

Use the Sum option to sum the values in the summary field of a custom free-form or tabular report. From the Report Design menu, choose Field/Place/Summary/Calculated/Sum or Field/Place/Regular/Sum. Select PerGroup for a summary each time the group changes or Overall for an overall summary. Use the cursor to place the field in its desired location, and press RETURN. Adjust the number of digits displayed with the left and right arrow keys. Then press RETURN. Adjust the number of decimal points displayed with the arrow keys, and then press RETURN to complete the placement of the field.

Summary

Sequence (from the Report Specification Menu):
Field/Place/Summary

Use the Summary option to place a summary field within a custom report. From the Report Specification menu, choose Field/Place/Summary. From the next menu that appears, select Regular to place a regular field or Calculated to place a calculated field, based on an expression. If you choose Regular, you must next choose the field to be placed from a list of fields; if you choose Calculated, you must enter an expression as the basis for the calculation.

From the next menu that appears, choose Sum, Average, Count, High, or Low, depending upon the type of summary you desire. Then select PerGroup for a summary each time the group changes or Overall for an overall summary. Use the cursor to place the field in its desired location, and press RETURN. Next, adjust the number of digits displayed with the left and right arrow keys, and then press RETURN. Finally, adjust the number of decimal points displayed with the arrow keys, and press RETURN to complete the placement of the field.

Suppress

Sequence (from the Report Specification Menu):
Setting/GroupRepeats/Suppress

Use the Suppress option to prevent the printing of all occurrences of repeated field values within a group. From the Report Specification menu, choose Setting/Group-Repeats/Suppress.

Symphony

Sequence:
Tools/ExportImport/Import/Symphony
Tools/ExportImport/Export/Symphony

Use the Symphony option to exchange files between Paradox and Symphony. To import a Symphony file into Paradox, choose Tools/ExportImport/Import/Symphony from the menu. From the next menu, choose Release 1.0 or Release 1.1 as desired. Next, enter the Symphony filename, and then enter a name for the new Paradox table.

To export a file from Paradox to Symphony, choose Tools/ExportImport/Export/Symphony from the menu. From the next menu, choose Release 1.0 or Release 1.1 as desired. Enter the name of the table that is to be exported to Symphony, and then enter a filename for the resulting Symphony file. Alphanumeric fields will become labels within cells; number fields will become numbers in cells with a general format; currency fields will become numbers within cells with a Symphony format; and date fields will become numbers with a date format.

Table

Sequence:
Tools/Copy/Table
Tools/Delete/Table
Tools/Rename/Table
Tools/More/Protect/Password/Table

Use these versions of the Table option to copy, rename, or delete tables. To copy a table, choose Tools/Copy/Table, and enter the name of the table to copy, followed by the new name for the copy. To delete a table, choose Tools/Delete/Table, enter the name for the table, and confirm the deletion by choosing OK from the next menu. To rename a table, choose the Tools/Rename/Table option and enter the name of the table, followed by the new name for the table.

To password-protect a table, choose Tools/More/Protect/Password/Table, and enter the name of the table. Enter the password when prompted to do so, and enter it a second time to confirm the correct spelling. If you wish, fill in the auxiliary password from the next screen that appears and then press Do-It! (F2); if no auxiliary passwords are necessary, simply press Do-It! (F2).

TableBand

Sequence (from the Report Specification Menu):
TableBand

Use the TableBand option, while you are designing or changing tabular reports, to insert, erase, and resize columns, to move columns to new locations, or to copy columns. From the Report Specification menu, choose TableBand. The following menu options will appear:

- Insert, to insert a new column

- Erase, to erase a column

- Resize, to change the width of a column

- Move, to move a column to another location

- Copy, to copy a column to a new location

Select the desired option. For more specifics on an option, see the option by name in this appendix.

TableLookup

Sequence (from the Edit Menu):
ValCheck/Define/TableLookup

Use the TableLookup option to compare field entries to a lookup table to determine their validity. From the Edit menu, choose ValCheck/Define. Place the cursor in the field that is to be compared to the lookup table, and press RETURN. Choose Table-Lookup, and enter the name of the table that contains the lookup values. The field in the lookup table must be the first field in the table and must have the same name and characteristics as the field to which it is being compared.

From the next menu that appears, select JustCurrentField to check entered values in the current field against the lookup table, or select AllCorrespondingFields to check and fill in values from all corresponding fields in the lookup table.

Finally, choose PrivateLookup (or FillNoHelp, if you last chose AllCorresponding-Fields) to check the validity while denying access to the lookup table, or choose HelpAndFill to check the validity while allowing browsing of the lookup table.

Tables (to List Available Tables)

Sequence:
Tools/Info/Inventory/Tables

Use this Tables option to list all available tables in a directory. Choose Tools/Info/Inventory/Tables. Enter a directory name, or press RETURN without a name for the current directory. All available tables will appear by name within a temporary table, along with the creation dates for each table.

Tables (for Forms)

Sequence (from the Form Design Menu):
Multi/Tables

Use this Tables option to place, remove, or move a form from another table to the form you are designing. From the Form Design menu, choose Multi/Tables. From the next menu to appear, choose Place (to add another table's form to the current form), Remove (to remove another table's form from the current form), Move (to move a form already placed), or DisplayOnly (to specify that a form is to be used for editing or just for display).

TableSize

Sequence:
Image/TableSize

Use the TableSize option to change the current table's size (in rows) in the workspace. Choose Image/TableSize. Use the up and down arrow keys to increase or decrease the number of visible rows, and then press RETURN to set the desired table size. Tables must occupy a minimum of two rows.

TablesOfGroups

Sequence (from the Report Specification Menu):
Setting/Format/TablesOfGroups

Use the TablesOfGroups option to arrange reports in tables of groups. When arranged in tables of groups, the table header appears just once, at the top of the page. To specify this formatting, choose Setting/Format/TablesOfGroups from the Report Specification menu.

Tabular

Sequence:
Report/Design/Tabular

Use the Tabular option to design a tabular custom report. Choose Report/Design, and enter the name of the table. Select a designator for the report, and then enter a description. Choose Tabular for the type of report, and the Report Specification menu will appear. Design the report as desired, and then press Do-It! (F2) to store the report.

Time

Sequence (from the Report Design Menu):
Field/Place/Time

Use the Time option to place a field containing the current time in a custom free-form or tabular report. From the Report Design menu, choose Field/Place/Time, and select one of two possible time formats that appear as a menu. Move the cursor to the desired location, and press RETURN to place the time field.

ToDOS

Sequence:
Tools/More/ToDOS

Use the ToDOS option to temporarily suspend Paradox and access DOS through a DOS "shell." Choose Tools/More/ToDOS, and in a moment the DOS prompt will appear. From the DOS prompt, enter **EXIT** to return to Paradox. (Note that the CTRL-O or ALT-O key combinations can also be used to access DOS.)

Tools

Sequence:
Tools

Use the Tools option of the main menu to choose from among various Paradox tools. Choose Tools. The menu that appears provides the following options:

- Rename, to rename Paradox objects
- QuerySpeed, to speed the performance of queries
- ExportImport, to exchange data between Paradox and other software
- Copy, to copy Paradox objects
- Delete, to delete Paradox objects
- Info, to show information such as filenames, table fields, and network users
- Net, to perform common network functions
- More, to provide access to additional tools through another menu

Select the desired option. For more specifics on an option, see the option by name in this appendix.

Type

Sequence (from the Graph Design Menu):
Type

Use the Type option of the Graph Design menu to choose the type of graph to display, or to mix types within a single graph. From the Graph Design menu, select Type. Then select the desired type of graph from the next menu to appear. The available types are Stacked Bar, Bar, 3-D Bar, Rotated Bar, Line, Markers, Combined Lines and Markers, X-Y Graph, Pie Graph, and Area Graph.

Undo

Sequence (from the Edit Menu):
Undo
CTRL-U

Use the Undo option, while you are editing, to undo changes made to a record. Press F10 for the Edit menu, and choose Undo. From the next menu that appears, choose Yes to undo your most recent edit. You can repeat the Undo option to undo successive changes, all the way back to the start of a session. (Note that while in CoEdit mode, you can only undo the most recent action.)

Update

Sequence:
Tools/More/Add/Update
Tools/More/MultiAdd/Update

Use the Update option to update a keyed table, using the records in another table as the source of the update. Choose Tools/More/Add; or to update more than one table simultaneously, choose Tools/More/MultiAdd. Enter a name for the source table (the table with records to be added); and in the case of MultiAdd, enter the name of the map table. Then enter a name for the target table (the table to add the records to).

If the target table has a key field, another menu will provide the choice of NewEntries, for adding records to the target table, and Update, for updating the target table records based on the source table records. Choose Update, and the target table(s) will be updated.

UserName

Sequence:
Tools/Net/UserName

Use the UserName option to change your user name while you are using Paradox on a network. Choose Tools/Net/UserName, and enter the new user name (of up to 15 characters). Then confirm the new name by choosing OK from the next menu that appears.

ValCheck (to Set or Clear Validity Checks)

Sequence (from the Edit Menu):
ValCheck

Use this ValCheck option to set validity checks on fields or to clear one or more validity checks from a field. From the Edit menu, choose ValCheck. Then choose Define to define or Clear to clear a validity check.

ValCheck (to Clear All Validity Checks for a Table)

Sequence:
Tools/Delete/ValCheck

Use this ValCheck option to clear all validity checks from a table by deleting the validity check file. Choose Tools/Delete/ValCheck, and enter the name of the table.

Paradox will proceed to delete the file that contains all of the validity checks for that table.

View

Sequence:
View

Use the View option to view an existing table. Choose View, and enter the name of the desired table. If a table is already visible in the workspace, the table that you select with View will appear underneath the existing table.

ViewGraph

Sequence (from the Graph Design Menu):
ViewGraph

Use the ViewGraph option of the Graph Design menu to show the current graph on the screen, to print the current graph, or to store an image of the graph in a disk file. From the Graph Design menu, select ViewGraph. From the next menu that appears, select Screen (to display the graph), Printer (to print the graph at the default print device), or File (to store the graph in a disk file).

VisiCalc

Sequence:
Tools/ExportImport/Import/VisiCalc
Tools/ExportImport/Export/VisiCalc

Use the VisiCalc option to exchange files between Paradox and VisiCalc or other software that can use the VisiCalc (DIF) format. To import a VisiCalc file into Paradox, choose Tools/ExportImport/Import/VisiCalc from the menu and enter the name of the file to be imported. Next, enter a name for the new Paradox table that will receive the VisiCalc data. Paradox will proceed to convert the VisiCalc file into a Paradox table.

To export a file from Paradox to VisiCalc, choose Tools/ExportImport/Export/VisiCalc from the menu. Enter the name of the table that is to be exported to VisiCalc, and then enter a filename for the resulting VisiCalc worksheet.

Wait

Sequence (from the Report Specification Menu):
Setting/Wait

Use the Wait option to force the printer to pause after each page of a custom report. From the Report Specification menu, choose Setting/Wait. With this option chosen, the user will be prompted to press a key before each successive page is printed. Then confirm the selection by choosing Yes from the next menu that appears.

Who

Sequence:
Tools/Info/Who

Use the Who option to list all users currently running Paradox on a network. Choose Tools/Info/Who, and a list of network users will appear in the form of a temporary table.

Width

Sequence (from the Report Specification Menu):
Setting/PageLayout/Width

Use the Width option to control the page width in a custom report. From the Report Specification menu, choose Setting/PageLayout/Width. Enter the desired width, measured in number of characters (from 2 to 2000).

Write

Sequence:
Scripts/Editor/Write

Use the Write option to write a new script with the script editor. Choose Scripts/Editor/Write, and enter a name for the script. If the name that you supply is already in use by a script, Paradox will warn you of this by requesting confirmation before overwriting the old script. When you have finished editing the script, press Do-It! (F2) to save the script and exit the script editor.

Write-Protect

Sequence:
Tools/More/Protect/Write-Protect

Use the Write-Protect option to protect a table against changes or to remove write protection. Choose Tools/More/Protect/Write-Protect, and enter the name of the desired table. From the next menu that appears, choose Set to write-protect the table, or choose Clear to remove the write protection.

Yes

Sequence:
Yes

Use the Yes option to tell Paradox not to perform a specific type of operation.

Zoom

Sequence:
Image/Zoom

Use the Zoom option to locate the cursor at a specific field, record number, or matching value. Choose Image/Zoom. From the next menu that appears, choose Field, Record, or Value to go to a specific field, record number, or value.

appendix B

USING THE CUSTOM CONFIGURATION PROGRAM (CCP)

You can use the Custom Configuration Program (CCP) to change the way Paradox operates on your computer. The CCP is a special-purpose script, written in PAL, that presents a series of Paradox menus. By selecting various choices on these menus, you can change various default settings and configurations used within Paradox. Items that can be changed with the CCP include the following:

- Video configurations (such as the kind of monitor) and screen colors desired

- Hardware configuration, such as type of monitor and memory usage

- Report settings, such as default page length and page widths, margins, printer setup strings, and printer types

- Graph settings, such as the type of graph, colors, titles, and scalings desired, and printer or screen settings for graphs

- Default settings, such as the desired default directory, whether blanks are treated as zeros, and autosave default values

- International settings, such as number and date formats used throughout Paradox

- Network settings, such as user names, private directory names, and desired autorefresh intervals

- PAL features, such as whether secondary indexes should be maintained incrementally, and whether external editors should be linked into the PAL environment

- ASCII features for setting the parameters to be used in importing and exporting ASCII files

Using the CCP is straightforward: you simply start the CCP and select your desired choices from the menus. The Return option can be used in all submenus to return to the CCP main menu. After choosing your selections, choose Do-It! from the CCP main menu (or press F2) to implement your selections and exit from the CCP.

STARTING THE CUSTOM CONFIGURATION PROGRAM

The CCP can be started from DOS or from within Paradox. From DOS, first switch to the directory containing the program, and enter

PARADOX CUSTOM

to load Paradox and run the CCP. Or if you are already within Paradox, press F10 to get to the menu, and choose Scripts/Play. When asked for the name of the script, enter **CUSTOM** (or press RETURN and select CUSTOM from the list of scripts). After you press RETURN the CCP will load.

When the CCP is first started, an introductory screen will appear briefly. Then, if Paradox senses the presence of a color graphics card in your computer, it will ask

Are you using a B&W monitor right now?
(Y for yes, N for no)

If you are using a monochrome monitor, enter **Y**; otherwise, enter **N**. (If a color graphics card is not in your system, you will not see this question.) The CCP will proceed to display its main menu with the following choices:

Tune Video Reports Graphs Defaults Int'l Net PAL Ascii Do-It! Cancel
Configure Paradox to run in protected mode; obtain machine information.

The Do-It! and Cancel options perform the same actions they do elsewhere in Paradox. The remaining options are used for the items described at the start of this appendix (and covered in more detail shortly). Select the options you want from the menus, and answer the prompts as desired.

You can change more than one setting during a single session with the CCP. If you select a setting and decide you don't want to make changes, you can use the ESCAPE key to back out of the setting and get back to the CCP main menu. If for some reason you don't want any changes during the entire session to take effect, you can choose Cancel from the CCP's main menu to cancel all changes and exit from the CCP.

SAVING YOUR CHANGES

When you have finished making your settings, choose Do-It! from the main menu, or press F2. You will now see the following menu choices:

HardDisk Network
Write .CFG file to the directory where the system files are located.

Choose HardDisk if the configuration (.CFG) file is stored on your hard disk, or choose Network if you store your configuration file on a local area network server. Once the changes have been stored, you will be returned to DOS.

TUNE

Use the Tune option of the CCP menu to optimally configure Paradox to your hardware, when Paradox cannot accomplish this task itself. Normally, Paradox automatically configures itself to any extended memory present in your computer. If for some reason Paradox cannot do this, it displays a message telling you to use the CCP to configure your hardware. If you have seen this message, you should use the Tune option from the CCP menu.

When you select Tune, the following menu options appear:

MachineInfo ProtectedMode Return
Information about your machine's configuration.

The Return option returns you to the CCP main menu. Choose MachineInfo to run a series of testing programs that will determine what kind of computer and monitor you have, what kind of memory is installed, what drives are present, whether a mouse is present, and what is contained in your CONFIG.SYS and AUTOEXEC.BAT files. The information about your machine can be displayed on the screen, printed, or saved to a text file.

Choose ProtectedMode to tell Paradox whether or not to run in protected mode. (If you have 1MB or more of extended memory, Paradox is likely to perform better using protected mode.) When you choose this option, another menu provides you with additional options titled Configure, DefaultMode, and Return (to return to the previous menu). You can use Configure to configure your copy of Paradox to run in protected mode. You can use the DefaultMode option to determine whether Paradox always starts in real mode, or in protected mode.

 If you have memory-resident programs such as SideKick in memory, exit the Custom Configuration Program and unload these programs before using the Configure option of the CCP. If a memory-resident program is present and you run Configure, your machine could lock up, causing a loss of any data in the memory- resident programs.

VIDEO

Use the Video option of the CCP menu to select your video settings, such as monitor type and screen colors. When you select Video, the following options appear:

Monitor Snow Colors NegativeColors FormPalette Return
Mono, B&W, or Color.

Use Monitor to select a monitor type. Paradox normally senses the monitor type automatically, but some combinations of hardware may require you to select a monitor type, overriding the choice that Paradox would make. Select Monitor, and then choose the appropriate type from the three choices (Mono, B&W, or Color). Mono indicates a monochrome monitor and monochrome adapter; B&W indicates a monochrome adapter connected to color graphics card; and Color indicates any type of color monitor and color graphics adapter card.

Use Snow to eliminate possible interference, or "snow," from the screen. If snow appears, select Snow and then Yes to eliminate it.

Video/Colors (version 3.5)

When you select Colors after selecting the Video option, the following menu appears:

Design Change PickSetting Tools Help Return
Create a new color setting.

Use Design to design a new color setting. In Paradox, you can have multiple color settings assigned to different names. When you select Design, you can then choose one of nine numbered color settings to modify, or you can choose the standard setting. Paradox then prompts you for a description for the setting, then the Color Design Screen appears (Figure B-1).

In Paradox version 3.5, the Color Design Screen is used for changing color settings of the various Paradox objects. You use the cursor keys to move the cursor to the desired object or area of the screen that you want to change, then you press RETURN to select that object or area. When you do this, the cursor appears in the Color Palette at the upper right side of the screen, and the current color combination will be flashing. Use the arrow keys to change the foreground and background colors as desired; then press RETURN to select the color combination for that particular area or object. You can repeat this process for any other area or object on the Color Design Screen.

Once you have made your desired color changes, press Do-It! (F2) to save the settings. Note that you use the PickSetting option of the same Video/Colors menu to place a newly designed color setting into effect.

Use Change to modify an existing color setting. When you choose Change, pick the desired setting by number from the menu that appears, and enter a description, the color design screen appears, as described above. Use the cursor keys to move the

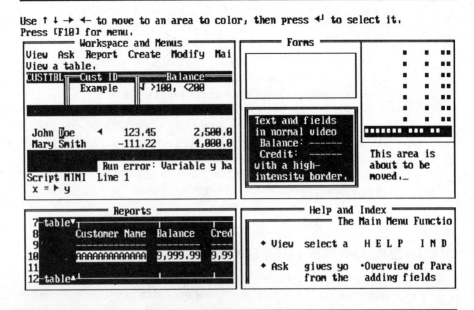

FIGURE B-1.   Color Design screen

cursor to the desired object or area of the screen that you want to change, then press RETURN to select that object or area. The cursor will move to the Color Palette at the upper right side of the screen, and the current color combination will be flashing. Use the arrow keys to change the foreground and background colors as desired; then press RETURN to select the color combination for that particular area or object. When done changing the colors for the setting, press Do-It! (F2) to save the settings.

Use PickSetting to select the color setting used by Paradox. When you select this option, a menu displaying the standard color setting and all color settings you have defined will appear; choose the desired setting by name from the menu.

You can use the Tools option to rename, copy, or delete existing color settings. The Help option displays a help screen regarding color selections, while the Return option returns you to the prior menu.

Video/Colors (version 3.0)

The Video/Colors command operates differently with version 3.0 of Paradox than it does with version 3.5. When you select Colors, another menu appears, offering these choices:

ExistingSettings Modify Help Return
Select, rename or delete a color setting.

In Paradox, you can have multiple color settings assigned to different names. The color setting currently in use is called the *current setting*. Paradox assumes you want to modify the current color settings. (You can use ExistingSettings to make active or to modify a color setting other than the current one.) Choose Modify to change the colors; then choose Return to get back to the Video menu. Make any other desired changes, and choose Do-It! from the CCP main menu (or press F2). The new colors will take effect the next time Paradox is started.

Use ExistingSettings to recall an existing color setting. When you select Existing-Settings, you see the following menu:

Select ChangeName Delete Help Return
Select an existing color setting to modify or make current.

The Select choice causes a list of available color settings to be displayed. The current setting will be highlighted, and the active setting will be preceded with an asterisk (*). When you first start the CCP, the active setting automatically becomes the current setting. To use a different setting as the current setting, highlight it from the list of choices, and press RETURN. If you want to create a new color setting, do so by choosing Video/Colors/Modify from the CCP main menu and then saving the color setting under a new name, as described shortly. It will then appear on the menu of choices provided by the Select option.

The ChangeName choice lets you rename a color setting you created and saved previously. Names for color settings can be up to 21 characters in length and must start with a letter, number, or $ or # symbol.

The Delete choice lets you delete a color setting you created and saved previously. Note that you cannot delete the Default and Compaq settings that are supplied with Paradox. If you delete the current setting, Paradox will ask you to choose another color setting. If you do not make this choice, Paradox will select the default setting.

From the Colors menu, choose Modify to make your desired changes to the screen colors. When you choose Modify, the first of ten screens will appear, displaying the colors of the various Paradox objects. You can use the PGUP and PGDN keys to move between the ten screens. The ten screens show the colors for the following objects:

- The Paradox main menu

- The menu prompts

- Prompted lists

- Query Forms

- Tables in CoEdit mode

- The Report Design screen

- The Form Design screen

- The help screens

- The Help Index

- The PAL debugger

Use the PGUP and PGDN keys to get to the screen you want to change. Once you are at the desired screen, select the element you wish to change from the menu. When you do so, a palette of available colors will appear in the upper-right corner of the screen, and the current color combination will be flashing. Use the arrow keys to change the foreground and background colors, as desired; then press RETURN to select the color combination for that particular screen.

Note that if you make changes to more than one of the ten screens, you can check those changes by viewing them in a summary screen before saving the changes. Pressing CTRL-END will take you directly to the summary screen.

Once you are satisfied with your changes, press F10 for a menu that provides two choices, Save and Cancel. Choose Save to add the modified setting to the list of color settings. You will be prompted for a name, which can be up to 21 characters in length. The saved setting automatically becomes the current setting; it will be made the active setting when you exit from the CCP and next restart Paradox. After the color settings are saved, you will be returned to the Video menu.

Use NegativeColors from the Video menu to specify colors that will be used for negative number and currency values. When you select NegativeColors, a menu with the following choices appears:

BothDifferent Numbers Currency Same
Color negative numbers and currency values differently than positive ones.

Choose BothDifferent to display both negative numbers and negative currency values differently than positive ones. Choose Numbers to distinguish negative numbers only; Currency to distinguish currency values only; or Same for no difference in the display between negative numbers or values and positive ones.

Use FormPalette from the Video menu to tell Paradox whether to automatically display the color palette while designing a form. Once you select Style/Color while designing a form, ALT-C can be used to make the color palette appear at the upper-right corner of the screen. From the Video menu, select Form/Palette. Then select On if you want the color palette to appear by default when designing a form; or select Off to hide the palette.

REPORTS

Use the Reports option of the CCP menu to select your report settings, such as page lengths and widths, margin settings, and printer setup strings. Note that changing report defaults will not affect existing reports; it will only affect the default settings for reports you create after making changes with the CCP. When you select Reports, the following options appear:

PageWidth LengthOfPage Margin Wait GroupRepeats
Setups FormFeed Return
Change the default width of the printed report page.

Use the PageWidth option to set the default width for each page in the report. If unchanged, the default is 80 characters. If you are using compressed print on a dot-matrix printer, you may want to change this to 132. You can enter any value between 10 and 2000. Once set, the value becomes the default; you can always change the value in an individual report by choosing Setting/PageLayout/Width from the Report Specification menu.

Use the LengthOfPage option to set the default page length. If unchanged, the default is 66 lines, which is standard for 11-inch-long paper. You can change this to any value between 2 and 2000; or you can enter C in response to the prompt for LengthOfPage. The letter "C" denotes continuous pages, which are usually used with mailing labels, fanfold checks, and similar continuous forms. If you are using a laser printer, you may need to change this option to match the page length of the printer. Once set, the value becomes the default; you can always change the value in an individual report by choosing Setting/PageLayout/Length from the Report Specification menu.

Use the Margin option to set the default left margin for the report. If unchanged, the default is 0, and Paradox begins printing at the far left edge of the page. You can enter any value between 0 and the current page width. Once set, the value becomes the default; you can always change the value in an individual report by choosing Setting/Margin from the Report Specification menu.

Use the Wait option to tell Paradox whether to pause after each printed page. This option is useful for manually fed printers, where a new sheet must be inserted for each page. After selecting Wait, choose No to print continuously without pausing, or choose Yes to tell Paradox to pause after each page. Once set, the choice becomes the default; you can always change the choice in an individual report by choosing Setting/Wait from the Report Specification menu.

Use the GroupRepeats option to indicate whether Paradox should include or suppress repeated group values. If unchanged, the default is Retain. With this setting, Paradox includes all group values in the report, whether they are repeated or not. After selecting GroupRepeats, choose Retain to include all group values, or choose Suppress to print repeated group values only for the first record in the group. Once set, the choice becomes the default; you can always change the choice in an individual report by choosing Setting/GroupRepeats from the Report Specification menu.

Use the Setups option to add, modify, or remove any printer port assignments and/or setup strings. When you choose the Setups option, a Paradox table named PRINTER appears. The current predefined printer setups are stored in this table. You can edit this table (using the same techniques as you would use to edit any table) to add, modify, or delete names, ports, and setup strings for printers. (See your printer manual for the setup strings needed for your particular printer.) Entering an asterisk after a name makes that setup the default setup. ASCII codes in setup strings can be entered with a backslash (\) followed by the three-digit ASCII value. Any setups that you store in this table will appear on a menu when you select Setting/Setup/Predefined while using the Report Specification. After making the desired changes to the PRINTER table, press Do-It! (F2) to store the changes and return to the Reports menu of the CCP.

Use the FormFeed option to tell Paradox whether to use form feeds or line feeds to advance each successive sheet of paper. After selecting FormFeed, choose No to use line feeds to advance each sheet of paper, or choose Yes to use form feeds after each page. (The default is form feeds.) Once set, the choice becomes the default; you can always change the choice in an individual report by choosing SetPrinter/Override/FormFeed from the Report Specification menu.

GRAPHS

Use the Graphs option menu to select default settings for graphs and to select printers or plotters used with graphs. When you select this option, the following menu appears:

GraphSettings Printers Screen Return
Modify the Paradox default graph settings.

Use GraphSettings to change the type of graph, titles, colors, axes, grids, legends, labels, and default pie-chart settings. When you select GraphSettings, the Customize Graph Type screen appears. You use this screen and its menu options in the manner described in Chapter 8 (see that chapter for more details). The only difference is, since you are in the CCP, the changes you make to the graph settings will become the defaults for graphs you create when you next load Paradox. Make the desired settings, and then choose Return from the menu to return to the Graphs menu of the CCP.

Use Printers to define the printers used for printing or plotting graphs. Note that graph printer definitions are completely independent of regular printer definitions. When you select Printers from the Graphs menu, the following menu appears:

1stPrinter 2ndPrinter 3rdPrinter 4thPrinter   Return
Choose or make changes to Printer 1 specifications.

From it you select the printer you wish to define. After you select the desired printer, the following menu appears:

TypeOfPrinter Settings Return
Choose manufacturer, model and mode for printer 1.

Use the TypeOfPrinter option to choose the printer make and model from a list of available printers. You can use the arrow keys to navigate through the list of printers, and press RETURN when the desired printer is highlighted.

Use the Settings option to select the desired printer port and to specify whether the printer should pause between pages. When you choose Settings, another menu will offer two choices: Device and PrinterWait. Choose Device to specify the desired port and any needed serial communications settings. Choose PrinterWait and then Yes to pause between pages, or choose PrinterWait and then No (the default) to tell Paradox not to pause between pages.

When you are done defining the printer or the printer settings, choose Return from the menu to return to the menu of printers. Then choose Return again to return to the Graphs menu of the CCP.

Use the Screen option of the Graphs menu to choose a display type for showing graphs. When you select the Graphs option, the following menu appears:

Auto CGA MCGA EGA VGA 8514 3270
Herc ATT Tandy 1000 Return
Detect display type automatically.

If you choose Auto (the default), Paradox automatically uses the maximum resolution supported by your hardware. You can select any of the other display types to override the choice made by Paradox. Note that any choice you make must be supported by your hardware; choosing VGA, for example, will have no effect if your system does not have a VGA graphics card. Once you have chosen the desired screen type, choose Return from the menu to return to the Graphs menu of the CCP.

DEFAULTS

Use the Defaults option of the CCP menu to change the default settings of various options within Paradox, including the working directory. When you choose Defaults from the CCP menu, the following menu appears:

SetDirectory QueryOrder Blank=Zero AutoSave DisableBreak Return
Set your DOS working directory.

Use the SetDirectory option to designate a default directory which will contain your Paradox objects. Once you select SetDirectory, you will be prompted for a directory name. Enter the name, and then choose Return to return to the CCP menu. Once you have set a directory, when you start Paradox the program will automatically switch to the directory you have named. Remember that during any individual session, you can use Tools/More/Directory from the Paradox main menu to change directories. If you set a DOS path to Paradox before loading the program, you can then load Paradox from any directory.

Use the QueryOrder option to determine whether the fields in an ANSWER table will rotate when you use CTRL-R to rotate the fields in the Query Form. Choosing QueryOrder causes a menu with two options to be displayed: ImageOrder and TableOrder. After choosing ImageOrder, when you use CTRL-R to rotate fields in a query, the fields in the ANSWER table will rotate to match the order of the fields in the query table. If you choose TableOrder (the default), the fields in the ANSWER table will always match the order of fields in the underlying table, and not that of the fields in the Query Form.

Use the Blank=Zero option to determine whether blank numeric values will be assigned a value of 0. Choose Blank=Zero and then choose Yes to treat blanks as zeros in numeric operations, or choose No to ignore blanks in numeric operations. Calculations involving blank fields will not work unless you choose Blanks = Zero Yes.

With versions of Paradox prior to version 3.5, an EMS option also appears on this menu. Use the EMS option to specify a percentage of expanded memory (EMS) that is to be allocated to a disk cache if you have 208K or more of expanded memory. The first 48K of expanded memory is always allocated to a virtual memory management system. Expanded memory in addition to the first 48K is normally divided between a disk cache (75%) and a temporary storage area (25%). You can modify this ratio by choosing the EMS option. When you select EMS, Paradox will ask for a percentage of expanded memory to allocate to the disk cache. Enter any desired amount between 0 and 100. If you perform much database work with very large tables, you may want to increase the percentage of memory allocated to the disk cache. Note that if you use a dedicated disk cache software program, you may want to set this value at 0 to avoid conflicts between Paradox and your disk cache software.

Use the AutoSave option to enable or disable the automatic saving of data to the hard disk. Choose AutoSave and then Yes to enable automatic saving of data to disk or No to disable the automatic saving of data. In most cases the only reason to disable autosave is to gain a slight speed increase if you are working with data on floppy disks.

Use the DisableBreak option to enable or disable the CTRL-BREAK key combination. CTRL-BREAK normally interrupts certain operations, such as editing sessions or reports. If you do not want to allow CTRL-BREAK to interrupt an operation, choose Disable-Break, and then choose Disable. To enable the CTRL-BREAK key combination, choose DisableBreak and then choose Enable.

INT'L

Use the Int'l option of the CCP menu to set your international number and date formats. When you choose Int'l, the following menu appears:

DateFormat NumberFormat Return
Specify the format to use for dates.

Use the DateFormat option to set the default date format for screen display and for reports. Choose DateFormat, and then choose one of three available formats from the menu that next appears. You can choose either mm/dd/yy (the default), dd-mon-yy (with the month spelled as a three-letter abbreviation), or dd.mm.yy.

Use the NumberFormat option to choose either U.S. format or International format for the default display of numbers. Choose NumberFormat and either USFormat or InternationalFormat from the next menu to appear. USFormat (the default) separates thousands with commas and places a period between whole digits (dollars) and decimal digits (cents). InternationalFormat separates thousands with periods and uses the comma to separate decimal digits from whole digits.

NET

Use the Net option of the CCP menu to change the default network settings. When you choose Net, the following menu appears:

UserName SetPrivate AutoRefresh Return
Specify a default user name.

Use the UserName option to specify your default user name. If the network software supports user names, Paradox will automatically read your user name from the network software. If your network software does not support user names (or if you don't like the user name assigned by the network software), you can use the UserName option to specify a different name. Select UserName and enter a name of up to 15 characters at the prompt. Press RETURN again to select the user name and return to the Net menu. Once you have made the change, it will take effect each time you start Paradox. If you want to change a user name just for one session, you can do so by choosing Tools/Net/UserName from the Paradox main menu.

Use the SetPrivate option to enter or change the location of your private directory. (It's a good idea to check with the network administrator before using this option; if you set your private directory to someone else's directory or to a shared directory, there will be problems with multiple access.) Choose SetPrivate, and enter the directory name, including the full path name. The change will take effect once you restart Paradox.

Use the AutoRefresh option to set the default automatic refresh interval. This interval is the rate (in seconds) at which Paradox refreshes, or updates, your screen to reflect any changes made by other users working with Paradox on the network. Choose AutoRefresh, and enter a value in seconds for the refresh interval. You can enter any value from 1 to 3600 (the default is 3), or you can leave the value blank, which turns off the automatic refresh feature. The value you enter becomes the default each time Paradox is started. If you want to change the interval for just one session, use Tools/Net/AutoRefresh from the Paradox main menu.

PAL

Use the PAL option to specify how external indexes are maintained or to link an external editor into the PAL environment. When you choose PAL from the CCP menu, the following menu appears:

MaintainIndexes Editor CalcDebug Return
Choose whether to incrementally update secondary indexes.

Use the MaintainIndexes option to specify whether indexes on keyed tables (QuerySpeed files) will be updated after each set of changes to a table, or only when they are outdated and about to be used. Choose MaintainIndexes and choose Yes to update the indexes after each update of the table, or choose No to update the indexes only when they are outdated.

Use the Editor option to link an ASCII text editor of your choice to the PAL environment. Choose Editor and then enter the command used to call your editor at the prompt. The change will take effect once you restart Paradox. Whenever you perform an action that would normally result in the Paradox editor becoming available (such as choosing Scripts/Editor from the main menu), your editor will appear instead. Keep in mind that you must set a DOS path to your editor.

Use CalcDebug to determine how errors in calculated fields are handled by Paradox. When you choose CalcDebug, another menu offers options named Toggle-Message, and ErrorString. Use the ToggleMessage option to turn on (or off) the error message that appears at the bottom of the screen when an error occurs in a calculated field. Use the ErrorString option to change the characters that appear in a calculated field when an error occurs.

ASCII

Use the ASCII option of the CCP menu to change the import and export defaults used with ASCII files. When you choose ASCII, the following menu appears:

Delimiter FieldsDelimited Separator ZeroFill ChooseDecimal Return
Change default delimiter or choose fields to be delimited.

Use the Delimiter option to change the default delimiters to a character of your choosing. Choose Delimeter, and you are prompted for the desired character to use as a delimiter. Use the FieldsDelimited option to determine which character fields are to be delimited. When you select FieldsDelimited, another menu provides two options: AllFields, and OnlyStrings. Choose AllFields if all fields are to be delimited, or OnlyStrings if only non-numeric fields are to be delimited.

Use the Separator option to choose a default separator for ASCII files that are imported or exported. When you select Separator, you will be prompted for the character that will serve as the separator. The default is the comma, which is used by many other software packages when creating ASCII files. You can use BACKSPACE to delete the comma and enter any character (except a space) as the desired separator.

Use the ZeroFill option to determine whether empty numeric fields in exported ASCII files will contain zeroes or blanks. Select ZeroFill, and from the next menu choose Nothing to leave empty numeric fields blank or Zeroes to fill empty numeric fields with zeroes. Nothing is the default value.

Use the ChooseDecimal option to select a default decimal separator for numeric fields in exported files. Either the period or the comma may be specified as a decimal separator. Select ChooseDecimal, and from the next menu that appears choose Period (the default) or Comma as desired.

DO-IT! AND CANCEL

The Do-It! and Cancel options in the CCP work in the same manner as in other parts of Paradox. Choosing Cancel exits the CCP without saving any changes you have made during the session. Choosing Do-It! (or pressing F2) saves changes made during the session and returns you to Paradox or to DOS (if you started the CCP from the DOS level). When you exit the CCP with Do-It! or F2, the changes will be written to your PARADOX.CFG configuration file. This file is normally read upon the startup of Paradox; hence, changes made during a CCP session will not be evident until you exit and restart Paradox.

INDEX